Alexander

GUINNESS WORLD RECORDS 2017

Welcome to **Guinness World Records** *2017. This year's edition is out of this world, and to prove it, we've enlisted the help of some truly inspirational record-breakers who know more than most people about pushing the boundaries. You'll find contributions from legendary astronauts Buzz Aldrin (pictured), Chris Hadfield and Al Worden, plus the current NASA Administrator Charlie Bolden. We talk to space scientists such as Dr Alan Stern, head of the recent Pluto missions, and even the US rock band OK Go, who filmed a music video in zero-gravity! And, of course, you'll find the latest superlatives from all your favourite Guinness World Records categories. There's something here for everyone. Enjoy!*

One of the most famous photographs ever, this portrait was captured during the **first manned landing on the Moon** in 1969. Pictured is US astronaut Buzz Aldrin, with fellow Moon walker – and photographer – Neil Armstrong and the *Eagle* lunar lander reflected in his visor. Read our interview with Buzz on pp.10–11.

CONTENTS

This year's edition is divided into 13 chapters, covering a vast spectrum of topics from the exploration of our universe to the latest sporting achievements. In between, you'll find subjects as diverse as 3D printing, robots, dinosaurs, killer plants, LEGO® Minifigures and mazes. We explore the history of pioneering journeys, from the 16th century right up to the present day, and celebrate some of Disney's remarkable animations. Elsewhere, you'll find a chapter dedicated to records that you could try for yourself at home – and another chapter covering records that you definitely *shouldn't* attempt!

Stunning photographs: Our picture team has been travelling the world to snap the most visually striking record holders. Every edition of *GWR* features more than 1,000 photos – many unique to us and seen for the first time.

Gallery: This photo-led feature offers a change of pace and gives you the chance to explore record-breaking in picture form.

Dateline: Running through the book, at the foot of the page, you'll find a chronological history of the universe... in 200 records!

Fun and informative: Our records are a unique mix of quirky facts and extraordinary stats that you won't find anywhere else.

Annotated images: We've added notes to some of the more complex imagery in the book, so that you can grasp the details of what you're seeing.

FAST FACTS

The *GWR* book was the result of a question: "Which is the fastest game bird in Europe?" (The answer: the red-breasted merganser and the eider) • The first edition went on sale in 1955 • It's the world's **biggest-selling annual book**

Factographics:
Each chapter kicks off with a special new feature that explores a topic visually. Facts and figures are given context with the help of spectacular photography and helpful infographics.

Fast Facts:
Bite-sized info that relates to the pages you're on at the time.

Longest worker ant
The elongated bodies of Australian giant bulldog ants (*Myrmecia brevinoda*), a species of Australian bull ant, measure as much as 3.7 cm (1.5 in) long. Bull ants lack advanced social structures, so each worker has evolved to be strong enough to forage alone.

DID YOU KNOW?
Ant colonies contain several different types – or "castes" – of ant, typically "worker", "queen", "drone" and "soldier". Workers – the most common – serve a small population of fertile males (drones), while soldiers defend the nest.

LONGEST COLUMN OF ANTS
Most ant colonies live in fixed nests on a site chosen by the queen, leaving only to mate or forage for food. There are some exceptions, however, such as the army ants (Eciton pictured) of Central and South America, and the driver ants (*Dorylus*) of Africa. These two genera are nomadic, with entire colonies leaving their nests in search of new foraging grounds. A colony on the move forms into a column that can be as much as 1 m (3 ft 3 in) wide and 100 m (328 ft) long. Army ant workers break up the column to form themselves into a living nest for their queen every night.

Largest ant genus
The genus *Pheidole* held 1,002 species when the last major survey was carried out in 2014, and new species are being discovered all the time. The smallest ant genus is *Nothomyrmecia*, which only contains one species, the dinosaur or dawn ant (*N. macrops*), which inhabits western and southern Australia. Some entomologists regard it as a living "fossil" on account of its primitive form.

Most dangerous ant
Myrmecia pyriformis, a species of bull ant found in coastal regions of Australia, has powerful jaws and a sting that dispenses a venom several times more potent than cyanide or arsenic. Bulldog ants have caused at least three human fatalities since 1936.

Largest colony of ants
The Argentine ant (*Linepithema humile*) was only introduced to Europe about 80 years ago but has spread rapidly, establishing a colony that stretches 6,000 km (3,700 mi) from northern Italy to the Atlantic coast of Spain.

Rarest male ants
It was initially thought that *Mycocepurus smithii* was one of the ant species that reproduced asexually, with all the ants in the colony being clones of the queen. Although this hypothesis has been proven wrong, no male specimens of *M. smithii* have ever been found. It has been speculated that they may be microscopically small, or that they only live for a very short period.

Highest thermotolerance
for an ant The Saharan silver ant (*Cataglyphis bombycina*, see **fastest ant**, right) does not begin foraging until the outside temperature has reached 46°C (115°F), and it can stay out in the scorching heat until its body temperature reaches 53°C (127°F). This adaptation allows it to avoid less heat-tolerant predators.

Farthest jump by an ant
The Indian jumping ant (*Harpegnathos saltator*) is the most accomplished of the jumping ants. Although only 1.9 cm (0.7 in) long, the Indian jumping ant can leap 10 cm (3.9 in) horizontally (over five times its own body length), and 2 cm (0.8 in) vertically. It achieves this via the synchronous activation of muscles in its middle and back pairs of legs.

Fastest ant
The Saharan silver ant (*C. bombycina*) can reach a speed of 1.8 km/h (1.1 mph). This is 100 times its body length every second. By comparison, Usain Bolt, the **fastest man**, "only" covers six body lengths per second. This extraordinary turn of speed minimizes heat to the Sun and also contributes to its body's convection (see left).

1.8 km/h

First written language Pottery from the neolithic Yangshao culture of Shaanxi Province, China, is inscribed with characters thought to represent numerals.

4 000

Tape measure: Wherever you see this icon, you're looking at a record holder shown at its actual size or scaled up.

100%

Do Try This At Home: Don't just read about records, break them! This interactive chapter offers up dozens of record ideas you can try from the comfort of your bedroom, kitchen, garden or gym. Go on, have a go!

FACTOGRAPHIC

ENGINEERING

For thousands of years, buildings were created from natural substances such as mud, ice, clay, stone and wood. Over time, however, humanity has amassed ever-more-inventive ways of developing innovative materials and techniques that have redefined the possibilities of architecture. Incredibly, eight of the top 10 tallest buildings in the world have been completed since the turn of the century – and virtuoso engineering is constantly rewriting the record books. Below, we present a snapshot of the 10 tallest buildings as of 2016 – with some class c older structures alongside, for comparison. The heights are calculated to the tallest "architectur?" point of the building, discounting fixtures such as antennae or flagpoles. This is the approach adopted by the Council on Tall Buildings and Urban Habitat (CTBUH) when measuring the world's tallest buildings.

ZIFENG TOWER
Location: Nanjing, China
Completed: 2010
Height: 450 m (1,476 ft)
Floors: 66 (plus seven below ground)
Elevator top speed: 7 m per sec (23 ft per sec)
Additional information:
• The design of the tower incorporates sky gardens that wind their way up the façade.

INTERNATIONAL COMMERCE CENTRE
Location: Hong Kong, China
Completed: 2010
Height: 484 m (1,588 ft)
Floors: 108 (plus four below ground)
Number of steps: 2,120
Elevator top speed: 9 m per sec (29 ft 6 in per sec)
Additional information:
• Highly energy-efficient for a building of such a size.

TAIPEI 101
Location: Taipei, Chinese Taipei
Completed: 2004
Height: 508 m (1,667 ft)
Floors: 101 (plus five below ground)
Number of steps: 2,046
Elevator top speed: 16.83 m per sec (55 ft 2 in per sec)
Additional information:
• The most steps climbed on a bicycle is 3,139, by Krystian Herba (POL) at the Taipei 101, in 2 hr 12 min on 22 Mar 2015. He went from the first floor to the 52nd floor, then took an elevator back down before climbing again, this time to the 91st floor.

ABRAJ AL-BAIT TOWERS (AKA MAKKAH ROYAL CLOCK TOWER)
Location: Mecca, Saudi Arabia
Completed: 2012
Floors: 120 (plus three below ground)
Elevator top speed: 6 m per sec (19 ft 8 in per sec)
Additional information:
• The Dokaae clock face is 43 m (141 ft) in diameter – the **largest clock face**
• The spire at the top of the building is capped with a gold mosaic crescent that weighs 35 tonnes (77,160 lb).

BURJ KHALIFA
Location: Dubai, UAE
Completed: 2010
Height: 828 m (2,717 ft)
Floors: 163 (plus one below ground)
Number of steps: 2,909
Elevator top speed: 10 m per sec (32 ft 9 in per sec)
Additional information:
• The fastest time to climb the Burj Khalifa is 6 hr 13 min 55 sec, by Alain Robert (FRA) on 29 Apr 2011.
• The fastest time to climb the Burj Khalifa on a bicycle is 2 hr 20 min 38 sec, by Vittorio Brumotti (ITA) on 18 Oct 2012.

DID YOU KNOW?
Originally 146.5 m (481 ft) tall, the Great Pyramid at Giza in Egypt is more than five times smaller than today's **tallest building**, the Burj Khalifa. But for 3,800 years, this 3rd-century-BCE edifice remained the tallest building on Earth.

Leaning Tower of Pisa
Height: 56.67 m (185 ft 11 in)
Completed: 1372

WILLIS TOWER
Location: Chicago, USA
Completed: 1974
Height: 442.1 m (1,451 ft)
Floors: 108 (plus three below ground)
Elevator top speed: 8.1 m per sec (26 ft 6 in per sec)
Additional information:
• Completed in 1973, formerly the Sears Tower, it was the tallest building in the world for 25 y

All measurements and

DO TRY THIS AT HOME...
IN YOUR BEDROOM

No matter how old we get, some toys and games will never lose their appeal. From juggling and yo-yoing to solving Rubik's Cubes and launching paper aircraft, what makes these playtime classics so enduring is the timeless challenge they present in the very moment of playing with them. Whether you're a novice or an adult that's always the chance to beat your personal best, or master the world's best. And the coolest thing about those records? That you can do them all in your very own bedroom – even in your pyjamas, if you so wish!

GUINNESS WORLD RECORDS 2017

1749 First lightning rod

DID YOU KNOW?
Dotted throughout the book are these Did You Know? panels, which tell you more about the featured record holders and give you a better understanding of the record categories. Also, look out for more trivia in the Fast Facts feature at the top of each spread.

1767

EDITOR'S LETTER

Compiling the world's best-selling annual book is made all the more challenging by having to decide what to leave out. Once again, over the past year we've seen about 1,000 people a week make claims…and even though only a small percentage of these applicants make it all the way through to becoming official Guinness World Records title holders, there are still too many new records to list in the book!

This time, the decision of what to include was made a little easier by focusing on one particular aspect of record-breaking: space exploration and astronaut pioneers. Recently, we've seen the confirmation of gravitational waves (see p.204), the *New Horizon* flyby of Pluto resulting in some amazing photographs (pp.14–15 and pp.20–21), the launch and landing of the **first reusable rocket** (p.204) and even the **first espresso brewed on the *International Space Station*** (*ISS*) (pp.104–05)!

This year, NASA also announced that it had received a record number of applications for its astronaut programme – an incredible 18,300 people. Clearly, there is currently a fascination with space travel not seen since the launch of the Space Shuttle back in the 1980s.

To help us with our out-of-this-world theme, we sought out some remarkable astronauts. Moon pioneer and Mars enthusiast Buzz Aldrin knows all about pushing the limits of what's possible. I'm honoured that he was able to provide this year's foreword (pp.10–11).

It was also a thrill to meet with Commander Chris Hadfield – best known for his "Space Oddity" video filmed from the *ISS*. Chris is one of the most inspirational figures I've had the joy of meeting and his Q&A (pp.12–13) is a must-read for anyone wanting to become a record holder.

Ronaldo

We caught up with football legend Cristiano Ronaldo (PRT) during his recent visit to London. He was in town for the premiere of the documentary movie *Ronaldo* (UK, 2015), and we took the chance to hand over his GWR certificate acknowledging him as the **most followed athlete on Twitter**, with 42,093,141 followers as of 11 May 2016.

The Rock

At the world premiere of the disaster movie *San Andreas* (USA, 2015) in London on 21 May 2015, the film's star Dwayne Johnson (USA/CAN) – aka "The Rock" – broke the record for the **most selfies taken in three minutes**. The WWE wrestler-turned-actor fired off 105 successful snaps with fans during his red-carpet walk. The event was also attended by director Brad Peyton.

Charlie Bolden, another ex-astronaut and now NASA Administrator, also provided words of wisdom on the importance of record-breaking for pushing the boundaries. You can find his contribution on p.5. We spoke to Samantha Cristoforetti – creator of that *ISS* espresso – about her record for the **longest time in space by a woman**. And float over to p.189 for a chat about reduced-gravity travel with OK Go frontman Damian Kulash, who talks about his band's experience filming a one-take music video inside a "vomit comet"!

GWR ON TV AND RADIO

We'd like to say a huge thank-you to all the TV and radio shows who invited our adjudicators into their studios in the past year. Congratulations, too, to all the famous faces who had a go at some record-breaking.

A LEAGUE OF THEIR OWN
Arsenal and Wales midfielder Aaron Ramsey recorded the **most hits of a golf ball on a golf club in 30 sec** (61) on 9 Jul 2015 on this popular sporting game show.

SCRAMBLED!
The **most hot dogs made in one minute** is 10, achieved by Luke Franks (UK), host of the CITV Saturday-morning kids show, on 20 Jan 2016.

FUN KIDS RADIO
On 30 Mar 2016, radio host Sean Thorne (pictured right) and Mark Heads (both UK) set the record for the **most soft toys caught blindfolded in 30 sec** (14).

IRELAND AM
To celebrate the launch of the Rugby World Cup, Ireland AM attempted the **most conversions in one minute (team)**, scoring 16 at the RDS Arena on 10 Sep 2015.

IT'S NOT ROCKET SCIENCE
TV science-show hosts Romesh Ranganathan, Rachel Riley and Ben Miller oversaw the record for the **longest line of balloons popped by laser** (200) in Jan 2016.

EXPLORING SPACE

Space travel is fairly new to us *homo sapiens* – it was only in 1961 that Yuri Gagarin became the **first human in space**. Setting near-impossible targets is part of being a space pioneer, so any aspiring record holder should listen to what these iconic figures have to say. In this year's book, you'll hear from superlative astronauts Buzz Aldrin, Chris Hadfield and Al Worden (see right). We were also honoured to hear from NASA Administrator – and former astronaut – Charlie Bolden:

"At NASA, we've been leading the world in historic firsts, from the first nation to successfully land on the Red Planet, to the first humans to land and walk on the Moon, to the first reusable spacecraft, nearly 16 years of continuous habitation aboard the International Space Station, *and record-shattering science missions with incredible space observatories that peer into other galaxies and spacecraft that travel to the farthest reaches of the Solar System. Now we're on a human journey to Mars and astronauts continue to break their own records for time spent in space, and we're developing cutting-edge new technologies as we learn to live and work in orbit and travel farther, not just to visit but to stay."*

Charles Bolden, NASA Administrator

1. GWR Editor-in-Chief Craig Glenday poses for selfies with Moon pioneer Buzz Aldrin...

2. ...and Chris Hadfield

3. GWR science consultant David Hawksett presents two certificates to Apollo 15's Al Worden

① ② ③

In addition to Space (p.14), we have chapters on Planet Earth (p.28), Animals (p.44), Humans (p.68), Toys & Games (p.138), Engineering & Architecture (p.156), Arts & Media (p.170), Science & Technology (p.190) and Sports (p.206).

WHAT'S NEW?
New chapters this year include Do Try This at Home... (p.118) – which is packed with easy-to-attempt record ideas using

Sport Relief 2016

Guinness World Records was proud to support Sport Relief 2016 – the UK-based charity event that, in March, raised £56.9 m for good causes. For our part in the event, we ratified the record for the **most cyclists completing a 1-km time trial in 1 hour** at the Lee Valley VeloPark in London. In total, 40 people took part, among them Olympians James Cracknell and Sally Gunnell, Mike Bushell from BBC Breakfast, the former Downing Street Press Officer Alastair Campbell and cyclists from a number of cycling clubs across London. Cracknell (pictured here on the left, in white) performed his lap – and a subsequent 140 laps – on a modified Chopper bicycle to raise further funds for the charity.

Lee Valley VeloPark Lee Valley VeloPark

SPORT RELIEF 2016

NICK KICKS
Host Roman Kemp accepted the certificate for the **most football penalty kicks scored by a team of mascots in one minute** (16), set on the Nickelodeon show on 26 Jan.

SATURDAY KITCHEN
TV chef James Martin (right) presented Theo Randall (UK) with his certificate for the **fastest time to make an omelette** (14.76 sec) on his TV show on 2 May 2015.

SKY SPORTS RUGBY
The **most apples crushed with the biceps in one minute** is 14, achieved by Drew Mitchell (AUS) and filmed by Sky Sports Rugby in Toulon, France, on 3 Mar 2016.

BLUE PETER
On 12 Nov 2015, in honour of GWR Day, *Blue Peter* presenter Radzi Chinyanganya modelled the world's **longest cape**, which stretched 44.27 m (145 ft 2.9 in).

TEXT SANTA
The **most jumpers put on in one minute** is 11, achieved by Paddy McGuinness and Olly Murs (both UK) to mark Christmas Jumper Day on 18 Dec 2015.

Oldest known galaxy
Galaxy GN-z11 has formed. It will be discovered in Mar 2016 by astronomers using the NASA/ESA *Hubble Space Telescope*. Its redshift – which is used to measure the distance to galaxies – is 11.09.

13,300 MYA ▶

DATELINE

EDITOR'S LETTER

ON THE ROAD WITH GWR

Our roving adjudicators have been hitting the streets of the UK to find the country's – and the world's – most Officially Amazing people. Among the places we visited this year was the Gadget Show Live event at the Birmingham NEC, where our very own Sofia Greenacre ratified the record for the **largest 3D-printed sculpture of a human** – a 2.05-m (6-ft 8.7-in) coloured 3D rendering by 3D-printers Backface (UK) of *Gadget Show* TV host Jon Bentley.

Sofia was also part of the GWR team at BRICK – the convention "Built for LEGO® Fans" – where we adjudicated a number of records. Pictured here is Kamil Dominowski (POL), who achieved the record for the **most LEGO bricks added to a base plate in 30 sec** – a total of 127 – at the London version of the BRICK show on 13 Dec 2015.

household items – and its flipside, Don't Try This at Home… (p.128), with records that you must certainly *not* have a go at unless you're a trained performer or stuntman!

Recordology (p.82) focuses on classic GWR subjects including eating, collecting, growing giant vegetables and building big things. And there's a special history of Journeys (p.104) – a chronological look at the story of humanity's need to explore the planet and beyond, from the deepest point on Earth to our nearest Solar System neighbours.

Another new feature is Dateline, which runs along the foot of most pages. This is effectively a history of the universe in just 200 records. It's no easy task to sum up the story of the past 14 billion years in 200 entries, so this is our review of history as seen through the lens of the superlative, from the **largest explosion** (the Big Bang)

Most ABBA songs played and identified in one minute

BBC Radio 2's *Friday Night is Music Night* – the UK's longest-running orchestral radio show, which first aired in 1953 – played host to a world record on 15 Jan 2016, when presenter Ken Bruce (UK, above right) named 13 ABBA songs played by pianist Robert Wells (SWE, above left).

to the aforementioned **first confirmation of the discovery of gravitational waves** in 2016.

The Gallery pages give our picture team the chance to showcase some exceptional photography. We cover subjects from Clouds (pp.34–35) to Videogames (pp.154–55) and Disney records (pp.184–85) to

MARATHON RECORDS

In Apr 2016, our adjudicators lined the course of the Virgin Money London Marathon to ratify records attempted by costumed runners. Pictured below are all the successful athletes, who between them raised thousands of pounds for charity. We've been a proud partner of the London Marathon since 2007, approving more than 230 world records over the past 10 years.

First News

Here at GWR, we love to share in the joys of record-breaking, and regularly helping us to spread the word is *First News*, the award-winning weekly national newspaper for young people. We were thrilled to be able to celebrate our 60th anniversary in 2015 with a record-breaking special, so a big thank-you to everyone at *First News* for their continued support!

- Film character (m) Sean Fitzpatrick (Elsa, *Frozen*), 2:39.08
- Nurse uniform (m) Alistair Smith, 2:45.37
- Scout uniform Mark Lambell, 2:58.44
- Plant Lee Goodwin (flower in pot), 3:02.43
- Astronaut suit (m) Martin Hewlett, 3:06.26
- Three-legged (m) Damian Thacker & Luke Symonds, 3:07.57
- Dinosaur (full body) Ben Evans, 3:08.07
- Book character (f) Naomi Flanagan (Tinker Bell), 3:08.34
- Bottle (m) Charlie Long, 3:09.37
- Human organ Michael Stevenson (prostate), 3:13.20
- Animal (f) Katie Godof (tortoise), 3:15.39
- Crustacean (m) Greg Trevelyan (lobster), 3:17.39
- Mascot (m) Francis Gilroy, 3:17.57
- Elf (m) Petr Hruska, 3:19.15
- Circus strongman (m) Steven Reading, 3:19.30
- Highland dress (m) Scott Boyd, 3:21.00
- Gingerbread man Richard Kell, 3:29.21
- Tap/Faucet (m) Thomas Langdown, 3:29.55
- Graduation gown (m) Owen Arthurs, 3:43.20

Oldest planet
An extrasolar planet in the globular cluster M4 forms some 5,600 light years from Earth. It is more than twice as old as the Solar System, and its discovery will be announced in Jul 2003.

FAST FACTS

The **most people in a nursery-rhyme relay** is 288, set at John Ball Primary School in London on 11 Jan 2016 • David Clare (UK) covered every location on a London Monopoly board on foot in a record 2 hr 37 min 7 sec on 20 Sep 2015

RECORD-BREAKER Q&As

The best part about working at GWR is getting to meet the most remarkable people (and animals!). It's been our pleasure over the years to host record holders at our London HQ for a Friday morning meet-and-greet with staff. Here are some of the visitors we've welcomed while making this book...

Kiran Shah
At 1.263 m (4 ft 1.7 in), Kiran is the world's **shortest stuntman**. He paid us a visit after filming *Star Wars VII: The Force Awakens* (USA, 2015).

Rev. Kevin Fast
Canadian strongman Kevin popped in to talk about his record-breaking antics pulling planes, fire trucks and Santa sleds. He once even pulled an entire house!

Lee Mack
The TV comedian wowed us with his darts skills, scoring the **most inner and outer bull's-eyes in one minute** (12) and the **most darts number 2s in one minute** (18).

Vincent Pilkington
The world's **fastest turkey plucker** showed why his record – one bird stripped of feathers in just 1 min 30 sec – has remained unbeaten since 1980.

Paddy Doyle
The UK's most prolific record holder attempted his 500th fitness challenge in May 2016. Paddy has been a regular fixture in GWR since the 1980s.

"Mr Cherry"
A six-time record-breaker (and star of our TV show *Officially Amazing*), "Mr Cherry" popped into the office after filming the most recent series in 2016.

Domes (pp.160–61). The book is full of awesome images from our roving photographers, who tour the world to illustrate our remarkable record holders.

Sports fans will notice a new approach to the final chapter of the book this year. We've decided to focus exclusively on all the latest significant sporting achievements from a range of events, presented as a series of single-page features. If it's classic sporting superlatives that you're after, just turn to pp.232–241 for Sports Reference, which lists absolute records across many different sports.

The last new feature to mention is Factographics. At the start of each chapter is a spread that examines one aspect of record-breaking in more detail, using photography and graphics to tell the story behind the records. Among the topics covered are the Moon (pp.16–17), Mount Everest (pp.106–07), the current top 10 tallest buildings (pp.158–59), and the financial side of the movies (pp.172–73) and sports (pp.208–09).

A big thank-you to all our consultants who have worked on this year's book, especially those making their GWR debut, including cruciverbalists Will Shortz and John Henderson, Shakespeare expert Stuart Hampton-Reeves, chess enthusiast James Pratt and cyberneticist Rohan Mehra. And finally, thanks to the thousands of claimants who applied this year. I hope you agree that it all makes for the most fascinating read...

Craig Glenday
Craig Glenday
Editor-in-Chief

Tim Peake
Astronaut Tim Peake ran the London Marathon in orbit on board the *International Space Station*! Strapped to a treadmill, he finished in 3 hr 35 min 21 sec – the **fastest time to complete a marathon in orbit (male)**. The record was confirmed by GWR's Marco Frigatti, who adjudicated the attempt from the European Space Agency's astronaut centre in Cologne, Germany.

Film character (f)
Faye Morse (Green Fairy, *Moulin Rouge*), 3:44.18

Imitation chainmail (upper body)
Chris Taylor, 3:48.45

Fast-food item
Ryan Deering (hot dog), 3:57.17

Mascot (f)
Rachel Bown (Happy Hippo), 3:58.57

Ghillie suit (f)
Corin Leach, 3:59.13

Chef outfit
Phil Olson, 4:07.17

Firefighter outfit (f)
Erin Fairhead, 4:09.32

Animal (full body) (f)
Gill Punt (polar bear), 4:21.08

Two-person costume
Chris Coulson & Thomas Church (horse and jockey), 4:21.21

Four-legged (m)
Charles Reynolds, Oliver Smith, Fraser Barrett, 4:44.18/19

Four-person costume
J Lafferty, M Palmer, S Clifford-Tucker, L Small (fire engine), 5:25.01/02

Carrying an 80-lb (36.2-kg) pack
Michael Barker, 5:43.24

Chainmail (upper body)
David Cooke, 5:45.51

Carrying a 100-lb (45.3-kg) pack
Christopher Shirley, 7:43.26

Greatest impact on Earth
A planet the size of Mars collides with the young Earth. Some of the debris from this cataclysm goes into orbit around Earth and collects together under its own gravity to form the Moon.

4,500 MYA

DATELINE

GWR DAY

You could say that every day is Guinness World Records Day, with records being attempted and achieved by someone, somewhere, at any moment. And you'd be right. Our dedicated GWR Day, though, was first staged in 2005 to mark our 50th anniversary and is an international celebration of records and record-breaking. The event, held in November each year, throws a spotlight on the thousands of people who choose this day to make their attempts, and the latest GWR Day saw more than 610,000 participants take part in just one record attempt alone, for the **most people sport stacking in multiple venues**. Featured here are some of the other successful attempts made to mark GWR Day…

Most pine boards broken in one minute (female)

GWR Day in Australia was featured live on the *Today* show, and Summerly Denny (AUS) rose to the occasion, breaking 215 pine boards at the Olympic Park in Sydney. Summerly attempted the record in order to raise awareness of cancer research; her father Glenn Coxon – who happens to hold the record for the **most pine boards broken in one minute (male)** – had recently undergone treatment for stage-four cancer.

Farthest basketball hook shot blindfolded

In one of seven records broken by the Harlem Globetrotters (USA) on GWR Day 2015 (see Ball Skills), "Big Easy" Lofton netted a ball from 50 ft 3.5 in (15.32 m) at Talking Stick Resort Arena in Phoenix, Arizona. Team-mate "Hammer" Harrison made the **longest underhand basketball shot**: 84 ft 8.5 in (25.81 m).

Most people sport stacking in multiple venues
The 10th annual World Sport Stacking Association STACK UP! proved, once again, to be the most attended Guinness World Records Day attempt. A total of 618,394 stackers – representing 2,691 schools and organizations from 31 countries – took part in the record, which challenges as many people as possible to participate in sport stacking. This relatively new sport requires people to stack and de-stack specially designed plastic cups. Attendance numbers varied, from the USA's 547,777 participants to the Philippines' 35, but everyone was a winner!

Fastest 100 m running on all fours
GWR Day clearly motivated Kenichi Ito (JPN) to regain a record that he had held until 2013. After studying the locomotion of patas monkeys, Ito worked out how best to run 100 m on all fours in the fastest possible way, clocking a new time of 15.71 sec in Setagaya, Tokyo, Japan.

Fastest tennis ball caught
Anthony Kelly (AUS) – a martial artist and Australia's most decorated Guinness World Records title holder – demonstrated his lightning reflexes on the *Today* show for GWR Day. At the Olympic Park in Sydney, Anthony caught a tennis ball fired from a machine at a distance of 6 m (19 ft 8 in). It was travelling at a scorching 119.86 mph (192.9 km/h) – a painful but impressive feat that brought his record total to 41.

LONGEST HUMAN TUNNEL SKATEBOARDED BY A DOG
Otto the skateboarding dog has perfected the art of whizzing through an arch of human legs, tilting and weaving to avoid mishaps. No surprise, then, that the English bulldog wowed fans in Lima, Peru, by skimming through a tunnel of 30 people for GWR Day. Otto's proud owners, Luciana Viale and Robert Rickards, were inspired to choose a bulldog after watching videos of former record star Tillman, another skateboarding bulldog. Otto is also a talented surfer.

FAST FACTS

YouTube rap star Dan Bull wrote an inspirational GWR song to encourage everyone attempting records on the day • Sport stacking is the most popular GWR Day activity: to date, more than 3.7 million people have taken part

MASS PARTICIPATION

GWR Day is *the* day to gather friends, family, colleagues or classmates to try for a listing in our book. Here are some of the group effort records that were set for GWR Day in the past (some have since been broken):

PEOPLE	RECORD	COUNTRY/YEAR
618,394	Most people sport stacking – multi venue	USA, 2015
25,703	Largest line dance – multi venue	China, 2014
3,032	Most children reading with an adult	UAE, 2008
1,934	Largest computer class – multi venue	India, 2006
1,554	Largest wheelbarrow race	Australia, 2009
1,348	Largest game of leapfrog	New Zealand, 2010
882	Largest sports lesson	N Ireland, UK, 2009
764	Largest gathering of people wearing bobble hats	N Ireland, UK, 2010
407	Most people flapping simultaneously	USA, 2012
368 (92 bands)	Largest gathering of ABBA impersonators	Australia, 2011

Largest gathering of people dressed as penguins

Smashing their previous record of 373, Richard House Children's Hospice (UK) gathered 624 participants for their Penguin Waddle event. They secured the title in a sunken amphitheatre – the Scoop at More London arts venue on London's South Bank. Staff from the hospice initiated the event to publicize and raise funds for their charity, which provides clinical and residential care for young patients and support for their families.

Fastest time to type a text message (SMS) on a mobile phone while performing head spins
He may have several breakdance records to his name, but it was by texting that Benedikt Mordstein (DEU) secured his latest world record. While maintaining a head spin, Mordstein typed out a seven-word text – the German proverb "Ein blindes Huhn findet auch ein Korn" ("Even a blind hen sometimes finds the corn") – doing so in just 56.65 sec in Freising, Germany.

Largest lipstick sculpture
On 10 Nov 2015, Agnè Kišonaitė (LTU) revealed her glamorous Lipstick Tower, built from 18,399 lipsticks. Agnè was sponsored by wtc more (HKG) to make a Christmas sculpture for their shopping mall, and she spent two months developing the 3.03-m-tall (9-ft 11-in) tower.

Most lit candles held in the mouth
In honour of GWR Day 2015, Dinesh Shivnath Upadhyaya (IND) beat his own personal best by stuffing 15 burning candles into his mouth. He continued the "mouth" theme with the **most toothpicks rotated in the mouth** simultaneously (49), the **most matchsticks extinguished with the tongue in one minute** (30), and the **most grapes stuffed in the mouth** (88).

Most pull-ups in 24 hours
Marine Corps veteran Guy Valentino (USA) completed 5,862 pull-ups in New York, USA, live on television in honour of both Guinness World Records Day and Veterans Day (11 Nov). The fitness enthusiast surpassed the previous record of 5,801 pull-ups with a nail-biting 12 min to go.

Most hula-hoops spun
Bree Kirk-Burnnand (AUS) whirled into the record books by keeping 181 hula-hoops spinning in Perth, Australia. She held the record for 10 days before it was reclaimed by previous holder Marawa Ibrahim (AUS), with 200 hoops!

DID YOU KNOW?
Alastair (right) also holds the absolute world record for the **tightest parallel park**. He slid his Fiat 500c into a parking space that was a mere 7.5 cm (2.95 in) wider than the car itself at the Autosport International show in Birmingham, UK, on 8 Jan 2015.

Tightest parallel park in reverse

British stunt driver and multiple record holder Alastair Moffatt was on peak form at Brooklands in Weybridge, Surrey, UK, when he attempted a parallel park... in reverse. Driving a classic Mini, he accelerated backwards to 40 mph (64 km/h) then pulled off a handbrake turn, spinning a full 180° and, in one seamless manoeuvre, sliding between two parked Minis. The space he slotted into was a mere 1 ft 1.3 in (34 cm) longer than the car he was driving, breaking the existing world record.

Brooklands, the birthplace of British motorsport, opened in 1907 and was the **first purpose-built motor racing circuit**.

FOREWORD: DR BUZZ ALDRIN

*"The children born between the years 2000 and 2010 will be the ones making the first landings on Mars. And it's those kids that we would like to ensure are enthusiastic about the future... **Dr Buzz Aldrin, lunar explorer and space pioneer***"

This edition of *Guinness World Records* takes as its inspiration two major themes of record-breaking: the conquest of space and pioneering adventures. And there is no one alive on Earth today more qualified to introduce these concepts than Dr Buzz Aldrin. A space scientist, astronaut and educator, Buzz occupies the space where these two worlds collide. He is the very definition of a space pioneer, holding records for, among other things, taking the **first selfie in open space** and, of course, for his central role in the **first manned landing on the Moon**.

During a trip to London to launch his book – *Welcome to Mars: Making a Home on the Red Planet* (2015) – Dr Aldrin met with GWR to receive his world record certificates. In an exclusive interview with Editor-in-Chief Craig Glenday, Buzz talked about his superlative achievements and his determination for humanity to reach our planetary neighbour.

"DR RENDEZVOUS"

Colonel Buzz Aldrin – born Edwin Eugene Aldrin Jr – was known to his NASA colleagues as "Dr Rendezvous". He was the first of the NASA astronauts to have a doctorate – in Buzz's case, in orbital dynamics – and his pioneering research and techniques on docking spacecraft in orbit are still employed today. A keen scuba diver, he also championed underwater training techniques to simulate the zero-gravity environment encountered during spacewalks.

Upon his return from the Moon, Buzz was awarded the Presidential Medal of Freedom and, in 2011, the Congressional Gold Medal. He continues to advocate space travel, and inspires a new generation of astronauts with his best-selling books and his commitment to education.

First manned lunar landing

Apollo 11 saw Buzz (Lunar Module Pilot) and Neil Armstrong (Commander) make the first human landing on the surface of the Moon – in the *Eagle* – at 20:18 UTC on 20 Jul 1969. While Michael Collins orbited in the Command Module, Neil and Buzz became the first humans to set foot on the Moon's surface – Neil at 02:56 UTC on 21 Jul, followed by Buzz at 03:11.

FAST FACTS
Buzz got his name from his sister, who mis-pronounced "brother" as "buzzer" • He changed his name legally to Buzz in 1988 • His mother's maiden name was Marion Moon • MTV named their Video Music Award statue "Buzzy" after him

First selfie in open space

On 13 Nov 1966, during the Gemini 12 mission, Buzz started the second of his three spacewalks. During the 2-hr 6-min tethered walk in open space he took photos of the visible star fields, but also turned the camera on himself to take the first self-portrait in open space.

"I just opened the hatch and looked around," said Buzz, "just like a sightseeing tourist would. I saw the camera and thought, 'I wonder what would happen if I took a picture of me', not knowing whether it would turn out at all! The lighting was not too well selected, but you could tell who it was."

Craig: Why did you choose to write a book about Mars?
Buzz: I wrote it because I think the idea of a transportation system between the Earth and the Moon that I had been working on was interesting for explorers. Or for adventure-travel tourism. But NASA wasn't interested in that! So I shifted my attention to a unique transportation system between Earth and Mars. Mars is our future – although I won't be around long enough to see it all happening!

Craig: When will we be able to land a human on Mars?
Buzz: I think at around 2040. This is two decades from the celebratory date of 20 Jul 2019 – 50 years from reaching the Moon.

Craig: How long would the journey to Mars be?
Buzz: I was reading the other day that people think we could get there in 30 days, maybe even quicker, but I think that's quite a bit in the future.

Craig: You're passionate about communicating science and astronomy to kids. How important is that to you?
Buzz: The children born between the years 2000 and 2010 will be the ones making the first landings on Mars. And it's those kids that we would like to ensure are enthusiastic about the future.

You don't want an education programme just for "geeks" – you know, people who only know math

and computers. You need the arts involved, so a number of us are calling [for] "S.T.E.A.M." education: Science, Technology, Engineering, Arts, Mathematics. We want to keep up with things, just like Guinness World Records wants to keep up with the latest records that are being set.

Craig: Talking of records, tell us about your experience on the Moon. What goes through your head when you first step off that ladder?
Buzz: One step at a time! And go down backwards, so that you can watch as you go down and not miss a step!

Craig: You described it in your autobiography as "magnificent desolation"...
Buzz: That was an overall impression of the entire progression of information, of discovery, of exploration... Compared to the history of humans, it was a magnificent achievement

for people to be out of their element and to land [on the Moon]. But looking around, nothing could have been more desolate than what we saw: the black sky, the sunlit terrain. Very clear. No atmosphere. No life. And up here, what we were looking at hadn't changed in thousands of years.

There isn't any place like that on the Earth. So, it is a desolate place we were visiting, but a magnificent achievement [to reach it].

And when you're out there on the surface and look up, you say, "Oh yeah! That's the Earth up there!"

Craig: What was it like seeing Earth from the Moon?
Buzz: Intellectually realizing that everyone else – living, or dead – is on the Earth except the three people up there at the Moon... that's a contrast. That's a record!

For more on the Moon landings, see pp.16–17.

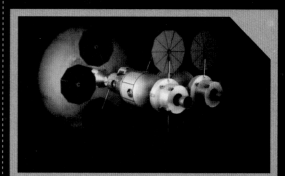

Cycling to Mars

Buzz is passionate about the planet Mars, and has devoted much of his time since his historic Moon landing trying to encourage humanity to set their sights on our Solar System neighbour as humanity's next frontier.

"If we took all the wasted effort that results in the discord on the Earth and put it into something positive, it would be a good turnaround of effort," Buzz told GWR. "The historical significance of people from the Earth beginning to populate another planet... I don't think people have any idea of how important that could be."

In his latest book, *Welcome to Mars*, Buzz explores the various options we have for – to quote the sub-title – "making a home on the Red Planet". "My way to get from Earth to Mars involves 'cycling'. It was discovered in 1985 and is still the best way of getting from Earth to Mars." By "cycling", Buzz means employing a fleet of spacecraft ("cyclers", artist's impression above) that would use the gravity of Mars and Earth to loop between the two planets with virtually no fuel consumption – and, potentially, continue to do so indefinitely. Much of his time is now devoted to securing the support and funds needed for this ambitious Martian dream.

Buzz continues: "Empires rise and empires fall. But I would not like to be remembered as being alive at a time when we were on the way down. We certainly need the public behind us."

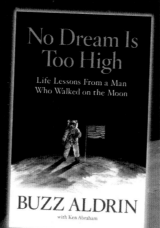

No Dream Is Too High
Life Lessons From a Man Who Walked on the Moon
BUZZ ALDRIN
with Ken Abraham

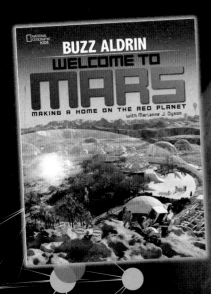

NATIONAL GEOGRAPHIC KIDS
BUZZ ALDRIN
WELCOME TO MARS
MAKING A HOME ON THE RED PLANET
with Marianne J. Dyson

"You are the future. You are going to achieve super things that are out of this world and that no one else has done before, and go to places that no one has ever gone. Earth isn't the only world for us any more."

INTERVIEW: CHRIS HADFIELD

> *If you get into Guinness World Records, it means that you've done something that's right on the edge of the human experience. Something that has pushed back the level of what we've achieved in the past. As an astronaut, I've been lucky enough to do several things that fit into that category...*
>
> *CDR Chris Hadfield*

If we earthlings had to identify a planetary ambassador – a truly exceptional figure to represent our race – then we would do well to choose the Canadian astronaut Chris Hadfield. An engineer, test pilot, Space Shuttle crew member, commander of the *International Space Station* and record-breaking musician, Chris embodies the very best of what it means to be human. His incredible resumé has given him a unique perspective on life, and when it came to finding inspirational figures to introduce this year's edition of *Guinness World Records*, Chris was an obvious choice.

Shortly before we went to press, GWR Editor-in-Chief Craig Glenday spoke with Chris about the need to set goals and aim to be the record-breaking best in the world, no matter what the activity or subject matter.

Craig: How important is the need to identify and break world records?
Chris: I think, through human nature, we respond well to a challenge. If someone says to you, "I can jump over that thing. I could lift that rock. If you and I ran from here to that tree, I'd beat you," it raises

Chris with his GWR certificate for **first music video filmed in space** (see far right). In his book, *An Astronaut's Guide to Life on Earth*, he talks of his love of music and how he recorded his album *Space Sessions: Songs from a Tin Can*.

COMMANDER CHRIS AUSTIN HADFIELD

Chris Hadfield was first inspired to become an astronaut as a nine-year-old child after watching the Moon landings on TV. With the Moon as his goal, he embarked on learning to fly – first gliders, then fighter jets – and later earned a degree in engineering and a masters in aviation systems.

In 1992, he joined the Canadian Space Agency's astronaut programme, and finally became the first Canadian to walk in space. He also learned Russian, reckoning that being able to speak the language of a superpower able to send humans into space would serve him well, which it did when he visited the *Mir* space station and flew on Space Shuttle and Soyuz missions. In Mar 2013, he took command of the *International Space Station* (*ISS*).

Since returning to Earth, Chris has written three books: *An Astronaut's Guide to Life on Earth* (2013), *You Are Here: Around the World in 92 Minutes* (2015), and the children's book *The Darkest Dark* (2016).

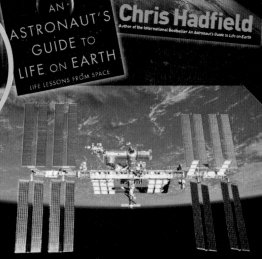

Largest space station

The *International Space Station*, which Chris commanded during Expedition 35 in 2013, is 72.8 m (239 ft) long and 108.5 m (356 ft) wide. With a volume of 916 m³ (32,350 cu ft) and weighing 419,455 kg (924,740 lb) – about the size of a Boeing 747 – it's the biggest habitable artificial satellite. It orbits c. 412 km (256 mi) above Earth.

Largest robotic arm in space

Chris was part of the team that installed Canadarm2 – the 17.5-m (57-ft) robotic arm that was attached to the *International Space Station* on 22 Apr 2001. The arm was fitted during a 7-hr spacewalk by Chris and US astronaut Scott Parazynski. (Pictured above is Chris' *ISS* crew.)

During the mission, Chris became the first Canadian to walk in space. "Doing spacewalks is extremely dangerous," he says. "And it's extremely hard. We prepare for [it] extensively. And like anything that you've prepared for for years and years that also has an element of danger to it, when the moment comes it's your whole focus... It's kind of your whole life in a moment. And it doesn't disappoint!"

a fundamental response within each of us that is just basic human nature. You might run faster in your life than you ever had for no greater purpose than the competition; it's just primordial to who we are. By having a book like *Guinness World Records*, it helps measure the best of us. And if you're a young person, it can challenge you to do something that otherwise you never would have attempted – a self-betterment that you might never have tried. Challenge is a wonderful thing to have in life. And, like everyone else on the planet, I have read through *Guinness World Records* and have been amazed by some of the things people have accomplished.

Craig: What does it take to be Chris Hadfield?
Chris: I think the most important thing is to give yourself a long-term goal that you think is probably impossible. But give

yourself that goal – maybe, "I want to climb Mount Everest," or "I want to climb the highest six peaks in the world," or "I want to invent a valve that will allow someone who has a heart attack to survive," or "I want to be able to do surgery on an eyeball so that a blind person can see" – whatever. Give yourself a goal in life that is right on the edge of impossible. Because even though you might not climb all those peaks, or invent that thing, the choices you're going to make in pursuit of that goal will actually change who you are. And you will be pursuing something that is in your heart.

In my case, I said, "I want to be an astronaut who walks on the Moon." Yet I never have. But it allowed me to choose the things I was going to do that led me through a life that has absolutely fascinated me and brought things out of me that I never would have otherwise been able to do. It allowed me to see and understand things that would have been denied me otherwise.

That's the real core of it: to challenge yourself. Not define yourself by that final success, but use it as the long-term lure that allows you to pursue – and succeed at – things on a daily basis.

For more on spacewalks, float over to pp.22–23.

First music video filmed in space

On 12 May 2013, Chris posted a video to YouTube of him singing a modified version of David Bowie's "Space Oddity", recorded during his last mission on board the *International Space Station* (*ISS*). The music video – the first filmed entirely in space – shows Chris floating around inside the *ISS* with his guitar, with Earth visible through the station's cupola window. The vocals and guitar were recorded on the *ISS*, while piano and other musical accompaniment were added by performers on Earth. The video was mixed with the help of the Canadian Space Agency.

Chris amassed some 770,000 followers on Twitter during his time on the *ISS* for his videos and photos of Earth from space, becoming a celebrity in the process.

He introduced the song with the post: "With deference to the genius of David Bowie, here's Space Oddity, recorded on Station. A last glimpse of the World." In Jan 2014, he added: "20 million hits! I am so delighted with the worldwide reaction to science & art, together."

Bowie tweeted "Hallo Spaceboy..." (the title of his 1996 hit single) in response to Chris's video.

> "That's the real core of it: to challenge yourself. Not define yourself by that final success, but use it as the long-term lure that allows you to pursue – and succeed at – things on a daily basis."

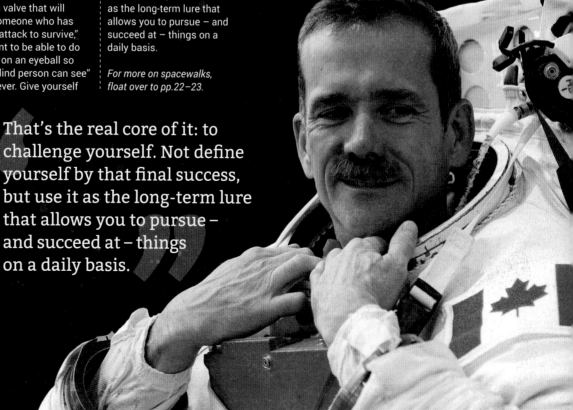

SPACE

DID YOU KNOW?
The name Pluto was suggested by an 11-year-old schoolgirl, Venetia Burney (UK). Her grandfather was the librarian at Oxford University and was able to pass on her idea to Pluto's discoverer, Clyde Tombaugh (USA), a few months after the discovery was announced.

3,825 MYA

Oldest volcanic rocks on Earth
A lava flow on the surface of the still-cooling Earth solidifies into a slab of igneous rock.
Its age will be confirmed in 2002 by researchers in Quebec, Canada.

CONTENTS

Smallest planet?

Discovered in 1930, Pluto was known for generations as the Solar System's **smallest planet**. This all changed in 2006, when the International Astronomical Union (IAU) revoked its planet status, changing it from the ninth planet – and the last entry in numerous classroom rhymes and mnemonics – to trans-Neptunian object "134340 Pluto". Recently, however, the campaign to return Pluto's planet status has been gaining ground, boosted by pictures such as this composite showing the relative scale of Pluto (right) and its moon Charon, taken by NASA's *New Horizons* spacecraft in 2015. Dr Alan Stern – Principal Investigator on the *New Horizons* mission – gives his thoughts on the debate on p.21.

First photosynthesis
Tiny, single-celled organisms – distant ancestors of present-day cyanobacteria – develop the ability to process nutrients using the light of the Sun as an energy source.

3,700 MYA

THE MOON

GWR presents a whistle-stop tour of our nearest cosmic neighbour – and the technology that enabled humanity to reach it.

The Moon is slightly more than a quarter the size of Earth in terms of diameter, and its elemental composition is very similar to that of our own planet. In fact, we're closely related: according to the giant-impact hypothesis, around 4.5 billion years ago a Mars-sized planet called Theia crashed into Earth, violently ejecting large amounts of debris into space. During the next million years or so, those rocky bits and pieces eventually coalesced to form the Moon. The Moon was thought to be unique until 1610, when Italian astronomer Galileo Galilei identified moons around Jupiter.

Mantle
Between the Moon's crust and inner core is a rigid zone known as the lithosphere, or upper mantle. It is approximately 620 km (385 mi) deep.

Partial melt
Separating the mantle from the innermost core is a partly molten layer of rocks and metals with a radius of roughly 480 km (300 mi).

Fluid outer core
Thought to be composed mainly of liquid iron. The outer core has a radius of around 330 km (205 mi).

Solid inner core
The heart of the Moon consists of a hard core with a radius of 240 km (150 mi), containing a high density of iron. It represents about 20% of the Moon; the cores of other planets in the Solar System can account for up to 50% of their size.

Crust
On average, the Moon's crust is 34–43 km (21–27 mi) thick, although it is as thin as 1 km (0.6 mi) in certain impact basins, and as thick as 60 km (37 mi) in the highlands on the far side. The surface of the Moon is called its regolith, and there are two main types: the bright ancient highlands, dominated by breccia, formed by asteroids and meteorites pulverising and melting the surface, and the darker maria (seas) that formed as basaltic lava flooded the lowlands.

The footprints left by the Apollo astronauts are all still there. There is no lunar atmosphere, which means that there is no wind or weather to erode them.

DID YOU KNOW?

The maximum distance between Earth and the Moon is around 406,700 km (252,711 mi). To understand the vast distance, consider this: the combined diameter of Mercury, Venus, Mars, Jupiter, Saturn, Neptune, Uranus and Pluto is 387,941 km (241,055 mi). This means you could fit all eight of our Solar System neighbours between Earth and the Moon!

The first men on the Moon were carried into space on a Saturn V rocket, still the **largest rocket** launched to date. On the launchpad, fully loaded with propellant – crucial to escape the pull of Earth's gravity – the rocket weighed some 2,900 tonnes (3,196 US tons). Here is the Saturn V shown to scale with two other record-worthy spacecraft.

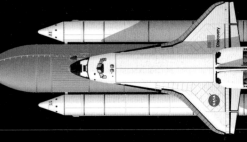
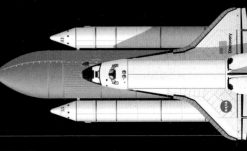

SATURN V (USA)
• Length: 110.6 m (363 ft)
• About 18 m (60 ft) taller than the Statue of Liberty and some 15 times heavier than a blue whale. Active from 1967 to 1973.

SPACE SHUTTLE (USA)
• Length: 56 m (184 ft)
• The first reusable spacecraft made its maiden flight on 12 Apr 1981, weighing 2,000 tonnes (2,204 US tons) at launch. Fuel alone was around 25 times heavier than the shuttle itself.

VOSTOK 1 (USSR, now Russia)
• Length: 30.8 m (101 ft)
• Carried Yuri Gagarin (USSR) on the first manned spaceflight on 12 Apr 1961.

An average USB memory stick is more powerful than the computers that were used to put a man on the Moon.

=

The mass of the Earth (5.98×10^{24} kg, or 1.3×10^{25} lb) is some 81 times greater than that of the Moon (7.34×10^{22} kg, or 1.6×10^{23} lb).

At approximately 3,474 km (2,158 mi), the diameter of the Moon is around 500 km (310 mi) smaller than the distance between Australia's west and east coast.

DID YOU KNOW?
The Apollo 11 astronauts couldn't get life insurance – too risky, apparently. So they signed photos that their families could sell in case the first Moon landing went wrong. The photos were date-stamped and posted to the families by a friend on 16 Jul 1969 – launch day.

DID YOU KNOW?
The surface gravity on the Moon is approximately one-sixth of the gravity on Earth. This means that astronauts would be able to jump six times higher on the Moon than here on Earth – were it not for their cumbersome and heavy spacesuits.

The Apollo Guidance Computer (AGC) circuitry was even more basic than the start/stop/defrost electronics used in modern toasters, having just 64 KB of memory and operating at 0.043 MHz.

A single Google search for "Apollo 11 mission" uses as much computing power as the entire Apollo 11 mission.

The Moon is moving away from Earth at a rate of **4 cm (1.5 in) per year.** This is roughly the length your fingernails will grow in the same amount of time.

4

3

2

1

0 cm

Largest extrasolar planet

Discovered in 2005, planet HD 100546 b has been estimated to be 600,000 mi (965,600 km) in diameter. It has a mass approximately 60 times that of Jupiter, and its size makes it very close to the boundary between giant planets and brown dwarf stars. In fact, it may turn out not to be a planet at all. It orbits the star HD 100546, aka KR Muscae, in the constellation Musca, approximately 320 light years away. The star itself is c. 10 million years old.

Most planets orbiting another star

HD 10180 (artist's impression above) is a star that is very similar to our Sun and about 120 light years away. Based on observations made at La Silla Observatory in Chile by Mikko Tuomi (UK), it has at least seven planets and possibly as many as nine.

Seven planets are also known to orbit KIC 11442793, a dwarf star about 2,500 light years away.

Smallest extrasolar planet
Kepler-37b orbits the star Kepler-37 at around 210 light years from Earth in the constellation Lyra. Its discovery by NASA's *Kepler* spacecraft was made public on 20 Feb 2013. Kepler-37b is only about 1,200 mi (1,930 km) across, smaller than the planet Mercury.

The **smallest extrasolar planet directly imaged by telescope** is the gas giant 51 Eridani b. It is about the same diameter as Jupiter (86,880 mi; 139,820 km) but twice its mass. It orbits the star 51 Eridani in the constellation Eridanus and was the first discovery, on 13 Aug 2015, by the Gemini Planet Imager at Stanford University, USA, which began searching for extrasolar planets in Nov 2014.

Youngest extrasolar planet
Infrared observations of the young star CoKu Tau 4 by NASA's *Spitzer Space Telescope* reveal a gap in the circumstellar disc of dust and gas that is likely to be a newly formed planet. The star, along with its possible planet, is located around 420 light years from Earth in the constellation Taurus, and is no more than 1 million years old.

Nearest extrasolar planet
On 7 Aug 2000, a team led by Dr William Cochran of the University of Texas McDonald Observatory (both USA) revealed evidence of a new world "in our own backyard", just 10.45 light years from the Sun. The gas giant, estimated to be 1.6 times the mass of Jupiter, orbits the star Epsilon Eridani. The exoplanet lies some 478 million km (297 million mi) from its central star, which is about the same distance as our Sun to the Asteroid Belt.

DID YOU KNOW?

Extrasolar planet OGLE-2005-BLG-390Lb takes about 10 years to orbit its chilly parent star, which is about one-fifth the mass of our Sun. The world is likely to have a thin atmosphere, like Earth, but its rocky surface is believed to lie concealed beneath vast frozen oceans.

TRIVIA

If we awarded a record for pinkest planet, it would surely go to the newly formed GJ 504b in the constellation of Virgo, which glows a magenta or cherry red (artist's impression below).

MOST DISTANT EXTRASOLAR PLANET

Near the centre of the Milky Way, at a distance of 21,500 ± 3,300 light years away from Earth, the planet OGLE-2005-BLG-390Lb orbits a red dwarf star. The low energy of its star, coupled with the size of its orbit (corresponding to between that of Mars and Jupiter around the Sun), means that the planet's surface temperature is just -220°C (-364°F). This makes OGLE-2005-BLG-390Lb the **coldest extrasolar planet**.

The OGLE part of its name derives from the Optical Gravitational Lensing Experiment. This uses ground-based telescopes to scan the central Milky Way for signs of a "microlensing event". In this phenomenon, light coming from a distant star is seen to dip if another star and its planet crosses in front of it. This is owing to the gravity of the nearer star and its planet.

DATELINE

 3,600 MYA

Oldest mountain range
The Barberton Greenstone Belt (also known as the Makhonjwa Mountains) begins to form in present-day South Africa. It is here, in 1875, that the first gold in the country will be discovered.

18 Space

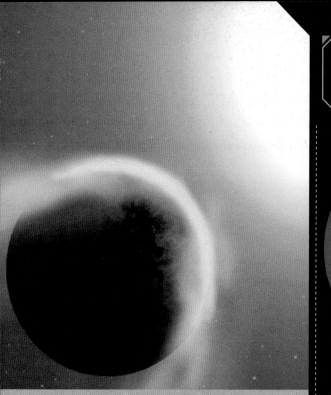

FAST FACTS

As of Feb 2016, there have been 2,085 confirmed discoveries of extrasolar planets • According to the National Academy of Sciences, there could be as many as 11 billion habitable, Earth-like planets in the Milky Way alone

First map of an extrasolar planet

In 2007, NASA's *Spitzer Space Telescope* observed the star HD 189733 and its planet, HD 189733 b, for 33 hr. The observations were converted into a temperature map with a range of 700–940°C (1,290–1,720°F). The map, pictured here, shows a warm spot on the planet's sunlit side.

Closest extrasolar planet to its parent star

Discovered by NASA's *Kepler* spacecraft in 2011, Kepler-70b orbits its host star, Kepler-70, at a distance of 0.006 astronomical units (about 898,000 km; 558,000 mi). Located c. 3,849 light years away in the constellation Cygnus, Kepler-70b orbits its star in just 5.76 hr and has an estimated surface temperature of around 6,930°C (12,500°F), making it the **hottest extrasolar planet**. It may be the rocky core remains of a gas giant.

to be subject to winds of up to 9,000 mph (14,500 km/h).

Earth-like extrasolar planet
More than 2,000 extrasolar planets in 1,300-plus systems have been spotted to date. Of these, Kepler-22b is the first potentially Earth-like example. Found in 2011, it is about 2.4 times the size of Earth and orbits its Sun-like star in about 290 days. The luminosity of this star and Kepler-22b's orbital distance suggest that it may occupy its star's habitable zone. If the planet has an Earth-like greenhouse effect, its surface temperature could be about 22°C (72°F).

DID YOU KNOW?

In 2015, the International Astronomical Union (IAU) ran a contest, open to the public, to give 14 stars and 31 extrasolar planets new names. So PSR B1257+12 became Lich and its planets are now Draugr, Poltergeist and Phobetor – characters from fantasy and folklore.

FIRST...

Planet hunter space mission
The *Convection Rotation and Planetary Transits* (*COROT*) spacecraft was launched on 27 Dec 2006 into a polar orbit 827 km (513 mi) above Earth. It was the first craft designed specifically to find planets around other stars and operated until Nov 2012, when it suffered an irreparable computer failure.

Extrasolar planet discovered orbiting a main-sequence star
Astronomers from the University of Geneva (CHE) announced the discovery of 51 Pegasi b on 6 Oct 1995. It orbits 51 Pegasi, a G5V main-sequence star – one that is in the process of fusing hydrogen into helium at its core, like our Sun.

The title of **windiest extrasolar planet** also goes to 51 Pegasi b, along with the gas giants HD 179949 b and HD 209458 b, which orbit other stars. All appear

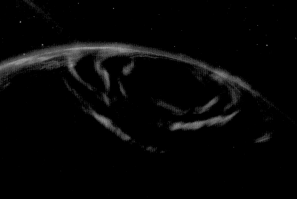

First confirmed discovery of an extrasolar planet

In 1992, astronomers announced the presence of two planets orbiting a pulsar named PSR B1257+12 (above), 980 light years from Earth. A pulsar is a rapidly spinning neutron star – the collapsed core of an exploded giant star – and emits intense radiation. PSR B1257+12's planets were designated "super-Earths" – more massive than Earth but much less massive than our gas giants – so this also marked the **first super-Earth extrasolar planet discovered**. PSR B1257+12 b, a third planet later confirmed in 1994 and now named Draugr, is the **lightest extrasolar planet**. Its mass is about 0.02 times that of Earth.

Oldest oil
The remnants of dead organisms lying on the seabed begin millions of years of transformation, crushed by the intense pressure from sediment deposits to form oil.

3,200 MYA

DATELINE

PLUTO

Shortest time from the discovery of a planet to its exploration by spacecraft
Pluto was discovered by US astronomer Clyde Tombaugh on 18 Feb 1930. It took just over 85 years – 31,193 days, to be precise – for it to be explored by spacecraft (see below).

Planet with the most chaotically rotating moons
Pluto has five known moons. Charon was discovered by American astronomer James Christy at the US Naval Observatory in Flagstaff, Arizona. Its discovery was announced on 7 Jul 1978. Nix and Hydra were discovered in 2005, and two others in 2011 and 2012, provisionally named S/2011 P 1 and S/2012 P 1.
    These last four are chaotically rotating moons. This means they tumble instead of rotating neatly along one axis. Saturn's moon Hyperion is the only other known chaotically rotating moon in the Solar System.

Pluto's largest moon is Charon, with a mean diameter of 1,212 km (753 mi) – more than half Pluto's diameter. Pluto is around eight times more massive than Charon; the two bodies orbit each other around a common centre of gravity between them. *New Horizons* came within 28,800 km (17,895 mi) of Charon on 14 Jul 2015.
    The **longest canyon on Charon**, as imaged by *New Horizons*, stretches at least

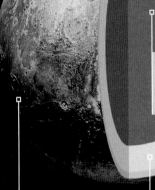

Most distant human remains
Around 30 g (1 oz) of the cremated remains of Clyde Tombaugh (1906–97) are being carried on board the *New Horizons* spacecraft in a canister (above) attached to the craft's upper deck. One of his final wishes was for his ashes to be sent into space.

Plutonian geology
The *New Horizons* flyby revealed stunning surface details that helped scientists better understand the composition of the planet

Rock core
A core of dense rock accounts for an estimated 70% of Pluto's diameter

Mantle of water ice
A sub-surface ocean of water ice that could be 100–180 km (62–112 mi) thick

Nitrogen ice surface
An estimated 98% of the surface is nitrogen ice, with traces of methane and carbon monoxide

Pluto at a glance

Discovery	1930	Atmospheric pressure at the surface	1 Pa
Mass	1.303 x 10^{22} kg	Density	1.860 g/cm^3
Volume	7.006 x 10^9 km^3	Surface gravity	0.66 m/s^2
Equatorial radius	1,187 km	Axial tilt	122.5°
Number of moons	5		(retrograde rotation)
Temperature	-240 to -218°C		

NEW HORIZONS
On 14 Jul 2015, the *New Horizons* spacecraft made the **first flyby of Pluto**. It launched from Cape Canaveral in Florida, USA, in Jan 2006, and, because of its mass of less than 0.5 tonnes (0.55 US tons), achieved the **fastest Earth departure speed for a planetary mission**: 58,338 km/h (36,250 mph). *New Horizons* passed the orbit of the Moon in just 9 hr and reached Neptune's orbit in 8.6 years. It made observations of Jupiter during its flyby in Feb 2007. The craft's suite of seven instruments includes the Venetia Burney Student Dust Counter, built by students at the University of Colorado.
    It is the **first mission to the outer Solar System led by a scientist** rather than a NASA centre, and is now en route to the Kuiper Belt Object (KBO) 2014 MU69 – an icy, rocky object – which it will encounter on 1 Jan 2019.

1,600 km (990 mi) across the surface of the moon and may extend farther, to its dark side.

Tallest mountain on Pluto
In 2015, a 5.25-km-tall (3.2-mi) mountain was discovered by the *New Horizons* team. It was named Matthew Alexander Henson, after the first African-American Arctic explorer.

DID YOU KNOW?
Pluto is part of the Kuiper Belt, a far-distant region of icy bodies that is a relic from the formation of our Solar System. Scientists believe that *New Horizons'* flyby of KBO 2014 MU69, almost a billion miles beyond Pluto, will reveal vital data about the evolution of the Solar System.

DATELINE

2,400 MYA

Longest ice age
The most severe ice age begins, and will last around 70 million years. During this period, the entire Earth will be covered in ice, possibly to a depth of 1 km (0.6 mi).

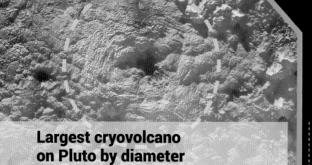

Largest cryovolcano on Pluto by diameter

A cryovolcano or ice volcano erupts liquids and vapour. Two geological features resembling cryovolcanoes have been found south of Pluto's icy Sputnik Planum. Results so far show Piccard Mons (below) to be around 200 km (125 mi) wide, and Wright Mons (above) 160 km (100 mi) wide. If these are cryovolcanoes, their eruptive material would probably be water ice, ammonia, nitrogen and/or methane.

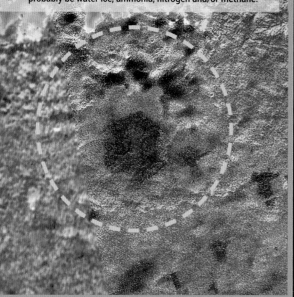

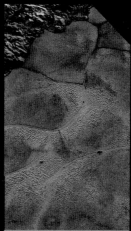

direction of Pluto. Part of this signal was reflected from Pluto and detected by the REX radar experiment on board the spacecraft. The technique, known as bistatic radar, can reveal surface properties of planetary bodies. During this successful experiment, *New Horizons* was 33 astronomical units from Earth, or 33 times the distance of Earth to the Sun.

TRIVIA
On 4 Jul 2015, the *New Horizons* team lost contact with the spacecraft – it had switched to the backup computer because of a problem. The team had to work round the clock to restore main computer function in time for the 14 Jul flyby.

Coldest glaciers in the Solar System

Close-ups of the vast, icy plain known as Sputnik Planum, in Pluto's "heart", show fluvial features reminiscent of glaciers on Earth. The surface here is thought to be composed mostly of nitrogen ice, with temperatures as low as 33 kelvin (-240°C; -400°F).

Largest crater on Pluto
Sputnik Planum, mostly in Pluto's northern hemisphere, measures around 1,050 x 800 km (650 x 495 mi). It is the site of active nitrogen glaciation, and the lack of impact craters indicates its surface is less than 10 million years old. Sputnik Planum is now believed to occupy a giant ancient impact basin filled with volatile ices.

Most distant bistatic radar experiment
Just after *New Horizons*' closest approach to Pluto, a radar signal from NASA's Deep Space Network on Earth was sent in the

Dr Alan Stern

The Principal Investigator on NASA's *New Horizons* mission to Pluto and the Kuiper Belt, Dr Alan Stern (fourth from right) shares his thoughts on Pluto's changing status as a planetary body.

"Times change. Back in 2006, a convention of astronomers declared Pluto no longer a planet, but planetary scientists never voted to agree. Now, following the exploration of Pluto by NASA's *New Horizons* in 2015, the pendulums of planetary experts and lay opinion are swinging strongly the other way.

"The arguments against Pluto were that it was too small, on too odd an orbit, and one of too many for schoolkids to remember their names. But after the advances and scientific progress of the last decade, from telescopic studies to the flyby of Pluto, we see new data overturning those old ideas.

"Since then, Pluto has been shown to be the largest known body in the deep outer Solar System beyond Neptune. And thousands of planets have been discovered orbiting other stars, many in orbits like Pluto's. These facts, along with the dizzyingly complex surface that Pluto showed *New Horizons*, and discoveries that Pluto has five moons (more than Earth, Mars, Venus and Mercury combined) – as well as blue skies, mountains, glaciers, a rocky interior and dunes – have tipped the scales back to planethood.

"We know that Pluto is not a comet a few kilometres across, either. It's huge, with a circumference of almost 7,500 km (4,600 mi) – as far as from Manhattan west across North America and the Pacific to Maui [in Hawaii]. In 2016, Pluto isn't seen just as a planet, but the largest of many small planets that inhabit our deep outer Solar System and probably are common to other star systems as well."

Largest "classical" crater on Pluto

The 250-km-wide (155-mi) impact basin Venetia Burney is a "classical" crater: one that has not been resurfaced with ice. This image shows the cratered interior of Venetia Burney, whose outer rim forms the line of hills visible at the bottom.

Oldest macroscopic organism
Grypania cf. spiralis, an ancestor of algae, is present in Michigan, USA. Meanwhile, other organisms, later called the "Gabonionta" or "Francevillian biota", are flourishing in Gabon, Africa. Both are visible to the naked eye.

2,100 MYA

DATELINE

SPACEWALKS

First spacewalk

Lieutenant-Colonel Alexei Leonov (USSR) performed the first EVA on 18 Mar 1965, spending 12 min 9 sec outside the *Voskhod 2* spacecraft. The spacewalk was a triumph, but Leonov had problems. Returning to the airlock, he found that his spacesuit had ballooned. He couldn't bend his arms or legs properly and had to release a little oxygen while in space to re-enter the craft.

Longest total time walking in space by a female astronaut
Sunita Williams (USA) has spent 50 hr 40 min on seven separate spacewalks from the *International Space Station* (*ISS*).

Oldest person to perform a spacewalk
On 19 Apr 2013, Russia's Pavel Vinogradov (b. 31 Aug 1953) performed a spacewalk from the *ISS* aged 59 years 231 days.

FIRST...

Spacewalk between spacecraft
On 20 Jul 1966, Michael Collins (USA) spacewalked from *Gemini 10* to the unmanned GATV-8 booster with a tether and Hand-Held Maneuvering Unit. The craft were 3 m (9 ft 10 in) apart. The day before, Collins flipped his camera around to take the **first selfie in space,** in the *Gemini 10* capsule. The same urge gripped astronaut Buzz Aldrin (USA) during the Gemini 12 mission, which took place later that year. On 13 Nov, he paused during a 2-hr spacewalk to take the **first selfie in open space**.

Internal spacewalk
On 22 Aug 1997, Russia's Anatoly Solovyev and Pavel Vinogradov carried out a spacewalk inside the depressurized *Spektr* module of the *Mir* space station, whose hull had been breached after striking an unmanned *Progress* supply vehicle. Their spacewalk, to inspect and initiate repairs, lasted 3 hr 16 min.

First spacewalk (female)

On 25 Jul 1984, Soviet cosmonaut Svetlana Savitskaya performed a spacewalk – more formally known as an extravehicular activity (EVA) – outside the *Salyut 7* space station as part of the Soyuz T-12 mission. Savitskaya and Vladimir Dzhanibekov spent 3 hr 30 min outside *Salyut 7*, carrying out maintenance repairs, including the **first welding in open space**.

First spacewalk in deep space

Al Worden (USA) was Command Module Pilot on Apollo 15, which returned to Earth on 7 Aug 1971. En route home, and still nearly 320,000 km (198,800 mi) from Earth, he performed the first spacewalk that was not in Low Earth Orbit, to retrieve film cassettes from cameras on the spacecraft. His EVA, on 5 Aug 1971, lasted for 39 min in all. Worden is pictured above receiving his GWR certificate in Feb 2016.

CHRIS HADFIELD, SPACEWALKER

Canada's Chris Hadfield is the man who charmed the world with his memorable take on David Bowie's "Space Oddity", filmed during his last mission on the *ISS* and immortalized as the **first music video filmed in space**. But GWR caught up with him in Nov 2015 to find out about another record-breaking feat.

During a 7-hr spacewalk on 22 Apr 2001, Chris and Scott Parazynski (USA) attached *Canadarm2* (the **longest robotic arm in space**) to the *ISS*. It was his first spacewalk, and it got off to a bad start: his visor's chemical anti-fogging solution got in his eyes, causing him to lose his vision, first in one eye, then the other.

"And then I was blind, in my spacesuit, outside on a spacewalk!" Years of extensive preparation helped him to keep a calm head, even when he was hanging on to the *ISS* for dear life. "OK, I can't see," he told himself. "But I can still feel. I can hear. I can talk. I can breathe. How am I going to solve this problem?" Luckily, his tears welled up and helped to dilute the contaminant within half an hour.

DATELINE 2,000 MYA
Largest impact crater on Earth
An asteroid or comet collides with Earth, creating a depression with an estimated diameter of 300 km (186 mi). Now known as the Vredefort crater, it is located near present-day Johannesburg in South Africa.

FAST FACTS

To date, more than 200 astronauts have performed a spacewalk • Spacesuits are white to reflect the heat of direct sunlight in space, which may exceed 275°F (135°C) • It takes about 45 min to don a spacesuit

DID YOU KNOW?

Spacewalks can last up to 8 hr, depending on the tasks being carried out – although the **longest spacewalk** (see below) was a little longer. For the first few hours, astronauts breathe pure oxygen, to remove nitrogen from their bodies. Otherwise they might develop gas bubbles, which can cause pain in the joints – aka the "bends".

First untethered spacewalk

NASA astronaut Captain Bruce McCandless II (USA) was the first person to perform an untethered spacewalk, from the Space Shuttle *Challenger*, on 7 Feb 1984. The walk was scheduled in order to test the Manned Maneuvering Unit, a backpack that cost $15 m (£10 m) to develop.

MOST...

Spacewalks

During five space flights, between 1988 and 1998, Anatoly Solovyev (RUS) made 16 spacewalks.

Spacewalks during a Space Shuttle mission

Robert Curbeam (USA) performed four spacewalks during the STS-116 mission by the Space Shuttle *Discovery* on 9–22 Dec 2006.

Spacewalks from one spacecraft

As of 3 Feb 2016, a total of 193 spacewalks had been staged outside the *ISS*. They were undertaken by 121 different astronauts and cosmonauts and lasted for 1,192 hr overall.

Longest spacewalk

American astronauts Jim Voss and Susan Helms spent 8 hr 56 min in space on 11 Mar 2001. Their job was to make room on the *ISS* for the Italian cargo module *Leonardo*. The module, which carried supplies and equipment for the station, was transported by the Space Shuttle *Discovery*.

Largest neutral buoyancy pool

NASA's Neutral Buoyancy Laboratory is situated at the Sonny Carter Training Facility near the Johnson Space Center in Houston, Texas, USA. The facility has a volume of 824,044 cu ft (23,334.33 m³) – nearly 10 times that of an Olympic swimming pool. The neutral buoyancy provided by the water simulates the effects of microgravity on an EVA.

Most people on a spacewalk

The Space Shuttle *Endeavour* launched in May 1992 (mission STS-49). The primary aim of the exercise was to repair the *Intelsat VI* satellite, which had partially failed. Retrieving the satellite proved problematic until Pierre Thuot, Richard Hieb and Thomas Akers (all USA) performed a spacewalk together and were able to capture *Intelsat VI* by hand while mission commander Daniel Brandenstein delicately positioned *Endeavour* to within a few feet of the stricken satellite. This marks the only occasion to date that three people have walked in space at the same time.

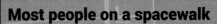

Largest marine animal structure
Dead and living stony corals begin to coalesce into what will become the Great Barrier Reef. Located off the coast of present-day Queensland in Australia, it will eventually measure 80,000 sq mi (207,200 km²).

600 MYA

VOYAGER

First and farthest
Launched in 1977, *Voyager 1* and *Voyager 2* were sent to study the giant outer planets Jupiter, Saturn, Uranus and Neptune. En route to Jupiter, *Voyager 1* captured the **first image of Earth and the Moon in a single frame from space**. It has now travelled into interstellar space, making it the **first probe to leave our Solar System**, on around 25 Aug 2012. As of 24 Mar 2016, *Voyager 1* was 20,078,268,831 km (12,476,057,841 mi) away from Earth and still sending data to Mission Control in the USA – the **longest communications distance**. With their radioisotope thermoelectric generators, the probes are the **most durable nuclear-powered interplanetary spacecraft**.

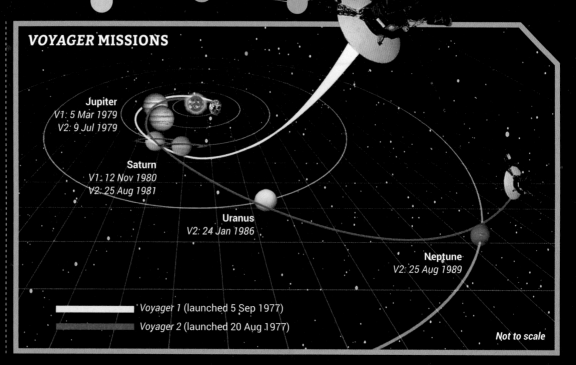

VOYAGER MISSIONS

Jupiter
V1: 5 Mar 1979
V2: 9 Jul 1979

Saturn
V1: 12 Nov 1980
V2: 25 Aug 1981

Uranus
V2: 24 Jan 1986

Neptune
V2: 25 Aug 1989

━━━━━ *Voyager 1* (launched 5 Sep 1977)
━━━━━ *Voyager 2* (launched 20 Aug 1977)

Not to scale

Jupiter: *Voyager 1* performed its flyby of Jupiter on 5 Mar 1979. After its closest approach, the probe turned to face the planet in the Sun's direction. In the **first observations of Jupiter's ring system**, it sighted a faint ring – the main component in the planet's ring system. This also has an inner torus (circle of gas) and two faint outer rings.

Io: On *Voyager 1*'s mission, navigation engineer Linda Morabito (USA) noticed a crescent protruding from Jupiter's moon Io. This marked the **first discovery of extraterrestrial volcanism**. Io is the **most volcanically active body in the Solar System**. Its volcanic plumes can reach hundreds of kilometres high.

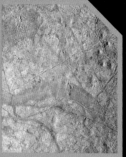

Europa: Jupiter's large, icy moon Europa has the **smoothest surface in the Solar System**. Its only prominent relief are ridges a few hundred metres high, as discovered by *Voyager 2* during its flyby in Jul 1979. Images of what looks like broken sea ice, refrozen, suggest that a subsurface ocean may exist on Europa.

Saturn: The structure of Saturn's rings – the **largest ring system of any planet** – results from the gravitational influence of its many moons. These countless particles of ice and dust have a mass of 4 x 10^{19} kg (9 x 10^{19} lb), equivalent to about 30 million Mount Everests. Saturn also has the **largest hexagon in the Solar System** – a cloud formation with 13,800-km-long (8,500-mi) sides at its north pole, first discovered by the two *Voyager* probes.

DID YOU KNOW?
Saturn's rings are kept in orbit by the gravities of its many moons. They are not permanent, but are being slowly eroded, partly by the constant rain of micrometeorites. Some scientists predict that in another 100 million years or so, the rings may have disappeared.

Planetary bodies not to scale

Oldest animal trails
Marine creatures, possibly resembling sea anemones, leave tracks on rocks in the Ediacaran Period. These are later found off Newfoundland, Canada.

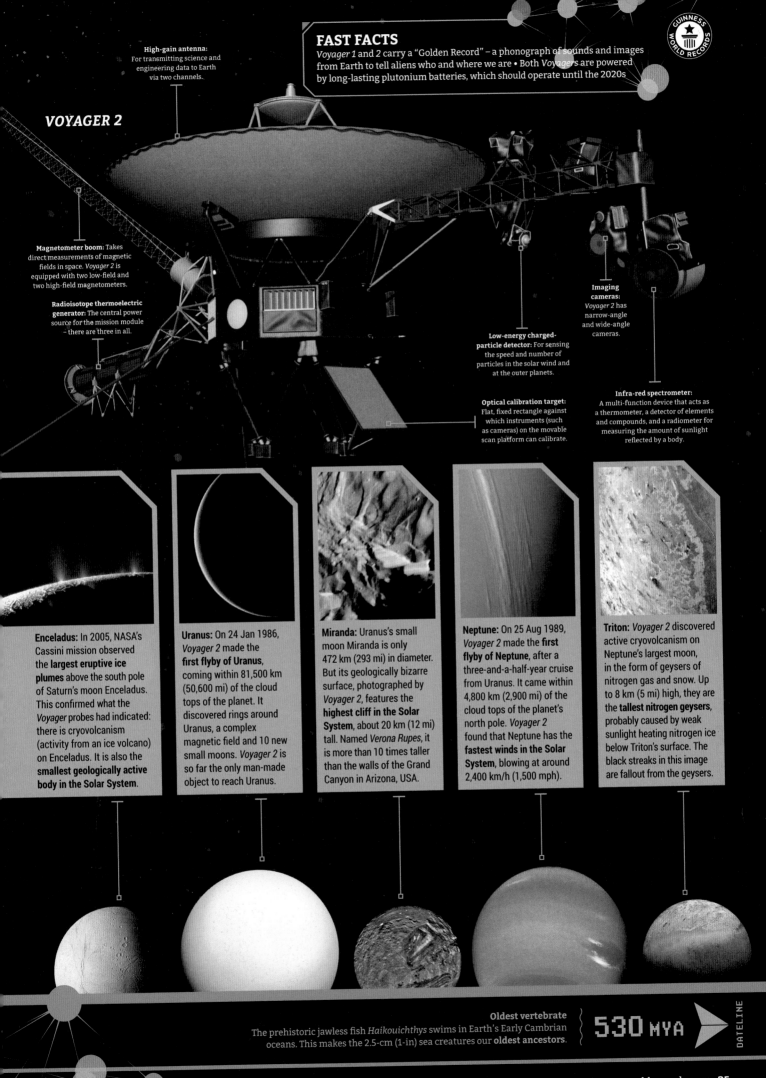

VOYAGER 2

High-gain antenna: For transmitting science and engineering data to Earth via two channels.

FAST FACTS
Voyager 1 and *2* carry a "Golden Record" – a phonograph of sounds and images from Earth to tell aliens who and where we are • Both *Voyagers* are powered by long-lasting plutonium batteries, which should operate until the 2020s

Magnetometer boom: Takes direct measurements of magnetic fields in space. *Voyager 2* is equipped with two low-field and two high-field magnetometers.

Radioisotope thermoelectric generator: The central power source for the mission module – there are three in all.

Imaging cameras: *Voyager 2* has narrow-angle and wide-angle cameras.

Low-energy charged-particle detector: For sensing the speed and number of particles in the solar wind and at the outer planets.

Optical calibration target: Flat, fixed rectangle against which instruments (such as cameras) on the movable scan platform can calibrate.

Infra-red spectrometer: A multi-function device that acts as a thermometer, a detector of elements and compounds, and a radiometer for measuring the amount of sunlight reflected by a body.

Enceladus: In 2005, NASA's Cassini mission observed the **largest eruptive ice plumes** above the south pole of Saturn's moon Enceladus. This confirmed what the *Voyager* probes had indicated: there is cryovolcanism (activity from an ice volcano) on Enceladus. It is also the **smallest geologically active body in the Solar System**.

Uranus: On 24 Jan 1986, *Voyager 2* made the **first flyby of Uranus**, coming within 81,500 km (50,600 mi) of the cloud tops of the planet. It discovered rings around Uranus, a complex magnetic field and 10 new small moons. *Voyager 2* is so far the only man-made object to reach Uranus.

Miranda: Uranus's small moon Miranda is only 472 km (293 mi) in diameter. But its geologically bizarre surface, photographed by *Voyager 2*, features the **highest cliff in the Solar System**, about 20 km (12 mi) tall. Named *Verona Rupes*, it is more than 10 times taller than the walls of the Grand Canyon in Arizona, USA.

Neptune: On 25 Aug 1989, *Voyager 2* made the **first flyby of Neptune**, after a three-and-a-half-year cruise from Uranus. It came within 4,800 km (2,900 mi) of the cloud tops of the planet's north pole. *Voyager 2* found that Neptune has the **fastest winds in the Solar System**, blowing at around 2,400 km/h (1,500 mph).

Triton: *Voyager 2* discovered active cryovolcanism on Neptune's largest moon, in the form of geysers of nitrogen gas and snow. Up to 8 km (5 mi) high, they are the **tallest nitrogen geysers**, probably caused by weak sunlight heating nitrogen ice below Triton's surface. The black streaks in this image are fallout from the geysers.

Oldest vertebrate
The prehistoric jawless fish *Haikouichthys* swims in Earth's Early Cambrian oceans. This makes the 2.5-cm (1-in) sea creatures our **oldest ancestors**.

530 MYA

DATELINE

BLACK HOLES

What is a black hole?

Black holes are the remnants of stars that ended their lives as supernovae. They are characterized by a region of space in which gravity is so strong that not even light can escape. Pictured right is a ground-breaking rendering of a black hole, painstakingly created by the makers of the movie *Interstellar* (USA, 2014) in collaboration with the US theoretical physicist Kip Thorne.

Densest objects in the universe

A "stellar" black hole (i.e., a black hole created from the gravitational collapse of a massive star) can be around 20 times the mass of our Sun. At its centre is the "singularity", where the mass of the dead star from which the black hole originated is compressed to a single point of zero size and infinite density. It is this singularity that generates the powerful gravitational field of a black hole. Many thousands of them are thought to exist in our galaxy alone. Scientists believe that supermassive black holes reside in the centres of most, if not all, galaxies and weigh more than a million Suns.

Heaviest black hole

In 2009, astronomers using NASA's Swift gamma-ray space telescope measured the mass of the supermassive black hole at the centre of the quasar S5 0014+81. (Quasars are star-like "extra-galactic" objects that are the most luminous objects in the universe.) The result – around 40 billion solar masses – means that this black hole is some 10,000 times larger than the supermassive black hole at the heart of our Milky Way galaxy.

First "rogue" black hole discovered

Markarian 177 is a dwarf galaxy some 90 million light years away. Studies using Hawaii's Keck Observatory in Jun 2013 strongly suggest that the bright object SDSS1133, associated with the galaxy, is a supermassive black hole that has been ejected from the galaxy's centre.

MOST SCIENTIFICALLY ACCURATE BLACK HOLE IN A MOVIE

Gargantua (above) is the fictional black hole in the movie *Interstellar* (released 5 Nov 2014). It was rendered using code called Double Negative Gravitational Renderer (DNGR), which was developed by visual effects company Double Negative in collaboration with renowned physicist Kip Thorne (USA, below).

It works by solving equations for bundles of light propagating around the curved space-time of a spinning black hole. The result is an accurate reproduction of the gravitational lensing effects an observer would see if they were there. While the initial black hole they produced was more realistic, director Christopher Nolan requested a few changes to make it more comprehensible to movie audiences – a decision that Thorne agreed with.

Closest black hole to Earth

A0620-00 is a binary system containing a low-mass star and a stellar black hole. The system is located approximately 3,000 light years away from Earth, in the constellation Monoceros. The black hole in this star system has a mass at least 3.2 times that of the Sun and could be as much as 15 times heavier. Once every 7.75 hr, it is orbited by a "K-type" star – one that, in stellar terms, has a relatively cool temperature. The artist's impression above shows the companion star caught in the black hole's gravitational pull.

Shortest distance between two black holes

In Mar 2009, a team of astronomers reported that the quasar SDSS J153636.22+044127.0 appears to contain a binary black hole at its centre. Revealed by spectral analysis of their light, the two black holes weigh the equivalent of 50 million and 20 million Suns, but are only one-third of a light year apart. This is less than 10% of the distance between our Sun and the nearest star, Alpha Centauri.

Farthest object ever visible to the naked eye

Gamma-ray bursts are the birth cries of black holes, created as supermassive stars exhaust their fuel and collapse to a singularity. On 19 Mar 2008, NASA's *Swift* satellite detected a gamma-ray burst from a galaxy 7.5 billion light years away. Some 30–40 sec after the detection by *Swift*, the optical counterpart of the gamma burst was picked up by telescopes on Earth. The flash from this incident – referred to by astronomers

First known example of a live birth
A mother and embryo placoderm (prehistoric armoured fish) perish, producing a well-preserved fossil in which the embryo is attached to its mother via an umbilical cord. Some 25 cm (9.8 in) long, the species will be named *Materpiscis attenboroughi*.

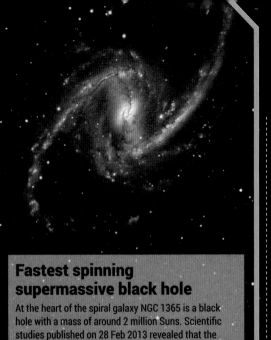

FAST FACTS

Black holes distort space and time: the closer you get to one, the more time slows down • Prof John Wheeler (USA) coined the term "black hole" in 1967 • The term for the way matter is shredded by the gravity of a black hole is "spaghettification"

Fastest spinning supermassive black hole

At the heart of the spiral galaxy NGC 1365 is a black hole with a mass of around 2 million Suns. Scientific studies published on 28 Feb 2013 revealed that the black hole is spinning at around 84% of the speed of light.

as GRB 080319B – was visible to the naked eye for approximately 30 sec. In technical terms, it had an apparent magnitude of 5.8, making it about as bright as the planet Uranus appears from Earth.

Apparent magnitude is a scale used in astronomy to describe the brightness of objects as seen from Earth. Confusingly, the numbers in the magnitude scale run backwards: the brighter the light from an astronomical object appears, the lower its apparent magnitude number will be.

Later the same year, on 16 Sep, NASA's *Fermi Gamma-ray Space Telescope* detected the **most powerful gamma-ray burst ever**, from 12.2 billion light years away in the direction of the Carina constellation. The event recorded by *Fermi* was as powerful as around 9,000 normal supernovae. The blast threw out material at speeds of 99.9999% of the speed of light.

Brightest quasar in the sky

Quasar 3C 273 is some 2.5 billion light years away in the constellation of Virgo.

Despite its distance, it has an apparent magnitude of 12.9 – bright enough for it to be seen with relatively modest telescopes. The extreme luminosity of this quasar is believed to be caused by the heating of a huge accretion disc (revolving disc of material) surrounding a supermassive black hole. If 3C 273 was just 30 light years away, it would shine as brightly as the Sun in our sky.

Most powerful X-ray flare from a black hole in the Milky Way

On 14 Sep 2013, astronomers using NASA's Chandra X-ray Observatory detected an increase in X-ray radiation of a factor of 400 from the supermassive black hole Sagittarius A*, located at the centre of the Milky Way galaxy. The flare was three times more powerful than the previous holder, which occurred in the same region in 2012.

It lasted for a couple of hours, which is consistent with one theory about its origins. Scientists have speculated that an asteroid was torn apart by the gravitational force of the black hole, and that its

Nearest supermassive black hole

Sagittarius A* is the supermassive black hole at the centre of our Milky Way, some 27,000 light years away from Earth. With a mass of around 4 million Suns, it is orbited by several massive stars. This image was taken by NASA's *Chandra* space telescope. The different colours represent X-rays of different energies. The "cloud" in the centre represents dust and gas at the centre of the galaxy emitting X-rays. Sagittarius A* is hidden in the very brightest part of the centre of this image.

debris was then heated as it spiralled into the event horizon, creating the flare.

Deepest note in the universe

Acoustic waves generated by a supermassive black hole in the centre of the Perseus cluster of galaxies, 250 million light years away, have given rise to a phenomenally deep note. The sound, which propagates through the extremely thin gas surrounding the black hole, is a B-flat, 57 octaves below middle C.

We can't hear this noise because sound waves cannot travel through the vacuum of space and so the black hole's rumblings are contained within the gas cloud. Also, the note produced is more than a

million billion times lower than the deepest note a human ear can detect.

These acoustic waves were discovered by an international team of astronomers led by Prof Andrew Fabian (UK) using observations recorded by the Chandra X-ray Observatory.

DID YOU KNOW?

An "event horizon" is the term astronomers use to describe the outer perimeter of a black hole. Beyond this boundary, nothing – not even light – can escape the black hole's pull and will be sucked in. It is perhaps the ultimate "point of no return".

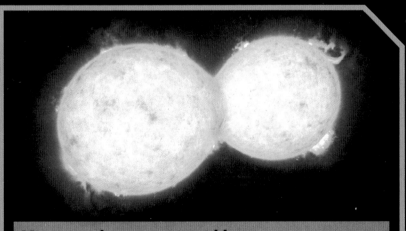

Most massive overcontact binary

VFTS 352 is a binary star system in the Tarantula Nebula in the Large Magellanic Cloud, some 160,000 light years away from Earth. The two stars have a combined mass of around 57 times that of the Sun and orbit each other so closely that they overlap and share material. Known as an "overcontact binary", these two massive stars are an estimated 12 million km (7.4 million mi) apart and orbit their common centre of mass once a day.

Largest galactic collision
A group of around 300 galaxies slams into a larger group of approximately 1,000 galaxies, resulting in Abell 754 – a turbulent giant galactic cluster with a diameter of approximately 1 million light years.

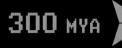

300 MYA

DATELINE

EARTH

240 MYA

Oldest known dinosaur
The small, meat-eating *Nyasasaurus parringtoni* thrives in Tanzania; analysis of fossils in 2012 reveals that it is the oldest dinosaur by 10–15 million years.

CONTENTS

Longest-burning methane crater

The Darvaza Crater, also known as the "Door to Hell", is located in a natural gas field in Turkmenistan and has been burning since 1971. It is believed that the ground caved in as a result of drilling and the crater was intentionally set alight in an attempt to burn off the leaking methane gas. It has burned continuously ever since.

In Nov 2013, fearless Canadian adventurer George Kourounis became the **first person to explore the Darvaza Crater** (inset). Wearing a heat-resistant aluminium suit and using a custom-made Kevlar climbing harness, Kourounis descended to the base of the fiery hole to collect rock samples. Later lab tests revealed bacteria living on the rocks, proving that life can survive extreme temperatures in excess of 1,000°C (1,830°F).

Longest dinosaur
At 39–52 m (128–170 ft) in length, *Seismosaurus halli* – a diplodocid sauropod dinosaur – is the lengthiest vertebrate to ever roam the Earth.

 154 MYA

DATELINE

EARTH

Our home planet carries us through space at more than 106,200 km/h (66,000 mph) relative to the Sun. We're also spinning on our axis, at around 1,600 km/h (1,000 mph) at the Equator – a dizzying fact! Among its companions in the Solar System, Earth is a real record-breaker: it's the **densest planet**, the **largest terrestrial planet** and the **most geologically active inner planet**.

DID YOU KNOW?

Iron, the **most common element** and bulk of Earth its inner core, gives our planet its strong magnetic field. Silicates – oxygen-silicon compounds – are the **most abundant minerals**, making up about 95% of the crust.

DID YOU KNOW?

At the bottom of the deepest gold mines, some 3.9 km (2.4 mi) below Earth's surface, the rock can reach 60°C (140°F). Each ton of rock yields less than a sugar cube-sized amount of gold.

HIGHEST POINT ON EARTH

Mount Everest in the Himalayas, on the Tibet-Nepal border, rises 8,848 m (29,029 ft) above sea level, a measurement obtained in 1954. The first efforts to measure the mountain – in 1852 – resulted in an exact figure of 29,000 ft (8,839 m), but surveyors at the time felt that the public would assume this was rounded off, so they added an extra 2 ft!

The Himalayas is the world's largest **mountain range**, containing 96 of the 109 peaks on Earth that are more than 7,300 m (24,000 ft) high. Formed by the collision of the Indian and Eurasian tectonic plates, the Himalayas still "grow" by about 1 cm (0.4 in) a year.

WHAT MAKES THE EARTH?

It took billions of years for Earth to change from a whirling mass of gas and dust to a habitable planet, creating the unique mix of elements listed below.

ELEMENT	WHERE FOUND	AMOUNT
1 Iron	Inner core (88.8%), outer core, crust	32.1%
2 Oxygen	Outer core, mantle, crust (46%)	30.1%
3 Silicon	Mantle, crust (27%)	15.1%
4 Magnesium	Mantle, crust	13.9%
5 Sulphur	Outer core	2.9%
6 Nickel	Inner and outer core	1.8%
7 Calcium	Crust	1.5%
8 Aluminium	Crust	1.4%
9 Trace elements		1.2%

FALLING THROUGH THE EARTH

Imagine you've drilled a tunnel through Earth and jumped in. Assuming no air resistance and an imperviousness to searing heat – in fact, assuming a *lot* of things! – how long would it take you to reach the other side? One theory – and there are many – suggests 42 min. Gravity accelerates you downwards, pulled by the mass of Earth's iron-rich core, which is what makes ours the **densest planet** in the Solar System. At the centre, while moving at around 800 km/sec (500 mi/sec), your body becomes weightless. As you pass the core, you'll start to feel the effects of gravity again, but now working against you, reducing your speed. Momentum will keep you going, though, and you'll arrive on the other side. Just be sure to grab on to something, or else you'll just fall back in again!

Everyone would fall through the Earth in the same time, whatever their weight

Total distance in freefall: 12,715 km (7,900 mi)

WORLD OF GOLD

If we extracted all the gold that sits at Earth's core, we could gold-plate our planet to a depth of 45 cm (18 in). However, it is rather hard to reach, at 2,800 km (1,740 mi) below our feet, where temperatures are upwards of 4,000°C (7,200°F). So it might be cooler and more effective to prospect in the ocean. Every litre (1.75 pints) of seawater contains around 13 billionths of a gram of gold, adding up to a total of 20 million tonnes of gold – more than three times the weight of the Great Pyramid at Giza.

BOWLING BALL EARTH

Mountains and deep valleys make up just 1/5,000th of the surface of our planet. It has been calculated that Earth would be smoother than a bowling ball, were it scaled down to the same size. However, Earth is not perfectly spherical like a bowling ball. As with all spinning planets, it bulges slightly in the middle: the Equator. Its diameter here is about 40 km (25 mi) wider than between the poles.

WATER, WATER, EVERYWHERE

According to the US Geological Survey, if all the water on, in and above Earth were gathered into a single drop, it would have a diameter of about 1,385 km (860 mi), just twice the length of the Grand Canyon. The fresh water that all life forms consume is surface water, taken mainly from rivers and lakes. This would combine into a single drop about 56 km (35 mi) wide.

RAINING CHAMPION

The speed of a typical raindrop is about 17 mph (27.3 km/h). This is slightly faster than the four-minute-mile pace but 6.5 mph (10.4 km/h) slower than Usain Bolt (above) in record-breaking mode. Raindrops are usually represented graphically in the shape of a teardrop, but in fact larger ones flatten out into a hamburger shape as they fall. Any that become much larger than 4.5 mm (0.17 in) break apart.

DID YOU KNOW?

HM survey ship *Challenger* first pinpointed and named the deepest part of the ocean (see below), within the Mariana Trench, in 1875. If Mount Everest were dropped into the trench, its peak would sit 2 km (1.2 mi) below the surface.

DEEPEST POINT ON EARTH

The Challenger Deep section of the Mariana Trench in the western Pacific Ocean plunges to 10,911 m (35,797 ft) below sea level. It is the site of the **deepest solo ocean descent** in a vessel, by James Cameron (CAN) in 2012, and of the **first manned descent** and **deepest ocean descent**, by Jacques Piccard (CHE) and Donald Walsh (USA) in 1960. The ocean depths represent one of the final frontiers; four times as many people have walked on the surface of the Moon (12) than have ventured to the bottom of the Challenger Deep.

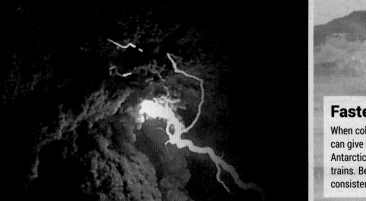

Fastest katabatic wind

When cold, dense air from high altitudes flows downhill under the force of gravity, it can give rise to so-called katabatic (or fall) winds. Around the coastal escarpment of Antarctica, katabatic winds can reach 300 km/h (186 mph) – as fast as China's high-speed trains. Because these winds are driven by the local geography, they are known for their consistency of direction. The term derives from the Greek word *katabasis* ("descending").

DID YOU KNOW?
The images here show dramatic volcanic lightning photographed during the unexpected eruption of Calbuco in Chile on 23 Apr 2015.
These thunderstorm clouds associated with volcanoes are often known as "pyrocumulonimbus" clouds ("pyro" meaning "fire").

First colour photograph of a green flash

Occurring after sunset, or just before sunrise, a green flash is essentially a mirage in which the highly refracted sunlight seems to produce a green spot at the top of the Sun. The first colour photographic proof of this elusive phenomenon was taken in 1960 by D K J O'Connell of the Vatican Observatory in Italy.

Highest storm surge

On 4 Mar 1899, Tropical Cyclone Mahina struck Bathurst Bay in Queensland, Australia. The associated storm surge – a rise in sea-water level caused by a combination of high winds and low pressure – was reported to be as high as 13 m (42 ft 7 in), with fish and dolphins found stranded on the top of 15-m-high (49-ft) cliffs. The surge resulted in the deaths of more than 400 people.

Most frequent occurrence of red rain

Since 1896, there have been sporadic reports of coloured rain in the Indian state of Kerala, on the Malabar Coast. From 25 Jul to 23 Sep 2001, Kerala saw multiple showers of red rain – the only place where this has occurred in three consecutive months. Scientists analysed red rain samples and, in 2015, concluded that the effect is brought about by spores from the microalgae species *Trentepohlia annulata*.

First description of crown flash

Seen as a bright patch above thunderstorms, crown flash was first described in 1885. It is probably caused by changing electrical fields within the thundercloud, to which plate- or needle-shaped ice crystals align, reflecting sunlight.

OLDEST DESCRIPTION OF VOLCANIC LIGHTNING

In volcanic eruptions that include a large ash plume, an electrical charge builds up in the air above the volcano and discharges as lightning. The first known description of volcanic lightning was written by Roman statesman Pliny the Younger, who witnessed the 79 CE eruption of Mount Vesuvius. He narrowly escaped with his life, and his famous uncle, Pliny the Elder, died trying to evacuate nearby towns.

153 MYA

Oldest flying bird
Archaeopteryx lithographica flourishes in what is now southern Germany; with feathers and wings but also claws and teeth, it is a key link between dinosaurs and birds.

FAST FACTS

On 3 Mar 1876, it rained raw meat near Rankin in Kentucky, USA • Tropical cyclones that form in the Atlantic or eastern Pacific are called hurricanes, while those that form in the western Pacific are called typhoons

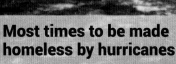

Most times to be made homeless by hurricanes

Melanie Martinez from Braithwaite, Louisiana, USA, was described as "America's unluckiest woman" after losing five different homes to five different hurricanes: Betsy (1965), Juan (1985), Georges (1998), Katrina (2005) and Isaac (2012). Hurricane Isaac hit Braithwaite on 29 Aug 2012 – the seventh anniversary of Hurricane Katrina.

Greatest pressure drop measured in a tornado

On 21 Apr 2007, a tornado hit a mobile mesonet vehicle that was gathering scientific data in the town of Tulia in Texas, USA. The vehicle's instruments recorded a pressure drop inside the vortex of 194 millibars. Tornadoes in the USA and Canada are rated – according to the damage they cause – on the Enhanced Fujita (EF) scale, ranging from 1 (mild) to 5 (total destruction). This tornado (aftermath pictured) was "only" an EF2.

Greatest rainfall in 24 hours
On 15 and 16 Mar 1952, some 1,870 mm (6 ft 1 in) of rain fell in 24 hr in Cilaos on Réunion island, in the Indian Ocean. The average rainfall for that month is nearer 167 mm (6.5 in).

Costliest tropical cyclone
On 29 Aug 2005, Hurricane Katrina laid waste to the coast of Louisiana and nearby states in the southern USA, causing around $108 bn (£59.9 bn) worth of damage.

Most intense hurricane
The category-5 Hurricane Wilma, which formed in Oct 2005, is the strongest on record. It had a low pressure centre of 882 millibars and sustained winds of 296 km/h (184 mph). As yet unconfirmed reports suggest that Hurricane Patricia, which struck Mexico in Oct 2015, may have been stronger still.

Even the largest hurricanes, however, are dwarfed by the tropical cyclones that form over the western and central Pacific. Typhoon Tip, which formed in Oct 1979, holds the record for **most intense tropical cyclone** with a low pressure of 870 millibars and wind speeds of 306 km/h (190 mph).

Most tornadoes spawned by a hurricane
Hurricane Ivan formed on 2 Sep 2004, becoming a category-5 storm in the Caribbean Sea. According to the National Climatic Data Center, it spawned 119 tornadoes in a three-day outbreak from 15 Sep.

DID YOU KNOW?
This ice-glazed car shows the chilling aftermath of an ice storm – in this instance, after a fall of freezing rain in Versoix, Switzerland, in 2012. To qualify as an ice storm, the rain must leave at least a 0.25-in-thick (6.35-mm) coating of ice on exposed surfaces.

Worst damage in an ice storm

In the first week of Jan 1998, a devastating ice storm hit eastern Canada and adjoining parts of the USA. It made travel impossible and cut off power to 3 million people – almost 40% of the population of Québec. The bill was an estimated CAN$4.3 bn ($3 bn; £1.8 bn) in Canada alone.

First known hominid
Orrorin tugenensis walks on two legs and is about the size of an adult female chimp. Scientists in the Kenya Palaeontology Expedition announce their discovery of its 6-million-year-old fossilized remains in Dec 2000.

6 MYA

guinnessworldrecords.com **33**

CLOUDS
GALLERY

Apart from adorning our skies with ever-shifting shapes and light effects, clouds are the meteorologist's friend. They help us predict weather systems, changes and extremes – vital in planning, logistics, travel and safety. They are formed from water droplets or ice crystals that are so light they can float in air, and begin life as water vapour rising from the ocean, lakes and rivers. Some clouds ride as high as a jet plane; others creep along the ground in a mist. They are named according to their shape and their height in the sky.

2

1

3

HIGHEST CLOUDS   1

Occurring at altitudes of around 50 mi (80 km), noctilucent clouds (top, in Stockholm, Sweden) are believed to be a mixture of ice crystals and meteor dust. They may be visible after sunset when, owing to their great height, they are still lit up by the Sun's rays. Nacreous or mother-of-pearl clouds (inset, in the Antarctic) are a rare form of *cirrus*, the **highest standard cloud form**, averaging 5.6 mi (9 km). Nacreous clouds may reach nearly 15 mi (24 km) in height.

LOWEST CLOUDS   2

Familiar grey-white *stratus* clouds have blurry edges that form patches or extensive layers below heights of around 2,000 m (6,560 ft). When drifting at ground level, they are known simply as "fog" (pictured here hanging over Daly City in California, USA). Layers of *stratus* may form from morning fog as it rises on warm air, which means a shower of light rain or snow is a likely prospect. If there are no other clouds above the *stratus* layer, the Sun or Moon may shine through.

CLOUDS WITH THE GREATEST VERTICAL RANGE   3

In the tropics, massive *cumulonimbus* clouds have been observed to reach a height of nearly 20,000 m (65,600 ft) – more than twice the height of Mount Everest. These giant towers, fuelled by strong updraughts of air, are named anvil-head *cumulonimbus* when they develop a typical flat-topped shape. This occurs when a cloud flattens out as it hits the thinner air of the stratosphere. *Cumulonimbus* clouds bring turbulence and thunderstorms.

HIGHEST OCCURRENCE OF DIAMOND DUST   4

Plateau Station, a (now disused) US research station on the central Antarctic Plateau, experiences the formation of diamond dust on average 316 days each year. These ground-level clouds of ice crystals occur when cold air underlies warmer air. Diamond dust is much thinner than fog, and can be seen as flashes of light when sunlight is reflected and refracted from the individual ice crystals. It is most common in the polar regions.

DATELINE   **5.9 MYA**   **Largest sea to dry up**
Geologic processes block the channel between the Atlantic Ocean and the Mediterranean Sea, transforming the latter into a dry salt basin.

6

DID YOU KNOW?
British amateur meteorologist Luke Howard (1772–1864) is known as the "namer of clouds". He knew that cloudwatching was the key to weather forecasting, and classified the three major cloud forms: *stratus* (Latin for "spread out"), *cumulus* ("heap") and *cirrus* ("curl of hair").

4

7

5

8

LARGEST SOLITON CLOUDS   5
Rare, solitary cloud forms called solitons maintain their shape while moving at a constant speed. The longest regular occurrence of this is known as the Morning Glory, which forms in the Gulf of Carpentaria, Australia. This backward-rolling cloud formation can be 1,000 km (620 mi) long, 1 km (0.6 mi) high and can travel at 60 km/h (37 mph). The Morning Glory regularly attracts gliders, who catch the updraught on the leading edge of the cloud.

SLOWEST CLOUDS   6
Lenticular clouds, which often form in the lee of mountain peaks or other geographical barriers, are stationary and remain in place while air moves through them. They occur singly or in layers at altitudes of up to 12,000 m (40,000 ft). As fast-moving, stable air is forced upwards by geographical features, its moisture content may condense to create these clouds. They are regularly misidentified as UFOs owing to their smooth, round or oval, lens-like shape.

MOST RECENTLY CLASSIFIED CLOUD FORMATION   7
The last cloud type to be recognized as distinct was *cirrus intortus* (meaning "twisted curl" or "ringlet") in 1951. This thin *cirrus* cloud forms high up into swirling or shapeless filaments. In 2009, a new type of cloud structure, *undulatus asperatus* (aka asperitas) was proposed by the Cloud Appreciation Society. It is characterized by an appearance resembling ocean waves and is relatively rare. These clouds tend to dissipate without causing storms.

LONGEST-LASTING MOUSTACHE CLOUD   8
One of the rarest clouds on Earth, horseshoe vortex or "moustache" clouds have not been observed to last much longer than one minute from formation to dissipation. They form when air rotates, which can lead to a tornado. But since the rotating air column is horizontal not vertical, no tornado occurs. Instead, an updraught turns the rotating cloud into a crescent shape. This phenomenon has been captured on camera only a handful of times.

Heaviest flying bird ever
Argentavis magnificens, a massive condor-like bird weighing 72 kg (158 lb) – heavier than a fully grown adult man – rules the skies over Miocene South America.

5 MYA

DATELINE

BIZARRE GEOLOGY

Largest geological feature discovered from space
Located in the part of the Sahara Desert that lies within Mauritania, the Richat Structure is a circular, multi-ringed sedimentary basin with a diameter of around 50 km (31 mi). Once thought to be an impact crater, it is now believed to be the eroded remains of an uplifted sedimentary dome. This distinctive "bull's-eye" feature was discovered from orbit by US astronauts Jim McDivitt and Ed White on the Gemini 4 mission in Jun 1965.

Newest ocean
In 2005, a rift some 56 km (35 mi) long opened up in the Afar Depression (the lowest point in Africa, also known as the Danakil Depression) in Ethiopia. In Nov 2009, scientists stated that their analysis showed the rift to be the start of the formation of a new ocean.

The tectonic processes occurring under Afar are the same as those on the ocean floor, at ridges where new crust forms and the existing crust is pushed apart.

Largest "stone forest"
The Grand Tsingy in western Madagascar is a 600-km² (230-sq-mi) "stone forest" of sharp limestone pinnacles dating from the Jurassic period (201.3–145 million years ago). Over time, this limestone has been eroded by rain, forming a landscape in which limestone peaks reach 90 m (295 ft) in height.

Longest "sailing stone" trails
The Racetrack Playa – a dry lake bed in Death Valley on the US Nevada-California border – is home to "sailing stones". The rocks here appear to have moved on their own, leaving trails across the surface up to 880 m (2,887 ft) long. Two

Largest cannonball concretions

Cannonball concretions are roughly spherical boulders formed by the natural cementation of sand by a mineral called calcite. The largest examples are 6 m (19 ft 8 in) across and are found in Rock City, Kansas, USA, as well as in central Wyoming and north-east Utah, USA, where they are associated with the Frontier Formation of the Late Cretaceous period (c. 100–66 million years ago).

scientists discovered the cause in Dec 2013 when checking on equipment put in place to research this phenomenon. All it takes is the heating up of a thin sheet of ground

ice and a light breeze. As the ice begins to break up, the rocks sometimes get caught up and moved in a process known as "ice shove".

Most natural arches in one region
Arches National Park in Utah, USA, has 2,067 natural arches with spans of 3 ft (90 cm) or more; the largest exceed 300 ft (97 m).

DID YOU KNOW?
Wave Rock (see below) is composed of granite dating back 2.7 billion years. It was formed as a result of the granite being eroded by acidic conditions in the soil that once covered it, rather than by water erosion. The feature belongs to the Yilgarn Craton, part of the original Australian landmass.

LONGEST NATURAL ARCH
Xian Ren Qiao (Fairy Bridge) is located north-west of Fengshan in Guangxi Province, China. A subclass of arch known as a natural bridge, Xian Ren Qiao was formed by the Buliu River carving through terrain composed of limestone. An expedition by the Natural Arch and Bridge Society in Oct 2010 measured its span at approximately 400 ft (120 m).

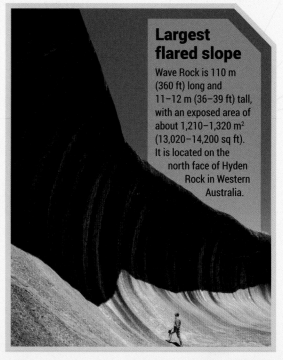

Largest flared slope

Wave Rock is 110 m (360 ft) long and 11–12 m (36–39 ft) tall, with an exposed area of about 1,210–1,320 m² (13,020–14,200 sq ft). It is located on the north face of Hyden Rock in Western Australia.

DATELINE

3.6 MYA

Oldest hominid footprints
Two or three hominids stride upright on the ashy plains of present-day Laetoli in northern Tanzania, leaving the earliest known human-like footprints. The track consists of some 70 prints in two parallel trails about 30 m (100 ft) long.

36 Earth

Highest natural arch

Tushuk Tash (meaning Pierced Rock, aka Shipton's Arch) is a natural arch of conglomerate material located west–north-west of K'ashih in Sinkiang, China. In 2000, an expedition from *National Geographic* measured the height of the arch to be around 1,200 ft (366 m) – about 165 ft (50 m) shorter than New York's Empire State Building.

and its tributaries, the cave has taken some 25 million years to form. It is home to around 200 indigenous species, mostly invertebrates.

Waterfall with the most natural bridges

Discovered in 1952, the Cave of the Three Bridges in Tannourine, Lebanon, contains a waterfall that plunges 255 m (836 ft) past three natural stone bridges. It cuts through 160-million-year-old Jurassic limestone.

Longest cave system

Mammoth Cave in Mammoth Cave National Park, Kentucky, USA, is a network of limestone chambers of which around 400 mi (640 km) have been explored so far. Created by the weathering action of the Green River

Deepest cave

On 10 Aug 2013, Ukrainian caver Gennady Samokhin extended the explored depth of the Krubera Cave in the Arabika Massif, Georgia, by 6 m (19 ft 8 in). Krubera, the only known cave with a depth greater than 2 km (1.2 mi), now has an official depth of 2,197 m (7,208 ft).

Largest concentration of methane explosion craters

In Jul 2014, a pilot flying over the Yamal Peninsula in north-west Siberia spotted a large hole c. 60 m (196 ft) across, 70 m (230 ft) deep and fresh in origin. Scientists believe that it formed after an explosion of methane hitherto trapped in the permafrost. Seven such craters have now been found; one was circled by around 20 smaller ones.

Largest slot canyon

Slot canyons evolve when hairline cracks in rock gradually become enlarged over millennia by quickly flowing water and flash floods. The US state of Utah is particularly rich in these formations, owing to its dry conditions and the presence of soft sandstone. The Narrows slot canyon in Zion National Park, Utah, is approximately 600 m (1,970 ft) deep, yet its walls are only 10 m (32 ft) apart at their widest points. The canyon snakes for 25 km (16 mi) through the Zion National Park (inset), and hikers take an average of 13 hours to traverse it.

First recognizable human
The tool-using *Homo habilis* evolves from a hominid such as *Australopithecus afarensis*, although it has smaller teeth and a larger brain than its ancestors. It lives in what is today eastern and southern Africa.

2.5 MYA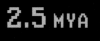

REEFS

Oldest coral reef

The Chazy Reef Formation is a fossilized coral reef that extends from Tennessee, USA, to Newfoundland, Canada. It originally formed around 450 million years ago in what was then the Iapetus Ocean. Its most significant outcrop occurs in Vermont at Isle La Motte, a rocky lake island that was once a substantial colony of stromatoporoid coral.

Deepest photosynthetic coral reef

In 1999, research at a deep-water reef called Pulley Ridge, located off the coast of Florida, USA, revealed a new type of coral ecosystem. Unlike all the deep-water reefs previously studied, Pulley Ridge has photosynthesizing algae. This is impressive, because its location on the sea floor at a depth of 80 m (262 ft) receives only 1% of the light that reaches the surface.

Deep-water corals are found everywhere from Norway to Nova Scotia, but their hard-to-reach locations mean that little is known about their ecosystems and life-cycles.

LONGEST REEF

The Great Barrier Reef, located off the coast of Queensland in north-eastern Australia, measures some 1,260 mi (2,027 km) from end to end. That's about the same as the distance from Miami to New York City or from Madrid to Rome.

The Great Barrier Reef is, in fact, a "reef system" – comprising some 2,900 separate colonies of living coral – that covers an area of 80,000 sq mi (207,200 km²). The reef is a diverse but fragile ecosystem, maintained by a delicate balance between the more than 5,000 species that call it home. Seemingly minor human interference can have dramatic effects. It is suspected, for example, that overfishing certain predators creates "plagues" of coral-eating starfish that kill off whole reefs.

LARGEST...

Reef system ever

A system of glass sponge reefs, 7,000 km (4,350 mi) from end to end, thrived in the Tethys Ocean during the Late Jurassic (157–145 million years ago). It was more than three times the length of the Great Barrier Reef. Such reefs were thought to be extinct, but living examples were discovered in the 1980s.

Largest raised coral atoll

A raised coral atoll is an island that forms as a normal, mostly submerged coral atoll, but is then lifted far above sea level by tectonic forces. The largest of these is Lifou Island in the south-west Pacific Ocean, which covers some 1,207 km² (466 sq mi) and is home to around 10,000 people.

The **largest system of glass sponge reefs** today is located off Canada's Pacific coast, covering around 700 km² (270 sq mi) of the sea floor in the Queen Charlotte Sound. It is home to sponges that are as tall as 21 m (69 ft) – that's more than four storeys high – and in excess of 9,000 years old.

Barrier reef system in the northern hemisphere

Barrier reefs are separated from the mainland or island

Oldest stone tools
In Africa, oval- and pear-shaped tools are made by chipping flakes from stone to create sharp or rounded edges. The oldest surviving samples of these "Acheulean" tools are later found in the West Turkana region of Kenya.

FAST FACTS

Technically, the word "reef" describes any underwater obstruction
• Corals are marine invertebrates (phylum Cnidaria) related to jellyfish
and anemones • Coral reefs are home to around 25% of all fish species

Largest atoll archipelago

The Tuamotu Archipelago in the central Pacific Ocean contains 75 coral atolls in a chain about 1,450 km (900 mi) long. The largest atoll, Rangiroa (pictured), covers an area of around 1,640 km² (633 sq mi), although only 79 km² (30 sq mi) of that is land.

Largest coral die-off

In 1998, a rise in ocean temperatures, triggered by an El Niño event, caused some 16% of the world's coral reefs to bleach and die. Bleaching is a phenomenon in which damaged reefs shed their symbiotic algae, leaving just the stone-like forms of the coral itself (above). A similar die-off happened in 2010, and many scientists believe that a third such event is currently taking place.

shore by a deep, and often wide, lagoon. Although large barrier reefs are common in the Pacific, the Caribbean is home to only a few. No reef system in the northern hemisphere is more extensive than the Belize Barrier Reef, which stretches from the coast of southern Mexico to northern Guatemala. It is second in size only to the Great Barrier Reef, the **largest reef system in the southern hemisphere** and the overall **longest reef** (see left).

Double barrier reef
Only six double barrier reefs – reefs formed as inner and outer layers – exist in the world today. Of these, the largest is the Danajon Bank, which is 272 km² (105 sq mi) in size. It lies between the islands of Cebu and Bohol in the Philippines.

Atoll reef
An atoll reef is an often more or less circular coral reef that encloses a shallow lagoon. The largest is Kwajalein Atoll, one of the Marshall Islands, which twists and turns for 176 mi (283 km) to enclose a lagoon of 1,100 sq mi (2,850 km²) – the **largest body of water enclosed by an atoll**. The lagoon is so large that observers cannot see the islands on one side from the other.

Although Kwajalein is the largest atoll, very little of it is above sea level. The **largest atoll by land area** is Kiritimati, part of the Line Islands chain in the central Pacific. This is a partially raised atoll (see left) whose islands cover an area of 235 sq mi (609 km²) around a small lagoon.

Fringing reef
This type of reef occurs close to the shore with no intervening lagoon. The largest is Ningaloo Reef in Western Australia, which is approximately 300 km (180 mi) long and some 100 m (330 ft) from the shore at its closest point.

Marine reserve
The Northwestern Hawaiian Islands Marine National Monument covers 356,879 km² (137,791 sq mi) of the Pacific. The reefs in this protected region – about the size of Germany – are home to more than 7,000 species, a quarter of which are found nowhere else.

DID YOU KNOW?
The Great Carrier Reef isn't the only reef with a warship in it. Kwajalein Atoll (see left) is home to the wreck of the German battleship *Prinz Eugen*, which sank while the US Navy was using it in nuclear tests during 1946. It was too radioactive to move and is now a popular dive site.

Largest artificial reef

In 2004, the US Navy decided that the 911-ft (277-m) aircraft carrier USS *Oriskany*, which had been rusting away in a navy shipyard since 1976, would be donated for use as an artificial reef. On 17 May 2006, after two years of work to remove toxic insulation materials, the *Oriskany* was sent to the bottom of the Gulf of Mexico by 500 lb (227 kg) of carefully placed explosives (below). The *Oriskany* has since attracted an abundance of marine life and become a popular diving site (left), commonly known as the "Great Carrier Reef".

Oldest musical instrument
In a campsite located in modern-day Ljubljana, Slovenia, a Neanderthal takes a segment of femur from a cave bear (*Ursus spelaeus*) and pierces it with four holes to create a bone flute.

43,000 BCE

DATELINE

RAINFORESTS

First use of a canopy raft in rainforest research

In Oct 1986, biologist Francis Hallé (FRA) led the first expedition to the canopy of the rainforest in Snake Creek, Guyana. His team used a canopy raft designed by pioneering French balloonist Dany Cleyet-Marrel, which was dropped on to the top of the rainforest canopy by an aerostat (a lighter-than-air craft such as an airship). The raft itself was a 580-m² (6,243-sq-ft) hexagon that used air-inflated beams and polyvinyl chloride netting. Weighing just 750 kg (1,653 lb), it was designed to rest on the rainforest canopy without damaging new growth. This first expedition, which also counted as field trials, allowed scientists to sample trees and plants and preserve them for later study.

Oldest terrestrial biome
Most of Earth's tropical rainforests have been established for at least a million years, although some are much older. They survived the last Ice Age, which ended around 10,000 years ago, because unlike the majority of the planet, the equatorial forests did not freeze over.

The **oldest rainforest** of them all is the Daintree Rainforest, located on the north-east coast of Queensland in Australia. It covers around 1,200 km² (463 sq mi) and is part of the Wet Tropics of Queensland, which was made a World Heritage Site in 1988 by the United Nations Educational, Scientific and Cultural Organization (UNESCO).

This area represents the largest single contiguous block of rainforest in Australia and is estimated to be 180 million years old.

Largest temperate rainforest
Temperate rainforests, which exist outside the Earth's tropics, generally form where relatively warm ocean temperatures impact inland climates. They have a much greater seasonal variation than tropical rainforests. The largest expanse of this biome on Earth is the Pacific Temperate Rainforests, which cover around 295,000 km² (113,900 sq mi) of the west coasts of the USA and Canada. These forests are only around a few thousand years old, having formed after the last Ice Age.

Largest coastal mangrove forest
The Sundarbans stretches for almost 6,000 sq mi (15,540 km²) across eastern India and Bangladesh, and acts as a natural barrier against tsunamis and cyclones that often blow in from the Bay of Bengal. The mangrove trees in this forest sometimes exceed 70 ft (21 m) in height, above islands of layered sand and grey clay. They have saltwater-tolerant roots.

Largest tropical forest reserve
The Tumucumaque National Park is located in the rainforest of the northern Amazonian state of Amapá in Brazil. Measuring some 38,875 km² (15,010 sq mi)

Largest natural pharmacy

Around 25% of all western pharmaceutical products come from ingredients in tropical rainforests, owing to their rich biodiversity. Indigenous tribes have utilized plants for medicinal purposes for millennia, but the western world only began to rediscover them in the second half of the 20th century.

in area, the reserve contains many endangered species of plant and animal. The creation of the park was announced on 22 Aug 2002 by Brazilian president Fernando Henrique Cardoso.

Largest river basin
The greatest river basin is that drained by the Amazon, covering

> **DID YOU KNOW?**
> The term "rainforest" describes any area with both a dense tree canopy and more than 140 cm (55 in) of annual rainfall. In addition to the well-known tropical rainforests, there are temperate rainforests in places such as north-west USA, Norway and Ireland.

Biome with the greatest biodiversity

The precise number of animal and plant species that exist in the world's tropical rainforests is unknown. Current estimates of biodiversity suggest that something in the range of 50–75% of all Earth's living species are concentrated in this habitat, which today covers around 6–7% of the planet's surface.

> **Oldest paintings**
> A group of Stone Age humans paint portraits of animals and imaginary beasts on the walls of a cave in what is now southern France.

FAST FACTS
Around 70% of plants identified as potential anti-cancer treatments are native to rainforests • If it were a country, the Amazonian rainforest would be the ninth largest • More than 20% of Earth's oxygen is made in the Amazon rainforest

vanilla family, this flower grows in the rainforests of Queensland, Australia, and is a saprophyte (i.e., it feeds on decaying organic material). It is not free-standing, but is supported by other trees.

Fastest declining biome
Tropical rainforests are shrinking more quickly than any other biome. A 2002 study using satellites revealed that around 5.8 million ha (14.3 million acres) of rainforest per year were lost from 1990 to 1997. Between 2000 and 2005, Central America lost 1.3% of its tropical rainforests each year; around two-thirds of its rainforests have become pasture since 1950.

Largest tree-cover loss by area
"Tree-cover loss" refers to the removal of trees, which may be within natural forests or tree plantations, and can result from factors such as mechanical harvesting, fire, disease or storm damage. According to data from the University of Maryland and Google published by Global Forest Watch, over the years 2001–14 Russia suffered the greatest tree-cover loss – largely boreal forests – with 40.94 million of its 761 million hectares lost.

In terms of the global impact of deforestation, however, it is Brazil and Indonesia (with some of Earth's most extensive tropical forests) that have historically come under scrutiny for their rates of deforestation. Brazil lost 38 million of its 519 million hectares of tree cover, ranking second globally after Russia in absolute tree-cover loss (mostly tropical forest) in 2001–14. More worryingly, and despite a drop in 2013, Indonesia's tree-cover loss rose by more than 30% in 2013–14 – the **largest deforestation by annual increase rate** – while that of Brazil rose by "only" 16% during the same time period. The two countries showed a less marked three-year average trend – 0.46% and 1.01% respectively – for the years 2012 to 2014.

Tallest tropical rainforest trees
Above the canopy of rainforests is the "emergent" layer, comprising a small number of very large trees. The tallest is the kapok tree (*Ceiba pentandra*), which grows to 60 m (196 ft), at a rate of around 4 m (13 ft) per year. It can be found mainly in southern Mexico, the southern Amazon and West Africa.

around 7,045,000 km² (2,720,000 sq mi). It has countless tributaries, including the Madeira, which at 3,380 km (2,100 mi) is the **longest river tributary**.

Perhaps unsurprisingly, the Amazon is the **widest river**. While not in flood, its main stretches reach widths of up to 11 km (7 mi) at their broadest.

The Amazon also has the **greatest river flow**, with an average discharge rate of about 200,000 m³/sec (7,100,000 cu ft/sec) – that's 80% of an Olympic swimming pool – into the Atlantic Ocean.

Tallest orchid
A height of 15 m (49 ft) has been recorded for the orchid *Galeola foliata*. Part of the

LARGEST TROPICAL RAINFOREST
The Amazon rainforest spans nine South American countries and covers some 5.5–6.2 million km² (2.1–2.3 million sq mi). This is necessarily an estimate, not only because the rainforest does not have distinct edges, but also because it merges with similar biomes across its indistinct boundaries. It is part of the Amazon biome – covering 6.7–6.9 million km² (2.5–2.6 million sq mi) – and includes the whole of the Amazon River Basin. Approximately two-thirds of the rainforest is in Brazil.

Highest concentration of uncontacted tribes
According to the human rights organization Survival International, there are approximately 100 uncontacted tribes in the world today. More than half of these are believed to live within the Brazil-Peru region of the Amazonian rainforest. Many of these tribes actively choose to have no contact with the outside world, sometimes by exhibiting hostility to outsiders, including neighbouring tribes.

KILLER PLANTS

Most fluorescent carnivorous plant

In a 2013 study, the peristome (the slippery ring of tissue at the opening to the pitcher) of the Khasi Hills pitcher plant (*Nepenthes khasiana*) of India was found to emit fluorescent light of a wavelength of 430–480 nanometres (i.e., blue light).

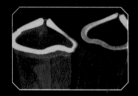

First plant species identified on Facebook
Up to 1.5 m (4 ft 11 in) long, the aptly named magnificent sundew (*Drosera magnifica*) is one of nearly 200 species of carnivorous plants in the taxonomic family Droseraceae. In 2012, amateur researcher Reginaldo Vasconcelos (BRA) had posted a photo on Facebook of a sundew plant that he had seen while exploring a jungle in Minas Gerais, south-eastern Brazil. In Jul 2015, the sundew was identified by experts as a hitherto-unknown species.

The **largest species of sundew** is *D. erythrogyne*, a climbing species endemic to Western Australia, which produces a lengthy scrambling stem that can grow to 3 m (9 ft 10 in) long. Of cosmopolitan distribution, sundews are carnivorous, famous for capturing and

Most dangerous tree

A member of the spurge family, the manchineel (*Hippomane mancinella*) grows in the USA's Florida Everglades and on the Caribbean coast. The sap that its trunk exudes is so acidic and poisonous that the merest contact with human skin causes a breakout of blisters; if it touches the eyes, it can cause blindness. Even standing under the tree in the rain is enough to cause blistering if the skin is wetted by raindrops containing any sap.

digesting insects and other small invertebrates. The plants trap their prey upon glistening drops of dew-like mucus at the tips of mucus-secreting tentacles on their leaves.

Most fireproof carnivorous plant
The cobra lily (*Darlingtonia californica*) is not a true lily, but a species of pitcher plant. It is native to the southern end of the Cascade Mountains range in northern California

and southern Oregon, USA. Brushfires regularly sweep through this area, and the cobra lily has evolved the ability to regrow its leaves and pitchers from its root after such a conflagration.

Largest prey of any carnivorous plant
Both *Nepenthes rajah* and *N. rafflesiana* have been known to eat large frogs, birds and even rats. These species are commonly found in the rainforests of Asia, in particular Borneo, Indonesia and Malaysia.

Most selective carnivorous plant
Nepenthes albomarginata attracts and feeds exclusively on the foraging termite *Hospitalitermes bicolor*. Growing in the rainforests of Malaysia and Indonesia, *N. albomarginata* is also the only plant to offer its own tissue to secure a meal. The plant grows a ring of edible white hairs ("trichomes"), which attract the termites. These insects frequently slip down the "throat" of the plant and are then

FASTEST ENTRAPMENT BY A CARNIVOROUS PLANT

Carnivorous plants trap their prey in movements considered to be among the fastest in the plant kingdom. On land, the clamshell-like leaves of the Venus flytrap (*Dionaea muscipula*, left) shut in one tenth of a second (100 milliseconds) from the moment they are stimulated, typically by insect prey moving into the trap. Underwater, the hinged trapdoor of the bladderwort (*Utricularia vulgaris*, right) captures its victim in 1/15,000th of a second. The bladderwort has no roots; its fleshy underwater leaf branches are filled with air and keep the plant buoyant, enabling it to float.

TRIVIA

Tomato leaves and stems contain a poison called tomatine, considered a natural pesticide. Apple seeds contain tiny doses of amygdalin – a cyanide and sugar compound.

DATELINE

9500 BCE

Earliest cultivated food crops
Neolithic farmers in south-west Asia begin sowing domesticated plants for human consumption, including pulses, cereal and flax.

42 Earth

Most poisonous common plant

Ricin – the poison of the castor oil plant (*Ricinus communis*) – is 6,000 times more toxic than cyanide and 12,000 times more toxic than rattlesnake venom. According to *The Merck Index: An Encyclopedia of Chemicals, Drugs, and Biologicals* (1997 edition), a dose of 700 micrograms (2.46 oz) is enough to kill a person weighing 72 kg (159 lb).

Most dangerous stinger

The fine white stinging hairs of New Zealand's tree nettle, aka ongaonga (*Urtica ferox*), inject toxins into the skin that are potent enough to kill dogs and horses. The hairs contain many skin irritants, notably histamine, 5-hydroxytryptamine (serotonin), acetylcholine and formic acid. On at least one occasion, in 1961, the plant is known to have killed a man just five hours after skin contact.

Largest freshwater blue-green algal bloom

In 1991–92, a 1,000-km (620-mi) stretch of Australia's Barwon-Darling River was contaminated by a toxic blue-green algal bloom. Such events are often caused by fertilizer run-off, which feeds a population explosion in colonies of blue-green algae (also known as cyanobacteria). These bacteria produce cyanotoxins – some of the most poisonous substances known to science. The Barwon-Darling River bloom, which was dominated by *Anabaena circinalis*, caused the deaths of domesticated livestock that drank the contaminated water, and led to a state of emergency being declared.

The **first animal poisoning caused by a freshwater blue-green algae** occurred in Lake Alexandrina, South Australia, in the late 19th century. Dogs, sheep, pigs, horses and cattle all died after drinking water from the lake, the surface of which had been covered with a scum of *Nodularia spumigena*.

digested. Unwittingly, however, surviving termites encourage more of their fellow prey to visit the plant by returning to their colony with the hairs.

Smallest family of carnivorous plants
The taxonomic family Cephalotaceae contains just a single species – the Australian pitcher plant (*Cephalotus follicularis*), which is also known as the Albany pitcher plant. A small species with deep reddish-purple pitchers, it stands only 20 cm (7.8 in) tall and is native to south-western coastal districts in Western Australia.

Most poisonous fungus
Amanita phalloides, known as the death cap mushroom, is responsible for 90% of fatal poisonings caused by fungi. The death cap is found worldwide, including North America and the UK.

Largest genus of pitcher plants

The genus *Nepenthes* contains some 150 species of tropical pitcher plants, plus hybrids and cultivars. The **largest meat-eating plant** is the giant montane pitcher plant (*N. rajah*, right), native to the state of Sabah on Borneo. The largest specimen was 41 cm (1 ft 4 in) tall (below). It was found on 26 Mar 2011 during a Sabah Society visit to Mesilau, on the east ridge of Mount Kinabalu on Borneo.

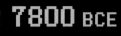

Oldest walled town
With some 2,000 people already calling it home, Jericho in the Middle East is one of the earliest settlements to construct a stone boundary. It is today the **oldest continually inhabited city**.

7800 BCE

DATELINE

guinnessworldrecords.com **43**

ANIMALS

DID YOU KNOW?
Male Komodo dragons primarily clash during the mating season between May and August. With muscular tails bearing their weight, they stand on their hind legs and grapple with their forelegs, wrestling until one of them is injured or too exhausted to continue.

7000 BCE

Oldest playable instrument
A seven-holed flute is carved from the leg bone of a crane in the village of Jiahu, near the Yellow River in China. In 9,000 years' time, when it is unearthed by archaeologists, the wind instrument will still produce a tune!

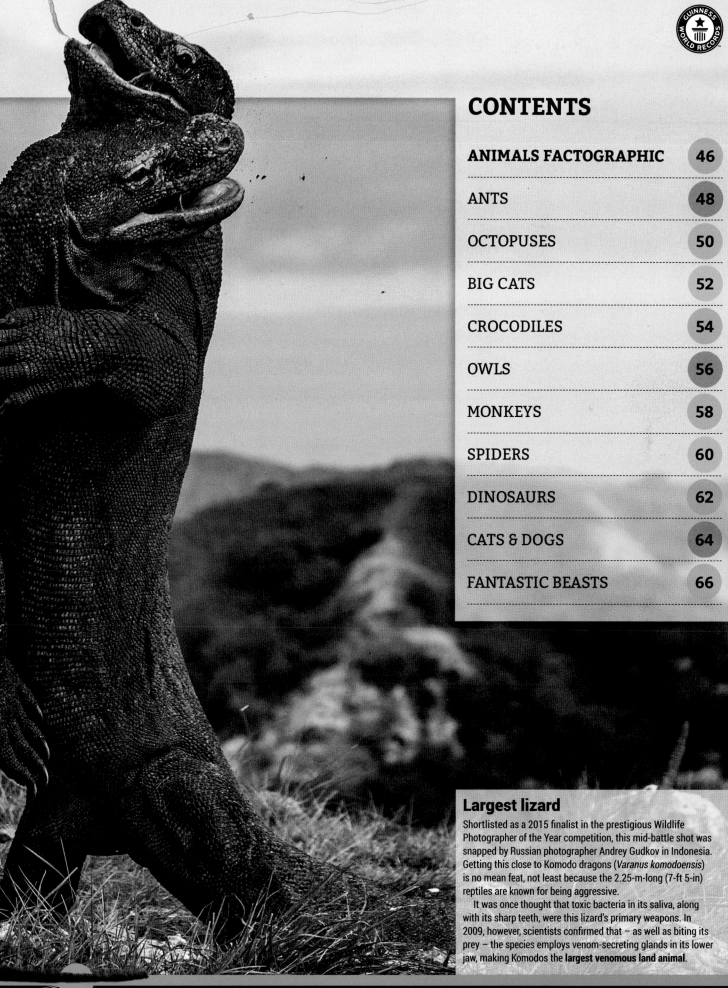

CONTENTS

Largest lizard

Shortlisted as a 2015 finalist in the prestigious Wildlife Photographer of the Year competition, this mid-battle shot was snapped by Russian photographer Andrey Gudkov in Indonesia. Getting this close to Komodo dragons (*Varanus komodoensis*) is no mean feat, not least because the 2.25-m-long (7-ft 5-in) reptiles are known for being aggressive.

It was once thought that toxic bacteria in its saliva, along with its sharp teeth, were this lizard's primary weapons. In 2009, however, scientists confirmed that – as well as biting its prey – the species employs venom-secreting glands in its lower jaw, making Komodos the **largest venomous land animal**.

First pottery kilns
Progressing from baking clay in the Sun, the Hassuna culture of northern Mesopotamia (modern-day Iraq) revolutionizes pottery by developing kilns that can reach 1,000°C (1,830°F).

6000 BCE

DATELINE

ANIMALS

The animal kingdom is remarkably diverse. Members range in complexity from gelatinous jellyfish and simple sponges to surprisingly complex water fleas and ultra-intelligent dolphins... and this is just the sea life! In size, the range is also extreme, from single-celled organisms to the mighty blue whale, the **largest animal ever**. Illustrated here is a selection of creatures noted for their superlative size, be it height, weight, wing-span or appetite, alongside each is a comparison to illustrate just how immense these animals are.

LARGEST WING-SPAN FOR A LIVING BIRD

On 18 Sep 1965, a male wandering albatross (*Diomedea exulans*) of the southern oceans was studied by members of the research ship USNS *Eltanin* in the Tasman Sea. It had a wing-span of 3.63 m (11 ft 11 in) – about twice the height of the average human, and nearly 10 times the wing-span of a blackbird (*Turdus merula*).

DID YOU KNOW?

Even newborn giraffes are taller than most humans, averaging 2 m (6 ft 6 in). The females give birth standing up, so their offspring (calves) start life with a thump, dropping around 2 m to the ground!

TALLEST MAMMAL

An adult male giraffe (*Giraffa camelopardalis*) typically measures 4.6–5.5 m (15–18 ft) in height. The tallest recorded specimen to date was 5.8-m-tall (19-ft) George, a Masai bull (*G. c. tippelskirchi*) originally from Kenya that was received at Chester Zoo in Cheshire, UK, on 8 Jan 1959. He was more than three times the height of an adult human.

DID YOU KNOW?

The elephant's trunk is a highly versatile tool. It's a nose, a digger, a hand and a supplementary foot. It can siphon up water, or be used to pull down whole trees and signal. It's strong enough to pull down whole trees and sensitive enough to pluck a berry from a branch.

LARGEST TERRESTRIAL MAMMAL

The adult male African elephant (*Loxodonta africana*) typically stands 3–3.7 m (9 ft 10 in–12 ft 1 in) at the shoulder. It weighs 4–7 tonnes (8,800–15,400 lb) – an average weight equivalent to 90 fully grown adult men. The tallest specimen known – a bull shot on 4 Apr 1978 – measured an unprecedented 4.42 m (14 ft 6 in) from shoulder to forefoot.

LARGEST FELINE CARNIVORE

The male Siberian tiger (*Panthera tigris altaica*) averages 3.15 m (10 ft 4 in) in length from nose to the tip of the extended tail. It also stands 99–107 cm (3 ft 3 in–3 ft 6 in) at the shoulder and weighs about 265 kg (580 lb). To maintain its weight, one tiger has to eat the equivalent of 17.3 ten-year-old boys every month!

LARGEST LIVING BIRD

Male examples of the North African ostrich (*Struthio camelus camelus*), a ratite (flightless) sub-species, have been recorded at 2.75 m (9 ft) tall and weighing 156.5 kg (345 lb). That makes the ostrich approximately 98,000 times heavier than the male bee hummingbird (*Mellisuga helenae*), the smallest bird.

x10,000 x10,000 x10,000
x10,000 x10,000 x10,000
x10,000 x10,000 x8,000

LARGEST PINNIPED

There are 34 known species of pinniped – aquatic mammals including seals, sea lions and walruses – the largest of which is the southern elephant seal (*Mirounga leonina*). Bulls average 5 m (16 ft 4 in) long and weigh some 2–3.5 tonnes (4,400–7,720 lb) – up to 50% of which can be blubber. As the bulkiest member of the taxonomic order Carnivora, the elephant seal is also the largest carnivore, some five times heavier than the average adult polar bear (*Ursus maritimus*) – the largest land carnivore. While several whales eat meat, they are not part of the Carnivora group, so, taxonomically speaking, are not carnivores.

ANTS

100%

Largest ant
Fulvus driver ant (*Dorylus fulvus*) queens (above) can measure as much as 5 cm (2 in) long once fully mature. The smallest driver ant workers, by contrast, are only 2.5 mm (0.1 in) long. The large, wingless queens travel with their workers in migratory groups that periodically split up to form new colonies.

Largest average size for an ant species
There is usually significant variation in size between the different castes of ants in a colony. A species with

DID YOU KNOW?
Justin O Schmidt put together his sting pain index as a side project while researching insect defences (and getting stung a lot in the process). He describes the sting of a bullet ant as being "like walking over flaming charcoal with a 3-inch rusty nail in your heel".

ANATOMY OF AN ANT

Spiracle: Ants do not have lungs. Oxygen enters the body through openings called spiracles and is piped directly to tissue.

Antennae: Sensory organs used to smell, touch and feel. They can also be used for communication.

Head

Mouth

Thorax: A muscular midsection to which the six jointed legs connect, along with wings in the flying (mating) phase.

Eye: The ant's compound eyes comprise numerous tiny lenses.

Gaster: Abdominal structure housing vital organs. Its telescoping segments allow the gaster to expand – for example, if the ant has fattened up to survive the winter.

Leg

Claws

Mandibles: Mouthparts used for cutting, digging and fighting, as well as passing food to the mouth; controlled by powerful muscles in the head.

a queen that is much larger than normal may not have unusually large workers, and vice versa.

Going on the mean body size (the average obtained from the measurements of workers, soldiers, drones and queens), the largest species is *Dinoponera gigantea*. Native to the Amazon rainforest in Brazil

and Peru as well as in coastal Guyana, it averages 3.3 cm (1.3 in) long.

Largest ant species ever
We know from fossils found in Messel, Germany, that queens of *Titanomyrma giganteum*, which lived in Europe around 50 million years ago, were 6 cm (2.4 in) long and had a wing-span of 15 cm (5.9 in).

Fewest chromosomes in an insect
Male ants are "haploid" (they have only one chromosome from each of their species' chromosome pairs), while female ants are "diploid" (possessing both parts of the pair). The Australian jack jumper ant (*Myrmecia pilosula*) has only a single pair, meaning that males of the species have just one chromosome.

The **most chromosomes recorded in an ant** is 94 (47 pairs). This figure was recorded from two different species – the dinosaur or dawn ant (*Nothomyrmecia macrops*) of Australia and *Platythyrea tricuspidata*, a species found in Indonesia.

Most aquatic ant
Polyrhachis sokolova, native to Queensland in Australia, Papua New Guinea and the island of New Caledonia, lives in mangrove forests

that are routinely inundated by the tide. Its nests are constructed with purpose-built air pockets for the safe storage of eggs, and its workers have developed the ability to swim underwater for prolonged periods – an adaptation seen in no other species of ant.

Fastest self-powered predatory strike
Odontomachus bauri – aka *the* trap-jaw ant – of South America can close its mandibles at a speed of up to 64 m/s (209 ft/s). In addition to using its mandibles to bite prey, the ant also utilizes them to escape danger, striking them against the ground to fling itself 8.3 cm (3.2 in) into the air and horizontally as far as 39.6 cm (1 ft 3.5 in). This is the equivalent of a human jumping 13.4 m (44 ft) straight up.

TRIVIA
A number of birds indulge in "anting", which involves crushing ants and rubbing them all over their plumage. Pictured is a hairy woodpecker (*Picoides villosus*) in a typical anting posture. The formic acid released from the ants helps to keep parasites away.

Most painful insect sting
In 1983, entomologist Justin O Schmidt (USA) published the first version of the Schmidt Sting Pain Index. The index ranks the bullet ant (*Paraponera clavata*) – native to Nicaragua and southwards through Central America to Paraguay – as the insect with the most painful sting, registering a maximum score of 4.0+ on Schmidt's four-point scale.

Smallest ant
Carebara bruni, a species of ant native to Sri Lanka, contains workers as tiny as 0.8 mm (0.03 in) long – 46 times smaller than the **longest worker ant** (see above right). The length of *C. bruni* is roughly the same as the thickness of a bank card.

5,700%

100%

DATELINE

5000 BCE

Oldest surgical procedure
A 50-year-old man in Ensisheim, France, undergoes trepanation – the process of removing bone from the top of the skull; the discovery of his body 7,000 years later provides the oldest evidence of surgery.

48 Animals

Longest worker ant

The elongated bodies of Australian giant bulldog ants (*Myrmecia brevinoda*), a species of Australian bull ant, measure as much as 3.7 cm (1.5 in) long. Bull ants lack advanced social structures, so each worker has evolved to be strong enough to forage alone.

Largest ant genus

The genus *Pheidole* held 1,002 species when the last major survey was carried out in 2014, and new species are being discovered all the time.

The **smallest ant genus** is *Nothomyrmecia*, which only contains one species, the dinosaur or dawn ant (*N. macrops*, see opposite page), which inhabits western and southern Australia. Some entomologists regard it as a living "fossil" on account of its primitive form.

Most dangerous ant

Myrmecia pyriformis, a species of bull ant found in coastal regions of Australia, has powerful jaws and a sting that dispenses a venom several times more potent than cyanide or arsenic. Bulldog ants have caused at least three human fatalities since 1936.

DID YOU KNOW?

Ant colonies contain several different types – or "castes" – of ant, typically "worker", "queen", "drone" and "soldier". Workers – the most common – serve a small population of fertile females (queens) and fertile males (drones), while soldiers defend the nest.

Farthest jump by an ant

The Indian jumping ant (*Harpegnathos saltator*) is the most accomplished of all jumping ants. Although only 1.9 cm (0.7 in) long, the Indian jumping ant can leap 10 cm (3.9 in) horizontally (over five times its own body length), and 2 cm (0.8 in) vertically. It achieves this via the synchronous activation of muscles in its middle and back pairs of legs.

Largest colony of ants

The Argentine ant (*Linepithema humile*) was only introduced to Europe about 80 years ago but has spread rapidly, establishing a colony that stretches 6,000 km (3,700 mi) from northern Italy to the Atlantic coast of Spain.

Rarest male ants

It was initially thought that *Mycocepurus smithii* was one of the ant species that reproduced asexually, with all the ants in the colony being clones of the queen. Although this hypothesis has been proven wrong, no male specimens of *M. smithii* have ever been found. It has been speculated that they may be microscopically small, or that they only live for a very short period.

Highest thermotolerance for an ant

The Saharan silver ant (*Cataglyphis bombycina*; see **fastest ant**, right) does not begin foraging until the outside temperature has reached 46°C (115°F), and it can stay out in the scorching heat until its body temperature reaches 53°C (127°F). This adaptation allows it to avoid less heat-tolerant predators.

LONGEST COLUMN OF ANTS

Most ant colonies live in fixed nests on a site chosen by the queen, leaving only to mate or forage for food. There are some exceptions, however, such as the army ants (*Eciton*, pictured) of Central and South America, and the driver ants (*Dorylus*) of Africa. These two genera are nomadic, with entire colonies leaving their nests in search of new foraging grounds. A colony on the move forms into a column that can be as much as 1 m (3 ft 3 in) wide and 100 m (328 ft) long. Army ant workers break up the column to form themselves into a living nest for their queen every night.

1.8 km/h

Fastest ant

The Saharan silver ant (*C. bombycina*) can reach speeds of 1.8 km/h (1.1 mph). This is 100 times its body length every second. By comparison, Usain Bolt, the world's **fastest man**, "only" covers six body lengths per second. This extraordinary turn of speed minimizes its exposure to the Sun and also contributes to its body's cooling by convection (see left).

First written language
Pottery from the neolithic Yangshao culture of Shaanxi Province, China, is inscribed with characters thought to represent numerals.

4000 BCE

DATELINE

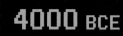

guinnessworldrecords.com **49**

OCTOPUSES

First octopus

Dating back some 296 million years, a fossilized octopod dubbed *Pohlsepia mazonensis* was unearthed in Illinois, USA. Formally described in 2000, it has been said to resemble a "globular splat"; however, with eight distinct arms, two eyes and what may be an ink sac, it possesses all the features associated with modern octopuses.

Largest octopus genus

There are more than 100 species within the rather uninspiringly named *Octopus* genus (opinions vary among biologists about the exact number). That's more than a third of all octopuses.

At the other end of the scale, there are three holders of the title of **smallest octopus family**. The see-through glass octopus (*Vitreledonella richardi*), the seven-arm octopus (*Haliphron atlanticus*) and the football octopus (*Ocythoe tuberculata*) – named for the shape of its mantle – are all the sole members of their respective families.

ANATOMY OF AN OCTOPUS

Eye

Mantle: What looks like the head is, in fact, the octopus's equivalent of our abdomen, containing all its major organs.

Funnel: Water can be pumped through the siphon as a means of propulsion.

Arm: Despite often being called "tentacles", an octopus's appendages are really arms/legs. Most have eight, but there are exceptions (see **most arms on an octopus** and **first hexapus**).

Suckers

Skin: Pigment-containing cells called chromatophores just under the skin enable the octopus to change colour to reflect its mood or to blend into its surroundings.

Beak: The mouth is located below the mantle where all the arms meet. Made of chitin, like a crab's exoskeleton, the beak is the only hard part of this creature's body. It is used to both latch on to and crush prey.

The seven-arm octopus also holds an exclusive record for **largest mantle**. On one specimen, this "body" section measured 0.69 m (2 ft 3 in) long, beating even that of the **largest octopus** (opposite) with an average 0.6-m (1-ft 11-in) mantle.

Most sociable octopus

While most octopuses lead quite solitary lives, the unclassified larger Pacific striped octopus, found off Nicaragua, can form groups of 30 to 40 individuals. Also going against normal octo-relations, they often share a den with a partner for several days while mating.

This unusually gregarious cephalopod is also the **most fecund octopus**. Whereas most octopus species reproduce once, females of this species can mate and gestate many times throughout their lives, laying and hatching multiple egg broods continuously.

Longest brooding period

All female octopuses are known for being very protective when it comes to their eggs, but no octopus

Greatest octopus mimic

Several species of octopus have been observed in the wild mimicking other animals by changing their colour and body shape, or even adapting their behaviour. However, none has mastered the art of impersonation better than the mimic octopus (*Thaumoctopus mimicus*, left), native to the Indo-Pacific and the Red Sea.

Studies reveal that this shape-shifter can imitate at least 16 other marine creatures, including flatfish (bottom right), sea snakes (top right), brittle stars, sea anemones, crabs and jellyfish.

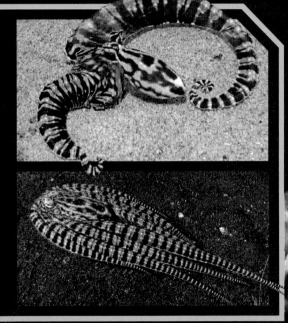

TRIVIA

As part of a 2008 study into animal dexterity, octopuses were given jam jars and Rubik's Cubes to see if they favoured a certain arm. Results showed that octopuses use six of their eight limbs equally to manipulate objects; the other two are reserved for locomotion.

{ **First timekeeping device**
The time stick – a primitive type of sundial – is developed by the ancient Mesopotamians. It tells the time by casting a shadow that changes length and position as the Sun "moves" overhead.

FAST FACTS

Octopi is not correct; the plural is octopuses or octopodes • Octopus wrestling was a popular sport in the USA in the 1960s • Octopuses have three hearts

– nor any other animal, for that matter – can lay claim to being more committed to brooding than the deep-sea species *Graneledone boreopacifica*.

In May 2007, one mother was sighted on a rocky wall at a depth of 1,400 m (4,600 ft) guarding eggs laid just a few weeks earlier. Subsequent visits confirmed her ongoing vigil, which continued to Sep 2011 – a staggering 53 months (nearly four-and-a-half years). A month later she was gone, and the 160 or so egg cases had all hatched.

Most arms on an octopus

As the name suggests, the majority of *oct*opuses have eight limbs, but there are exceptions. One far-from-ordinary common octopus (*Octopus vulgaris*), found off Japan, boasted 96 arms. It's now preserved for posterity at the Marineland aquarium in Shima, Japan.

Most bioluminescent octopus

While many squid species have evolved to emit light to attract prey and mates in the gloomy ocean depths, *Stauroteuthis syrtensis*, aka the glowing sucker octopus (above), is one of very few octopuses to display the trait. Adapted suckers on the arms have been observed glowing blue-green, primarily at 470 nanometres – a wavelength that travels well through water.

Most venomous mollusc

A 2009 study found that all octopuses are venomous to some degree, but the blue-ringed octopuses (*Hapalochlaena*), found off Australia and south-east Asia, pack enough neurotoxin to paralyse or kill 10 adult humans!

There are also accounts of octopuses with *fewer* arms. The **first hexapus** documented was a lesser octopus (*Eledone cirrhosa*), caught in 2008 near Wales, UK. It was christened Henry after King Henry VIII, who is famed for having six wives. Other six-legged octopuses have been spotted, but they are widely accepted to be genetic mutants rather than a distinct species.

Deepest octopus

The dumbo octopus (*Grimpoteuthis*) has been sighted at 7,000 m (23,000 ft) below the surface, where it is able to withstand pressures of 695 atmospheres – that's the equivalent of 695 kg (1,530 lb) weighing down on a fingernail. Although typically measuring 20–30 cm (7.8–11.8 in) in length, one jumbo dumbo was 1.8 m (5 ft 10 in)!

LARGEST OCTOPUS

The giant Pacific octopus (*Enteroctopus dofleini*) has an average arm-span of 16 ft (5 m). In terms of individual specimens, however, the largest on record boasted an arm-span of 31 ft 5 in (9.6 m) – longer than an anaconda – and weighed in at 600 lb (272 kg). The giant Pacific octopus has a diet of crustaceans and small fish, but will occasionally take on bigger meals such as sharks (below).

First use of the wheel
The ancient Mesopotamians begin using wheeled carts as a means of transport; previously, humans had rolled along heavy objects on logs.

c. 3500 BCE

DATELINE

BIG CATS

Highest-living predators on land

Hidden cameras have photographed the rare and seldom-seen snow leopard (*Panthera uncia*, pictured) at altitudes of 19,000 ft (5,800 m). During the early 1990s, a puma (*Puma concolor*) was observed at the same altitude in the South American Andes mountains.

The **largest-ever lion subspecies** was the American lion (*Panthera leo atrox*), which once inhabited North America but became extinct c. 11,000 years ago. Some 25% larger than the largest modern-day African lions, it had a head-and-body length of 1.6–2.5 m (5 ft 3 in–8 ft 2 in), stood 1.2 m (3 ft 11 in) at the shoulder and weighed up to 350 kg (773 lb).

Highest bite force in a big cat in proportion to size

The bite of a jaguar (*Panthera onca*) is proportionately stronger than that of any other big cat. A 100-kg (220-lb) jaguar can bite with a force of 503.57 kg (1,100 lb 3 oz) at the canine teeth, and 705.79 kg (1,556 lb) at the carnassial notch on its fourth upper premolar and first lower molar teeth.

Most prolific man-killing leopard

The "Leopard of Panar" was deemed responsible for

Smallest leopard

The adult male Arabian leopard (*Panthera pardus nimr*) weighs approximately 30 kg (66 lb) and the female 20 kg (44 lb) – far lighter than any of its other eight subspecies. This critically endangered cat has only recently been recognized.

killing more than 400 people during the early 20th century in Kumaon, northern India. It was finally dispatched by renowned Anglo-Indian hunter Jim Corbett in 1910.

Largest wild cat

Male Siberian, or Amur, tigers (*Panthera tigris altaica*) normally have a length of 2.7–3.3 m (8 ft 10 in–10 ft 10 in) from nose tip to tail tip, a shoulder height of 1–1.07 m (3 ft 3 in–3 ft 6 in), and may weigh up to 306 kg (674 lb).

The **largest species of sabre-toothed cat** or machairodont, all of which are now extinct, was *Smilodon populator*, which lived in South America from around 1 million to 10,000 years ago. It stood 1.56 m (5 ft 1 in) at the shoulder, while the biggest males may have exceeded 500 kg (1,100 lb).

FIRST WHITE LIGERS

In Dec 2013, at Myrtle Beach Safari in South Carolina, USA, a white Bengal tigress called Saraswati (pictured) gave birth to the first confirmed white ligers. The father was a white African lion.

Myrtle Beach is also home to the **largest living cat**, Hercules (inset). An adult male liger, he is 10 ft 11 in (3.33 m) long, stands 4 ft 1 in (1.25 m) at the shoulder and weighs 922 lb (418.2 kg).

DID YOU KNOW?

A "liger" is a cross between a male lion and a tigress. A lioness and male tiger cross results in a "tigon". Other hybrid crosses within the feline family include a "jagulep" (a male jaguar-leopardess mix) and a lijagulep (a mix between a male lion and female jagulep).

DATELINE

3300 BCE

Oldest tattoos
"Ötzi the Iceman" dies from an arrow wound during the Bronze Age. When his well-preserved body is discovered in 1991 – in the Alps between Austria and Italy – it is found to be covered with 61 tattoos.

FAST FACTS
Snow leopards can cover seven times their body length in one leap • No two tigers have the same pattern of stripes • The roar of a lion can be heard 5 mi (8 km) away • Cheetahs don't roar; instead, they purr

First hybrid of big and small cats
Near the end of the 19th century, matings between pumas (*Puma concolor*) and leopards (*Panthera pardus*) in captivity at German animal collector Carl Hagenbeck's private zoo, the Tierpark in Hamburg, resulted in the birth and survival into adulthood of several puma-leopard hybrids.

First three-species big cat hybrid in captivity
The UK's London Zoo displayed a female "lijagupard" in 1908. Her mother had been a jagupard (a hybrid of a male jaguar and leopardess) born at Chicago Zoo in Illinois, USA, and her father a lion. She resembled a slim, long-limbed lioness but was dappled with large brown rosettes.

DID YOU KNOW?
Cats have three eyelids. As well as the top and bottom lids, there is a third lid, known as the nictitating membrane. It originates at the corner of the eye near the nose and moves across the eye from side to side. In a healthy cat, it is tucked away at the side of the eye.

Lowest-frequency big-cat roar
The roar of the lion (*Panthera leo*), native to Africa and Asia, has a lower frequency than that of any other big cat. A lion's roar is delivered in bouts, lasting up to 90 sec and consisting of up to 50 calls with a fundamental frequency of 40–200 Hz. From 1 m (3 ft 3 in) away, it would record 114 dB on a sound-level meter.

The **least dangerous big cat to humans** is the snow leopard (*P. uncia*). To date, only two confirmed attacks have been recorded.

Most social big cat
Most big cats are solitary creatures, but the lion (*P. leo*) is famously social, living in groups of individuals known as prides. Most prides consist of five to six lionesses, their cubs and one or two lions, but there is evidence of prides with as many as 30 individuals.

First confirmed sighting of a white lion
Long familiar in traditional South African folklore, the white lion was first sighted in 1938, when one specimen was seen by Joyce Little in Timbavati (now a private game reserve) on the western edge of South Africa's Kruger National Park.

Oldest living leopard in captivity
A black leopard (*Panthera pardus*) named Ivory, b. 23 Sep 1991, was aged 24 years 58 days as of 20 Nov 2015. He is owned by Donna Martin and Working Wildlife (both USA) and lives in Frazier Park, California, USA.

Largest "small" cat
It may be the fourth-largest cat species – only the lion, tiger and jaguar are bigger – but the puma is generally not classified as a "big cat". Specimens typically grow to 2.75 m (9 ft) in length, while an adult male may weigh 100 kg (220 lb 7 oz). The puma is also the **mammal with the most common names**. Its 40-plus titles include cougar, mountain lion, catamount and painter.

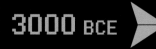

Longest-burning fire
A coal seam in New South Wales, Australia, is struck by lightning and catches fire. It is still burning, some 5,000 years later.

3000 BCE

DATELINE

CROCODILES

Largest crocodile in captivity

This saltwater crocodile (*Crocodylus porosus*) – known to his keepers as Cassius – was captured in 1984 after going on a boat-smashing spree near Darwin, Australia. Cassius was found to be an impressive 18 ft (5.48 m) long when measured in 2011 at his home in Marineland Melanesia wildlife zoo on Green Island, Queensland.

Largest crocodile ever

Sarcosuchus imperator, a monster crocodile that walked the Earth some 110 million years ago, weighed 8 tonnes (17,600 lb) and was 11–12 m (36–39 ft) long. Reaching this immense size required more than 50 years of growth.

Largest crocodile in captivity (ever)

Although Cassius (above) is the largest crocodile in captivity today, the largest ever was a 6.17-m (20-ft 3-in) saltwater crocodile captured in Bunawan, Philippines, on 3 Sep 2011. This crocodile was named Lolong and housed at Bunawan Eco-Park. Lolong did not adapt well to life in captivity, however, and died on 10 Feb 2013.

The **oldest crocodilian in captivity (living)** is Muja, an American alligator (*Alligator mississippiensis*). It is not known how old he was on arrival (fully grown) at Belgrade Zoo, but the 78 years 219 days he has lived there to 18 Apr 2016 are enough to secure him this record. Muja survived the aerial bombing of the zoo during World War II.

The **oldest crocodilian in captivity (ever)** was Hakuna, an African slender-snouted crocodile (*Mecistops cataphractus*) at Blijdorp Zoo in Rotterdam, Netherlands. He and his mate, Matata, were acquired in 1929 – a gift from singer and dancer Josephine Baker. While Matata died in 2014, Hakuna lived there for a total of 85 years until his death on 19 Feb 2015.

Largest crocodile genus

The genus *Crocodylus*, the true crocodiles, contains 12 individual species and is represented on every continent other than Europe and Antarctica.

Rarest crocodilian

According to a 2002 study, there are fewer than 200 Chinese alligators living in the wild. Native to the lower Yangtze River in China, this species has struggled with habitat destruction and hunting by local farmers.

Newest crocodile species

The desert or sacred crocodile (*C. suchus*) of West Africa looks almost identical to the Nile crocodile (*C. niloticus*), but genetic analysis carried out in 2011 proved that it is only distantly related.

Largest crocodilian eggs

The false gharial (see below) lays eggs that are around 10 x 7 cm (3.94 x 2.76 in). That's about the same diameter as a baseball.

The **smallest crocodilian eggs**, by contrast, are laid by the Chinese alligator (*A. sinensis*). These are as little as 5.23 cm (2 in) long and 3.27 cm (1.3 in) wide – smaller than a hen's egg.

Unsurprisingly, Chinese

Most human fatalities in a crocodile attack?

In his 1962 book *Wildlife Sketches Near and Far*, the Canadian naturalist Bruce Stanley Wright recounted a deadly saltwater crocodile encounter on Ramree Island in Burma during World War II. On 19 Feb 1945, as the story goes, Allied troops (below) forced 1,000 Japanese prisoners of war to cross 10 mi (16 km) of mangrove swamps, where they fell prey to *C. porosus*. After a night of frenzied feeding by the crocodiles, only 20 men emerged alive. New research by the National Geographic Channel, however, has cast doubt on the story, or at least on the extent of the deaths.

Smallest crocodilian family

The family Gavialidae contains only two species: the gharial (*Gavialis gangeticus*, below) and the false gharial (*Tomistoma schlegelii*). The former is native to Bangladesh, India and Pakistan, while the latter lives in south-east Asia. Until recently, the false gharial was thought to be a type of crocodile, hence the name.

DATELINE

2600 BCE

First autograph
A Sumerian scribe named "Adu" uses a reed to etch his cuneiform signature into a clay tablet in what is now Tell Abu Salābikh, Iraq.

FAST FACTS

The roar of an American alligator, the **loudest crocodilian**, can reach 92 dB • The word "crocodile" comes from the Greek for "pebble worm" • Crocodiles can swim faster than they can run

Fastest crocodile

The freshwater crocodile (*Crocodylus johnstoni*) of northern Australia can run at speeds of 17 km/h (10.56 mph). Scary as this sounds, the "freshie" (as it is commonly known) generally uses its speed to run away from people, not towards them.

TRIVIA

Crocodiles have a powerful biting force (see below), but their jaws can be kept shut with a regular rubber band: the muscles that *open* the mouth are much weaker than those that clamp it shut.

alligators also produce the **smallest crocodilian hatchlings**, with an average length of 20 cm (7.9 in), and are, as adults, the **smallest alligators** – with an average length of just 1.5 m (4 ft 11 in) for males.

Most restricted distribution for a crocodile

While some crocodiles are spread over vast areas (the saltwater crocodile ranges from southern India to western Australia), others have adapted to life in a very restricted habitat. The most extreme example of this is the Cuban crocodile (*C. rhombifer*), which lives only in Cuba's Zapata Swamp, an area of 4,354 km² (1,681 sq mi).

First plane crash caused by a crocodile

On 25 Aug 2010, a small passenger plane crashed on approach to Bandundu Airport in the Democratic Republic of the Congo. When emergency services reached the crash site, they found a lone survivor who explained that the crash had been caused by a crocodile. A passenger had smuggled one on board in a sports bag, and when it broke loose the panicked passengers caused a stampede that unbalanced the aircraft. The crocodile was subsequently hacked to death with a machete.

DID YOU KNOW?

The 5.5-m (18-ft) Brutus has become something of a celebrity with tourists on Australia's Adelaide River, where he can be lured into view by an offering of buffalo meat. The saltwater crocodile is missing one front leg following a shark attack.

LARGEST CROCODILIAN

Adult male estuarine or saltwater crocodiles (such as Brutus, right) can grow to at least 7 m (23 ft) long and often weigh more than 1 tonne (2,205 lb). People have claimed to have seen 10-m (32-ft 10-in) individuals in the wild, but no conclusive evidence of such giants exists.

The saltwater species also holds the record for **strongest bite force for a crocodile**. Any animal (or person!) unlucky enough to get caught, such as the doomed boar, inset left, can be subjected to a bite force of 11,216 N (2,521 lbf) – equivalent to being crushed under the weight of a mid-sized car.

Tallest pyramid
Construction begins on the iconic Great Pyramid of Giza in Egypt. It will take 20 years to complete the 146.7-m-tall (481-ft 3.5-in) structure, later classified as one of the seven wonders of the ancient world.

2560 BCE

DATELINE

guinnessworldrecords.com 55

OWLS

Newest species of owl

The Seram masked owl (*Tyto almae*) was formally described and named in 2013. It was first made known to science back in 1987, however, when a specimen was photographed (but not collected) in the wild by a visiting expedition. It is native to, and named after, the Indonesian island of Seram.

Earliest known owl species

Berruornis orbisantiqui dates back to the mid/late Palaeocene epoch, some 60–57 million years ago. Its fossils have been found in deposits at Reims in north-eastern France. This ancestor was about the same size as today's largest eagle owls, which are the **largest owls** of any kind alive (see right).

Largest owl ever

The Cuban giant owl *Ornimegalonyx* is known from fossils of four closely related species native to Cuba and dating from approximately 10,000 years ago. Standing 1.1 m (3 ft 7 in) tall, and probably weighing well in excess of 9 kg (19 lb 13 oz), *Ornimegalonyx* is believed to have been flightless, or almost flightless.

Largest owl clutch

In general, the snowy owl (*Nyctea scandiaca*, pictured below) lays the largest clutch, with many 11-egg clutches known. However, a single northern hawk owl (*Surnia ulula*) in Finland has been recorded as laying a clutch of 13 eggs.

Largest owl genus

The genus *Otus*, containing most of the scops owls, is found worldwide, with 46 distinct species recognized. Some authorities consider a few subspecies to be separate species in their own right, raising this total to as many as 51.

Of those species whose populations have been scientifically estimated, the **most abundant owl** is the little owl (*Athene noctua*). Native to much of temperate Europe, northern Africa and Asia eastwards to the Korean peninsula, it is thought to number some 5,000,000–15,000,000 individuals worldwide.

The **owl species with the greatest distribution range** is the common barn

Most northerly owl

The snowy owl is native to the Arctic regions of Eurasia and North America. It heads north in search of food and is one of very few birds to spend much of the year in the high Arctic zone. Snowy owls have even been recorded on Canada's Ellesmere Island, at 82°N, in the bitter-cold darkness of mid-winter.

DATELINE

c. 2281 BCE

Longest reigning pharaoh
Phiops II, aka Pepi II or Neferkare, becomes ruler of Egypt at the age of six and will remain in power for allegedly 94 years. This also potentially makes his the **longest ever reign** of any monarch.

56   Animals

FAST FACTS

Owls' eyes are tube-shaped and cannot move • A group of owls is called a "parliament" • A barn owl can eat 1,000 mice per year • Unusually for birds, female owls are bigger than males and often have brighter plumage

LARGEST OWL

The European race of the eagle owl (*Bubo bubo*) has an average body length of 66–71 cm (2 ft 2 in–2 ft 4 in) and a weight of 1.6–4 kg (3 lb 8 oz– 8 lb 13 oz). It also has the **greatest wing-span for an owl**: at more than 1.5 m (4 ft 11 in), this is about the same as the arm-span of a 14-year-old child.

Eagle owls will eat almost anything that moves, from beetles to roe deer fawns. The major part of their diet consists of mammals (such as rats, mice, foxes and hares), but birds of all kinds are also taken, including crows, ducks, grouse, seabirds and even other owls.

100%

owl (*Tyto alba*). It has a near-global distribution, estimated by the International Union for Conservation of Nature to cover 63,300,000 km² (24,440,000 sq mi), and is absent only from Antarctica.

This bird also has the **most subspecies for an owl**. It is generally split into at least 27 subspecies.

Smallest owl family
There are two taxonomic families of owl alive today (plus several prehistoric ones): Strigidae and Tytonidae. The smallest is Tytonidae – the barn owls and bay owls – with 19 species.

100%

Smallest owl

The elf owl (*Micrathene whitneyi*, right) of south-western USA and Mexico averages 12–14 cm (4.7–5.5 in) long and weighs less than 50 g (1.76 oz). It typically nests in a hole made by another bird, or in cavities in trees. Sometimes, a woodpecker and elf owl may even nest in the same bush. Only marginally larger is the least pygmy owl (*Glaucidium minutissimum*), weighing around 50 g (1.76 oz) and with a total length of 15 cm (5.9 in).

Oldest cypress tree
A specimen of *Cupressus sempervirens* takes root in the city of Abarkuh in Iran; later named Sarv-e-Abarkuh, it will continue to flourish into the 21st century.

2000 BCE ▶ DATELINE

MONKEYS

54 kg

Largest baboon

Adult male chacma baboons (*Papio ursinus*) can grow to a length of 115 cm (3 ft 9 in) – not including a tail of up to 84 cm (2 ft 9 in) – and can weigh as much as 40 kg (88 lb).

Although native to South Africa, these baboons are found all over southern Africa. An isolated troop has even been discovered living in the Namib Desert, Namibia, where there is no surface water for eight months every year. This makes the chacma baboon the **most drought-resistant monkey**.

Smallest Old World monkey

At the opposite end of the scale from the mandrill (left) are two closely related species of talapoin: the Angolan or southern talapoin (*Miopithecus talapoin*) and the Gabon or northern talapoin (*M. ogouensis*). These talapoins have a total length of no more than 45 cm (1 ft 5 in), and weigh c. 800 g (1 lb 12 oz). They typically live in swamps and mangrove forests, and are excellent swimmers.

Noisiest land animal

The fearsome screams of the howler monkey (genus *Alouatta*) of Central and South America have been described as a cross between the bark of a dog and the bray of a donkey increased a thousandfold! The males have an enlarged bony structure at the top of the windpipe that enables the sound to reverberate. Once in full voice, they can be heard clearly up to 3 mi (4.8 km) away.

Heaviest night monkey

As their name suggests, South America's night monkeys, or douroucoulis, are the world's only nocturnal monkeys. Of the 11 species currently recognized, the heaviest is Azara's night monkey (*Aotus azarae*), which weighs about 1.25 kg (2 lb 12 oz), with males being slightly heavier than females.

Most herbivorous monkey

The gelada (*Theropithecus gelada*) is a large, baboon-like monkey native to Ethiopia. Despite its fearsome appearance and huge canine teeth, this species is exclusively vegetarian, with grass making up 90% of its diet (the rest is seeds and roots). The gelada's diet is an adaptation to its habitat in the verdant highlands of northern Ethiopia, where plant life is abundant enough to support herds of up to 700 individuals.

Encroaching human activity and drought have drastically reduced the gelada population over

Largest monkey

The male mandrill (*Mandrillus sphinx*) of equatorial West Africa has a head-and-body length of 61–76 cm (2 ft–2 ft 6 in). Males average 25 kg (55 lb) but can weigh 54 kg (119 lb). The mandrill's distinctive blue rump, red face and yellow beard make it one of the most colourful mammals.

The **largest New World monkey**, meanwhile, is the highly endangered woolly spider monkey (*Brachyteles arachnoides*) – aka muriqui – of Brazil, with a head-and-body length of 46–63 cm (1 ft 6 in–2 ft) and weighing up to 15 kg (33 lb).

SMALLEST MONKEY

Adult pygmy marmosets (*Cebuella pygmaea*, juveniles pictured), found in the upper Amazon, grow to an average weight of 119 g (4.20 oz) – about the same as a mid-sized orange. Despite their size – typically 136 mm (5.3 in) long excluding tail, which is usually longer than the body – pygmy marmosets can leap 5 m (16 ft 5 in) into the air!

1900 BCE

First alphabet
Egyptian masons carve an inscription into a limestone block using the earliest known form of phonetic writing system.

DATELINE

FAST FACTS
The word "monkey" is thought to derive from "mannikin", the Dutch for "little man" • A group of monkeys is a "troop" • The **first mammal in space** was a monkey called Albert II in 1949 • 2016 was the Chinese Year of the Monkey

KNOW YOUR PRIMATES
What's the difference between apes, monkeys and prosimians?

APE
Apes are tailless, and typically larger – and more intelligent – than other primates. This superfamily comprises the "great apes" (bonobos, chimpanzees, gorillas and orang-utans) and "lesser apes" (gibbons).

MONKEY
Monkeys usually have tails, and many of the approximately 260 known species are arboreal (live in trees). Monkeys are divided into two main groups: "Old World" (Africa and Asia) and "New World" (Americas).

PROSIMIAN
Prosimians are a group of more primitive primates that includes lemurs, lorises, bushbabies, pottos and tarsiers. They are mostly nocturnal and arboreal, hunting for insects and small mammals in the trees.

55 km/h

Fastest primate
The patas monkey (*Erythrocebus patas*) of western and eastern Africa can reach speeds of 55 km/h (34 mph). With their long slender limbs, these quadrupedal (all-fours) Old World monkeys are sometimes referred to as "primate cheetahs".

TRIVIA
Spider monkeys (*Ateles*) use their muscular, tactile, prehensile ("grasping") tail as a fifth hand. Pictured here is one such monkey extending its reach by grasping on to a branch with its tail.

the last few decades, but it is still thought to be the **most abundant monkey**, with a population of around 200,000 individuals.

Most northerly baboon
The sacred or hamadryas baboon (*Papio hamadryas*) is native to the Horn of Africa and the most south-westerly portion of the Arabian Peninsula. The **most southerly baboon**, and also the **most southerly non-human primate**, is the chacma baboon (*P. ursinus*, see opposite page), which

has a range that extends as far south as the Cape of Good Hope in South Africa.

Most southerly marmoset
Marmosets are a group of New World monkeys that, along with tamarins, make up the family Callitrichidae. Almost all marmosets and tamarins live in the Amazon rainforest. The notable exception is the black-tailed marmoset (*Mico melanurus*), which has a range that extends from the south-central Amazon in Brazil to the edges of the

Chaco plains in Paraguay. It is thought that the black-tailed marmoset's range is a result of deforestation in the Amazon, which forced it to adapt to new habitats.

Newest monkey
The most recent species of monkey to have been scientifically recognized is the white-cheeked macaque (*Macaca leucogenys*). Native to the tropical forests of south-eastern Tibet, it was officially described in Mar 2015 and is distinguished from other local macaques by the white whiskers on its cheeks, the shape of the male's genitals and a ruff of fur around its neck.

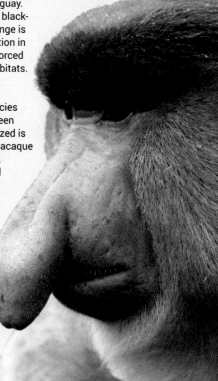

Most northerly primate
Japanese macaques (*Macaca fuscata*) live near Nagano in the mountainous Jigokudani area of Japan. Humans aside, they are the northernmost population of primates. Also known as snow monkeys, they survive the -15°C (5°F) winters by warming themselves in hot volcanic springs.

Longest nose on a primate
The proboscis monkey (*Nasalis larvatus*), found only on the island of Borneo, has a pendulous nose up to 17.5 cm (7 in) long in elderly male specimens. Often large enough to hang over the mouth, it becomes red and swollen when the monkey is in danger or excited. It also acts as a resonator when the monkey makes its characteristic honking warning sound.

Oldest love song
A love song is etched into a stone tablet in the ancient city of Ugarit (modern-day Ras Shamra in Syria); lost until the 1950s, its first performance to modern audiences comes on 6 Mar 1974.

1800 BCE

DATELINE

SPIDERS

Earliest fossil spiders

Found in coal deposits in North America and Europe, the remains of the suborder of primitive spiders known as Mesothelae date from the Carboniferous period, 359–299 million years ago. They probably used their silk for covering their eggs or as a groundsheet, since web-weaving is considered to have evolved much later.

Mesothelae, of which there is only one living family, also possess the **most spinnerets for a spider**: four pairs. Originally evolving from limbs, these organs produce the silk that spiders use for creating webs and linings.

Largest fossil spider

A preserved female specimen of *Mongolarachne jurassica* has a body approximately 24.6 mm (1 in) long, with front legs around 56.5 mm (2.2 in) long. It lived in what is now northern China some 164 million years ago, during the Mid-Jurassic era.

Most venomous spider

The venom of the Sydney funnel-web (*Atrax robustus*), which lives in and around the city of Sydney, Australia, is fatal to humans at a concentration of just 0.2 mg per kg of body weight. The spider owes its lethal poison to a quirk of evolution: although it preys on insects, its venom acts in a way that is especially deadly to humans. At least 14 people have died as a result of Sydney funnel-web bites, some in as little as 15 min.

Earliest orb-weaver spider

Modern orb-weaver or orb-web spiders spin large, strong, complex webs. The earliest known species, *Cretaraneus vilaltae*, was described in 1990 from an exoskeleton discovered in Spain. It lived 140 million years ago in the Early Cretaceous period.

The **oldest cobweb** also dates from the Cretaceous period. In 2009, brothers and amateur fossil hunters Jamie and Jonathan Hiscocks found a web preserved in amber on a beach in East Sussex, UK.

First herbivorous spider

Bagheera kiplingi was formally classified in 1896 from a male specimen. It took another 110 years to identify the first female specimen because of the species' extreme sexual

Largest spider eyes

The ogre-faced (aka gladiator or net-casting) spider, of the genus *Deinopis*, has bulging eyes measuring up to 1.4 mm (0.055 in) across. The eyes do not produce very good images but are excellent at gathering light for night vision – helpful, as this stick-like, tropical arachnid is a nocturnal ambush hunter. It catches prey in a net-like web that it holds suspended from its four front legs; any prey touching the trap is instantly enveloped.

LARGEST SPIDER

First discovered in 1804, this heavyweight ambush hunter is native to the coastal rainforests of Suriname, Guyana and French Guiana. The record leg-span for a male goliath bird-eating spider (*Theraphosa blondi*) is 28 cm (11 in). The specimen was collected by members of the Pablo San Martin Expedition at Rio Cavro, Venezuela, in Apr 1965, and was large enough to cover a dinner plate.

A two-year-old spider of the same species, bred by Robert Bustard and reared by Brian Burnett of Alyth in Perthshire, UK, also had a leg-span of 28 cm in Feb 1998.

DID YOU KNOW?

When goliath bird-eaters feel threatened, they make a hissing sound by rubbing together the bristles on their legs. This is called stridulation and is audible up to 4.5 m (15 ft) away. While bites are very painful, they are not typically dangerous to humans.

100%

1500 BCE

DATELINE

First all-weather clock
A timekeeping device called a *clepsydra* is first used in Ancient Egypt. It works by allowing water to drain from a container at a steady rate. It is not accurate by modern standards, but unlike a sundial it works on overcast days.

FAST FACTS
If attacked, tarantulas flick small barbed hairs, which can cause temporary blindness in humans • Antarctica is the only continent with no spiders • Gram for gram, spider silk is around five times stronger than steel

TRIVIA
The goliath bird-eating spider has no need of a web. Instead, it sneaks up and pounces on prey – such as birds, frogs or mice – injecting venom via fangs that can exceed 2.5 cm (1 in) long.

Most widespread widow spider
In the genus *Latrodectus*, the brown widow (*L. geometricus*), believed to be native to South Africa, has been inadvertently distributed by humans almost worldwide. Introduced populations have been recorded in 14 countries, from the USA to the Far East and Australia. There is evidence that it has begun to displace the more venomous native black widow (*L. hesperus*) in certain areas of southern California, USA.

dimorphism (differences between male and female). This jumping spider, or salticid, lives in Mexico, Guatemala and Costa Rica, and feeds on protein- and fat-rich nubs called Beltian bodies, found at the tips of acacia leaves.

The spider is named after the black panther Bagheera, who features in Rudyard Kipling's *The Jungle Book*, and the author himself.

Rarest spider
Counts of the Kauai cave wolf spider (*Adelocosa anops*) have never exceeded 30 specimens. It lives in total darkness in caves on the island of Kauai, Hawaii, USA, and has no eyes.

Noisiest spider
The male European buzzing spider, *Anyphaena accentuata*, vibrates his abdomen against a leaf to make a buzzing sound and attract a female – though she can only detect it from the vibrations.

The male of the American species *Lycosa gulosa* taps his palps and abdomen on dry leaves to produce an equally audible purr.

Least venomous spider
Uniquely among modern-day spiders, the cribellate or hackled orb-weavers lack venom glands. Instead, they wrap their prey in silk and douse them with digestive enzymes to liquefy them.

Smallest spider webs
The webs of the so-called midget spiders can be less than 10 mm (0.39 in) across. Among their 44 tiny species is *Patu marplesi*, which has a body length of 0.3 mm (0.011 in), making it the **smallest spider**.

Largest spider venom glands
The glands of South America's *Phoneutria nigriventer* each measure up to 10.2 mm (0.4 in) long and 2.7 mm (0.1 in) in diameter and contain as much as 1.35 mg (0.000044 oz) of venom. The venom can cause paralysis and asphyxiation in humans and the contents of one spider's glands are enough to kill 225 mice.

Strongest spider webs
Discovered in Madagascar, Darwin's bark spider (*Caerostris darwini*) weaves the strongest known spider silk, with a tensile strength of up to 520 MJ/m³ (megajoules per cubic metre) – making it twice as tough as any previously described silk. *C. darwini* also spins the **largest webs** – up to 2.8 m² (30 sq ft) – which can stretch between two river banks.

Highest living spider
The Himalayan jumping spider (*Euophrys omnisuperstes*), or "highest of all", was first discovered in 1924 at 6,700 m (21,980 ft) on Mount Everest in Nepal. It was living under stones frozen to the ground. First described in 1975, it is thought to feed on tiny insects blown by the wind from lower altitudes.

First documented war
The Egyptians defeat the Hittites at the Battle of Kadesh. Pharaoh Ramses II has the campaign written up in a series of propaganda bulletins that are distributed throughout his kingdom.

1274 BCE

DATELINE

guinnessworldrecords.com 61

DINOSAURS

First scientific description of a dinosaur

Megalosaurus bucklandii ("great fossil lizard") was described in 1824. Workmen uncovered remains of this bipedal flesh-eater some time before 1818 in a quarry near Woodstock in Oxfordshire, UK.

First stegosaur

Huayangosaurus taibaii lived during the Middle Jurassic period – 165 million years ago – in the area of Huayang (Sichuan) in China. It was formally described and named in 1982. The **dinosaur with the longest spikes** was *Loricatosaurus*, a genus of herbivorous stegosaur that lived 160–164 million years ago in what is now England. As fossils, these spikes, set on the tail, are 1 m (3 ft 3 in) long but may have been covered by a horny sheath, which might have doubled their length. They were probably used as weapons and perhaps also utilized to attract mates.

Dinosaur with the most teeth

The duck-billed hadrosaurs were herbivores with toothless beaks. In the side of their jaws, however, they had as many as 960 self-sharpening cheek teeth for chewing tough plants.

Longest dinosaur

A diplodocid excavated in New Mexico, USA, in 1980 was estimated to be 39–52 m (128–170 ft) long based on comparisons of individual bones. Named *Seismosaurus halli* ("earth-shaking lizard"), it was finally reconstructed at the Wyoming Dinosaur Center, USA, in 1999 and found to be 41 m (134 ft) in length.

Smallest dinosaur species

The feathered *Microraptor zhaoianus* measured 39 cm (1 ft 3.3 in), of which 24 cm (9.4 in) was the tail. A fossil of the diminutive species discovered at Chaoyang in Liaoning Province, China, in 1999 is estimated to be 110–120 million years old.

LARGEST PLESIOSAUR

The carnivorous marine reptile *Liopleurodon* grew to 25 m (82 ft) in length. It had a short neck, a 3-m-long (10-ft) head and four powerful flippers. It lived in the Mid to Late Jurassic period, some 150–165 million years ago, but was not technically a dinosaur; it belonged to an order of reptiles called Sauropterygia. Plesiosaurs were divided into two distinct suborders: the short-necked Pliosauroidea, which included *Liopleurodon*, and the long-necked Plesiosauroidea.

LARGEST...

"Ostrich" dinosaur

The largest species of ostrich dinosaur or ornithomimosaur (named after their superficial outward similarity to an ostrich) was *Deinocheirus mirificus*. It lived 69–71 million years ago during the Late Cretaceous period in what is today Mongolia. It is currently known from three specimens, the largest of which measures 11 m (36 ft) in length and weighs 6.36 tonnes (14,020 lb).

DID YOU KNOW?

The neck of *Omeisaurus tianfuensis* (see below) comprised 17 elongated bones and measured four times its body length. By way of comparison, the neck of a modern-day giraffe contains only seven bones and is just twice as long as its body.

Dinosaurs not to scale!

LONGEST DINOSAUR TAIL

The sauropod *Diplodocus* lived during the Late Jurassic period, c. 145 million years ago, in present-day North America. Its tail grew to 13 m (42 ft 8 in) long and may have acted as a counterbalance to its lengthy neck.

LONGEST DINOSAUR TAIL RELATIVE TO BODY SIZE

Leaellynasaura amicagraphica was 3 m (9 ft 10 in) long, but its 2.25-m (7-ft 4-in) tail was three times the length of its head, neck and body. It lived 120–125 million years ago.

WIDEST DINOSAUR

Distinguished by the large club at the end of its tail, *Ankylosaurus* was up to 2.5 m (8 ft) wide. The entire back was covered with bony plates, studs and spikes, as was the head, including the eyelids.

DINOSAUR WITH THE LONGEST NECK RELATIVE TO BODY SIZE

Omeisaurus tianfuensis had a neck some 9.1 m (30 ft) long but only a 2.3-m (7-ft 6-in) body. It lived in the Jurassic era, some 160–164 million years ago.

DATELINE

1271 BCE

First peace treaty
After three years of war, Egyptian pharaoh Ramses II and Hattusili III, king of the Hittites, agree to a peace treaty. Copies of the treaty are made on silver tablets in both Akkadian cuneiform and Egyptian hieroglyphics.

FAST FACTS

Dinosaurs roamed the Earth for 165 million years (humans have been here for about 2 million years) • British scientist Richard Owen coined the word "dinosaur" ("terrible lizard") in 1841 • Most dinosaur species were vegetarian

The arms of *Deinocheirus mirificus* measured 2.4 m (7 ft 10 in) long – the **longest arms for a bipedal dinosaur**. Each hand had three large-clawed fingers.

Feather-winged raptor
Formally described and named in Oct 2015, *Dakotaraptor steini* was 5–6 m (16 ft 4 in–19 ft 8 in) long. The existence of feathers on this dinosaur's wings (i.e., forelimbs) was confirmed by the presence of a row of bumps along a ridge on the lower edge of the forearm bone called the ulna. Known as ulnar papillae, or quill knobs, these bumps are also present in modern-day birds, as bases for the reinforced attachment of the wing feathers (remiges).

Four-winged dinosaur
The only recorded specimen of *Changyuraptor yangi* was discovered in China's Liaoning Province and formally described and named in 2014. A fully grown adult, the specimen measured some 1.2 m (3 ft 11 in) long and is estimated to have weighed 4 kg (8 lb 13 oz) when alive – making it approximately the same

Highest percentage of intact dinosaur remains

In the summer of 2000, the fossilized remains of a 77-million-year-old duck-billed dinosaur were discovered in northern Montana, USA. Dubbed "Leonardo", the 7-m-long (23-ft) *Brachylophosaurus* was the fourth dinosaur ever found to be classified as a mummy. Some 90% of its body was covered in fossilized soft tissue, including skin, muscles, scales and footpads, and its last meal was preserved in its stomach. The creature was three or four years old when it died.

size as a turkey. Belonging to the microraptor group of dinosaurs, it is called a four-winged dinosaur because its forelimbs and hind

limbs bore long true flight feathers, and it may have been able to fly. It lived in the Early Cretaceous period some 125 million years ago.

Largest fossilized excrement from a carnivore

Currently residing in the Royal Saskatchewan Museum in Regina, Saskatchewan, Canada, the largest coprolite (fossilized faeces) from a carnivore recorded to date is that of a *Tyrannosaurus rex*. Discovered in 1995, the prehistoric ordure measures 50 cm (1 ft 7.6 in) across and weighs more than 7 kg (15 lb 6 oz). Analysis of the droppings provides insights into dinosaurs' diet, eating habits (for example, whether they gulped or chewed their food) and how long food remained in their gut.

Largest collection of dinosaur eggs

As of Nov 2004, the most extensive collection of dinosaur eggs numbered 10,008 individual samples. It is held at the Heyuan Museum in Guangdong Province, China. All of the eggs come from the Late Cretaceous era (c. 100~66 million years ago) and include eggs from oviraptorid and duck-billed dinosaurs.

HEAVIEST CERATOPSIAN
The massive three-horned herbivore *Triceratops horridus* weighed 14 tonnes (30,860 lb). It lived 66–68 million years ago, during the Late Cretaceous period, in what is now North America.

HEAVIEST DINOSAUR
Most scientists agree that the heaviest dinosaur was probably *Argentinosaurus*, a titanosaurid from Argentina. Based on its vast vertebrae, it is estimated to have weighed some 100 tonnes (220,460 lb).

LARGEST CARNIVOROUS DINOSAUR
Spinosaurus roamed the present-day Sahara around 100 million years ago. It measured some 17 m (56 ft) long and weighed 7–9 tonnes (15,430–19,840 lb).

Largest ziggurat
A terraced temple, known today as the Ziggurat of Chogha Zanbil, is built for King Untas of the Elamites in what is now Iran. It is roughly 100 m (328 ft) long on each side and 50m (164 ft) tall.

1250 BCE

DATELINE

CATS & DOGS

Smallest cat ever
Tinker Toy, a male blue point Himalayan-Persian, measured only 7 cm (2.75 in) tall and 19 cm (7.5 in) long when fully grown (aged 2.5 years). The unusually tiny feline was owned by Katrina and Scott Forbes of Taylorville in Illinois, USA.

Shortest living cat (height)
A nine-year-old female Munchkin cat named Lilieput measured 5.25 in (13.3 cm) from the floor to the shoulders on 19 Jul 2013. She is owned by Christel Young (USA) of Napa in California.

Fastest cat breed
The Egyptian Mau has been called a "feline greyhound" for its ability to reach speeds of 48 km/h (29.8 mph). It is also superb at leaping, thanks to its powerful, muscular hind legs. Despite its name, it is of European-American origin.

Longest jump by a cat
Alley, a rescue cat owned by Samantha Martin (USA), made a flying leap of 6 ft (1.82 m) in Austin, Texas, USA, on 27 Oct 2013.

Greatest mouser
Towser (b. 21 Apr 1963), a female tortoiseshell owned by Glenturret Distillery Ltd in Perth and Kinross, UK, caught an estimated 28,899 mice. She averaged three mice per day until her death on 20 Mar 1987.

Wealthiest cat
When Ben Rea (UK) died in May 1988, he left his entire £7-m ($12.5-m) fortune to Blackie, the last surviving of the 15 cats with whom he had shared his mansion.

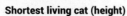

Tallest domestic cat (ever)
Savannah Islands Trouble, aka "Trouble", was 48.3 cm (1 ft 7 in) tall when measured at the Silver Cats Cat Show in Reno, Nevada, USA, on 30 Oct 2011. He was owned by Debby Maraspini (USA) and died on 15 Aug 2012. Trouble was an F2 Savannah cat, a breed produced from a domestic/African serval (*Leptailurus serval*) cross. These cats are officially recognized as domestic, but owe their exotic looks, strong markings and long legs and body to their wild forebears.

Most tricks by a cat in one minute
Didga (AUS) and her owner Robert Dollwet (USA) performed 20 tricks in Tweed Heads, Australia, on 10 Sep 2015. Pictured from the top, she is seen giving a high five, rolling over, skateboarding and jumping on to Robert's hands. Didga, who was adopted from a cat shelter, can even take on the challenge of a real skateboarding park.

LONGEST CAT (LIVING)
Ludo, owned by Kelsey Gill (UK), measured 118.33 cm (3 ft 10.6 in) long on 6 Oct 2015 in Wakefield, UK. Ludo is one of the oldest American breeds: a Maine Coon, named after the US state. There is a myth – impossible in reality, but encouraged by its typical brown tabby colouring and abundant fur – that it resulted from matings between semi-wild cats and raccoons. The Maine Coon's robust health and companionable, lively personality has ensured its popularity as a family pet for well over a century.

DATELINE

850 BCE

Oldest bridge
A slab-stone single-arch bridge is built over the River Meles in Smyrna (Izmir in modern-day Turkey). It will continue to be used into the 21st century.

FAST FACTS

Palaeolithic humans in east Asia domesticated dogs about 15,000 years ago by breeding aggression out of wolves • Cats were domesticated at least 9,000 years ago, probably by being given food in return for helping to control rodents

Tallest female dog

Lizzy, a Great Dane, stood 96.41 cm (3 ft 1.96 in) tall in Fort Myers, Florida, USA, on 14 Nov 2014. She was measured aged seven years, but owner Greg Sample says she was this tall by the age of three. He calls her a "show-stopper", adding that she always attracts attention when they're out and about.

Smallest dog ever

A dwarf Yorkshire terrier owned by Arthur Marples (UK) was 7.11 cm (2.8 in) tall and 9.5 cm (3.7 in) long.

A female Chihuahua called Milly, owned by Vanesa Semler (USA), measured 9.65 cm (3.8 in) tall on 21 Feb 2013, and is the **smallest dog (living)**.

Heaven Sent Brandy, a female Chihuahua belonging to Paulette Keller (USA), is the **smallest dog by length**: 15.2 cm (6 in) from nose to tail tip on 31 Jan 2005.

Tallest dog ever

Zeus (USA), a Great Dane, measured 111.8 cm (3 ft 8 in) on 4 Oct 2011. He lived in Otsego, Michigan, with Denise Doorlag and family.

Fastest time for a dog to retrieve a person from water over a 25-m distance

Jack the Black vom Mühlrad is a Newfoundland working for the German rescue organization DLRG. With his handler Hans-Joachim Brückmann (DEU), he took 1 min 36.81 sec to retrieve a

person from the Kaarster See lake in Germany on 11 Jun 2013.

Fastest time to climb 20 stairs on hind legs

Walking on his back paws, Chinese poodle Arsenal scaled 20 steps in just 7.47 sec on the set of CCTV's *Guinness World Records Special* in Beijing, China, on 9 Jan 2016. Arsenal's owner, Xu Ligang (CHN), had to tell the eager pooch to "slow down" during the attempt, fearing that he might lose his balance.

First litter of "test-tube dogs"

Seven healthy puppies (five pure beagles and two beagle-cocker spaniel crosses), conceived by *in vitro* fertilization (IVF), were born to a surrogate female in summer 2015.

Wealthiest dog

In 1931, Ella Wendel of New York City, USA, bequeathed $15 m (£10.5 m) to her standard poodle, Toby. After her death, Toby was looked after by three servants.

Longest tail on a dog

Keon, an Irish wolfhound owned by Ilse Loodts (BEL), revealed the full extent of his 76.8-cm (2-ft 6.2-in) tail in Westerlo, Belgium, on 18 Aug 2015. Ilse applied for the record on Keon's behalf when her sons realized that his tail surpassed that of the previous record holder, a fellow wolfhound, by just over 4.5 cm (1.7 in).

Most tricks by a dog in one minute

Smurf and his proud owner Sarah Humphreys (UK) performed 32 tricks in Hertfordshire, UK, on 7 Aug 2015. Pictured from the top, Smurf is shown holding, rolling over, bowing and jumping over Sarah's arm. Talented Smurf is a film and TV star. For his role in the film *Sightseers* (UK, 2012) he won the Palm Dog award at Cannes.

First Olympic Games
The Olympic Games are held for the first time in July, when Koroibos, a cook from Elis in southern Greece, wins the foot race. They are inaugurated to honour the god Zeus.

776 BCE

DATELINE

guinnessworldrecords.com **65**

FANTASTIC BEASTS

Largest breed of cattle
Chianina cattle were brought to the Chiana Valley in Italy from the Middle East in pre-Roman times. Four types of the breed exist, the largest of which is the Valdichiana Chianina, found on the plains and low hills of Arezzo and Siena. Bulls average 1.73 m (5 ft 8 in) at the shoulder and weigh 1,300 kg (2,866 lb), but some Chianina oxen have reached 1.9 m (6 ft 2.8 in).

Tallest cow ever
Blosom, owned by Patricia Meads-Hanson (USA), measured 1.9 m (6 ft 2.8 in) from the hoof to the withers (the ridge between the shoulder blades) in Orangeville, Illinois, USA, on 24 May 2014.

Largest hamster species
The European or common hamster (*Cricetus cricetus*) has a head-and-body length of up to 34 cm (1 ft 1.4 in), plus a tail length of up to 6 cm (2.3 in), yielding a total length of around 40 cm (1 ft 3.7 in).

Oldest manatee in captivity
Snooty (b. 21 Jul 1948) was aged 67 years 254 days as of 31 Mar 2016. Snooty was brought to the South Florida Museum in Bradenton, Florida, USA, as a calf in 1949. He lives in a 60,000-US-gal (230,000-litre) pool with two other manatees. Snooty's longevity owes much to the fact that he lives in a controlled environment. In the wild, factors such as algal blooms, boat strikes and fishing debris see most manatees die before they reach the age of 10.

Although widely distributed in the wild across Eurasia, the species is critically endangered in certain European countries. It can live for eight years in captivity.

Rarest domestic horse hybrid
In his book *The Variation of Animals and Plants Under Domestication* (1868), naturalist Charles Darwin (UK) described a unique three-species specimen. He wrote: "Many years ago I saw in the Zoological Gardens [of London] a curious triple hybrid, from a bay mare, by a hybrid from a male ass and female zebra. This animal when old had hardly any stripes; but I was assured by the superintendent, that when young it had shoulder-stripes, and faint stripes on its flanks and legs. I mention this case more especially as an instance of the stripes being much plainer during youth than in old age." This hybrid's father was a fertile male donkra (a rare hybrid, resulting from a male donkey mating with a female zebra).

Rarest marsupial pet
A male mountain pygmy possum (*Burramys parvus*) was found in the kitchen of a ski-lodge in eastern Victoria's Australian Alps in Aug 1966. It became the pet of mammalogist

LARGEST HORN SPAN ON A GOAT (LIVING)
Rasputin is an eight-year-old Walliser black-necked goat (*Capra hircus*). The distance between the tips of his horns measured 1.35 m (4 ft 5.1 in) in Lienz, Tyrol, Austria, on 5 Jun 2015.

- **Largest horn span on a steer (living):** 9 ft 9.25 in (2.97 m), for Lazy J's Bluegrass (USA), a Texas longhorn (*Bos taurus*) living in Greenleaf, Kansas, USA, as of 4 Oct 2014. That's greater than the height of Sultan Kösen (TUR), the **tallest living man**.
- **Longest horns on a steer:** 10 ft 4.75 in (3.16 m), for a Texas longhorn steer named Gibraltar, bred and owned by Dickinson Cattle of Texas, USA.
- **Longest horns on a bull:** 4 ft 6 in (1.37 m), with a circumference of 2 ft 6 in (0.76 m), for a bull named Gopal, on 21 Aug 2002. The bull is owned by Bhagwan Mahavir Pashu Raksha Kendra Anchorwala Ahinsa Dham animal protection centre in Gujarat, India.
- **Longest horn on a sheep:** 1.91 m (6 ft 3.1 in), for a Marco Polo sheep (*Ovis ammon polii*). The species is indigenous only to the Pamir Mountains bordering Tajikistan, Afghanistan, Pakistan and China.

DATELINE

510 BCE

First permanent theatre
The outdoor Theatre of Dionysus is built in Athens, Greece. With an estimated capacity of 17,000 people, the theatre is "in the round", with stone rows built up a slope overlooking the stage.

Dr John Seebeck (AUS). The possum was the first scientifically recorded living specimen of its species. Until then, the mountain pygmy possum had been known to science only from fossil remains dating back 20,000 years and was thought long-extinct.

Smallest species of Amazon parrot

Amazon parrots from Mexico, South America and the Caribbean islands are popular pets. Almost 30 species are currently recognized. The smallest of these is the black-billed amazon (*Amazona agilis*), which is just 25 cm (9.8 in) long and native to mountainous rainforests in the centre of the island of Jamaica. Once a common species, its numbers have fallen owing to deforestation, specimen collection for the pet trade and poaching for food. It is categorized as vulnerable by the International Union for Conservation of Nature (IUCN).

Longest rabbit

Darius, a Flemish giant rabbit owned by Annette Edwards (UK), was found to be 4 ft 3 in (129.5 cm) long when measured for an article in the UK's *Daily Mail* newspaper on 6 Apr 2010. He is shown above with Georgia Hadley, who was then six years old.

Most wool sheared from a sheep in one shearing

A total of 41.1 kg (90 lb 9.7 oz) was sheared from Chris – an errant overgrown sheep rescued by animal charity RSPCA ACT (AUS) – by national shearing champion Ian Elkins in Weston Creek, Australian Capital Territory, on 3 Sep 2015. When found, Chris was so woolly from living in the wild for several years that he could barely stand and was in urgent need of a trim to prevent infection. The shearing took approximately 45 min.

Last Mascarene parrot
As accepted by the IUCN, the last Mascarene parrot (*Mascarinus mascarin*) was a pet owned by King Maximilian I Joseph of Bavaria. He kept it in his royal gardens and menagerie at Munich in Germany, where it lived until at least 1834, by which time it was very old. This species was native to Réunion, one of the Mascarene Islands in the Indian Ocean, but the last account of wild specimens there dates from the 1770s.

3.9 km/h

Fastest 10 m on hind legs by a horse

Desert Kismet (UAE), a 16-year-old grey gelding, covered a distance of 10 m (32 ft 9 in) on his hind legs in 9.21 sec at Dubai Polo & Equestrian Club in Dubai, UAE, on 10 Feb 2016. Desert Kismet is owned by H H Sheikha Maryam bint Mohammed bin Rashed Al Maktoum and trained by Rui De Sousa (above).

Highest jump by a llama

Caspa, owned by Sue Williams (UK), cleared a bar set at 1.13 m (3 ft 8.4 in) during DogFest at Arley Hall in Cheshire, UK, on 14 Jun 2015. The bar was part of a standard horse jump, on which heights were marked at regular intervals.

Largest empire (by percentage)
The Achaemenid (aka Persian) Empire accounts for around 49.4 million of the world's 112.4 million people – or 44%. It includes parts of Central Asia, the Mediterranean, North Africa, Thrace and Macedonia.

490 BCE

DATELINE

guinnessworldrecords.com **67**

480 BCE

Largest naval battle
In September, the Battle of Salamis takes place off the coast of Greece, near the port of Piraeus. An estimated 200,000 men are divided between 800 vessels in the defeated Persian fleet and 370 in the victorious fleet of the Athenians and their allies.

CONTENTS

100%

Largest gape

No one likes to be called a big mouth... but in the case of Bernd Schmidt (DEU), it's actually a record-breaking compliment! The gap between his incisors measured 8.8 cm (3.46 in), as officially ratified at a dental practice in Wendlingen, Germany, on 17 Jan 2015. The measurement was confirmed by dentist Silvia Locklair. Bernd's son had asked him to submit an attempt after seeing this record listed in the 2015 edition of *Guinness World Records*.

The History of the Peloponnesian War, by Greek politician Thucydides, is the earliest work to try to recount and understand past events. Its eight books detail the political and military developments of the 431–404 war between Sparta and Athens.

First history book

400 BCE

DATELINE

BODY PARTS

The complex, multi-functional, yet extraordinarily neat machine that is the human body usually runs so efficiently that we don't think about what it's doing at any given moment – like right now. Even while you're scanning this page, your brain is receiving oxygen to help you concentrate, your skin is keeping microbes at bay and your eyes are making the super-quick movements required for reading. No wonder several of the body's hidden components are record-breakers – shown here at actual size.

LONGEST BONE

Excluding a variable number of sesamoids (small rounded bones), the adult human has 206 bones, compared with about 300 in children (as they grow, some bones fuse together). The thigh bone, or femur, is the longest. It usually makes up 27.5% of a person's stature, and may be 50 cm (1 ft 8 in) long in a 180-cm-tall (5-ft 11-in) man.

The **longest recorded bone** was a femur measuring 76 cm (2 ft 6 in) that belonged to a German giant named Constantine (aka Julius Koch). It was measured by doctors after his death in 1902.

The femur is also the **strongest bone**, and ounce for ounce is stronger than steel. A rod of steel of comparable size would weigh four or five times as much.

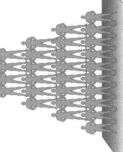

The femur supports the body's whole weight in all activities, from standing to extreme sport. The American College of Sports Medicine states that, in a healthy adult female, it can support more than 30 times the body weight!

LARGEST ORGAN

Skin, which protects all other organs and body systems, and regulates temperature and moisture, is itself an organ. An average adult is covered in 1.5–2 m² (16–21.5 sq ft) of skin. But if the lungs were fully stretched out, they would cover 80–100 m² (861–1,076 sq ft) – about half a tennis court!

Lungs

=

=

Skin

32 sheets of A4 paper

1,603 sheets of A4

The skin has three layers: the outer, waterproof epidermis; the dermis with hair follicles, blood vessels and sweat glands; and the subcutis or fat layer.

SMALLEST BONE

Named after its shape, the stapes or stirrup bone is one of three auditory ossicles ("tiny bones") in the middle ear. The others are the malleus (hammer) and incus (anvil). These transmit sound vibrations, and their absence would mean significant hearing loss.

The stapes measures some 2.6–3.4 mm (0.1–0.13 in) long and weighs 2–4.3 mg (0.030–0.066 grains). It forms the **smallest joint**, with the incus bone, and is controlled by the body's **smallest muscle**, the stapedius, less than 1.27 mm (0.05 in) long.

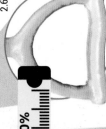

930%

100%

LARGEST ARTERY

The aorta distributes oxygenated blood around the body. It typically measures 3 cm (1.18 in) in diameter where it leaves the heart, at the left ventricle – as wide as the orange circle on the right. It passes blood to the heart's coronary arteries, before feeding vital organs, via the arterial network, from the head to the pelvic area. Here, it narrows to about 1.75 cm (0.68 in) wide, and divides into the iliac arteries, which carry blood to the legs.

AORTA

Besides the aorta, the pulmonary artery is the other main artery, carrying de-oxygenated blood only to the lungs.

The aorta wall is very elastic, allowing it to pulsate in rhythm with the heartbeat and helping to propel blood around the body.

The vena cava, which returns blood to the heart from the rest of the body, is the **largest vein**, with a diameter of 1.2–2 cm (0.47–0.78 in).

The heart, about the size of your clenched fist, pumps blood around a 150,000-km (93,200-mi) system of blood vessels – long enough to wrap round the world more than three times.

The heart is made of involuntary muscle, so it works all by itself – all the time. Beating 100,000 times a day, it clocks up 3 billion beats over an average lifetime.

100%

100%

100%
As well as being the **largest internal organ** (see below right), the liver is also the body's **largest gland**. Glands secrete substances such as hormones and release them into the bloodstream; in the case of the liver, it secretes bile, which helps us digest fats.
The liver is divided into four parts, or "lobes", of differing size and shape. The liver's functions include fighting off infection, removing toxins from the blood, and storing nutrients, vitamins and blood sugar. At any one time, it contains about 13% of your blood (0.57 litres or 1 pint in a fully grown adult).
100%
Three pairs of extraocular muscles in the orbit (eye socket) anchor each eye, moving it up and down and side to side, and rotating it.

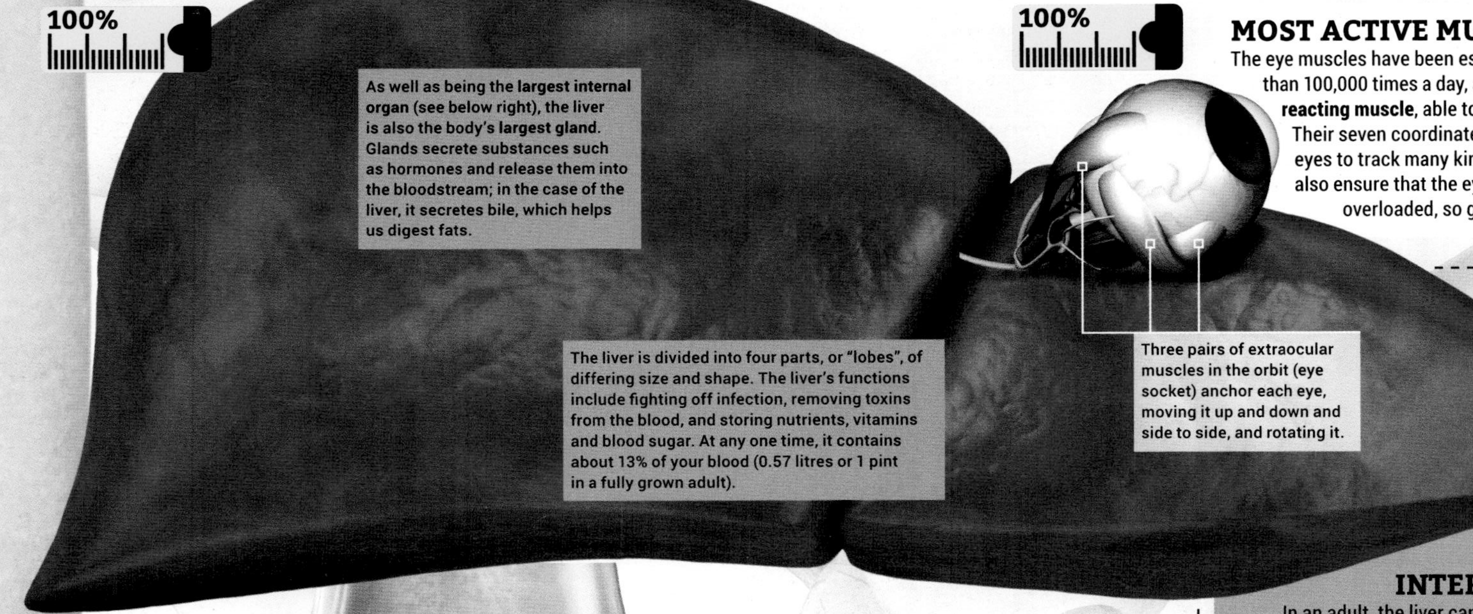

MOST ACTIVE MUSCLE

The eye muscles have been estimated to move more than 100,000 times a day, and are the body's **fastest-reacting muscle**, able to contract in 0.01 sec. Their seven coordinated movements allow the eyes to track many kinds of moving object. They also ensure that the eye's receptors are not overloaded, so good vision is maintained.

LARGEST INTERNAL ORGAN

In an adult, the liver can weigh 1.2–1.5 kg (2 lb 10 oz–3 lb 5 oz) – the equivalent of four FIFA-approved soccer balls. Located behind the lower ribs, it performs more than 100 separate vital functions. It is the only organ that can regenerate itself, so one person can donate a portion of their liver, which will then grow back to normal size. What's more, the donated part will grow to the right size in the recipient!

=

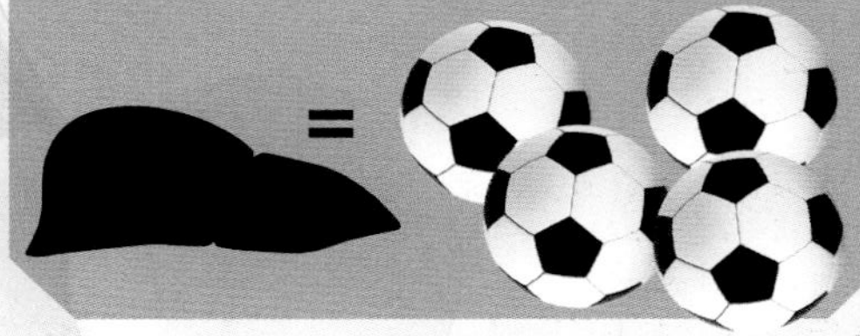

LARGEST SESAMOID BONE

Sesamoid bones are bones that act like pulleys in the complex arrangements of tendons around some joints. Most are only a few millimetres wide and shaped like eggs or sesame seeds (the name "sesamoid" comes from "sesamum", the Latin for sesame seed). The body's largest is the patella or kneecap, which protects the ends of the femur and tibia (shin bone) where they meet at the knee joint. The average human kneecap is 44 mm (1.73 in) wide and 36 mm (1.41 in) from top to bottom.

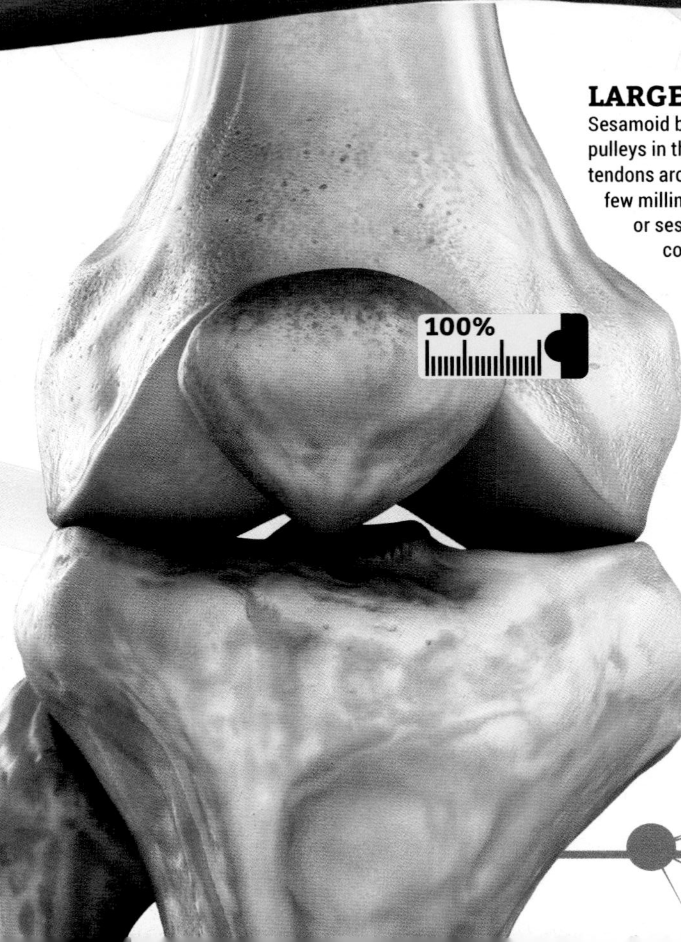

100%

DID YOU KNOW?

Bones contain a core of bone marrow, a soft tissue. Red marrow makes new blood cells; yellow marrow is essentially fat, and found in a long bone like the femur. Children's bone marrow is mostly red; in adults it is half red, half yellow.

The inside of our larger bones have a spongy appearance. It's between the microscopically thin walls of this honeycomb-like material that marrow is found.
Blood vessels and nerves run through our bones. Red and white blood cells are formed inside bone, then carried around the body via the bloodstream.

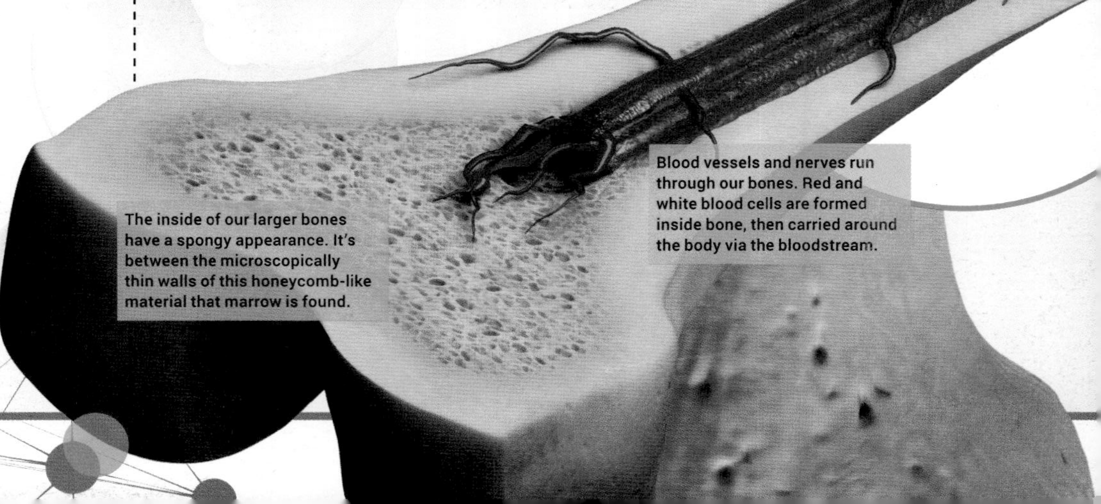

BODY MODIFIERS

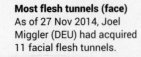

Most flesh tunnels (face)
As of 27 Nov 2014, Joel Miggler (DEU) had acquired 11 facial flesh tunnels.

Largest flesh tunnel (ear)
Kalawelo Kaiwi (USA) had a 10.5-cm (4.13-in) flesh tunnel in his ear lobe verified at a natural health clinic in Hawaii, USA, on 14 Apr 2014.

Largest lip plate
Ataye Eligidagne's (ETH) lip plate spanned 19.5 cm (7.7 in) in width and 59.5 cm (23.4 in) in circumference, as verified in Oct 2014. The previous maximum width of these clay plates was 15 cm (6 in).

Most facial piercings
Axel Rosales (ARG) had 280 piercings on his face, as of 17 Feb 2012.
On the same day, Francesco Vacca (USA) revealed the **most piercings in the tongue**: 16.

DID YOU KNOW?
Depending on the image chosen, tattooing may involve the skin being pierced with the tattooist's needle between 50 and 3,000 times a minute. A tattoo ages along with its owner, growing faded, with any words becoming progressively harder to read over time.

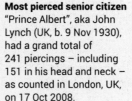

MOST TATTOOED SENIOR CITIZEN (FEMALE)
Charlotte Guttenberg's (USA) tattoos cover 91.5% of her body, as revealed in Melbourne, Florida, USA, on 3 Jun 2015. She told GWR that her "gallery" began with a tattoo of a butterfly, a birthday present to herself in 2006. Since then, and about 1,000 tattooing hours later, Charlotte's body art has burgeoned into floral and animal imagery, symbols from Shintoism and an emperor dragon winding around her leg. While her inspiration is Japanese culture, she has added a few details of her own, such as delicate Victorian mittens. She plans to continue with a full head tattoo, a "secret garden" below her hair.

Most body modifications (female)
"The Mexican Vampire Lady", aka Maria Jose Cristerna (MEX), has 49 body modifications, including significant tattoo coverage, a range of transdermal implants on her forehead, chest and arms, and multiple piercings in her eyebrows, lips, nose, tongue, ear lobes, belly button and chest. With 96% tattoo coverage on her body, as of 8 Feb 2011, she is also the **most tattooed female (living)**.

Most surgical-needle piercings in one session
On 14 Dec 2014, Russ Foxx applied 4,550 needles to Matthew Menczyk (both CAN) in 8 hr 12 min at Wicked Tattoo & Piercing in Maple Ridge, British Columbia, Canada.

Most pierced senior citizen
"Prince Albert", aka John Lynch (UK, b. 9 Nov 1930), had a grand total of 241 piercings – including 151 in his head and neck – as counted in London, UK, on 17 Oct 2008.

Most tattooed senior citizen (male)
Tom Leppard (UK) has 99.9% of his body covered in a leopard-skin design, consisting of dark spots on a yellow background.

Longest tattoo session (multiple people)
"Alle Tattoo", aka Alessandro Bonacorsi (ITA), completed a session of 50 hr 8 min in Palermo, Italy, on 10–12 Oct 2014.
With Riccardo Rivieccio (ITA), Alle Tattoo also achieved the **most tattoos in 12 hours by a team of artists**: 836 tattoos by 12 artists, on 26 Oct 2013.
And on 10 Oct 2015, Alle Tattoo arranged the **most people to form a tattooed sentence**: 77. They spelt out "Step by step together for a world of peace happiness family passion art love tattoo and music."

Most tattoos of...
• Squares: Matt Gone (USA) had 848 squares tattooed

Most pierced woman
On 4 May 2000, Elaine Davidson (BRA/UK) was verified as having 462 piercings: 192 on her facial area and 270 on (and inside) her body. As of 8 Jun 2006, Elaine had accumulated the **most piercings in a lifetime (female)**: 4,225. Elaine is constantly adding and replacing jewellery, mostly in her face.

DATELINE
341 BCE
First use of a crossbow
The use of a crossbow is documented for the first time at the Battle of Ma-Ling in Linyi, China. It is probably a single-shot weapon held with a pistol-style grip.

72 Humans

FAST FACTS
Stone Age people probably inked themselves with natural dyes • From the 1770s, circuses became centres of tattooing in Europe and the USA • Early tattooed attractions, such as Englishman John Rutherford, started touring in the 1820s

Most tattooed man
The ultimate in multi-layered tattooing is represented by Lucky Diamond Rich (AUS, b. NZ), who has spent more than 1,000 hr having his body inked by hundreds of tattoo artists. First, he had a full collection of colourful designs from around the world tattooed over his entire body. But that was just for starters. He next opted for a 100% covering of black ink, including eyelids, the skin between the toes, inside the ears and even his gums. He is now being tattooed with white designs on top of the black, and coloured designs over the white!

over his body, including 201 on his head, as counted on *Lo Show dei Record* in Italy on 7 Jul 2014.

• **A cartoon character**: Lee Weir (NZ) had been tattooed with 41 portraits of Homer Simpson, as of 5 Jun 2014.

• **Bones**: "Rico", aka Rick Genest (CAN), has 139 human bones tattooed on his body, reproducing part of his skeleton, as verified in Milan, Italy, on 27 Apr 2011.

• **Insects**: As of the same date, "Rico" also had 176 insect tattoos on his upper body and head.

DID YOU KNOW?
Lucky began his tattooing odyssey when travelling with a circus. He first had a small juggling club inked on his hip, then collected more tattoos as he moved about. He now pushes the boundaries of tattooing with his layering concept.

Most body modifications (couple)
Victor Hugo Peralta (URY) and his wife Gabriela Peralta (ARG) have 84 modifications, verified on the set of *Lo Show dei Record* in Milan, Italy, on 7 Jul 2014. These consist of 50 piercings, 14 body implants, eight microdermals, five dental implants, four ear expanders, two ear bolts and one forked tongue.

Most pierced man
As of 5 Aug 2010, Rolf Buchholz (DEU) had 453 piercings, including 158 around his lips, 31 in his ears, 25 in his eyebrows, eight in his nose, two in his tongue, three in his chest and four in his navel. On 16 Dec 2012, Rolf's piercing total of 481, added to two subdermal "horn" implants and 33 other body transformations, made a tally of 516 – the **most body modifications (male)**.

Largest group of life-size statues
A group of 6,000–8,000 life-size clay soldiers and other figures – later known as the "Terracotta Army" – are created for Emperor Qin Shi Huangdi's tomb near Xi'an in China. They will be discovered in 1974.

221 BCE

DATELINE

MEDICAL MIRACLES

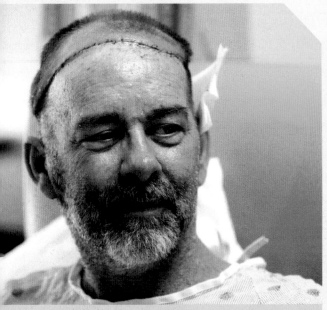

First skull and scalp transplant

Following treatment for leiomyosarcoma (a rare form of cancer), James Boysen (USA) was left without the top of his skull. A 15-hr operation on 22 May 2015 saw him receive partial skull and scalp grafts involving painstaking microsurgery. He also received a new kidney and pancreas. The procedure took place at Houston Methodist Hospital in Texas, USA, and involved surgical teams from both that hospital and the Anderson Cancer Center.

Youngest organ donor
On 1 Dec 2015, Hope Lee (UK) donated her kidneys and liver cells just 74 min after her birth.

Most transplanted organ
In 2013 – the most recent year for which statistics are available – the kidney was the most widely transplanted organ. According to the Global Observatory on Donation and Transplantation, 79,325 kidney transfer operations were performed that year, out of a total of 118,127 transplants – about 67% of all such operations.
According to the same source, in 2013 Norway was the **country with the most transplanted organs per million population**.

Most extensive skull implant using 3D printing

In Nov 2013, neurosurgeon Bon Verweij and maxillofacial surgeon Marvick Muradin (both NLD) replaced about 90% of a skull using 3D-printing technology. The patient, a 22-year-old woman, suffered from a medical condition that made her cranial bone thicken. The growing bone was putting pressure on her brain, affecting vital body functions. The operation took place at the University Medical Center Utrecht in the Netherlands and lasted 23 hr.

More than 95 organs were transplanted per million citizens.
As of the same year, Spain was the **country with** **the most organ donations from deceased people**, with 35.3 organs donated per million of the population.

Most sensitive bionic skin

A bionic component is something that replaces or enhances a part of the human body with an electronic or electromechanical implant. In 2014, researchers from institutions in Seoul, South Korea, and Cambridge, Massachusetts, USA, announced a breakthrough in the field of synthetic bionic skin. The material takes the form of thin, rubbery sheets with a lattice of electronic sensors that can measure three sensory elements – temperature, pressure and moisture.

DID YOU KNOW?
This bionic skin may even be adapted in terms of sensitivity: for fingers, the density of sensor weave will be higher than in areas such as the wrist. When activated, the sensors generate small amounts of electrical current, which can be used to stimulate nerves in the body.

FIRST...

Bionic bone implant
In Jul 2006, scientists at University College London, UK, announced that early clinical trials at Mount Vernon Hospital in Middlesex, UK, had been completed for a method of attaching a titanium rod directly to human bone. While rods and pins have long been used in broken-bone repair, this was the first time that the metal rod protruded through the skin. The aim is to enable direct attachment of prosthetic limbs to residual bone, rather than strapping them to the limb as a whole.

Bionic brain prosthesis
The hippocampus is the part of the brain that forms and stores long-term memories. Professor Theodore Berger (USA) has developed a working hippocampal prosthesis. In 2011 – in collaboration with Sam Deadwyler and Robert Hampson at Wake Forest Baptist Medical Center in North Carolina, USA – it was successfully tested with

DATELINE

200 BCE

First battery
An unknown inventor in what is now Baghdad, Iraq, discovers that by placing a copper cylinder and an iron rod in a ceramic pot filled with acid, it is possible to generate around 1.5 volts of electricity.

74 Humans

DID YOU KNOW?
Frank the artificial human is currently housed at the Smithsonian National Air and Space Museum in Washington, DC, USA. There, he converses with human museum-goers through a laser-scanned copy of Prof Bertolt Meyer's own face.

Most bionic body parts in an artificial human

"Frank" (short for "Frankenstein") is an experiment to show that a functioning artificial human body can be made from bionic parts. Unveiled on 17 Oct 2013, Frank – who has 18 individual bionic body parts – was inspired by Prof Bertolt Meyer (above), now of Chemnitz University of Technology in Germany, and created by Darlow Smithson Productions and Shadow Robot (both UK).

live rats. The prosthesis uses electrodes to record both from the input and output nerve bundles of a damaged hippocampus. The input was analysed by an external processor array and appropriate responses were then generated to stimulate an output pattern. This mimicked the way in which a healthy hippocampus functions. In 2013, the prosthesis

was successfully tested on primates. The breakthrough opens up the possibility of repairing brains damaged by diseases such as Alzheimer's.

Bionic eye to overcome macular degeneration
In Jul 2015, Ray Flynn (UK) became the first person to have a bionic eye implanted to recover the sight he had partially lost from macular degeneration. The operation took place at the Manchester Royal Eye Hospital, UK. Macular degeneration is the most common cause of sight loss in the developed world.

Child to survive "internal decapitation"
In Oct 2015, 16-month-old Jaxon Taylor (AUS) suffered the fracture of his first two vertebrae and their ligaments as a result of a car accident. This meant that his head was separated from his neck, a trauma known as "internal decapitation". This is fatal in 68% of cases, with survivors usually suffering paralysis. Fortunately, Jaxon's spinal cord did not snap. Surgeon Dr Geoffrey Askin and his team at the Lady Cilento Children's Hospital in Brisbane, Australia, were able to repair Jaxon's injury with complete success.

Most organs transplanted in a single operation

Six-month-old Italian Alessia di Matteo (2003–05) underwent the transplant of eight organs in a 12-hr operation at Holtz Children's Hospital at University of Miami/Jackson Memorial Hospital, USA, on 31 Jan 2004. The organs were the liver, stomach, pancreas, small and large intestine, spleen and both kidneys. Tragically, Alessia died of complications within a year.

FIRST PROSTHETIC HAND CONTROLLED BY THE BRAIN

In Sep 2015, the USA's Defense Advanced Research Projects Agency (DARPA) developed the first prosthetic hand that could be controlled directly by the brain. It could also transmit tactile sensations (i.e., a sense of touch) allowing users to pick up delicate objects without damaging them. The hand was implanted in a 28-year-old man who had been paralysed for 10 years as a result of a spinal-cord injury. The prosthetic limb was developed by DARPA in collaboration with scientists from the Applied Physics Laboratory at Johns Hopkins University in Maryland, USA.

100%

Oldest analogue computer
A Greek inventor builds a complex mechanical computer, known today as the Antikythera Mechanism. The computer is lost in a shipwreck and not rediscovered until 1901.

100 BCE DATELINE

OLDEST...

Qualified pilot

George Neal (CAN, 21 Nov 1918–4 Apr 2016) was still regularly flying light aircraft at the age of 96 years 193 days, as verified on 2 Jun 2015. George, who had his first flying lesson at the age of 16, had a remarkable 45-year career as a test pilot with de Havilland, and went on to fly his own aircraft: a DHC-1 Chipmunk.

Band

The Golden Senior Trio (all JPN) is a jazz ensemble whose members had an average age of 83 years 19 days, as of 5 Jul 2015. Seen above, with GWR adjudicator Kaoru Ishikawa, they are: Naoteru Nabeshima (vibraphone, 89 years 52 days old, above left), Zensho Otsuka (piano, 81 years 140 days old, centre) and Naosuke Miyamoto (bass, 78 years 234 days old, right). All have maintained a passion for music from their early days and formed the band on 18 Sep 2008. Their repertoire crosses genres and includes a jazz version of Beethoven's Piano Sonata No.8 in C minor, Op.13 ("Pathétique").

Person (ever)

Jeanne Louise Calment (FRA) lived for 122 years 164 days. Born on 21 Feb 1875, Jeanne died at a nursing home in Arles, France, on 4 Aug 1997.

In 1990, she survived hip surgery aged 114 years 11 months, making her the **oldest surgery patient**.

The **oldest man ever** was Jiroemon Kimura (JPN, b. 19 Apr 1897), who died on 12 Jun 2013 aged 116 years 54 days.

Person to climb Everest

Yuichiro Miura (JPN, b. 12 Oct 1932) reached the peak of Everest on 23 May 2013 at 80 years 223 days. This also made him the **oldest person to climb a mountain over 8,000 m**.

Tamae Watanabe (JPN, b. 21 Nov 1938) became the **oldest woman to climb Everest** when she summitted – for the second time – on 19 May 2012, at the age of 73 years 180 days.

Abseiler

Aged 101 years 55 days, Doris Cicely Long MBE (UK, b. 18 May 1914) abseiled down the Spinnaker Tower in Portsmouth, UK, on 12 Jul 2015.

Woman to row across any ocean solo

Diana Hoff (UK, b. 1 May 1944) was 55 years 135 days old at the start of her crossing of the Atlantic east to west solo, in *Star Atlantic II*, between 13 Sep 1999 and 5 Jan 2000.

English Channel swimmer

Otto Thaning (ZAF, b. 13 Mar 1941) crossed from Shakespeare Beach in Dover, UK, to Wissant Bay near Calais in France in 12 hr 52 min, aged 73 years 177 days, on 6 Sep 2014.

The **oldest English Channel swimmer (female)** is Sue Oldham (AUS, b. 24 Nov 1945), who made the crossing in 17 hr 11 min, aged 64 years 257 days, on 8 Aug 2010.

Person to fly in zero gravity

At 86 years 90 days old, Ugo Sansonetti (ITA, b. 10 Jan 1919) took a zero-gravity flight

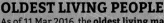

OLDEST LIVING PEOPLE

As of 11 Mar 2016, the **oldest living man** was Israel Kristal (ISR, left), who was aged 112 years 178 days, as verified by the Gerontology Research Group and Jewish Records Indexing. Mr Kristal was born on 15 Sep 1903 in the village of Maleniec, near Żarnów in Russia (now Poland). Since 1950 he has lived in Haifa, Israel.

Susannah Mushatt Jones (USA, b. 6 Jul 1899, right) was 116 years 303 days old as of 4 May 2016. Ms Jones lives in Brooklyn, New York City, where she received her certificate just before her 116th birthday, which she celebrated with two parties. She is the **oldest living person**.

Oldest synagogue
The Wadi Qelt Synagogue is erected as part of the Hasmonean Winter Palace complex on the road between Jericho and Jerusalem in the Middle East. It will be toppled by an earthquake in 31 BCE.

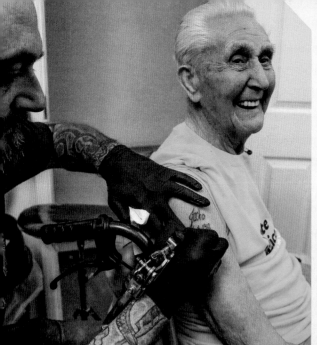

Person to receive their first tattoo

On 6 Apr 2016 – to celebrate his 104th birthday – Jack Reynolds (UK, b. 6 Apr 1912) had a tattoo of his own design, reading "Jacko 6.4.1912", inked on his upper arm at Pete Who's Tattoos in Chesterfield, UK. A relaxed Jack commented, "I'd rather be doing this than having a haircut." *Good Morning Britain* (ITV, UK) took up his story and filmed him receiving his GWR certificate at home the next day.

FAST FACTS

The study of ageing and the elderly is known as "gerontology", from the Greek *geron* ("old man") and *logos* ("explanation") • Of the 50 people aged 110 or more, 23 were born in Japan • The odds of you reaching 120 years old are 1 in 10 billion

Silver sports stars

The **oldest bodybuilder** is Jim Arrington (USA, b. 1 Sep 1932, left), aged 83 years 6 days when competing at a professional bodybuilding competition in Venice, California, on 7 Sep 2015. Jim, who has been bodybuilding for more than 40 years, came fourth out of more than 60 contestants.

Competitive sprinter Hidekichi Miyazaki (JPN, b. 22 Sep 1910, right) was 105 years and one day old when he ran in the Kyoto Masters Athletics Autumn Competition in Kyoto, Japan, on 23 Sep 2015, the third consecutive year that he has become the **oldest sprinter**. Mr Miyazaki ran the 100 m race in 42.22 sec.

on a modified Boeing 727 in Fort Lauderdale, Florida, USA, on 10 Apr 2005.

Person to land on the Moon
On 4 Feb 1971, Alan Shepard (USA, b. 18 Nov 1923) was 47 years 78 days old when he walked on the Moon during the Apollo 14 lunar mission.

Person to release a new album
Aged 97 years 74 days, Dame Vera Lynn (UK, b. Vera Welch, 20 Mar 1917) launched compilation album *National Treasure – The Ultimate Collection* (Decca) on 2 Jun 2014.

Australian artist Herbert Henry "Smoky" Dawson MBE (19 Mar 1913–13 Feb 2008) is the **oldest person to release an album of new material**. He was 92 years 156 days old when *Homestead of My Dreams* came out on 22 Aug 2005.

Winner of an EGOT
Known as the "Grand Slam of Show Business", EGOT is an acronym for the feat of winning an Emmy, a Grammy, an Oscar and a Tony. Only 12 individuals have earned an EGOT, the oldest being British actor/director John Gielgud (14 Apr 1904–21 May 2000), who achieved his in 1991 at the age of 87 years 133 days. He won: a Tony in 1961 (Best Director of a Drama: *Big Fish, Little Fish*); a Grammy in 1979 (Best Spoken Word, Documentary or Drama Recording: *Ages of Man*); an Oscar in 1982 (Best Actor in a Supporting Role: *Arthur*); and finally an Emmy in 1991 (Outstanding Lead Actor in a Miniseries or Special: *Summer's Lease*).

DID YOU KNOW?
Research mission STS-95 returned space pioneer John Glenn to orbit 36 years, eight months and nine days after he became the first American to orbit the Earth. On 20 Feb 1962, he circled the globe three times in 4 hr 56 min.

Astronauts

On 29 Oct 1998, John Glenn (USA, b. 18 Jul 1921, right) became the **oldest astronaut** at the age of 77 years 103 days, when he was launched as payload specialist on the STS-95 Space Shuttle mission. In nine days, the crew conducted nearly 80 experiments.

The **oldest astronaut (female)** is Barbara Morgan (USA, b. 28 Nov 1951, inset), who was 55 years 253 days old when she lifted off on the STS-118 mission to the *International Space Station* (*ISS*) on 8 Aug 2007. Morgan's roles included educator and robotic-arm operator.

OLDEST SUPERCENTENARIANS

A "supercentenarian" is anyone who is aged 110 years or more. As of 4 May 2016, there were 49 women in the 50 oldest living supercentenarians and only one man.

	Name	Born	Age
1	Susannah Mushatt Jones (USA)	6 Jul 1899	116 yr 303 days
2	Emma Morano-Martinuzzi (ITA)	29 Nov 1899	116 yr 157 days
3	Violet Brown (JAM)	10 Mar 1900	116 yr 55 days
4	Nabi Tajima (JPN)	4 Aug 1900	115 yr 274 days
5	Chiyo Miyako (JPN)	2 May 1901	115 yr 2 days
6	Eudoxie Baboul (FRA)	1 Oct 1901	114 yr 216 days
7	Ana Vela-Rubio (ESP)	29 Oct 1901	114 yr 188 days
8	Mitsue Toyoda (JPN)	15 Feb 1902	114 yr 79 days
9	Marie-Josephine Gaudette (ITA)	25 Mar 1902	114 yr 40 days
10	Yukie Hino (JPN)	17 Apr 1902	114 yr 17 days

Source: Gerontology Research Group

Longest-lasting empire
After thwarting Antony and Cleopatra at the Battle of Actium in 31 BCE, Octavian dissembles the Roman Republic and appoints himself Emperor Augustus. The new Roman Empire will endure for 503 years.

27 BCE

DATELINE

FAMILY VALUES

Highest age of 12 living siblings

The 12 children of Magnus and Elsebeth Olsen (DEN) – all of whom were born in the Faroe Islands between 1920 and 1938 – had a combined age greater than a millennium: 1,025 years 41 days. The five sisters and seven brothers had their combined age confirmed on 27 Aug 2014.

HIGHEST AGE OF...

A parent and child
Sarah Knauss (USA, 1880–1999) was once the **oldest living woman**. On 30 Dec 1999, the 119-year-old and her 96-year-old daughter Kathryn Knauss Sullivan (USA, 1903–2005) had a total mother-daughter age of 215!

The **highest combined age for a living parent and child**, meanwhile, is 210 years 48 days, set by Jamaican mother and son Violet Brown (b. 10 Mar 1900) and Harland Fairweather (b. 15 Apr 1920) on 21 Apr 2015. Violet is also believed to be the last living subject of Queen Victoria.

Nine living siblings
Francesco Melis and his wife Eleonora Mameli (both ITA) welcomed their first child,

Consolata, into the world on 22 Aug 1907. Over the next 27 years, she would be joined by eight brothers and sisters. By 20 Jun 2014, with Consolata aged 106, the nine siblings' total age was 837 years 6 days.

Three generations to run a marathon
At the Tokyo Marathon on 22 Feb 2015, a Japanese grandfather, daughter and grandson, with a combined age of 173 years 163 days, raced their way into the record books. Shigetsugu Anan and Yasuko Nakatake both crossed the line in 6 hr 42 min 28 sec, while the youngest member of their group, Suguru Nakatake, finished 2 sec earlier.

MOST...

Living generations
On the birth of her great-great-great-great grandson in 1989, Augusta Bunge (USA) became the matriarch of a seven-generation family.

Quadruplets born to the same mother
Valentina Vassilyev, who

Oldest couple to marry (aggregate age)

The combined age of the oldest couple to marry is 194 years 280 days. The landmark was achieved by lovestruck couple George Kirby (UK, b. 13 Jun 1912) and Doreen Kirby (UK, Luckie, b. 6 Sep 1923) when they were married in Eastbourne, East Sussex, UK, on 13 Jun 2015.

lived in Shuya, Russia, in the 18th century, gave birth to four sets of quads. She also bore seven sets of triplets and 16 pairs of twins. Her overall total of 69 children easily makes her the **most prolific mother**.

Centenarian siblings
The Clarke family (IRL) lays claim to five centenarians: Joseph, Charles, Patrick, James and Margaret. The record was confirmed on Margaret's 100th birthday on 30 May 2014.

MOST SIBLINGS WITH THE SAME BIRTH WEIGHT

Oliver, Keanu and Phoenix, three of the four sons of Megan and Luke Bell from Queensland, Australia, all weighed precisely 7 lb 8 oz (3.4 kg) when they were born between 2007 and 2013. Incredibly, the Bells' first son, Hayden, was born only one ounce heavier, weighing in at 7 lb 9 oz (3.43 kg) in 2006.

DATELINE

40 CE

Longest Roman aqueduct
Roman engineers complete a 275-m-long (902-ft) aqueduct – known today as the Pont du Gard – to supply the settlement of Nemausus (present-day Nîmes in France) with clean drinking water.

78 Humans

FAST FACTS
The British royal family celebrates each new baby with a 41-gun salute
• Among OECD countries, Turkey has the largest average household:
4.11 people vs the average 2.63 • In the USA, the average marrying age is 28

Most family members to complete a marathon

The majority of us cheer on loved ones from the sidelines at a marathon, but not the Hughes family (IRL). On 27 Oct 2014 at the Dublin Marathon, 30 relatives (27 pictured) from multiple generations took to the track. The fastest was Hillary Hughes, who ran a time of 3 hr 34 min 28 sec.

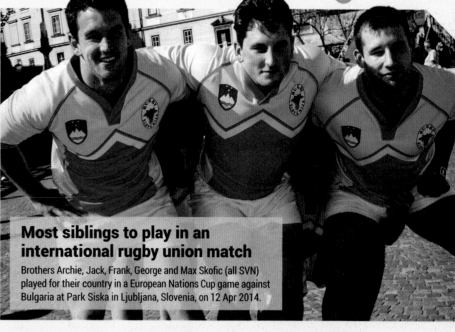

Most siblings to play in an international rugby union match

Brothers Archie, Jack, Frank, George and Max Skofic (all SVN) played for their country in a European Nations Cup game against Bulgaria at Park Siska in Ljubljana, Slovenia, on 12 Apr 2014.

Siblings to marry siblings from another family

Between 1977 and 1996, five daughters of Narandra Nath and Taramoni Roy married five sons of Trarpoda Karmaker and Khana Rani Roy (all BGD).

Family members on the Hollywood Walk of Fame

In 2004, continuing a long lineage of acting talent, *E.T.* child star Drew Barrymore (USA) became the seventh member of her family to be honoured with a gold star. She joined her great uncle Lionel Barrymore, who boasts two stars, along with great aunt Ethel, grandfather John, grandmother Dolores Costello, great-grandfather Maurice Costello and her father John D Barrymore, who each have one. That's eight gold stars for the family altogether.

Most siblings to compete in a motorsport competition

Brothers Arto, Matti, Ari, Jyrki, Markus and Pasi Hintsala (all FIN) went head to head at the annual Vehkamaan motor race in Liminka, Finland, on 14 Aug 2010.

Oldest adoptee

Proving that it's never too late to be adopted, Mary Banks Smith (USA, left) was aged 76 years 96 days when a court in Dallas, Texas, declared her the daughter of Muriel Banks Clayton (USA, right) on 9 Jun 2015. In doing so, Muriel also became the **oldest adoptive parent**, aged 92 years 322 days. Both women were delighted by the long-coming affirmation, with Mary commenting: "I feel very happy. She has been Mom for a long time, and now it's official."

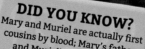

DID YOU KNOW?
Mary and Muriel are actually first cousins by blood; Mary's father and Muriel's mother were siblings. After her father died and her mother was institutionalized, Mary was taken in by various relatives, but aged 14 she moved to live with Muriel, where she felt happiest.

Most leap-year generations in one family

Every four years, Peter Anthony Keogh (IRE, b. 1940, centre), his son Peter Eric (UK, b. 1964, right) and his granddaughter Bethany (UK, b. 1996, left) have their birthdays on 29 Feb.

First documented volcanic eruption
Mount Vesuvius erupts, destroying of the town of Pompeii, Italy. The Roman politician and writer Pliny the Younger writes two letters to his friend, the historian Tacitus, detailing the events and their aftermath in great detail.

79 CE

BODY EXTREMES

Tallest man ever
When last measured, on 27 Jun 1940, Robert Pershing Wadlow (USA) was 272 cm (8 ft 11.1 in) tall. His shoe size was 37AA, or UK size 36 – equivalent to 47 cm (18.5 in) long – and his hands measured 32.3 cm (12.7 in) from the wrist to the tip of his middle finger. These are the **largest feet ever** and the **largest hands ever**, respectively.

Largest afro
Tyler Wright (USA) is the proud owner of a head of hair that measures 25.4 cm (10 in) high, 22.9 cm (9 in) wide and 177 cm (5 ft 10 in) in circumference. Tyler's afro was measured in St Louis, Missouri, USA, on 19 Jun 2015, when he was 12 years old.

The **largest afro (female)** belongs to Aevin Dugas (USA). It measured 16 cm (6.3 in) high, 21 cm (8.27 in) wide, and had a circumference of 139 cm (4 ft 7 in) when verified on the set of *Lo Show dei Record* in Rome, Italy, on 31 Mar 2012.

TALLEST...
• **Man** and **person**: Currently, the tallest living human is Sultan Kösen (TUR), who measured 251 cm (8 ft 2.8 in) on 8 Feb 2011. For the **tallest man ever**, see above.
• **Woman**: Siddiqa Parveen (IND) measured at least 222.2 cm (7 ft 3.4 in) tall in Dec 2012. Owing to Siddiqa's ill health and her inability to stand upright, it's impossible to ascertain her exact stature; however, Dr Debashish Saha, who performed the measurements, estimated her standing height to be at least 233.6 cm (7 ft 8 in).

LONGEST...

• **Beard ever**:
When he died in 1927, Hans N Langseth's (NOR) beard measured 5.33 m (17 ft 6 in) long. The record-breaking facial hair was presented to the Smithsonian Institution in Washington, DC, USA, in 1967.

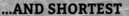

• **Beard on a living person**: Sarwan Singh (CAN) had a beard measuring 2.495 m (8 ft 2.5 in) long as of 8 Sep 2011. Sarwan leads the congregation of the Guru Nanak Sikh temple, located in Surrey, British Columbia, Canada.
• **Fingernails on a pair of hands ever (male)**: The nails of Melvin Boothe (USA) had a combined length of 9.85 m (32 ft 3.8 in) when measured on 30 May 2009.
• **Fingernails on a pair of hands ever (female)**: Lee Redmond (USA) started to grow her fingernails in 1979. She carefully manicured them to reach an overall length of 8.65 m (28 ft 4.5 in), as confirmed on the set of *Lo Show dei Record* in Madrid, Spain, on 23 Feb 2008.

...AND SHORTEST
• **Woman**: Jyoti Amge (IND, far left) measured 62.8 cm (24.7 in) tall on 16 Dec 2011.
• **Man**: Since *GWR 2016*, we have said a farewell to Chandra Bahadur Dangi (NPL, 1939–2015). At 54.6 cm (21.5 in) tall, he remains the **shortest man ever**. Chandra, who was mobile, was shorter than the shortest non-mobile living man, though the opposite is usually true. After his death, GWR re-opened separate categories for the record. The **shortest living man (mobile)** is once more Khagendra Thapa Magar (NPL, centre left), who stood 67.08 cm (26.4 in) tall on 14 Oct 2010. The **shortest living man (non-mobile)** is Junrey Balawing (PHL, near left), who was 59.93 cm (23.6 in) tall on 12 Jun 2011.

DATELINE

112 CE

First shopping mall
Located in Rome, Italy, Trajan's Forum includes a covered market area with 150 shops and offices set over six gallery levels. It is designed by the architect Apollodorus of Damascus.

80 Humans

FAST FACTS

Hair retains a short-term record of the substances in the bloodstream – which is why it is so useful as forensic evidence • Of all the mammals, only primates have fingernails • The human tongue "print" is unique – just like a fingerprint

Youngest female with a full beard

Harnaam Kaur (UK, b. 29 Nov 1990) was aged 24 years 282 days when she was confirmed to have a full beard, in Slough, UK, on 7 Sep 2015. Harnaam began to grow facial hair at the age of 11. She is an avid body- confidence and anti-bullying activist.

The **longest beard on a woman** is that of Vivian Wheeler (USA, right). Her facial hair measured 25.5 cm (10.04 in), from follicle to tip, on the set of *Lo Show dei Record* in Milan, Italy, on 8 Apr 2011. "It really helped to have a Guinness World Record," Vivian told GWR. "It showed me I could be proud of being me. It made me feel like I had a chance in society."

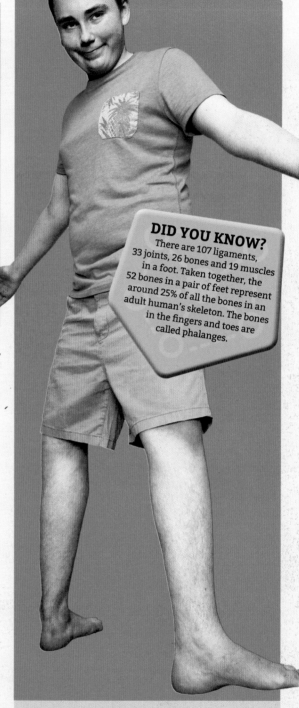

DID YOU KNOW?
There are 107 ligaments, 33 joints, 26 bones and 19 muscles in a foot. Taken together, the 52 bones in a pair of feet represent around 25% of all the bones in an adult human's skeleton. The bones in the fingers and toes are called phalanges.

• **Hair (male)**: In 1949, Indian monk Swami Pandarasannadhi was reported to have hair 26 ft (7.92 m) in length. This may have been caused by a scalp condition called plica neuropathica, which makes the hair so matted that it cannot be untangled.
• **Hair (female)**: The hair of Xie Qiuping (CHN) measured 5.627 m (18 ft 5.54 in) on 8 May 2004. She began growing her lengthy locks in 1973.

• **Moustache**: When measured for Italy's *Lo Show dei Record* in Rome on 4 Mar 2010, the moustache of Ram Singh Chauhan (IND) was 14 ft (4.29 m) long.
• **Nose on a living person**: The nose of Mehmet Özyürek (TUR) measured 8.8 cm (3.46 in) long from the bridge to the tip when recorded on 18 Mar 2010.
• **Tongue**: Nick Stoeberl (USA) had a tongue 10.1 cm (3.97 in) long, from its tip to the middle of the closed top lip, as of 27 Nov 2012.
• **Tongue (female)**: Chanel Tapper's (USA) tongue measured 9.75 cm (3.8 in) long on 29 Sep 2010.

HEAVIEST...

• **Man ever**: Jon Brower Minnoch (USA, 1941–83) weighed over 1,400 lb (635 kg; 100 st) when assessed in Mar 1978.
• **Woman ever**: Rosalie Bradford (USA, 1943–2006) was reported to have a peak weight of 1,200 lb (544 kg; 85 st) in Jan 1987.
• **Living woman**: As of 13 May 2010, Pauline Potter (USA) weighed 643 lb (291.6 kg; 46 st).

Longest eyebrow hair

Zheng Shusen (CHN) has one eyebrow hair that extended to 19.1 cm (7.5 in) when measured at Manzhouli, Inner Mongolia, China, on 6 Jan 2016.

The **longest ear hair** is only marginally shorter. Anthony Victor (IND) has hair sprouting from the centre of his outer ears (middle of the pinna) that measures 18.1 cm (7.12 in) at its longest point.

Greatest foot rotation

Maxwell Day (UK) is able to rotate his right foot through 157°, as verified in London, UK, on 23 Sep 2015. Maxwell was discovered at the *Minecraft* conference Minecon 2015 – he saw a picture of the previous record holder and told a Guinness World Records team member that he could break the record. In fact, Maxwell can rotate both his feet, although he can "only" rotate his left foot 143°.

First use of gas warfare
Persian forces attacking the Roman garrison of Dura-Europos in eastern Syria dig tunnels to try to gain access. They ignite bitumen and sulphur crystals to fill the tunnels with noxious fumes.

254 CE

DATELINE

guinnessworldrecords.com **81**

RECORDOLOGY

DID YOU KNOW?
Wally is the creation of English illustrator Martin Handford. The bobble-hatted boy goes by many names: he's known as Waldo in North America, Charlie in France, Walter in Germany, Willy in Norway, Holger in Denmark, Hugo in Sweden and Ubaldo in Italy!

330 CE

Oldest travel guide
An anonymous traveller writes the *Itinerarium Burdigalense*, a guide for pilgrims going from France to Jerusalem. It gives recommendations for hostels, inns and stables along the route.

CONTENTS

Largest gathering of people dressed as Wally

Where's Wally? If you were at the Street Performance World Championship at Merrion Square West in Dublin, Ireland, on 19 Jun 2011, you would have seen him everywhere! In total, 3,872 participants donned Wally's trademark specs, bobble hat and red stripes. And it was all in a good cause: proceeds raised from the sale of Wally outfits on the day were subsequently donated to Africa Aware, an Irish charity working in Malawi.

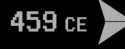

Longest pole-sitting overall
St Simeon the Stylite, a Christian mystic and hermit, dies atop the 15-m (50-ft) pillar on which he had sat for the previous 39 years. He came down just once, so that the pole could be slightly increased in height.

459 CE DATELINE

PICTURE THIS!

Every year, the *Guinness World Records* Picture Editors criss-cross the planet in search of the most striking record-holder images. To celebrate the work of our global team of photographers, we present here 10 of our favourite images snapped for the last few editions of the book. These iconic record holders are not only inspiring, fascinating ambassadors for GWR, they also symbolize the diversity and scope of record-breaking...

FARTHEST EYEBALL PROTRUSION

Kim Goodman (USA) is a truly *eye*-conic record holder! She is able to pop her peepers out of their sockets by an eye-watering 12 mm (0.47 in), as confirmed in Istanbul, Turkey, in 2007.

FASTEST COMPLETION OF THE BOG SNORKELLING TRIATHLON (FEMALE)

The fastest time to complete the World Bog Snorkelling Triathlon is 2 hr 45 min 40 sec and was achieved by Natalie Bent (UK) at the 2010 World Bog Snorkelling Triathlon in Llanwrtyd Wells, Wales, UK, on 11 Jul 2010.

Running
12 km (7.5 mi)

Bog snorkelling
82 m (270 ft)

Cycling
31 km (19 mi)

MOST BIG MACS EATEN

In 2012, Donald A Gorske (USA) celebrated his 40th anniversary as a customer of the fast-food chain McDonald's by consuming his 26,000th Big Mac! Donald is such a fan of the burger chain that he's eaten at one of their outlets every single day since 17 May 1972. If you took the beef from all the Big Macs that Donald's eaten in his lifetime, you'd be faced with a single 2.3-tonne (5,200-lb) burger patty measuring a mammoth 2.6 m (8 ft 6 in) wide and 50 cm (19.6 in) thick!

TALLEST AND SHORTEST DOGS

In 2007, we brought together the mightiest and meekest dogs for a photo shoot in Sacramento, California, USA. At 107 cm (42.2 in) to the shoulder, Great Dane Gibson was 10 times taller than Chihuahua Boo Boo, at just 10.16 cm (4 in)!

DID YOU KNOW?

It took Kevin Fast 1 min 16 sec to pull the plane 8.8 m (28 ft 10 in). Among the muscle-bound pull the muscle-bound minister's other records are **heaviest house pulled** (35.8 tonnes; 79,145 lb) and **most cars pulled simultaneously** (15).

HEAVIEST AIRCRAFT PULLED

On 17 Sep 2009, Reverend Kevin Fast of Ontario, Canada, pulled a CC-177 Globemaster III weighing an incredible 188.83 tonnes (416,299 lb). He hauled the aircraft at the Canadian Forces Base in Trenton, Ontario. Coincidentally, the Globemaster III weighed almost exactly the same as the **largest blue whale** ever measured (190 tonnes/419,000 lb on 20 Mar 1947).

LARGEST WALKING ROBOT

Fanny is a radio-controlled robot dragon measuring 15.72 m (51 ft 7 in) long by 8.2 m (26 ft 10 in) tall. She was made by Zollner Elektronik AG (DEU) in Zandt, Germany, for an annual folklore festival. The terrifying creature is powered by a 2-litre turbo diesel engine and weighs 11 tonnes (24,250 lb) – about the same as 158 Komodo dragons, at c. 70 kg (154 lb) the real-world's largest lizard.

LARGEST COLLECTION OF *STAR WARS* MEMORABILIA

Steve Sansweet (USA) has collected so many pieces of memorabilia relating to his favourite movie franchise that he can't log them fast enough. As this packed picture shows, he has a lot of *Star Wars* items: 92,360 at the last official count. However, he owns an estimated 500,000 items in total, making his official count a mere 18.4% of his actual collection.

■ Uncounted
■ Counted

MOST PIERCED WOMAN AND MOST PIERCED SENIOR CITIZEN

This incredible portrait of Elaine Davidson (UK, b. BRA; left) and John Lynch (UK, right) shows the extent of their piercings. At the last count, the pierced pair possessed a combined total of 703 rings, studs and rods. Assuming 7.5 g (0.26 oz) per piercing, this equates to enough metal to produce 354 soda cans!

LARGEST MONSTER TRUCK

Bigfoot 5 is 4.7 m (15 ft 6 in) tall with 3-m-tall (10-ft) tyres. Built in 1986 as one in a series of 17 by Bob Chandler of St Louis, Missouri, USA, *Bigfoot 5* is now permanently parked in St Louis, and makes occasional appearances at local shows. Tipping the scales at a whopping 38,000 lb (17,236 kg), it's equivalent in weight to three bull African elephants!

FASTEST 30 M ON A SCOOTER BY A DOG

Norman the Scooter Dog, owned by Karen Cobb (USA), set this unusual speed record in Marietta, Georgia, USA, on 12 Jul 2013. The pawesome pooch covered 30 m (98 ft) on a scooter in 20.77 sec – averaging a speed of 5.2 km/h (3.2 mph). It has been estimated that the average dog is as intelligent as a two-year-old child – and even capable of basic arithmetic!

FOOD

Largest vegetable stew

On 21 Mar 2015, Knorr Fine Foods (EGY) served up a stew weighing 4,155 kg (9,160 lb 3 oz), which took 12 hr to prepare in Cairo, Egypt. One of Egypt's national dishes, *foul* (aka *ful* or *foule*) includes cooked fava beans optionally seasoned with lemon juice and a mix of herbs and spices.

Fastest time to eat a 12-inch pizza

Kelvin Medina (PHL) ate a pizza in 23.62 sec in Taguig, Philippines, on 12 Apr 2015.

Greatest weight of Carolina Reaper chillies eaten in one minute

Russel Todd (USA) scoffed 70 g (2.5 oz) of Carolina Reaper chillies in 60 sec in New York, USA, on 26 Apr 2015. That's some feat: the Carolina Reaper is the **hottest chilli**. Grown by the PuckerButt Pepper Company (USA), it averages 1,569,300 units on the Scoville heat scale.

Most expensive sandwich

The "Quintessential Grilled Cheese" was selling for $214 (£132.64) at Serendipity 3 in New York, USA, as of 29 Oct 2014.

Most sausages produced in one minute

Liam O'Hagan of O'Hagan's Sausages (both UK) made 44 sausages in 60 sec at a charity event in Chichester, UK, on 2 Nov 2015.

Largest cupcake mosaic

The Spar Group Ltd (ZAF) put together a 138.56-m² (1,491.44-sq-ft) cupcake mosaic in Durban, South Africa, on 5 Sep 2015. Comprising 33,660 cupcakes, it was created as a tribute to the Springboks for the Rugby World Cup 2015 as well as a fund-raiser for Childhood Cancer Awareness Month.

MOST ICE-CREAM SCOOPS BALANCED ON A CONE

Dimitri Panciera (ITA) carefully balanced 121 scoops of ice-cream on a single cone in Forno di Zoldo, Italy, on 20 Sep 2015. In doing so, he topped his own record of 109 scoops, set in the same location on 20 Jul 2014 at the Gelatiamo festival, an annual celebration of the ice-cream that the Val di Zoldo area produces.

When it comes to cones, though, one towers above all the rest. The **tallest ice-cream cone** measured 3.08 m (10 ft 1.26 in) and was made by Hennig-Olsen Is AS and Trond L Wøien (both NOR) at Kristiansand, Norway, on 26 Jul 2015.

DATELINE

650 CE

Largest hoard of Anglo-Saxon treasure
A veteran soldier buries 5 kg (11 lb) of gold in Staffordshire, UK. The hoard creates a sensation when it is uncovered in 2009.

86 Recordology

FAST FACTS

Americans eat 100 acres (40.4 ha) of pizza every day • Hot dogs were among the first foods eaten during the Apollo 11 Moon mission • Heinz sells 11 billion single-serve packets of ketchup each year

Longest sausage

S.C. Carrefour Romania S.A. and Aldis SRL Calarasi (both ROM) created a 62.75-km-long (38.99-mi) sausage in Ploieşti, Romania, on 1 Dec 2014. That's nearly two-and-a-half times the length of all the corridors in the US Pentagon!

Most limes sliced in half in one minute

On 19 Mar 2015, Julio César Távara (PER) halved 100 limes in 60 sec at *Reporte Semanal* (Latina TV) in Lima, Peru. Julio César works in a seafood restaurant near Piura in Peru and his nickname is "The Limes Ninja".

Largest…
Cheese sculpture: On 18 Sep 2015, the Melt fast-food eatery in Hollywood, California, USA, carved a 1,524-lb (691.27-kg) cheeseburger out of a block of Wisconsin cheddar.

Glass of beer: Angus Wood and Ed Dupuy of Stod Fold Brewing Company (all UK) served up a 2,082-litre (550-US-gal) glass of ale – equivalent in volume to 26 bathtubs of beer – in Halifax, West Yorkshire, UK, on 6 Jul 2014.
Rice cracker: On 26 Oct 2014, JCI Noda (JPN) unveiled a 2.35-m² (25.3-sq-ft) rice cracker in Noda, Chiba, Japan.

Sticky rice cake: On 13 Apr 2015, Salakhet Siem Reap (KHM) made a sticky rice cake weighing 4,040 kg (8,906 lb 10 oz) – the weight of six dairy cows – in Siem Reap, Cambodia.

Pulled pork: The Pork Association (AUS) produced a 707-kg (1,558-lb 10-oz) portion of pulled pork – the weight of two grand pianos – in the Australian city of Sydney on 14 Apr 2015.

Largest pizza

With a surface area of 1,261.65 m² (13,580.28 sq ft), this gigantic pizza (also the **largest gluten-free pizza**) was nearly five times the size of a tennis court! It was prepared by Dovilio Nardi, Andrea Mannocchi, Marco Nardi, Matteo Nardi and Matteo Giannotte (all ITA) from NIPfood at the Fiera di Roma trade fair in the Italian capital city of Rome on 13 Dec 2012.

DID YOU KNOW?

This gargantuan, 100% gluten-free pizza was named "Ottavia" in homage to Octavian Augustus, the first Roman emperor. A gluten-free diet has been credited with a variety of health benefits, such as improving cholesterol levels, promoting digestive health and increasing energy levels.

Oldest Viking boats
A defeated Viking raiding party buries its dead in a longship on the island of Saaremaa, Estonia. The remains of this ship represent the oldest evidence of Viking seafarers.

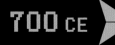

700 CE

DATELINE

GARDEN GIANTS

Heaviest pumpkin
Beni Meier of Switzerland won the 2014 European Championship Pumpkin Weigh-off with a homegrown specimen weighing 1,054 kg (2,323 lb 10 oz) – as heavy as 15 fully grown men. The gargantuan gourd was authenticated by the Great Pumpkin Commonwealth in Ludwigsburg, Germany, on 12 Oct 2014.

Largest rose bush
A specimen of the rose bush Lady Banks (*Rosa banksiae*) located in Tombstone, Arizona, USA, has a trunk circumference of 13 ft 5 in (4.09 m), stands some 9 ft (2.75 m) tall and covers 8,000 sq ft (743 m²).

Most blooms on an orchid
In all, 91 blooms were counted on an orchid grown by Shi Yuanfeng (CHN), as verified in Benxi, Liaoning, China, on 20 May 2014.

Most tomatoes from a single plant
Surjit Singh Kainth (UK) harvested 1,355 tomatoes from just one of his plants in Coventry, West Midlands, UK, on 11 Sep 2013.

Largest cashew tree
A cashew tree in Natal, Brazil, reputedly planted by a local fisherman in 1888, covers an area as large as 28 tennis courts – c. 7,500 m² (80,700 sq ft) – and yields up to 80,000 fruit (and "nuts") per year.

HEAVIEST FRUIT & VEG

FRUIT/VEG	WEIGHT	GROWER	DATE
Apple	1.849 kg (4 lb 1.2 oz)	Chisato Iwasaki (JPN)	24 Oct 2005
Avocado	2.19 kg (4 lb 13.2 oz)	Gabriel Ramirez Nahim (VEN)	28 Jan 2009
Beetroot	23.4 kg (51 lb 9.4 oz)	Ian Neale (UK)	7 Sep 2001
Broccoli	15.87 kg (34 lb 15.7 oz)	John and Mary Evans (both USA)	1993
Cabbage	62.71 kg (138 lb 4 oz)	Scott A Robb (USA)	31 Aug 2012
Cantaloupe melon	29.4 kg (64 lb 13 oz)	Scott and Mardie Robb (both USA)	16 Aug 2004
Celery	33.9 kg (74 lb 11.7 oz)	Ian Neale (UK)	23 Sep 2011
Cherry	21.69 g (0.76 oz)	Gerardo Maggipinto (ITA)	21 Jun 2003
Courgette	29.25 kg (64 lb 7.7 oz)	Bernard Lavery (UK)	1990
Fig	290 g (10.2 oz)	Mehtap Omer (UK)	24 Aug 2014
Garlic head	1.19 kg (2 lb 10 oz)	Robert Kirkpatrick (USA)	1985
Gooseberry	64.49 g (2.27 oz)	Kelvin Archer (UK)	21 Aug 2013
Grapefruit	3.210 kg (7 lb 1 oz)	Cloy Dias Dutra (BRA)	9 Nov 2006
Lemon	5.265 kg (11 lb 9.7 oz)	Aharon Shemoel (ISR)	8 Jan 2003
Mango	3.435 kg (7 lb 9.1 oz)	Sergio and Maria Socorro Bodiongan (both PHL)	27 Aug 2009
Parsnip	7.85 kg (17 lb 4.9 oz)	David Thomas (UK)	23 Sep 2011
Peach	725 g (1 lb 9 oz)	Paul Friday (USA)	23 Aug 2002
Pear	2.948 kg (6 lb 8 oz)	J A Aichi Toyota Nashi Bukai (JPN)	11 Nov 2011
Plum	323.77 g (11.42 oz)	Minami-Alps City JA Komano Section Kiyo (JPN)	24 Jul 2012
Potato	4.98 kg (10 lb 15.6 oz)	Peter Glazebrook (UK)	4 Sep 2011
Pumpkin	1,054 kg (2,323 lb 10 oz)	Beni Meier (CHE)	12 Oct 2014
Radish	31.1 kg (68 lb 9 oz)	Manabu Oono (JPN)	9 Feb 2003
Sweet potato	37 kg (81 lb 9 oz)	Manuel Pérez Pérez (ESP)	8 Mar 2004
Turnip	17.78 kg (39 lb 3.2 oz)	Scott and Mardie Robb (both USA)	1 Sep 2004

HEAVIEST...

WATERMELON
Chris Kent of Sevierville, Tennessee, USA, grew a watermelon that weighed 350 lb 8 oz (159 kg). It was verified at the Operation Pumpkin festival held in Hamilton, Ohio, USA, on 4 Oct 2013.

ONION
On 12 Sep 2014, Tony Glover (UK) presented an onion that weighed 8.5 kg (18 lb 11.8 oz). The eye-wateringly large vegetable was presented at the Harrogate Autumn Flower Show in Harrogate, North Yorkshire, UK.

CARROT
Peter Glazebrook (UK) grew a carrot to a world-beating weight of 9.1 kg (20 lb 1 oz). As with Tony Glover's gigantic onion (see left), the record was verified at the Harrogate Autumn Flower Show, UK, on 12 Sep 2014.

CUCUMBER
On 26 Sep 2015, at the Malvern Autumn Show at the Three Counties Showground in Malvern, UK, David Thomas (UK) presented a cucumber weighing an astonishing 12.9 kg (28 lb 7 oz).

DATELINE

717 CE

Oldest family business
Buddhist monk Garyo Houshi sets up a *ryokan*, a traditional inn, in the village of Awazu, Japan, near a spring reputed to have healing powers. The current owner is Houshi's 46th-generation descendant.

100%

Heaviest strawberry

Koji Nakao (JPN) cultivated a 250-g (8.82-oz) strawberry that measured 8 x 12 cm (3.15 x 4.72 in) and had a circumference of 25–30 cm (9.84–11.81 in). It was weighed in Fukuoka, Fukuoka Prefecture, Japan, on 28 Jan 2015.

TALLEST PLANTS

PLANT	HEIGHT	GROWER	DATE
Amaranthus	8.48 m (27 ft 10 in)	Jesse Eldrid (USA)	25 Oct 2007
Basil	3.34 m (10 ft 11.5 in)	Anastasia Grigoraki (GRC)	4 Jul 2012
Bean (speckled butterbean)	14.1 m (46 ft 3 in)	Staton Rorie (USA)	7 Nov 2003
Cactus (homegrown)	24 m (78 ft 9 in)	Sri Dharmasthala Manjunatheshwara College of Dental Sciences (IND)	23 Dec 2009
Coleus	2.5 m (8 ft 4 in)	Nancy Lee Spilove (USA)	31 Oct 2004
Collard	4.06 m (13 ft 4 in)	Woodrow Wilson Granger (USA)	24 May 2007
Cosmos	3.75 m (12 ft 3 in)	Cosmos Executive Committee (JPN)	17 Oct 2003
Cotton	9.75 m (32 ft)	D M Williams (USA)	15 Jul 2011
Daffodil	1.55 m (5 ft 1 in)	M Lowe (UK)	1979
Dandelion	1.77 m (5 ft 10 in)	Jo Riding and Joey Fusco (both CAN)	12 Sep 2011
Fuchsia (climbing)	11.4 m (37 ft 5 in)	Reinhard Biehler (DEU)	13 Jun 2005
Kale	5.54 m (18 ft 2 in)	Gosse Haisma (AUS)	1987
Lupin	1.96 m (6 ft 5.1 in)	A H Fennell (IRL)	1993
Papaya tree	13.4 m (44 ft)	Prasanta Mal (IND)	2 Sep 2003
Parsley	2.37 m (7 ft 9.3 in)	David Brenner (USA)	10 Jun 2009
Pepper	4.87 m (16 ft)	Laura Liang (USA)	1999
Petunia	5.8 m (19 ft 1 in)	Bernard Lavery (UK)	1994
Rose (climbing)	27.7 m (91 ft)	Anne and Charles Grant (both USA)	1 Aug 2004
Rose bush (supported)	5.66 m (18 ft 7 in)	Robert Bendel (USA)	12 Oct 2009
Sugar cane	12.5 m (41 ft)	Hoovayya Gowda (IND)	21 Jun 2014
Sunflower	9.17 m (30 ft 1 in)	Hans-Peter Schiffer (DEU)	28 Aug 2014
Sweetcorn (maize)	10.74 m (35 ft 3 in)	Jason Karl (USA)	22 Dec 2011
Thistle	2.4 m (8 ft)	Christine Sadler (CAN)	26 Aug 2010

LONGEST...

Beetroot
On 26 Sep 2015, at the Three Counties Showground in Malvern, Worcestershire, UK, Joe Atherton (UK) presented a 7.212-m-long (23-ft 7.9-in) beetroot. By way of contrast, the reticulated python – the **longest snake** – grows to around 6.25 m (20 ft 6 in).

The year before, at the same competition, Joe submitted the **longest parsnip**, which measured 6.28 m (20 ft 7.2 in).

Bottle gourd
Alan Eaton (CAN) presented a 3.797-m-long (12-ft 5.5-in) bottle gourd (*Lagenaria siceraria*) at Bracebridge Fall Fair in Ontario, Canada, on 19 Sep 2015.

Cucumber
Ian Neale (UK) grew a 1.07-m-long (3-ft 8-in) cucumber for presentation at the Royal Bath & West Show in Shepton Mallet, UK, on 26 Sep 2011.

Radish
Jamie Courtney-Fortey, Gareth Fortey and Kevin Fortey (all UK) grew a radish measuring 2.235 m (7 ft 4 in) in Cwmbran, Gwent, Wales, UK, as verified on 25 Oct 2015.

SWEDE
In Sep 2013, Ian Neale (UK) unveiled a prize-winning 54-kg (119-lb) swede at the UK National Giant Vegetable Championship held during the Malvern Autumn Show.

LEEK
Paul Rochester (UK) presented a 10.6-kg (23-lb 6-oz) leek at the Malvern Autumn Show on 26 Sep 2015. Paul says that the secret to his success is playing music to his vegetables, a tip his father Wilfred gave him.

CAULIFLOWER
Big-veg specialist Peter Glazebrook (UK) grew a cauliflower that weighed 27.48 kg (60 lb 9.3 oz) on 21 Apr 2014. He is seen here with his wife, Mary.

Oldest university
The University of Karueein is founded in Fez, Morocco, and remains a seat of learning to this day. Its specialist subjects are Islamic studies and Arabic linguistics.

859 CE

DATELINE

CHOCOLATE

Most expensive chocolate bar sold at auction

When British explorer Robert Falcon Scott embarked on the *Discovery* expedition to Antarctica in 1901, many supplies were donated by a range of everyday brands keen to be associated with the adventure. Products included Colman's English mustard, Bird's custard and some 3,500 lb (1,590 kg) of Cadbury's chocolate and cocoa. One of the 10-cm-long (4-in) chocolate bars, still unwrapped and stored in a cigarette tin, sold for £470 ($687) to an anonymous buyer at Christie's auction house in London, UK, on 25 Sep 2001.

Oldest chocolate

In 2007, anthropologist John Henderson (USA) found traces of cacao in pottery fragments dating to 1150 BCE near Puerto Escondido in Honduras. It's thought the cacao was fermented and drank as a mildly alcoholic beverage.

Although cacao-based drinks may have emerged centuries before, the **earliest recipe for chocolate drink** dates from 1631.

Published in *Chocolate: or, an Indian Drinke*, penned by Spanish physician Antonio Colmenero, the book expounded the food's health benefits, claiming it could cure coughs and sickness, and even aid conception.

First white chocolate

White chocolate was introduced by Nestlé in 1930, and marketed in Switzerland under the name "Galak". The bar was gradually introduced in other countries under various names, including Milky Bar and Alpine White.

First Valentine's box of chocolates

Richard Cadbury (UK), the eldest son of John Cadbury, who founded the now iconic brand, was the first chocolate-maker to commercialize the association between the confectionery and romance, producing a heart-shaped box of chocolates for Valentine's Day in 1868.

TRIVIA

Chocolate is derived from the fruit ("pods") of the cocoa, or cacao, tree *Theobroma cacao*, native to the tropics of Central and South America. Cocoa beans are actually seeds from the trees' pods (below); after harvesting, the beans are fermented and dried.

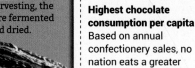

Tallest chocolate Santa Claus

Mirabello shopping centre in Cantù, Italy, commissioned a 5-m-tall (16-ft 4.8-in) cocoa-based effigy of Father Christmas in 2011. Built over three weeks by six chocolatiers from Tosca, a family-run confectioner in Cremona, Italy, the supersized, sugar-glazed Santa was hollow, yet still weighed a massive 1.7 tonnes (3,750 lb) – about the same as 20 real-life Santa Clauses!

Highest chocolate consumption per capita

Based on annual confectionery sales, no nation eats a greater amount of chocolate than Switzerland. In 2015, the average Swiss person consumed an estimated 9.3 kg (20 lb 8 oz).

Chocolate bar with the most flavour variants

To date, the standard four-finger KitKat chocolate bar has been made available in more than 120 flavours. The variations include cucumber, wasabi, watermelon and salt, and, of course, milk chocolate.

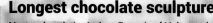

Longest chocolate sculpture

Master chocolatier Andrew Farrugia of Malta used up more than 780 hr and around 1,285 kg (2,830 lb) of Belgian chocolate sculpting what must be the most delicious train ever made. The intricately detailed *Belcolade Express*, named in honour of the Belgian chocolatier sponsor, was sculpted to celebrate Brussels Chocolate Week 2012 and stretched an incredible 34.05 m (111 ft 8 in) – longer than a fully grown blue whale.

Standing 50 cm (1 ft 7 in) high, the train featured a modern electric locomotive at one end and a classic steam loco at the other. Pictured is Farrugia (on the right) at the unveiling ceremony for the 6.5-million-calorie creation at Brussels-South station in Belgium on 19 Nov 2012.

DATELINE

 870 CE

Largest ancient castle
Construction begins on Prague Castle (in the present-day Czech Republic).
When completed, the castle covers an area of 18 acres (7.3 ha).

90 Recordology

Largest box of chocolates

On 2 Apr 2008, confectionery retailer Thorntons and prop-maker Russell Beck Studio (both UK) created a bumper box of chocolates that towered 5.04 m (16 ft 6 in) tall. Tipping the scales at 1,690 kg (3,725 lb) – the weight of a small car – it was 6,760 times heavier than a standard 250-g (8.8-oz) box of Thorntons Moments.

LARGEST CHOCOLATE...

Easter egg
In 2011, Le Acciaierie Shopping Village in Cortenuova, Italy, unveiled a chocolate egg weighing 7,200 kg (15,873 lb) and standing 10.39 m (34 ft 1 in) tall. At more than twice the height of a typical London double-decker bus, this *eggs*-treme creation is also the **tallest Easter egg**.

Truffle
A titanic truffle weighing 802 kg (1,768 lb 2 oz) – the equivalent of 11 adult men – was made by Mirco Della Vecchia, Andrea Andrighetti, Rimini Fiera, Fabbri 1905, Icam and Martellato (all ITA) in Rimini, Italy, on 21 Jan 2012. The 1-m-wide (3-ft 3-in) truffle was concocted from dark chocolate, cream and Amarena cherries.

Rabbit
Some 6,000 chocolate bars were axed and chiselled into shape to produce a behemoth bunny at the annual Chocofest event, held in Gramado, Brazil. Training agency Senac-RS (BRA) unveiled the final 3,850-kg (8,488-lb) sculpture on 12 Apr 2014. The rabbit was posed with a chocolate football in honour of the 2014 FIFA World Cup, which was hosted by Brazil.

Bell
Bonbons Verdier of Serres-Castet in France crafted a gold-coated chocolate bell weighing 293 kg (645 lb 15 oz) on 16 Jun 2011. The 1.51-m (4-ft 11.4-in) bell had to be moved into the shade to prevent it melting in the intense summer heat; electric fans were also deployed to keep the record-breaking choc cool.

Sculpture
Aficion Chocolate (CHN) crafted a building 4.08 m (13 ft 4.6 in) long on 30 Sep 2015. Weighing 10,187 kg (22,458 lb 7 oz), this edible edifice outdid the previous record by 1,900 kg (4,188 lb).

Crafted by Andrew Farrugia (see choc train opposite), the **tallest chocolate sculpture** recreated the Burj Khalifa at Dubai Airport, UAE, on 27 Nov 2014. At 13.5 m (44 ft 4.2 in) high, it was 61 times smaller than the real **tallest building**.

Meanwhile, the Namba Walk mall in Osaka, Japan, made the **largest chocolate-candy sculpture** in 2012: a 267.4-kg (589-lb 8-oz) sugar-coated heart.

FAST FACTS
The **oldest person ever**, Jeanne Louise Calment (FRA), who lived to 122, partly put down her long life to eating chocolate • White chocolate is not technically chocolate as it has no cocoa solids

TOP OF THE CHOCS
Chocolate is seriously big business. Here we take a look at the biggest-selling chocolate confectionery brands...

	Brand	Maker	Revenue (2014)
1	Cadbury	Mondelēz International Inc (USA)	$6,238,900,000
2	Kinder	Ferrero Group (LUX/ITA)	$4,602,100,000
3	Hershey's	The Hershey Company (USA)	$3,214,400,000
4	M&M's	Mars Inc (USA)	$3,207,100,000
5	Snickers	Mars Inc (USA)	$2,980,100,000
6	Milka	Mondelēz International Inc (USA)	$2,631,900,000
7	KitKat	Nestlé SA (CHE)	$2,606,400,000
8	Galaxy/Dove	Mars Inc (USA)	$2,573,300,000
9	Ferrero Rocher	Ferrero Group (LUX/ITA)	$2,210,800,000
10	Reese's	The Hershey Company (USA)	$2,161,000,000

Source: Euromonitor International, estimated figures

LARGEST CHOCOLATE COIN
Tipping the scales at 658 kg (1,450 lb 10 oz), this colossal chocolate 1-Euro coin was presented at the Cioccoshow fair in an event organized by the BF Servizi SRL (ITA) in Bologna, Italy, on 15 Nov 2012 to mark Guinness World Records Day. The coin had a diameter of 1.96 m (6 ft 5.17 in) – more than the height of the average male adult – and was 17 cm (6.69 in) thick. The outsized confectionery took 22 hr to prepare, after which sculptors Stefano and Tommaso Comelli (both ITA) spent a further 12 hr carving it into shape.

Oldest parliament
A great assembly (the *Althing*) is held in Iceland, gathering men from all the island's clans to decide on matters of law. The Althing, Iceland's parliament, still meets today.

930 CE

DATELINE

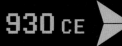

COLLECTIONS

Largest collection of sunglasses

In 1999, "Auntie" Betty Webster (USA) began wearing and collecting novelty sunglasses while working as a restaurant hostess in Kamuela, Hawaii, USA. Her running total of 1,506 individual designs was verified there on 2 Oct 2015. Known throughout the islands as the "Hostess with the Mostess", Betty colour-coordinates her sunglasses with her outfits and is always on the lookout for new designs, while fans and followers regularly contribute to her collection.

Autographed golf balls
As of 1 Mar 2015, Joe Galiardi (USA) had 204 golf balls, all signed by different professional golf players.

Comic books
On 6 Aug 2015, Bob Bretall (USA) updated his record for the third time, with 101,822 publications. He began buying comics as a child and adds (and reads) around 100 titles a month.

Corkscrews
Ion Chirescu (ROM) had acquired 23,965 pieces over 10 years, up to 18 Jun 2015. In Aug 2015, he opened a museum in Bucharest, Romania, to house them.

***The Dark Eye* memorabilia**
Alexander Grimme (DEU), a devotee of the role-playing game, had assembled 2,848 print items, artworks, videogames, miniatures and more by 11 Apr 2015.

***Doctor Who* memorabilia**
Beginning in 1974 with a yellow "Bump and Go" Marx Dalek received for Christmas, Ian O'Brien (UK) has 2,021 *Doctor Who* items, as verified on 25 Jul 2015.

Dragon-related items
Born in the year of the dragon, Huang Xiaojing (CHN) had spent 40 years gathering 3,201 different dragon-related objects, as of 18 Apr 2015.

Jade
Lam Chung Foon (HKG) had collected 7,176 exquisite pieces of jade art and jewellery by 20 Jun 2015. He also has the **largest collection of candles**: 6,360, verified on 23 Dec 2011.

***Lupin the Third* memorabilia**
Books, magazines, figurines, collectable cards, keychains, guitar tabs and toys comprise the 2,281 items related to the Japanese animation character, gathered by Dario Calabria (ITA) up to 12 Apr 2015.

DID YOU KNOW?
Coprolites are highly valued by palaeontologists for what they contain: materials such as bone and plant matter and pollen. These indicate the plants and animals that coexisted with the creature that deposited the dung, and reveal much about extinct ecosystems.

LARGEST COLLECTION OF COPROLITES

George Frandsen (USA) owns 1,277 coprolites, or fossilized faeces, as documented at the South Florida Museum in Bradenton, Florida, USA, on 1 Aug 2015. His prehistoric poo comes from 15 states in the USA and eight countries worldwide. George began finding the fossils on camping trips to Utah as a youngster. A prize piece is "Precious" (below right), his largest true-to-form coprolite, weighing in at 1.92 kg (4 lb 3.5 oz). It was found in South Carolina and dates from the Miocene epoch, 23.8–5.3 million years ago. It is naturally glossy, feels and smells like rock, and was produced by a huge crocodilian species around 6 m (20 ft) long. "Coprolite" comes from the Greek for "dung stone".

DATELINE

960 CE

First paper money
Chinese merchants of the Song Dynasty (960–1279) begin to use banknotes as currency. Secret cyphers are included within the design to try to prevent counterfeits.

FAST FACTS

Collectors have "proper" names based on their speciality, such as archtophilists (teddy bears), deltiologists (postcards), pannapictagraphists (comic books), planganologists (dolls) and sucrologists (sugar packets).

DID YOU KNOW?

In 2011–14, actress Debbie Reynolds's collection of 3,500 film costumes was auctioned in the USA. She had spent decades gathering iconic pieces, and paid $200 (£80) for "that" dress worn by Marilyn Monroe in *The Seven Year Itch* (USA, 1955). The dress sold for $4.6 m (£2.85 m).

Swamp Thing memorabilia

The DC Comics character has loomed large in the life of John Boylan (USA), as testified by his collection of 797 items – among them 501 comics – on 21 Mar 2015. John's favourites include a *Swamp Thing* TV crew-member jacket and original comic-book art.

Rackets

On 1 Jul 2015, Igor Kucej (SVK) unveiled his display of 1,260 historic wooden tennis rackets, all made between 1890 and 1985.

Skylanders memorabilia

The 4,100 *Skylanders* items collected by Christopher Desaliza (USA), as of 27 Jan 2015, include all versions of all the figures, plus cards, covers, lanyards and posters.

Tea glass holders

The containers for tea glasses are often collected as works of art in their own right. As of 11 Apr 2015, Sergey Kruglov (RUS) had amassed 1,921 holders, each distinctively crafted in metal or enamel.

Videogames

Joel Hopkins (AUS) had 17,466 games to his name as of 12 Jan 2016.

ANIMAL COLLECTIONS

It may begin with a gift, an ornament or a plush toy, or simply with a fondness for a certain kind of animal. But soon a collector will be the custodian of an entire menagerie...

	Theme	Number	Collector	Date verified
1	Mouse and rat	47,398	Christa Behmenburg (DEU)	13 Oct 2014
	Rabbit	28,423	Steve Lubanski and Candace Frazee (USA)	25 Mar 2011
	Cat	21,321	Carmen de Aldana (GTM)	14 Mar 2011
	Owl	18,055	Dianne Turner (USA)	20 Dec 2005
	Pig	16,779	Anne Langton (UK)	13 Jul 2011
2	Cow	15,144	Ruth Klossner (USA)	9 Jun 2015
	Penguin	11,062	Birgit Berends (DEU)	14 Mar 2011
	Frog	10,502	Sheila Crown (UK)	12 May 2002
	Crocodile	6,739	Andrew Gray (UK)	2 Sep 2015
	Chicken	6,505	Cecil and Joann Dixon (USA)	28 Jun 2006
	Elephant	5,779	Janet Mallernee-Briley (USA)	8 Apr 2008
	Monkey	5,680	Wang Lingxian (CHN)	1 Mar 2005
	Horse	2,762	Edgar Rugeles (COL)	26 Aug 2013
	Giraffe	2,443	Susa Forster (DEU)	5 Aug 2005
3	Sheep	1,365	Tyesha Elam (USA)	13 Nov 2015

Largest collection of hamburger-related items

As of 20 Sep 2014, "Hamburger Harry", aka Harry Sperl (DEU), had amassed 3,724 items on a burger theme, verified in Daytona Beach, Florida, USA. Harry owns the burger mobile from the movie *Good Burger* (USA, 1997), along with two burger beds and one burger waterbed. His prize possession is a hamburger Harley-Davidson motorcycle, aka *Hamburger Harley*, a 1987 HD Sportster built in 1993. He also has hamburger toys, books, CDs, statues, posters, bags, games and clothing.

Brightest supernova
Exploding star SN 1006 exceeds the luminosity of Sirius – today's **brightest star seen from Earth** – by up to 1,500 times. It remains visible for two years.

1006 ▶ DATELINE

guinnessworldrecords.com **93**

MASS PARTICIPATION

Largest pantomime animal race

An eclectic mix of 63 two-person pantomime animals, including horses, camels and Rudolph the Reindeers, stepped up to the starting line at Newcastle Racecourse, UK, on 31 Aug 2015. The wacky racers were raising funds for local charity St Oswald's Hospice as part of an event that was organized by The Great North Gallop (UK).

MOST PEOPLE...

Caber tossing
On 8 Aug 2015, a group of 69 people simultaneously launched a volley of near-6-m (20-ft) wooden poles known as "cabers" into the air. The mass feat of strength took place at the 70th Fergus Scottish Festival and Highland Games, an annual event in Ontario, Canada.

In a zorbing relay
Each running inside a big plastic zorb ball, 237 people completed a 50-m (164-ft) leg of a course within the required 10 sec on 25 Apr 2015. That means a total

of 11.85 km (7.3 mi) was covered in the attempt, put on by Hong Kong-based company GP22 (CHN).

Wearing hair in a beehive
With brushes, hairspray and almost 50 stylists at hand, Discovery Italia gave 261 women beehive hairdos in Milan, Italy, on 19 Mar 2015. The distinctive bouffant hairstyle is believed to have originated in 1960, when Chicago-based salon owner Margaret Vinci Heldt (USA) was challenged to conceive an original coiffure to see in the new decade.

A more dramatic change of hairstyle was chosen by Pedal for Hope (CAN), to raise money for the Canadian Cancer Society. On 16 May 2015, a total of 267 people gathered at Peterborough Airport, Ontario, to say goodbye to their locks and set a new record for the **most heads shaved simultaneously**.

Making "sand angels"
Freshwater West beach in Pembrokeshire, UK, was imprinted with 352 "sand angels" – the seaside take

on "snow angels" – on 6 Jun 2015. Keep Wales Tidy arranged the event to promote the nation's pristine coast, plus its 41 Blue Flag beaches.

Twerking simultaneously
American hip-hop star Big Freedia, aka Frederick Ross,

was just one of 406 people to twerk their way into the record books on 15 Nov 2014. The event took part at the eighth Annual Central City Festival held in New Orleans, Louisiana, USA.

Eating breakfast in bed
Talk about dedication to customer service... The Sheraton Langfang Chaobai River Hotel served up its "Color Your Plate" breakfast – which includes pastries, fruit, orange juice and yoghurt – to 418 guests on 16 Aug 2015. It was an al-fresco affair, with 225 beds laid out on the hotel's lawn in Beijing, China.

Dressed as Catrinas and Catrines
At a fiesta staged in Cuauhtémoc, Mexico, on 1 Nov 2014, La Catrina Fest MX (MEX) assembled

Most bodies painted

The Polish telecoms company PLAY gathered 497 party-goers at the Woodstock Festival in Kostrzyn nad Odrą, Poland – one of Europe's largest music events – and smothered them in paint on 31 Jul 2015. This bettered PLAY's own en-masse body-painting record, achieved at wwthe same event in 2014, by 99 people.

Most people riding a surfboard

Surf's up! If you've ever tried surfing, you'll know how difficult it is... So imagine trying to get 66 people riding a surfboard at the same time. That's exactly what Visit Huntington Beach and the Epic Big Board Ride (both USA) achieved at Huntington Beach, a surfing hotspot in California, USA, on 20 Jun 2015. At 12.83 m (42 ft 1.5 in) long and 3.37 m (11 ft 1 in) wide, the Big Board upon which they rode was also confirmed as the world's **largest surfboard**. Not a bad way to celebrate International Surfing Day.

DID YOU KNOW?
Making the big board required a group effort. It was designed with CAD software by Australian board-maker Nev Hyman. The parts were then manufactured by mouldCAM in Rhode Island, USA, while assembly was handled by boat-builders Westerly Marine in California, USA.

Oldest working brewery
The monks of Weihenstephan Abbey in Bavaria (now part of Germany) are given permission to open a brewery near Freising. It will still be operating 976 years later, although no longer staffed by monks.

509 people decked out in traditional skeleton costumes. The event was held to celebrate Mexico's annual Day of the Dead festival, at which deceased loved ones are remembered.

Riding unicycles
Balance and co-ordination – not to mention a total of 1,682 unicycles – were all required to secure this record on 1 Nov 2014. Staged by Taoyuan County Government (Chinese Taipei), the 500-m (1,640-ft)

race event was celebrating the region's newly acquired Special Municipality status.

Stargazing
As part of a nationwide science week in Australia, 1,869 astronomy lovers, wielding telescopes and binoculars, were brought together by Mt Stromlo Observatory, the Australian National University and the Canberra Astronomical Society on 21 Aug 2015 to study the night sky. This gathering in Australia's capital city was just one of 37 around the country that

evening, which attracted a combined 7,960 visitors – the **most people stargazing in multiple locations**. The event was threatened by cold weather and cloudy skies, but the passion for stars, and records, paid off.

Twirling batons
On 21 Sep 2015, a gathering of 2,002 members of the Osaka Baton Twirling Association (JPN) performed at the Japanese city's central gymnasium. The dizzying display was the centrepiece of the 25th Osaka Baton Twirling Competition.

Popping bubble wrap
In all, 2,681 boy scouts assembled at Denver Area Council's Camporee on 19 Sep 2015 to pop bubble wrap together. They easily wrapped up the record, more than doubling the previous best of 1,011 people, set in Jan 2015. The feat took place at the Peaceful Valley Scout Ranch in Elbert, Colorado, USA.

Modelling on a catwalk
On 4 Jul 2015, eRetailer Very.co.uk and Culture Liverpool (both UK) joined forces to organize a unique fashion show. Comprising both professional models and runway wannabes, a total of 3,651 people strutted their stuff down Liverpool's Pier Head riverside promenade to set this record in style.

LARGEST LESSONS
Extraordinary examples of en-masse education...

Subject	Organizer	People	Date
Art	Lions Club Int'l District 323G1 (IND)	14,135	11 Nov 2014
Zumba	City of Mandaluyong (PHL)	12,975	19 Jul 2015
Cookery	One Plus One Natural Flour (CHN)	6,334	20 Dec 2015
Maths	Mattecentrum and En Bra Start (both SWE)	3,611	18 Nov 2015
Magic	Israel Cagliostro Oxman (ISR)	1,476	1 Jun 2015
Chemistry	Technopolis (BEL)	1,018	5 May 2015
Soccer	Knocklyon Utd Football Club (IRL)	686	23 May 2014
Hockey	Cundall Manor School (UK)	509	21 Mar 2015
Welding	Three Fires Council and Boy Scouts of America (both USA)	275	11 Apr 2015
Segway	Sony Pictures Entertainment (USA)	108	11 Apr 2015

LARGEST YOGA LESSON
A staggering 35,985 people adopted a cross-legged "lotus" position in honour of the inaugural International Day of Yoga on 21 Jun 2015. Organized by the Government of India's Ministry of AYUSH (Ayurveda, Yoga and Naturopathy, Unani, Siddha and Homeopathy), dedicated to natural wellbeing pursuits, the event took place on a 1.4-km (0.8-mi) stretch of the Rajpath in the heart of New Delhi. As well as soldiers, civil servants and students (see Fast Facts), even India's Prime Minister, Narendra Modi (left), demonstrated his flexibility.

First use of rockets
Chinese scholar and military engineer Zeng Gongliang describes the use of "fire arrows" – simple gunpowder rockets launched from crossbows – by the armies of Song Dynasty China.

1042

DATELINE

COSPLAY

LARGEST GATHERING OF PEOPLE DRESSED AS...

Comic-book characters
Conventions for comics fans are where cosplayers go to see and be seen, with large events attracting huge numbers of costumed attendees. An impressive 1,784 dressed-up comic-book heroes and villains gathered at the Salt Lake Comic Con in Salt Lake City, Utah, USA, on 25 Sep 2015.

Daleks
Many cosplayers put hundreds of hours of work into their creations, and when they're copying something from a movie or TV show, the end result can be hard to distinguish from the original. This made it all the more terrifying when a force of 95 Daleks, Doctor Who's seemingly indestructible enemy, rolled on to the grounds of the National Space Centre in Leicester, UK, on 29 Nov 2008, waving their eyestalks and barking "Exterminate!" at anything that moved.

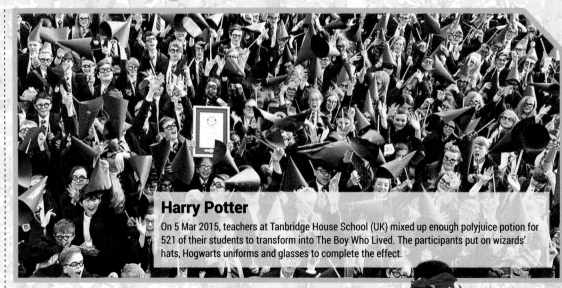

Harry Potter
On 5 Mar 2015, teachers at Tanbridge House School (UK) mixed up enough polyjuice potion for 521 of their students to transform into The Boy Who Lived. The participants put on wizards' hats, Hogwarts uniforms and glasses to complete the effect.

***Dragon Ball* characters**
Although cosplay has its origins in American sci-fi fandom, it grew into the cultural phenomenon it is today as part of the Japanese anime and manga scene. The manga *Dragon Ball* and its anime offshoot *Dragon Ball Z* are particularly popular with cosplayers. On 1 Nov 2012, the Saló del Manga comic festival in Barcelona, Spain, hosted 307 *Dragon Ball* characters as part of an event staged by Editorial Planeta (ESP).

Robin Hood
The UK's Camping and Caravanning Club hit the target on 27 Aug 2011, when 1,215 people dressed up as the legendary archer. The attempt took place at the Newark Showground in Nottinghamshire, UK, during the annual National Feast of Lanterns camping rally.

Rosie the Riveter
We can do it! Inspired by the rallying cry of America's iconic female war worker, 1,084 boiler-suited women and girls gathered at the World War II Home Front National Historical Park in California, USA, on 15 Aug 2015.

***Star Trek* characters**
As part of Destination *Star Trek* in London, UK, convention organizers Media 10 Limited (UK) gathered 1,063 *Star Trek* cosplayers for an event on 20 Oct 2012. Most participants wore starfleet uniforms, but the crowd also included Klingons, Borg and a variety of alien monsters from the original series.

Superheroes
On 2 Oct 2010, exactly 1,580 caped crusaders, web-slingers and

Spider-Man
On 28 Jul 2015, a charity event organized by recruitment firm Charterhouse drew 438 spider folk to the streets of Sydney, Australia. Donations raised by the masked web-slingers went to support health charity Life Education. The organizers settled on the classic red, blue and black costume of *The Amazing Spider-Man*, the favourite of Spider-Man purists, shunning the myriad other costumes that Spidey has worn in his various reboots and cameo appearances.

> **DID YOU KNOW?**
> Although what we would call cosplay has been around since the 1930s, the term "cosplay" itself is relatively new. It was coined by film-maker Nobuyuki Takahashi (JPN) at the 1984 World Science Fiction Convention in Los Angeles, California, USA.

DATELINE 1187 — Largest monolithic church
Work begins on the church of Medhane Alem in Lalibela, Ethiopia. Rather than building up, the builders dig down, carving the church out of a uniform piece of bedrock. It measures some 10 m (32 ft) high from the bottom of the pit in which it sits.

FAST FACTS
Cosplay is a portmanteau of "costume" and "play" • The World
Cosplay Summit attracted teams from 26 different countries in 2015
• Competitive cosplayers have to create their own costumes

Santa Claus

An astonishing 18,112 Santas came together at the Nagar Sakthan Thampuran Ground, Kerala, India, on 27 Dec 2014. They were taking part in an event organized by Thrissur Citizenry and Thrissur Archdiocese (both IND) to raise money for local charities.

The Hulk

On 13 Jul 2012, an incredible 574 visitors and local inhabitants turned up dressed as the Hulk on the streets of Castleblayney in Ireland, at the annual Muckno Mania Festival.

other costumed heroes assembled at Paramount Studios in Los Angeles, USA, in an event to promote the film *Megamind*.

Videogame characters
People have been enjoying game cosplay for almost as long as games have had characters to dress up as. The Särkänniemi theme park in Tampere, Finland, mustered 491 gaming cosplayers on 7 Sep 2013. The park is no stranger to gaming, having opened up an Angry Birds Land attraction in 2012.

Zombies
A 15,458-strong horde of the shambling undead groaned and lurched its way through the streets of Minneapolis in Minnesota, USA, on 11 Oct 2014, as part of the annual Zombie Pub Crawl.

PETER PAN

As part of a charity event organized on 29 Aug 2014 by recruitment firm Goodman Masson, 280 people donned the green tunic and tights of The Boy Who Wouldn't Grow Up in London, UK. The event was staged to raise money and publicity for Great Ormond Street Hospital for Children, a much-loved institution and the favourite philanthropic cause of J M Barrie, the author of *Peter Pan*. The Pan-tastic gathering took place on the steps of St Paul's Cathedral.

Largest New World civilization
The Inca Empire reaches its greatest extent, stretching along the Pacific coast of South America from what is now southern Colombia to central Chile. Its population is estimated to be around 10 million.

1200

DATELINE

BIG STUFF

Largest wheelbarrow

At 11.28 m (37 ft) long and with a wheel diameter of 2.81 m (9 ft 2.6 in), this super-sized wheelbarrow took a team of 10 people more than 300 hr to plan and build. It was constructed by Heimatverein Boke e.V. (DEU) and it was presented and measured in Boke, Germany, on 14 May 2015.

DID YOU KNOW?
The body of this record-breaking instrument is constructed of birch plywood, and the neck and head are of pine, as are all four tuning pegs. The ukulele has the correct fret spacing required to produce notes separated by a semitone, as is the case on a normal-sized uke.

LARGEST...

Bean bag
Yogibo (USA) presented a 211-ft-wide (64.3-m) bean bag with a volume of 1,406.23 cu ft (39.82 m³) at Nashua, New Hampshire, USA, on 15 Sep 2015.

Cheese slicer
Kristen Gunstad (NOR) unveiled a 7.79-m-long (25-ft 6.6-in) slicer at the ski resort in Kvitfjell, Norway, on 7 Mar 2015.

Colouring book
You'd need a lot of felt tips for the 10-m² (107.63-sq-ft) colouring book produced by the Zielona Sowa Publishing House (POL). Its size was confirmed at the National Stadium in Warsaw, Poland, on 24 May 2014.

Horseshoe
Kentucky Derby Museum (USA) has made a horseshoe 2.06 m (6 ft 9.1 in) wide and 2.13 m (6 ft 11.8 in) tall. It was measured at Eagle Sign & Design in Louisville, Kentucky, USA, on 9 Sep 2015.

Lunch box
A 2.6-m-wide (8-ft 6-in) lunch box with a capacity of 8.47 m³ (299.11 cu ft) was produced by Altus Viljoen and Wilgenhof Men's Residence (both ZAF). It was measured in Stellenbosch, South Africa, on 12 Apr 2015.

Magazine (single edition)
The River Group and Polestar (both UK) produced a version of the Aug 2015 issue of *Healthy* magazine that measured 2.35 m (7 ft 8.52 in) wide by 3.05 m (10 ft 0.28 in) tall. Its size was ratified in Sheffield, UK, on 30 Jun 2015.

Largest folding chair
Retailer Intermarché and manufacturer Neyrat Peyronie (both FRA) collaborated to produce a collapsible chair 4.77 m (15 ft 7.8 in) tall. The high seat was presented and measured in Bondoufle, France, on 27 May 2015.

Largest ukulele
Lawrence Stump (USA, below) has created a tunable and playable ukulele 3.99 m (13 ft 1 in) long, as verified in Lansing, Michigan, USA, on 11 Dec 2015. The instrument was built using the same methods and materials as a standard-size soprano ukulele – although it is 7.5 times larger.

DATELINE 1250

First gun
Anecdotal evidence suggests that firearms are in use in China and northern Africa, although the first documentary evidence for gun construction will not emerge until the following century.

FAST FACTS
You could accommodate more than 25,500 conventionally sized sandwiches in the **largest lunch box** (see p.98) • The **largest TV remote control** (below) is around 24 times larger than its real-life counterpart and took 68 days to build

Largest TV remote control
Brothers Suraj and Rajesh Kumar Meher (both IND) created this 4.5-m-long (14-ft 9.1-in) television remote control, which was measured in Sambalpur, India, on 21 Sep 2015. It is fully operational and was shown to work on a normal-sized TV.

Largest ice-cream scoop
Dimitri Panciera (ITA) served up a gigantic ice-cream scoop in Forno di Zoldo, Italy, on 20 Sep 2015. It measured 1.95 m (6 ft 4.7 in) long and 58 cm (1 ft 10.8 in) wide, with a depth of 17 cm (6.6 in). The super-sized scoop has a working mechanism to eject the ice-cream.

Mortar and pestle
Measured in Macael, Spain, on 28 Mar 2015, the largest mortar is 3.29 m (10 ft 9.5 in) high and has a diameter of 3.07 m (10 ft 0.8 in) at its mouth. Its pestle is 4.73 m (15 ft 6.2 in) long and 0.85 m (2 ft 9.4 in) at its broadest point. The über-utensil was created by Ayuntamiento de Macael (ESP).

Piggy bank
Even the keenest savers would struggle to fill the 8.03-m-long (26-ft 4.1-in), 5.58-m-tall (18-ft 3.7-in) piggy bank created by Kreissparkasse Ludwigsburg (DEU). It was measured in Ludwigsburg, Germany, on 18 May 2015.

Poster
Fareed Lafta (IRQ) has created a 7,164.78-m² (77,121.05-sq-ft) poster, as verified in Karbala, Iraq, on 26 Feb 2016. The poster, which depicted a map of Iraq, was 99.58 m (326 ft 8 in) long and 71.95 m (236 ft) wide. It was put on display at Karbala Stadium.

Umbrella
Jiangxi Kuntak Industrial Co Ltd (CHN) have made an umbrella 22.9 m (75 ft 1.5 in) in diameter. It was unveiled at Xingzi in Jiangxi Province, China, on 3 Aug 2015.

LONGEST MONSTER TRUCK
Brad and Jen Campbell (both USA) of Big Toyz Racing have created the *Sin City Hustler*, a 32-ft-long (9.7-m) monster truck. Measured in an aircraft hangar at Last Stop in White Hills, Arizona, USA, on 10 Jul 2014, it stands 12 ft (3.6 m) tall, weighs a hefty 15,000 lb (6,800 kg) – about the same as a bull elephant – and can accommodate 12 passengers. It packs a powerful 750-hp engine, but owing to its considerable weight the *Sin City Hustler* only has a maximum speed of around 45 mph (72.4 km/h). The titanic truck is currently operated by Russ Mann (USA).

First forensic autopsy
As part of an investigation into the suspected murder of a nobleman, Italian physician Bartolomeo da Varignana performs the first medico-legal autopsy. He will later be involved in other legally required autopsies.

1302 DATELINE

SMALLTOWN BIG STUFF

GALLERY

The big country that is the USA showcases many big ideas – and sometimes in small places. In particular, the town of Casey in Illinois is dotted with some of the world's largest items, all from the workshop Big Things in a Small Town, set up by Jim Bolin. Besides those pictured, Jim has spearheaded the **largest knitting needles** (13 ft long, or 3.98 m), the **largest crochet hook** (6 ft 1.5 in long, or 1.86 m) and the **largest wind chime** (42 ft long, or 12.8 m). Meanwhile, Ohio is home to the **largest yo-yo**, and Michigan to the **largest chainsaw** and **tallest tyre sculpture** (all pictured).

LARGEST PITCHFORK **1**

On 20 Oct 2015, Jim Bolin established a new record in Casey for his pitchfork, which measured 8 ft 4 in (2.56 m) wide and 61 ft 2 in (18.64 m) long. That's more than 12 times longer than a conventional pitchfork, or about the same as the length of a bowling alley. It is now on display outside Richards Farm Restaurant. Bolin designed the enormous farming tool to fit with the restaurant's rustic decor and symbolize Casey's agricultural community. It weighs 1,940 lb (880 kg).

LARGEST CLOGS **2**

Traditional wooden shoes originated in the Netherlands, but the largest pair resides in Jim's home town. On 20 Oct 2015, he presented clogs measuring 11 ft 5 in (3.5 m) long, 5 ft 10 in (1.77 m) wide and 4 ft 10 in (1.48 m) tall, outstripping the previous (Dutch) record by more than a *foot* all round. The shoes, made of 61 layers of pine, weigh about 1,500 lb (680 kg) each. Jim and two team-mates carved them by chainsaw then sanded and lacquered them to a glossy finish.

LARGEST GOLF TEE **3**

On 29 Jan 2013, Jim unveiled his gargantuan golf tee, based on the normal-sized version used at Casey Country Club. It stands 30 ft 9 in (9.37 m) tall, with a head diameter of 6 ft 3 in (1.91 m) and a shaft width of 2 ft 1 in (64 cm). Jim and his staff at Bolin Enterprises, Inc. made the tee from yellow pine boards glued together into a large block, and shaped it with chainsaws. (Some of his team took chainsaw lessons beforehand!) The tee is permanently set up at the Country Club.

LARGEST ROCKING CHAIR **4**

A wood-and-steel rocking chair, 56 ft 1 in (17.09 m) tall and 32 ft 9 in (9.99 m) wide, brought Jim Bolin, his team and his town another record on 20 Oct 2015. Each piece was weighed as the chair was constructed, giving a total weight of 46,200 lb (20,955 kg). A "dove of hope" is carved on the wooden head rest. The big rocker is one more episode in the USA's history of giant chairs, which began modestly with a 12-ft (3.6-m) Mission chair built by the citizens of Gardner, Massachusetts, in 1905.

DATELINE

1311

Tallest building
At 160 m (524 ft 11 in), the UK's Lincoln Cathedral overtakes the Great Pyramid of Giza to become the world's tallest building. Construction on the cathedral began in 1088. It will retain the record until 1549, when its spire collapses.

LARGEST MAILBOX (VOLUME) **5**

On 20 Oct 2015, Jim and his team debuted yet another Casey landmark – a giant version of a standard US mailbox. It has an internal volume of 5,743.41 cu ft (162.63 m³) and has a stairway inside the post stand so that visitors can climb up to the box. It's designed to accept mail (which, when deposited, raises a red flag), and Jim intends to use the interior space to set up a museum of mail history. The box is located in Casey's downtown business district.

LARGEST YO-YO **6**

On 15 Sep 2012 in Cincinnati, Ohio, Beth Johnson (USA) demonstrated a wooden yo-yo named *Whoa-yo* that she had spent three years constructing. Measuring 11 ft 10 in (3.62 m) in diameter and weighing 2.3 US tons (2.09 tonnes), the giant disc plunged 120 ft (36.5 m) on a rope attached to a 75-US-ton (68-tonne) crane before rebounding. The mighty *Whoa-yo* had crashed on three trial runs, but Beth's perseverance and skilful repair work finally paid off.

TALLEST SCULPTURE IN THE SHAPE OF A TYRE **7**

One of Michigan's most celebrated landmarks is an 80-ft (24.4-m) sculpture of a Uniroyal Giant tyre in Allen Park, off Interstate 94. The eight-storey roadside icon was built as a Ferris wheel for 1965's New York World's Fair, when 2 million visitors rode the 24 gondolas. The 12-US-ton (10.8-tonne) tyre has a fibre-glass surface with 6-in-deep (15-cm) treads, and equates to 960 actual Uniroyal tyres – ideal if you had a 200-ft-tall (61-m) vehicle!

LARGEST CHAINSAW **8**

In 1996, a working chainsaw measuring 22 ft 11 in (6.98 m) long and 6 ft (1.83 m) high was built by Jim "Hoolie" DeClaire of Moran Iron Works, Inc., in Onaway, Michigan. Affectionately named *Big Gus*, the super-size saw has since been on display at Da Yoopers Tourist Trap at Ishpeming in Michigan. It weighs almost 4 US tons (3.6 tonnes) and is powered by a V8 engine, although for safety reasons – it's located by a highway – *Big Gus* is rarely fired up to full capacity.

Worst pandemic
A devastating outbreak of the pneumonic form of plague (bacterial infection), known as the Black Death, draws to a close having claimed some 75 million lives worldwide.

1351 DATELINE

BALL SKILLS

Longest tennis volley rally

Angelo A Rossetti and Ettore Rossetti (both USA) exchanged 30,576 volleys of a tennis ball (without the ball hitting the ground) at the Weston Racquet Club in Weston, Connecticut, USA, on 8 Aug 2015. The two brothers once achieved the **longest tennis rally**, although the current record (50,970 strokes), set on 20 Jul 2013 in Bayreuth, Germany, is held by Frank and Dennis Fuhrmann (both DEU).

Most consecutive soccer ball headers while treading water

Jhoen Lefont Rodriguez (CUB) executed 1,503 consecutive soccer ball touches with the head – while afloat. He achieved the record in the swimming pool of the Hotel Nacional de Cuba in Havana, Cuba, on 10 Aug 2013.

Longest duration to spin a basketball on the toe
On 12 Mar 2015, in Wilbur-by-the-Sea, Florida, USA, Bernie Boehm (USA) spun a basketball for 25.52 sec.

Bernie can surf, too. On 31 Aug 2013, this sporty multi-tasker achieved the **longest duration to spin a basketball while surfing** – 33.25 sec – on the set of *Officially Amazing* at Ponce Inlet in Daytona Beach, Florida, USA.

One ball too easy for you? The **longest duration to spin two basketballs on one finger (maintaining spin)** is 4 min 31 sec. Chen Weiwei (CHN) achieved this revolutionary performance, spinning both balls, one on top of the other, on the set of *Lo Show dei Record* in Milan, Italy, on 7 Jul 2014.

Most hits of a golf ball on a club in 30 seconds
Soccer player Aaron Ramsey (UK) racked up 61 hits of a golf ball on a golf club in 30 sec on the set of *A League of Their Own* (UK) in London, UK, on 9 Jul 2015.

On the same TV show, former Premier League star Jamie Redknapp (UK) recorded the **greatest height to control a soccer ball**. He brought under control a ball that he had kicked to a height of 18.6 m (61 ft).

Longest duration spinning a basketball on the nose

"Scooter" Christensen of the Harlem Globetrotters kept a basketball spinning on his nose for 7.7 sec in Phoenix, Arizona, USA, on 5 Nov 2015. This was one of seven records set by the Globetrotters in celebration of GWR Day 2015. The others include: the **longest basketball shot blindfolded** (69 ft 6 in, or 21.18 m) by "Thunder" Law; the **most slam dunks in one minute by an individual** (15) by "Zeus" McClurkin; the **farthest kneeling basketball shot made backwards** (60 ft 7.5 in, or 18.47 m) by "Handles" Franklin; and the **most basketball three-pointers made by a pair in one minute** (19) by "Ant" Atkinson and "Cheese" Chisholm (all USA).

1373 } **Oldest treaty still in force**
On 16 Jun, diplomats from England and Portugal sign the Anglo-Portuguese Treaty of Alliance, a peace deal that will endure through countless global conflicts and many changes of government. It is still in effect today.

Most soccer ball rolls around the face in one minute

Victor Rubilar (ARG) rolled a soccer ball around his face 35 times in the Turkish city of Istanbul on 2 Nov 2013. The head-turning record was made in collaboration with Maltepe Park shopping centre (TUR). Victor also shares the record for **most soccer balls juggled**: five. His total, set in 2006, was equalled by Marko Vermeer (NLD) in 2014.

Most ping-pong balls juggled with the mouth
In his performances, Tony Fercos (USA, b. CZE) is able to blow and catch seven ping-pong balls in succession with his mouth in a single cycle. Each ball is fed into his mouth, "spat" high into the air and caught back in his mouth.

Farthest distance travelled with a soccer ball balanced on the head
On 22 Oct 2011, Abdul Halim (BGD) walked 15.2 km (9.44 mi) with a soccer ball atop his head. He made 38 laps of the 400-m track at the Bangabandhu National Stadium in Dhaka, Bangladesh.

The **longest time to balance a soccer ball on the shin** is 1 min 55 sec, achieved by Sinan Öztürk (DEU) in Mittweida, Saxony, Germany, on 13 Nov 2014.

Most bowling balls held simultaneously
Chad McLean (USA) clung on to 13 regular bowling balls (as approved by the World Tenpin Bowling Association) in Brigham City, Utah, USA, on 2 Nov 2015. He held four balls on his fingers, cradled seven in his arms and clamped two between his lower legs.

Heaviest balls rotated on the back of the hand
Xie Jiajun (CHN) rotated two balls weighing 4.5 kg (9 lb 14.7 oz) – which roughly equates to the combined weight of seven NBA basketballs – on 9 Jan 2016. This bettered his previous record, set in 2015, by 0.31 kg (10.9 oz).

Most "around the world" tricks in one minute
In this trick, a performer has to tap a soccer ball in the air then circle the same foot around it. Football freestyler John Farnworth (UK, below) holds the absolute record, with 85 tricks achieved in London, UK, on 3 Oct 2008.

The **most "around the moon" tricks in one minute** is 61, by Adrian Fogel (DEU) on 14 Feb 2010 in Nordhorn, Germany. For this, the ball is placed on the back of the neck and flicked up, during which time the person's head must complete one full revolution.

Most "around the worlds" in one minute (female)

Laura Biondo (ITA/VEN) completed 57 "around the world" tricks (see left) in Edinburgh, UK, on 18 Jul 2013. On the same day, she also set the one-minute record for **most soccer ball touches with the head (female)**: 206.

LONGEST DURATION TO CONTROL A SOCCER BALL ON A SLACKLINE

Most of us find it hard enough to perform "keepie-uppies" at the best of times. But to do it in mid-air? On 14 Dec 2015, in Brentford, London, UK, John Farnworth kept a soccer ball airborne for 29.82 sec while maintaining his balance on a slackline (left).

The footie freestyler also achieved the **most full-volley rebounds in 30 seconds** – 28 – at the National Football Museum in Manchester, UK, on 25 Aug 2015; Farnworth demonstrates the trick below.

Worst outbreak of "dancing mania"
In July, a large number of men and women in Aachen, Germany, break into frenzied dancing. Many dance until they collapse from exhaustion. This medieval illness has never been fully explained.

1374

DATELINE

guinnessworldrecords.com   **103**

JOURNEYS

DID YOU KNOW?
"'There's coffee in that nebula'... ehm, I mean... in that #Dragon.'" Cristoforetti's *Star Trek*-nodding tweet refers to the *Dragon* cargo craft, seen through the window, bringing the **first espresso machine in space** (dubbed "ISSpresso") to the *ISS* in May 2015. Using a 3D-printed microgravity cup, she was able to enjoy fresh coffee in orbit!

> **Largest palace**
> Ming Emperor Zhu Di orders the construction of a new palace in Beijing, China. This vast complex of some 980 buildings, today known as the Imperial Palace, requires more than a million workers and a decade to complete

GUINNESS WORLD RECORDS

CONTENTS

Longest continuous spaceflight by a woman

On 23 Nov 2014, European Space Agency (ESA) astronaut Samantha Cristoforetti (ITA) set off from Baikonur Cosmodrome in Kazakhstan for the *International Space Station* (*ISS*). Her job was to carry out research into weightlessness, but, after her Apr 2015 return flight was delayed, she also ended up breaking the women's record for the longest continuous time in space. It wasn't until 11 Jun 2015 that she touched down again, 199 days 16 hr 43 min after she left Earth. She's seen here sporting a *Star Trek* uniform, surrounded by the seven windows of the space station's cupola.

Oldest reading glasses
A resident of medieval London throws the broken horn frames of his glasses in the trash heap. When found more than 500 years later, they are regarded as the oldest known pair of reading glasses.

1450 ▶

EVEREST

For many adventurers, the ultimate journey on Earth is to the summit of Everest – at 8,848 m (29,029 ft), the world's **highest mountain**. But beforehand comes months of planning (not to mention fund-raising). When you get there, you have to spend weeks acclimatizing to the thinner air and fluctuating temperatures. And it demands extraordinary psychological toughness, too – several climbers have commented that getting to the top is "90% mental". But when you're there, you're on the roof of the world. Here, we look at some of the challenges facing those who wish to take on this epic adventure...

DID YOU KNOW?
It's approximately a mile (1.6 km) from the summit of Mount Everest. Not far, then – but it usually takes climbers that final push. In the final push to the summit, they can usually takes climbers around 12 hr to complete that final push.

THE ENERGY YOU'LL NEED
To get to the top of Everest, climbers have to build up huge reserves of energy. In the final push to the summit, they can use up 20,000 calories. That's the equivalent calorific content of 225 bananas. Or nine Margherita pizzas. Or 46 large steaks. Or even 66 cheeseburgers (right)!

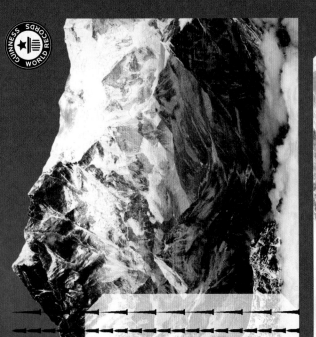

HIGHEST MOUNTAIN
The peak of Everest stands at 8,848 m (29,029 ft). That's just below the average cruising altitude of passenger jets, more than 10 times the height of the **tallest building** – the Burj Khalifa in Dubai, UAE – and some 20 times taller than New York City's Empire State Building. Located in the eastern Himalayas on the Tibet-Nepal border, it was revealed as the highest mountain in 1856 by the Survey Department of the Government of India. In 1865, the then British Surveyor General of India suggested that it be renamed after his predecessor, Colonel Sir George Everest.

LARGEST EVEREST CLEAR-UP
Since 2008, the Nepali Eco Everest Expeditions have seen annual trips to the mountain to clear away garbage from previous climbs. Some 12,000 kg (26,455 lb) of ropes, tents, food packaging, oxygen bottles, gas canisters and other discarded items have been removed. A record 6,000 kg (13,228 lb) was cleared in 2009, including 700 kg (1,543 lb) of debris from a helicopter that had crashed in 1973. This total also included 115 kg (253 lb) of frozen human waste – visualized here in the equivalent weight of house bricks.

HOW MUCH IT ALL COSTS

It can easily cost $45,000 (£29,450) to climb Everest, although for trips by Western operators the price can exceed $65,000 (£42,550). The sum varies according to how basic the trek is, whether or not you are supported, and whether you climb the north side (from Tibet) or the south side (from Nepal). Expenses include:

Travel: $500–$7,000 (£330–£4,580) to fly in to Kathmandu and on to base camp

Yaks: $150 (£98) each per day, at least $2,400 (£1,570)

Porters: $75 (£49) each per day, at least $1,350 (£880). Both are needed to carry kit to and from base camp

Sherpas: $5,000 (£3,270) each, plus their bottled supplemental oxygen, at $550 (£360) per bottle

Climbing permit (per climber): $7,000 (£4,580) from the north side; $11,000 (£7,200) from the south side

Supplies and gear: $12,000 (£7,850), including clothing, food, a Nepali cook at base camp, supplemental oxygen and a medical kit ($1,000, or £650)

Campsite maintenance: $2,000 (£1,300)

Sources: *thebmc.co.uk*; *alanarnette.com*; *grindtv.com*

CONQUERING MOUNT EVEREST

Increasing numbers of climbers attempt to scale Everest each year, but it still represents one of the ultimate challenges. Here are some of its pioneering conquerors.

DATE	RECORD
29 May 1953	First ascent: Edmund Percival Hillary (NZ) and Tenzing Norgay (IND/Tibet)
16 May 1975	First ascent (female): Junko Tabei (JPN)
8 May 1978	First ascent without supplemental oxygen: Reinhold Messner (ITA) and Peter Habeler (AUT)
20 Aug 1980	First solo summit: Reinhold Messner (ITA)
21 May 2004	Fastest ascent: Pemba Dorje Sherpa (NPL) in 8 hr 10 min (south side)
11 May 2006	Most ascents (female): six, by Lakpa Sherpa (NPL)
11 May 2011	Most ascents: 21, by Apa Sherpa, equalled by Phurba Tashi Sherpa (both NPL) on 23 May 2013
19 May 2012	Most ascents in one day: 245 climbers

GEARING UP

Pictured here is David Liaño González (MEX), the first person to climb Everest from both sides in one season. He reached the peak from Nepal on the south side on 11 May 2013 and returned to the peak on 19 May, climbing from Tibet on the north side. As David attests, choosing the right equipment is vital for increasing your chances of a successful climb. For our photoshoot, David dressed as he did on his climbs and talked us through the various bits of kit that helped him make his record-breaking summits.

Climbers take clothing that can be worn as layers, so they can adapt to weather changes and new stages of a climb. For the 8,000-ers (mountains of 8,000 m or more), a warm, all-in-one down suit is vital, with a hood to shield the face.

This lightweight, expandable backpack can accommodate clothes, a sleeping bag, provisions, water, camera and other accessories.

Most climbers take supplemental oxygen bottles and a mask for their climb. At the summit, oxygen levels are only around one-third of those at sea level. Without extra oxygen, the brain cannot focus and the body quickly tires.

For summit day, thin inner gloves are enclosed in two separate mittens; the outer one is waterproof. Mittens are better than finger gloves, as the latter make the fingers more vulnerable to the cold. Inside the inner glove are chemical hand-warming packs.

Climbing rope should be both strong and light. Some types of rope are treated to prevent them from becoming heavy in wet conditions.

This lightweight ice axe is attached to a wrist leash – a useful way of keeping the axe secure when attempting steeper sections of the climb.

Clip-on glacier crampons are essential for a sure grip on rock and ice. At the higher reaches of the mountain, climbers wear both an inner and outer boot. The high outer boot helps prevent snow and ice from getting inside.

EXPLORATION 1500–1970

JOURNEYS

Over the course of this chapter, we plot the history of record-breaking journeys. As you navigate through this chronology of exploration, you'll notice that the number of journeys per century increases greatly as we near the present day. That has much to do with our knowledge of the globe, and technical improvements in equipment, vehicles and vessels – as well as the increased enthusiasm for record-breaking. But over the centuries, much has remained the same: endurance, self-belief and sheer bravery are still essential provisions for anyone embarking on a journey of thousands of miles.

1642: *Dutch explorer Abel Tasman discovers a country he names Van Diemen's Land, later called Tasmania after him. During his voyages, he also discovers New Zealand, which Englishman Captain James Cook will reach in 1769 and map in detail. Tasman sails to Fiji and Tonga and maps the northern coast of Australia, but as he does not establish useful trade or shipping routes, his voyages are deemed a failure at home.*

▲ **1871:** British brothers John (above) and Robert Naylor complete the **first recorded walk from John O'Groats to Land's End**. They cover an average of 25 mi (40 km) per day, but make many diversions for sightseeing en route. Owing to these, they cover 1,372 mi (2,208 km) – more than double the distance of the journey as the crow flies. The book about their walk (right) is published only in 1916.

▲ **1522:** The **first circumnavigation** of the world is accomplished on 8 Sep, when the Spanish ship *Vittoria*, under the command of Juan Sebastián Elcano (ESP), reaches Seville in Spain. The ship had set out from Sanlúcar de Barrameda in Andalucía, Spain, on 20 Sep 1519, along with four others as part of an expedition led by the Portuguese explorer Ferdinand Magellan. They round Cape Horn, cross the Pacific Ocean via the Philippines and return to Europe after sailing around the Cape of Good Hope. *Vittoria* is the only ship to survive, and of the 239 Europeans who set out, only 18 return.

1577–80: Sir Francis Drake circles the globe, becoming the **first person to captain a complete circumnavigation**, and the first Englishman to do so. The journey lasts more than 1,000 days, and allows Drake to covertly raid Spanish treasure ships en route. Of the five ships that set sail, only his flagship – originally known as *Pelican* but renamed the *Golden Hind* in 1578 – makes it back.

1607–11: *English explorer Henry Hudson makes four voyages, attempting to find a trade route to Asia via the Arctic. He fails to do so, but his maps of North America contribute significantly to existing navigational knowledge.*

1620: *In Sep, the Pilgrim Fathers set sail for the New World from the English port of Plymouth on the ship* Mayflower. *They go on to found Plymouth Colony, the first permanent colonial settlement in New England.*

MAD.ᴸᴸᴬ BARÉ.

▲ **1766–69:** Disguised as a man, Jeanne Baret works as an assistant botanist on the first French round-the-world voyage, under Admiral Louis Antoine de Bougainville. She becomes the **first female to circumnavigate the globe** and helps discover a wealth of new plants during her extensive botanical field work.

1889: *The 300-m-tall (984-ft) Eiffel Tower is completed in Paris, France. Initially constructed as the entrance to the World's Fair, which is staged in that year, the wrought-iron edifice remains the world's* **tallest structure** *until the erection of the 319-m (1,046-ft) Chrysler Building in New York City, USA, 41 years later. As of 2016, it is still the tallest structure in Paris.*

1903: At 10:35 a.m. on 17 Dec, Orville Wright (USA) flies the 9-kW (12-hp) chain-driven *Flyer I* – which he has built with his brother Wilbur – for 120 ft (36.5 m) in Kitty Hawk, North Carolina, USA. He flies at an altitude of 8–12 ft (2.4–3.6 m) in the **first power-driven flight**.

DATELINE

1455 Oldest mechanically printed full-length book
The Gutenberg Bible is printed in Mainz, Germany, c. 1455 by Henne zum Gensfleisch zur Laden, commonly known as Johannes Gutenberg (c. 1398–1468).

FAST FACTS

Magellan is famed as the first circumnavigator, but he didn't make it all the way home: he was hacked to death in the Philippines • The **first power-driven flight** lasted 12 sec • John O'Groats is named after Jan de Groot, a Dutch ferryman

1900   **1950**   **1970**

▶ **1911:** The **first successful expedition to the South Pole** reaches its goal at 11 a.m. on 14 Dec. The Norwegian party of five men is led by Captain Roald Amundsen (right). They reach the Pole after a 53-day march with dog sledges from the Bay of Whales.

▲ **1953:** At 11:30 a.m. on 29 May, Edmund Percival Hillary (NZ, above left) and Indo-Tibetan Tenzing Norgay (b. Namgyal Wangdi, above right) complete the **first ascent of Everest**. They are shown here on the day before their historic achievement.

▶ **1924:** The **first aerial circumnavigation** is made by two US Army Douglas World Cruiser (DWC) seaplanes from 6 Apr to 28 Sep, starting and ending at Seattle, Washington, USA. The *Chicago* is piloted by Lts Lowell H Smith and Leslie P Arnold, while Lts Erik H Nelson and John Harding (all USA) fly the *New Orleans*.

▲ **1933:** Between 15 and 22 Jul, Wiley Post (USA) carries out the **first solo flight around the world** in *Winnie Mae*, a Lockheed Vega. He covers 15,596 mi (25,099 km), starting and ending in New York City, USA.

▲ **1950:** At 8,091 m (26,545 ft), Annapurna I is the 10th-tallest mountain in the world and is situated in the Nepalese Himalayas. It is **first summitted** on 3 Jun by Maurice Herzog and Louis Lachenal (both FRA).

1961: Cosmonaut Flight Major Yuri Alekseyevich Gagarin (USSR) flies into space in *Vostok 1* on 12 Apr on the **first manned spaceflight**. The take-off is from the Baikonur Cosmodrome in Kazakhstan at 6:07 a.m. GMT and the landing at Smelovka, near Engels, in the Saratov region of Russia, 118 min later.

1963: Junior Lt Valentina Vladimirovna Tereshkova (USSR) becomes the **first woman in space**. She takes off in *Vostok 6* from the Baikonur Cosmodrome at 9:30 a.m. GMT on 16 Jun.

▲ **1969:** "The *Eagle* has landed." Neil Armstrong and Buzz Aldrin (both USA) become the **first men on the Moon**, on 21 Jul. Armstrong steps on to the lunar surface at 2:56:15 GMT, followed by Aldrin at 3:11 GMT.

▲ **1969:** The **first person to row any ocean solo** is John Fairfax (UK, above), who crosses the Atlantic Ocean east to west in *Britannia* between 20 Jan and 19 Jul 1969. In the same year, Robin Knox-Johnston (UK) becomes the **first person to sail around the world** (solo and non-stop), in his yacht *Suhaili*. He leaves Falmouth, UK, on 14 Jun 1968, in the *Sunday Times* Golden Globe Race, and returns on 22 Apr 1969.

Oldest android design

Leonardo da Vinci (ITA) sketches a humanoid robot. His ideas for the finished model are lost, but some of his other drawings show a human knight with anatomically correct joints operated by cables and pulleys.

1495 ▶ DATELINE

EXPLORATION 1971–1995

JOURNEYS

▲ **1974:** David Kunst (USA, above) completes the **first confirmed circumnavigation on foot** on 5 Oct. He had begun on 20 Jun 1970 and covers 23,250 km (14,450 mi) across four continents. George Matthew Schilling (USA) is reputed to have walked around the world from 1897 to 1904, although this is unproved.

▲ **1980:** Italy's Reinhold Messner becomes the **first person to climb Everest solo**, reaching the summit on 20 Aug. It takes him three days to reach the top from his base camp at 6,500 m (21,325 ft). The climb is made all the more difficult by the fact that he does not use bottled oxygen.

▲ **1983:** George Meegan (UK) completes the **fastest walk along the Pan-American Highway** on 18 Sep. He covers 30,608 km (19,019 mi) in 2,426 days after setting out on 26 Jan 1977. His journey takes him from the southernmost point of South America to the northernmost point of North America.

▲ **1978:** Japanese explorer and mountaineer Naomi Uemura becomes the **first person to reach the North Pole in a solo expedition** across the Arctic sea ice, at 4:45 a.m. GMT on 1 May. He travels 770 km (478 mi), setting out on 7 Mar from Cape Edward, Ellesmere Island, in northern Canada. The expedition is dog-assisted and is supported with resupplies.

CERTIFICATE

The first female to ascend Everest is Junko Tabei (Japan, b. 22 September 1939) who reached the summit on 16 May 1975

A commemorative award to celebrate the 60th anniversary of Guinness World Records

OFFICIALLY AMAZING

1955 **60** 2015

▲ **1975:** On 16 May, Junko Tabei (JPN) becomes the **first woman to climb Mount Everest**. She will go on to become the **first woman to climb the Seven Summits** (the highest peak on each continent) when she tops Puncak Jaya (aka Carstensz Pyramid) on 28 Jun 1992.

▲ **1982:** On 29 Aug, Sir Ranulph Fiennes (above left) and Charles Burton (above right, both UK) return to Greenwich, London, UK, having completed the **first surface circumnavigation via both Poles**. They had set out from Greenwich on 2 Sep 1979, crossing the South Pole on 15 Dec 1980 and the North Pole on 10 Apr 1982. In all, their epic trek covers 35,000 mi (56,000 km).

1535

Tallest suit of armour
A 2.057-m (6-ft 8-in) suit of armour made at around this time was once thought to have been worn by John of Gaunt, 1st Duke of Lancaster, in the 14th century. In fact, it is German in origin. It is on display in the White Tower at HM Tower of London, UK.

FAST FACTS

In 2011, a whale graveyard was found near the Pan-American Highway in Chile
• The North and South Poles have switched some 400 times in 330 million years
• The Atlantic Ocean is growing, but the Pacific Ocean is shrinking

1985   **1990**   **1995**

▲ **1985:** Between 30 Jun and 20 Aug, Hanspeter Beck (AUS) unicycles 6,237 km (3,876 mi) from Port Hedland in Western Australia to Melbourne in Victoria. His 51-day 23-hr 25-min journey represents the **fastest unicycle ride across Australia**.

▲ **1986:** Richard G "Dick" Rutan and Jeana Yeager (both USA) complete the **first circumnavigation by aircraft without refuelling** in 9 days, from 14 to 23 Dec. Their unique aircraft *Voyager* is designed and built by Dick's brother Burt.

▶ **1986:** On 5 Aug, Patrick Morrow (CAN) becomes the **first person to climb the Seven Summits** – the highest mountains on all seven continents – according to the Carstensz list, which recognizes the highest point in Oceania as Puncak Jaya (aka Carstensz Pyramid) in Indonesia.

▲ **1988:** Wearing buoyant 4.2-m-long (13-ft 9-in) skis, Rémy Bricka (FRA) carries out the **fastest "walk" across the Atlantic Ocean** in 59 days, from 2 Apr to 31 May. He covers 5,636 km (3,502 mi), towing a platform of supplies and essentials such as a water still.

1989 and 1991: The record for the **first and fastest man and woman to have circumnavigated the Earth by car** covering six continents under the rules applicable in 1989 and 1991 embracing more than an equator's length of driving (24,901 road miles; 40,075 km), is held by Saloo Choudhury and his wife Neena Choudhury (both India). The journey took 69 days 19 hours 5 minutes from 9 September to 17 November 1989. The couple drove a 1989 Hindustan "Contessa Classic" starting and finishing in Delhi, India.

▲ **1989:** Robert Swan (UK) becomes the **first person to walk to both Poles** when the eight-man "Icewalk" expedition arrives at the North Pole under his leadership on 14 May. Three years earlier, on 11 Jan 1986, he had led the three-man "In the Footsteps of Scott" expedition to the South Pole.

▲ **1992:** The **fastest crossing of the Atlantic Ocean** is 2 days 10 hr 34 min 47 sec, by the 68.1-m (223-ft) luxury yacht *Destriero* from 6 to 9 Aug. The gas turbine-propelled vessel maintains an average speed of 53 knots (98 km/h; 60 mph). The skipper is Cesare Fiorio (ITA).

1993: On 7 Jan, Erling Kagge (NOR) completes the **first solo expedition to the South Pole**. His 1,400-km (870-mi) unsupported surface trek from Berkner Island takes him 50 days.

▲ **1994:** Børge Ousland (NOR) performs the **fastest solo unsupported trek to the North Pole** in 52 days, from 2 Mar to 23 Apr. He sets out from Cape Arkticheskiy on the Russian archipelago of Severnaya Zemlya. The feat also makes him the **first person to make a solo and unsupported journey to the North Pole from land**.

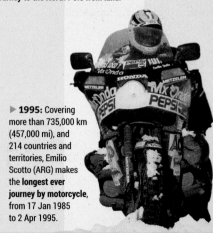

▶ **1995:** Covering more than 735,000 km (457,000 mi), and 214 countries and territories, Emilio Scotto (ARG) makes the **longest ever journey by motorcycle**, from 17 Jan 1985 to 2 Apr 1995.

Oldest botanical garden (same location)
The Orto Botanico in Padua, Italy, is created. As of 2016, the original design remains – a circular central plot (symbolizing the world) surrounded by a ring of water – and the site is still dedicated to scientific research.

1545 ▶ DATELINE

1996   **1999**   **2000**

▲ **1996:** Peter Bird (UK) spends the **longest collective time at sea in an ocean rowboat**: 940 days. From 1974 to 1996, he covers 34,238 km (21,275 mi) rowing across the Atlantic Ocean, from east to west; the Pacific Ocean, from east to west; and the Pacific Ocean, from west to east.

▲ **1999:** Emmanuel Coindre (FRA) embarks upon the first of seven epic adventures at sea – the **most solo ocean crossings** – by traversing the Atlantic Ocean, east to west, in a pedal-boat. He goes on to row the Atlantic, east to west, in 2001, west to east in 2002 and east to west in 2004, before recording the **fastest solo row across the Atlantic (west to east)**, also in 2004, in 62 days 19 hr 48 min (pictured above). He rows the Pacific Ocean, west to east, from Chōshi in Japan to Coos Bay in Oregon, USA, in 2005, taking 129 days 17 hr 22 min. Lastly, he completes the **fastest solo row across the Indian Ocean** in 56 days 7 hr 29 min 11 sec, from 30 Nov 2013 to 25 Jan 2014.

▲ **2000:** Between 31 May and 6 Sep, Colin Bodill (UK) records the **fastest circumnavigation by microlight**. He rounds the globe in his Mainair Blade 912 Flexwing microlight in 99 days, starting and landing at Brooklands airfield in Weybridge, Surrey, UK. En route, Bodill flies alongside another record-breaker, Jennifer Murray (UK), who registers the **fastest circumnavigation by helicopter (female)** in the same time, and between the same dates.

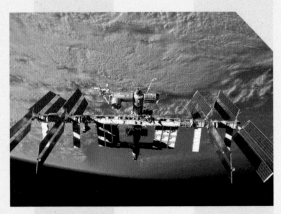

▼ **1999:** On 10 Jan, Antoine De Choudens (FRA) becomes the **first person to complete the Three Poles Challenge without supplementary oxygen on Everest**, having embarked on his feat on 25 Apr 1996.

▼ **2001:** Erik Weihenmayer (USA) was born with retinoschisis, an eye condition that left him completely blind by the age of 13. Despite this, on 25 May he becomes the **first blind man to climb Mount Everest**. As of Apr 2016, he is still the only blind person to have done so. Erik is also an accomplished rock climber, skier and paraglider.

▲ **1998:** Construction begins on the *International Space Station* (ISS). With a final cost in excess of $100 bn (£66.7 bn), it will become the most **expensive man-made object**.

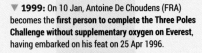

▶ **1998:** David Hempleman-Adams (UK) becomes the **first person to complete the Adventurers Grand Slam**, a gruelling challenge that involves climbing the Seven Summits (the highest peak on every continent) and trekking to both the North and South Pole from the coast. He begins his quest in 1980 and completes it 18 years later when he and fellow adventurer Rune Gjeldnes (NOR) walk to the North Pole from Mar to May 1998.

1999: Robert Hansen of Kittery, Maine, USA, completes the **longest solo and unsupported journey on a snowmobile**, from 12 Jan to 9 Feb. He covers 7,993 km (4,967 mi) from Medway, Maine, to International Falls, Minnesota, USA, and back.

DATELINE ▶ **1556** 〉 **Highest death toll from an earthquake**
An estimated 830,000 people perish in the quake (or *dizhen*) that strikes the Shaanxi, Shanxi and Henan provinces in China on 2 Feb.

FAST FACTS

Oceans can hold approximately 50% more carbon than Earth's atmosphere • No country owns Antarctica • The *ISS* has 15 pressurized modules (seven US, five Russian, two Japanese and one European)

2001   **2004**   **2005**

2004: Sarah and Sally Kettle (both UK) carry out the **first row across any ocean by a mother and daughter team**. They cross the Atlantic Ocean, east to west, in *Calderdale – The Yorkshire Challenger* between 20 Jan and 5 May.

2001: The **first married couple to reach both Poles** – Mike and Fiona Thornewill (both UK) – arrive at the North Pole on 5 May, having reached the South Pole by ski on 4 Jan 2000. Both trips are air-supported and the couple are accompanied by team-mate Catharine Hartley (UK). The latter leg also earns Fiona Thornewill and Hartley another record for **fastest ski journey to the North Pole (female):** 55 days.

2002: Aviator Steve Fossett (USA, 1944–2007, right) completes the **first solo circumnavigation by balloon**, between 19 Jun and 2 Jul in the *Bud Light Spirit of Freedom*. He takes off and lands in Australia.

2002: Embarking on the **longest unicycle journey**, Lars Clausen (USA) sets out from Tillamook, Oregon, USA, on 22 Apr. His double crossing of the country finishes in Los Angeles, California, on 12 Nov, having covered 14,686.8 km (9,125.9 mi) across 48 states.

2002: Tina Sjögren (SWE) becomes the **first woman to complete an unsupported journey to the South Pole** on 1 Feb. Along with her husband Thomas, she achieves the journey (from the Hercules Inlet) in 63 days, starting on 30 Nov 2001.

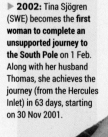

2005: Park Young-Seok (KOR) reaches the North Pole on foot on 30 Apr, becoming the **first person to achieve the Explorers Grand Slam**. This involves climbing the highest mountains on all seven continents, the 14 mountains over 8,000 m (26,246 ft), and reaching the North and South Poles on foot. His quest had begun when he summitted Everest on 16 May 1993.

2005: Between 1 and 3 Mar, Steve Fossett completes the **first solo circumnavigation by aircraft without refuelling**. It takes him 67 hr 1 min, in the *Virgin Atlantic GlobalFlyer*, starting and finishing at Salina, Kansas, USA. The aircraft, which is built by Scaled Composites, carries nearly 5 tonnes (11,000 lb) of fuel.

2005: On 18 Jul 2005, Flávio Jardim and Diogo Guerreiro (both BRA) complete their trip from Chuí to Oiapoque on the Brazilian coast, as part of the Blue Destination Expedition. At 8,120 km (5,045 mi), this is the **longest windsurfing journey**. They began on 17 May 2004.

First assassination by firearm
On 23 Jan, James Hamilton of Bothwellhaugh, Scotland – a follower and supporter of Mary, Queen of Scots – uses a carbine to kill James Stewart, 1st Earl of Moray and Regent of Scotland. **1570**

guinnessworldrecords.com **113**

EXPLORATION 2006–2009

JOURNEYS

▲ **2007:** Starting in Atalaya, Peru, and finishing in Belém, Brazil, Martin Strel (SVN) swims the entire length of the Amazon River in 67 days, between 1 Feb and 8 Apr. The 5,268-km (3,273-mi) achievement marks the **farthest open-water swim**. The distances he covers each day vary from 9 km (5.5 mi) to 127 km (79 mi).

▲ **2006:** Dee Caffari (UK) becomes the **first female to circumnavigate the world solo, sailing westbound and non-stop**, on 18 May. Setting out from Portsmouth, UK, on 20 Nov 2005, she takes 178 days 3 hr 5 min 34 sec to complete the voyage, unsupported, in the 22-m (72-ft) monohull *Aviva*. Almost three years later, Caffari becomes the **first female to sail non-stop around the world in both directions**, on 16 Feb 2009.

▲ **2007:** On 23 May, Jennifer Murray and Colin Bodill (both UK) accomplish the **first circumnavigation via both Poles by helicopter**. They set off from Fort Worth in Texas, USA, in a Bell 407 helicopter on 5 Dec 2006. Their flight is also the **fastest circumnavigation via the Poles by helicopter**, taking 170 days 22 hr 47 min 17 sec.

▲ **2006:** Between 19 Nov and 28 Dec, Hannah McKeand (UK) takes 39 days 9 hr 33 min to ski from Hercules Inlet, at the edge of the Antarctic continent, to the South Pole – the **fastest solo, unsupported and unassisted journey to the South Pole (female)**. The pole is situated at an altitude of 2,834 m (9,298 ft). The entire journey is uphill, and McKeand carries all her own supplies to ensure an essential daily intake of 6,000 calories.

2006: The three extreme points on Earth are Mount Everest, the North Pole and the South Pole (aka the Three Poles). On 24 Apr, Cecilie Skog (NOR) registers the **fastest time to complete the Three Poles challenge (female)** when she claims the North Pole. It takes her 1 year 336 days to achieve her feat.

▲ **2007:** Aged 18 years 301 days, Samantha Larson (USA) becomes the **youngest female to climb the Seven Summits, including Carstensz**, on 4 Aug.

▲ **2007:** On 6 Oct, Jason Lewis (UK) completes the **first circumnavigation using human power**, a 13-year journey without wind or motor assistance. Jason is joined by various supporters and friends for some stages of his mammoth trek.

DATELINE

1580

Longest castle siege
The cathedral fort of Ishiyama Hongan-ji in modern Osaka, Japan, is attacked by the warlord Oda Nobunaga in Aug 1570. It is defended by Ikkō-ikki warrior monks until Aug 1580, when the complex is finally burned down.

FAST FACTS

Antarctica's Gamburtsev Mountains are buried under ice up to 4,800 m (15,750 ft) thick • The top 3 m (10 ft) of the ocean holds as much heat as Earth's atmosphere • The last year that no one climbed Everest's summit was 1974

Note: Guinness World Records no longer accepts applications from adventurers under the age of 16

2008   **2009**

▲ **2009:** Sarah Outen (UK, b. 26 May 1985) is aged 23 years 310 days when she sets out to row across the Indian Ocean from 1 Apr to 3 Aug. Her 7,740-km (4,810-mi) crossing between Australia and Mauritius, in *Serendipity*, makes her the **youngest person** and **first woman to row the Indian Ocean solo**.

▲ **2008:** On 28 Sep, Rob Thomson (NZ) completes the **longest journey by skateboard**, in Shanghai, China. He begins the 12,159-km (7,555-mi) trip in Leysin, Switzerland, on 24 Jun 2007 and crosses part of Europe, the entire USA and China west to east, wearing out three sets of wheels and three skateboard decks.

▲ **2009:** Between 8 May and 13 Nov, Mick Dawson and Chris Martin (both UK) row from Chōshi in Japan to the Golden Gate Bridge in San Francisco, California, USA, aboard *Bojangles*. Their epic venture lasts 189 days 10 hr 39 min and makes them the **first team to row the Pacific Ocean west to east**.

▲ **2009:** On 27 Aug, Michael Perham (UK, b. 16 Mar 1992) becomes the **youngest person to circumnavigate by sailing solo, non-stop and unsupported**. He is aged 16 years 244 days when he sets out from Portsmouth, UK, in *TotallyMoney.com* on 15 Nov 2008.

▶ **2008:** Francis Joyon (FRA) arrives in Brest, France, on 20 Jan, at the end of the **fastest circumnavigation sailing solo**: 57 days 13 hr 34 min 6 sec. He makes the 38,900-km (24,170-mi) voyage in the 29.5-m (97-ft) trimaran *IDEC II*. On 16 Jun 2013, Joyon also accomplishes the **fastest single-handed transatlantic sailing**; he covers 5,333 km (3,314 mi) in 5 days 2 hr 56 min.

◀ **2009:** Ray Zahab, Kevin Vallely and Richard Weber (all CAN) reach the South Pole from Hercules Inlet in Antarctica on 7 Jan, after 33 days 23 hr 30 min – the **fastest unsupported and unassisted journey to the South Pole by a team**. Their personal best is trekking 55.56 km (34.5 mi) in a day.

Oldest stock exchange
A stock exchange in Amsterdam, Netherlands, is set up for trading in printed shares of the United East India Company of the Netherlands.

1602 ▶ DATELINE

EXPLORATION 2010–2015
JOURNEYS

▲ **2010:** Alan Bate (UK) completes the **fastest circumnavigation by bicycle (male)** between 31 Mar and 4 Aug. His total journey time is 125 days 21 hr 45 min, during which he cycles 29,467.91 km (18,310.51 mi) and travels more than 42,608.76 km (26,475.85 mi), including transfers. His epic ride begins and ends at the Grand Palace in Bangkok, Thailand.

► **2010:** Ed Stafford (UK) becomes the **first person to walk the length of the Amazon River.** He accomplishes the trip in 2 years 4 months 8 days (860 days), finishing on 9 Aug. He walks 145 mi (233 km) from the Pacific Ocean to the source of the Amazon, then follows the river for 4,345 mi (6,992 km), totalling 4,490 mi (7,225 km) coast to coast.

▲ **2010:** On 3 Jan, Katie Spotz (USA, b. 18 Apr 1987) is aged 22 years 260 days when she sets off from Dakar, Senegal, to paddle across the Atlantic east to west. After a 70-day voyage, she arrives in Georgetown, Guyana, on 14 Mar – the **youngest female to row across any ocean solo.**

▲ **2011:** On 13 Jan, Christian Eide (NOR) reaches the South Pole after a trek of 24 days 1 hr 13 min – completing the **fastest solo, unsupported and unassisted journey to the South Pole.** He sets off on the 1,150-km (715-mi) adventure on 20 Dec 2010, starting at the Hercules Inlet, on the south-western edge of the Ronne Ice Shelf. Eide covers an average of 47 km (29 mi) per day – although on his last day, he manages to ski 90 km (56 mi). He is shown above reflected in the mirrored ball that stands at the South Pole.

► **2010:** Vernon Tejas (USA) climbs the combined Kosciuszko and Carstensz lists of summits in 133 days. Tejas begins by climbing Vinson Massif on 18 Jan, and after ascents on Aconcagua, Carstensz Pyramid, Kosciuszko, Kilimanjaro, Elbrus and Everest, reaches the top of the last summit – Denali, aka Mount McKinley – on 31 May. This is the **fastest time to climb the Seven Summits, including Carstensz.** He is shown here at the top of Everest, with his Lapstick guitar.

FAST FACTS

The Himalayas formed 60 million years ago; rock at its summit contains 450-million-year-old fossils from the ocean bed • Kibo, the highest peak of Kilimanjaro, is a dormant volcano; its two other peaks are extinct volcanoes

2012   **2013**   **2014**   **2015**

▲ **2014:** Matthew Guthmiller (USA, b. 29 Nov 1994) becomes the **youngest person to circumnavigate by aircraft solo**. He ends his trip on 14 Jul in El Cajon, California, USA, aged 19 years 227 days.

▲ **2012:** Gábor Rakonczay (HUN) crosses the Atlantic Ocean east to west in his 7.5-m-long (24-ft 7-in) canoe in 76 days. Departing from Lagos in Portugal and arriving at the Caribbean island of Antigua on 25 Mar, he is the **first canoeist to paddle an ocean**.

▲ **2013:** British-American Vanessa Audi Rhys O'Brien completes the combined Kosciuszko and Carstensz lists in 295 days, starting with Everest on 19 May 2012 and ending with Kilimanjaro on 10 Mar 2013. This marks the **fastest time to climb the Seven Summits, including Carstensz (female)**. (See p.116 for the male record.)

▶ **2012:** On 21 Jul, Erden Eruç (TUR) completes a journey of 5 years 11 days 12 hr 22 min – the **first solo circumnavigation of the globe using human power**. He rows, kayaks, hikes and cycles across three continents and three oceans to return to his starting point: Bodega Bay in California, USA.

▼ **2013:** The Triple Seven Summits are the three highest mountains on each continent. Christian Stangl (AUT) reaches his last summit, Shkhara, 5,193 m (17,040 ft) tall, on the Georgia–Russia border, on 23 Aug to become the **first person to climb the Triple Seven Summits**.

▲ **2015:** Simon Chalk (UK) accomplishes his ninth ocean row on 3 Jan – the **most ocean rows by one person**. His crossings have been solo and in teams, and over the Atlantic and Indian oceans.

▶ **2013:** On 23 May, Phurba Tashi Sherpa (NPL, right) ascends the world's highest peak for the 21st time. He equals the record for the **most conquests of Everest**, set by Apa Sherpa (NPL) on 11 May 2011.

2013: David Liaño González (MEX) is the **first person to climb Everest from both sides in one season**. He climbs from Nepal on the south side on 11 May, and from Tibet on the north side on 19 May, making use of bottled oxygen both times.

▲ **2015:** Callum Gathercole (UK, b. 15 May 1995) is aged 20 years 219 days at the start of his Atlantic crossing on 20 Dec – the **youngest person to row across any ocean solo**.

Oldest continuously used national flag
The design of the flag of Denmark – a white Scandinavian cross on a red background – is adopted. It acquires its square shape in 1748. In Denmark, it is called the "Dannebrog" or "Danish cloth".

1625 ▶ DATELINE

DO TRY THIS AT HOME...

DID YOU KNOW?
Christian shouted the word "Tor!" – the German for "goal" – for his record attempt. His feat was part of a radio contest to find a sports fan who could shout the longest "goal" in the style of Latin American soccer commentators who stretch their vowels.
Goooooooooaaaa!

First operational pendulum clock
Although Italian inventor Galileo had conceived of a pendulum-driven clock before he died, the first working model isn't patented until some 20 years later, by astronomer and horologist Christiaan Huygens (NLD).

CONTENTS

Longest shout

This chapter is all about records that you can try yourself at home – proving that you don't need to be an Olympic athlete or Hollywood megastar to be a record-breaker. One have-a-go hero is Germany's Christian Kinner, holder of the record for the world's longest-lasting shout – the kind of feat that anyone can try. With the help of radio station Sportradio Sport1.fm, soccer fan Christian – a dedicated follower of Borussia Dortmund – let rip with a shout that lasted for an impressive 43.56 sec in Munich, Germany, on 25 Apr 2015. Back of the net!

If *you* want something to shout about, why not try breaking some of the records that follow on the next eight pages?

Oldest continuing periodical
The first issue of *Philosophical Transactions* is published by Britain's science academy, the Royal Society, on 6 Mar. It will go on to number Isaac Newton and Charles Darwin among its acclaimed contributors.

1665 ▶

DATELINE

DO TRY THIS AT HOME...
IN YOUR KITCHEN

If you thought that the kitchen was only good for making your dinner and washing the dishes, think again: it's also the perfect place to cook up some records! From common utensils to everyday foods such as eggs, sugar and rice, there are record-breaking opportunities in every cupboard and drawer – and even the fruit bowl. Whether you're a pro chef with lightning-quick prep skills or a gourmand with an acclaimed appetite, there really is something on the menu for everyone.

EGGS

Most crushed with the head in one minute	142	Scott Damerow (USA)
Most cracked with one hand in one minute	32	Ross McCurdy (USA)
Most crushed by sitting in one minute	72	Michaël Levillain (FRA)
Most crushed with the wrist in two minutes	78	Antonio Almijez (ESP)
Fastest time to crush 10 with elbows pointing forwards	12.64 sec	Mauro Vagnini (ITA)
Fastest time to move six from a box to egg cups using the feet	21.15 sec	Ashlee Carlisle (USA)
Fastest time to balance a dozen	1 min 6.45 sec	Brian Spotts (USA)

BANANAS

Most peeled and eaten in one minute	8	Patrick Bertoletti (USA)
Most snapped in one minute	99	Ashrita Furman (USA)

SUGAR CUBES

Most balanced on the chin (single stack)	17	Silvio Sabba (ITA)
Tallest tower	208 cm (6 ft 10 in)	Camille Courgeon (FRA)

SPOONS

Most balanced on the body	52	Etibar Elchiev (GEO)
Most twisted in one minute	14	Ashrita Furman (USA)
Most balanced on the face	31	Dalibor Jablanović (SRB)

CREAM CRACKERS

Fastest time to eat three	34.78 sec	Ambrose Mendy (UK)

JELLY CANDIES

Most jelly beans moved using a straw in one minute	36	Andrew Kamil Mourad (LBN)
Fastest time to sort 30 jelly beans using chopsticks	23.39 sec	Silvio Sabba (ITA)
Fastest time to sort 30 jelly babies using chopsticks	27.42 sec	Stephen Kish (UK)

M&M'S/SMARTIES

Most eaten in one minute with chopsticks	65	Kathryn Ratcliffe (UK)
Largest mosaic	13.8 m² (148.6 sq ft)	Jackson McKenzie (USA)
Fastest time to sort 500 g (17.6 oz) of Peanut M&M's	2 min 12 sec	Stephen Kish (UK)
Fastest time to sort 30 using chopsticks	31.5 sec	Yinger Guan (CHN)

DATELINE

1670

Oldest elected Pope
Clement X (ITA, b. Emilio Altieri) becomes leader of the Catholic Church aged 79 years 290 days. He will hold the position until his death just six years later.

ONIONS

Fastest time to eat a raw onion	29.5 sec	Yusuke Yamaguchi (JPN)
Fastest time to peel 50 lb	2 min 39 sec	Bob Blumer (CAN)
Most peeled and sliced in one minute	615 g (21.6 oz)	Masanori Fujimura (JPN)

FERRERO ROCHER

Most eaten in one minute	9	Peter Czerwinski (CAN)
		Patrick Bertoletti (USA)
Fastest time to eat 15	2 min 22 sec	Peter Czerwinski (CAN)
Most stacked	12	Silvio Sabba (ITA)
Fastest time to eat one with no hands	8.04 sec	Thomas Gangstad (NOR)

CONDIMENTS

Fastest time to drink a bottle of ketchup (396 g/13.9 oz)	32.37 sec	Benedikt Weber (DEU)
Most mustard drunk in 30 seconds	416 g (14.7 oz)	André Ortolf (DEU)
Fastest time to drink 200 ml (6.7 fl oz) of mustard	20.8 sec	Ashrita Furman (USA)

LEMONS

Fastest time to drink one litre of lemon juice through a straw	24.41 sec	Stephen Dechert II (USA)
Fastest time to peel and eat one	8.25 sec	Ashrita Furman (USA)
Fastest time to peel and eat three	28.5 sec	Jim Lyngvild (DEN)
Most caught blindfolded in 30 seconds (team of two)	15	Ashrita Furman and Bipin Larkin (both USA)
Most caught blindfolded in one minute (team of two)	33	Ashrita Furman and Bipin Larkin (both USA)

RICE & PASTA

Most uncooked rice grains moved with chopsticks in one minute	38	Silvio Sabba (ITA)
Most rice grains eaten with chopsticks in one minute	23	Rob Beaton (USA)
Most rice grains eaten with chopsticks in three minutes	134	Bob Blumer (CAN)
Most tortellini made in three minutes	25	Francesco Boggian (ITA)
Fastest time to eat a bowl of pasta (100 g/3.5 oz) with sauce	41 sec	Peter Czerwinski (CAN)

COCKTAIL STICKS

Most peas eaten in 30 seconds	40	Ashrita Furman (USA)
Most peas eaten in one minute	86	Paolo Verri (ITA)
Most sweetcorn eaten in three minutes	236	Ian Richard Purvis (UK)
Most baked beans eaten in five minutes	271	Ashrita Furman (USA)

Most prolific hanging judge
Lord Chief Justice George Jeffreys (UK) sentences some 320 rebels to death on the grounds of treason for participating in the Revolt of the West. These trials will come to be known as the Bloody Assizes.

1685

DATELINE

DO TRY THIS AT HOME...
IN YOUR BACKYARD

If it's a nice day outside, there's no reason to stay cooped up indoors because there are hundreds of record-worthy feats awaiting you in your very own backyard. As well as a great excuse to get some fresh air and boost your vitamin D levels, this is the perfect setting to attempt some sporty activities that require a bit more space. So dig out those long-forgotten toys you never thought you'd use again and get training. What if you don't have a garden? No problem – why not pack a picnic, head to the local park and turn your record attempt into a family day out?

FRISBEE/FLYING DISC

Longest duration aloft (male)	16.72 sec	Don Cain (USA)
Longest duration aloft (female)	11.81 sec	Amy Bekken (USA)
Longest distance thrown (male)	250 m (820 ft 2 in)	Christian Sandstrom (SWE)
Longest distance thrown (female)	138.5 m (454 ft 7 in)	Jennifer Griffin (USA)
Longest throw at a target	45.7 m (150 ft)	Brodie Smith (USA)
Most throws at a target in one minute	27	Loic Dumont (FRA)
Most catches behind the back in one minute	24	Tim and Daniel Habenicht (both USA)
Most cones hit in one minute	12	Brodie Smith (USA)

HULA HOOPS

Most spun simultaneously	200	Marawa Ibrahim (AUS)
Most caught and spun in one minute	236	Liu Rongrong (CHN)
Most rotations by a team of three in one minute	50	Paul Blair (USA), Pan Bo and Ding Hemei (both CHN)
Most rotations while on a trampoline in one minute	130	Ken Kovach (USA)

SPACE HOPPER

Fastest 100 m	30.2 sec	Ashrita Furman (USA)

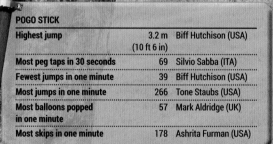

POGO STICK

Highest jump	3.2 m (10 ft 6 in)	Biff Hutchison (USA)
Most peg taps in 30 seconds	69	Silvio Sabba (ITA)
Fewest jumps in one minute	39	Biff Hutchison (USA)
Most jumps in one minute	266	Tone Staubs (USA)
Most balloons popped in one minute	57	Mark Aldridge (UK)
Most skips in one minute	178	Ashrita Furman (USA)

SOCCER BALL

Fastest 100 m with a ball balanced on the head	18.5 sec	Daniel Cutting (UK)
Most "around the Moon" tricks in one minute	61	Adrian Fogel (DEU)
Most "around the world" tricks in one minute	85	John Farnworth (UK)
Most juggled simultaneously	5	Victor Rubilar (ARG) Marko Vermeer (NLD)
Longest time spun on one finger	4 min 21 sec	Raphael Harris (ISR)
Fastest time to complete 50 passes (team of two)	29.7 sec	Jonathan Gomez (TTO) and Keith Considine (UK)

WATER BALLOONS

Farthest throw and catch (without bursting)	38.8 m (127 ft 4 in)	Ashrita Furman and Bipin Larkin (both USA)
Most caught and held in one minute	22	Ashrita Furman and Bipin Larkin (both USA)
Most thrown at a person in one minute	32	Ashrita Furman and Bipin Larkin (both USA)

First confirmed periodic comet
British astronomer Edmond Halley realizes that a comet first documented back in 240 BCE actually passes Earth in a 75-year cycle. He successfully predicts that the next flyby of Halley's Comet will be in 1758.

TRAMPOLINE

Most consecutive somersaults	3,333	Brian Hudson (UK)
Most backwards somersaults in 30 seconds	30	Shane Connor Smith (USA)
Most forward somersaults in one minute	40	Jed Evans (UK)
Most high front drops in one minute	26	Ken Kovach (USA)
Most seat drops in one minute	49	Oleksandr Nakonechny (UKR)
Most backwards tucks in one minute	30	Hu Zichao (CHN)

SKIPPING ROPE

Most backwards skips in 30 seconds	135	Hijiki Ikuyama (JPN)
Most triple unders in one minute	113	He Chunyan (CHN)
Most consecutive triple unders	423	Shozo Hamada (JPN)
Most consecutive quadruple unders	78	Akitoshi Moriguchi (JPN)
Fastest 100 m skipping	15.3 sec	Alain Trottier (USA)

BASKETBALL

Most circles around the waist in 30 seconds	68	Corey Rich (USA)
Most bounces in one minute	444	Thaneswar Guragai (NPL)
Longest time spinning three	7.5 sec	Thomas Connors (UK)
Longest time spinning on one finger (using one hand)	10 min 33 sec	Ruben Alcaraz (ESP)
Longest time spinning on the head	18.1 sec	Mehmet Kekeç (DEU)

MICRO SCOOTER

Highest bunny hop	80 cm (2 ft 7 in)	Marc Vinco (FRA)
Most tailwhips in one minute	57	Daniel Barrett (USA)
Most backflips in one minute	12	Dakota Schuetz (USA)

TENNIS BALLS

Most caught blindfolded in one minute	11	Anthony Kelly (AUS)
Most bounces on a racket handle in one minute	185	Florian Zoller (AUT)
Longest time to control one with a racket	4 hr 8 min 16 sec	Palmer Campbell (USA)
Most held in one hand	23	Mahadeo Bhujbal (IND)
Longest time to bounce one on the head	1 hr 1 min 2 sec	Tomas Lundman (SWE)
Longest time to control one using the feet	5 hr 28 min 59 sec	Jacek Guzowski (POL)

DIABOLO

Most catches in one minute	16	Wang Yueqiu (CHN)
Most juggling catches on the back in one minute	67	Chen Yun (CHN)
Most spins around the leg in one minute	117	Adrian Hidalgo (ESP)
Most consecutive bounces around the neck	126	Harvey Woods (UK)
Longest duration to juggle four around the leg	1 min 21 sec	Peng Zhan (TPE)
Longest grind	1 min 35 sec	Harry Feachen (UK)

Oldest restaurant
Restaurante Botín opens its doors in the centre of Madrid, Spain. Customers have to bring their own food and wine, which is then cooked on the premises. The eatery is still open today.

1725

DO TRY THIS AT HOME...
IN YOUR BEDROOM

No matter how old we get, some toys and games will never lose their appeal. From juggling and yo-yoing to solving Rubik's Cubes and launching paper aircraft, what makes these playtime classics so enduring is the timeless challenge they present in the very moment of playing with them. Whether you're a newbie or an old hand, there's always the chance to beat your personal best, or indeed the world's best. And the coolest thing about these records? You can do them all in your very own bedroom – even in your pyjamas, if you so wish!

GOLF BALLS
Most stacked in a tower	9	Don Athey (USA)

JUGGLING BALLS
Most catches in one minute (three)	422	Zdeněk Bradáč (CZE)
Most juggled	11	Alex Barron (UK)
Longest duration (three, blindfolded)	6 min 34 sec	David Rush (USA)
Longest duration (four)	2 hr 46 min 48 sec	Zdeněk Bradáč (CZE)

PAPER AIRCRAFT
Most made and caught in one minute (team of 10)	25	Airbus Group (FRA)
Most consecutive times to hit a target	13	Fumihiro Uno (JPN)
Most caught by mouth in one minute	17	Ashrita Furman and Bipin Larkin (both USA)
Farthest flight	69.14 m (226 ft 10 in)	Joe Ayoob and John Collins (both USA)

MR POTATO HEAD
Fastest time to assemble	6.62 sec	Samet Durmaz (TUR)
Fastest time to assemble while blindfolded	16.17 sec	Zoe Jayne Whalley (UK)

RUBIK'S CUBE (3x3x3)
Fastest time to solve	4.90 sec	Lucas Etter (USA)
Fastest time to solve with one hand	6.88 sec	Feliks Zemdegs (AUS)
Fastest time to solve while blindfolded	21.05 sec	Kaijun Lin (CHN)
Fastest time to solve with the feet	20.57 sec	Jakub Kipa (POL)
Fewest moves to complete	19	Tim Wong (USA) and Marcel Peters (DEU)

YO-YO
Farthest distance to "walk the dog"	6.85 m (22 ft 5 in)	Arron Sparks (UK)
Most "hop the fence" tricks in one minute	144	Arron Sparks (UK)
Most "reach for the Moon" tricks in 30 seconds	27	Arron Sparks (UK)
Most "eli hops" in 30 seconds	71	Hiroyuki Suzuki (JPN)
Most tricks in one minute	51	Hans Van Dan Elzen (USA)

TIDDLYWINKS
Longest wink shot	9.52 m (31 ft 3 in)	Ben Soares (UK)
Highest wink shot	3.49 m (11 ft 5 in)	Adrian Jones (UK)
		David Smith (UK)
		Ed Wynn (UK)

First lightning rod
American polymath Benjamin Franklin invents the lightning rod. It works on the principle that a metal rod fixed to the top of a building, and continuing underground, will draw a lightning strike that would otherwise harm the building.

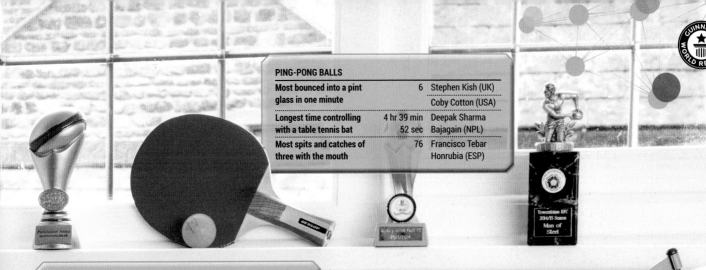

PING-PONG BALLS

Most bounced into a pint glass in one minute	6	Stephen Kish (UK) Coby Cotton (USA)
Longest time controlling with a table tennis bat	4 hr 39 min 52 sec	Deepak Sharma Bajagain (NPL)
Most spits and catches of three with the mouth	76	Francisco Tebar Honrubia (ESP)

SPORT STACKING

Fastest 3-3-3 stack	1.418 sec	William Orrell (USA)
Fastest 3-6-3 stack	1.824 sec	William Orrell (USA)
Fastest cycle stack	5.000 sec	William Orrell (USA)
Fastest 3-6-3 relay	12.212 sec	Chandler Miller, William Orrell, William Polly and Zhewei Wu (all USA)

JENGA

Fastest 30-level tower (team of two)	2 min 51.04 sec	Tyler and Ryan Measel (both USA)

PLAYING CARDS

Fastest time to arrange a deck	36.16 sec	Zdeněk Bradáč (CZE)
Most held in a fan	326	Ralf Laue (DEU)
Tallest house of cards	7.86 m (25 ft 9 in)	Bryan Berg (USA)
Fastest time to learn and recall a deck	21.19 sec	Simon Reinhard (DEU)

LEGO®

Tallest tower built with one hand in one minute	48	Chris Challis (UK)
Tallest tower built in one minute	131	Andy Parsons (UK)
Most bricks picked up with a brick in 30 seconds (one hand)	37	Megane Scott (UK) Nardy Nafzger (NLD)

COINS

Fastest time to stack 25	14.71 sec	Stephen Kish (UK)
Most stacked in one minute	69	Silvio Sabba (ITA)
Most balanced in a pyramid	880	Aleksandr Bendikov (BLR)
Most stacked	253	Dipak Syal (IND)

Most prolific composer
Georg Philipp Telemann (DEU) dies, leaving behind a body of work that includes 12 sets of church services for a year, 40 operas, 44 passions and more than 600 orchestral suites, plus concertos and other chamber music.

1767

DATELINE

DO TRY THIS AT HOME...
IN YOUR GYM

How better to overcome the boredom of endless reps at the gym than by aiming for a world record? Whether you're running on a treadmill, pumping iron or pummelling a punch bag, there are Guinness World Records titles to suit every ability. Featured here are just a small selection of the hundreds of categories that we monitor, so if you don't see something that you want to attempt, don't worry – just apply to our Records Managers at www.guinnessworldrecords.com and they'll do their best to help...

ROWING MACHINE (CONCEPT II)

Fastest 2,000 m (male)	5 min 36.6 sec	Rob Waddell (NZ)
Fastest 2,000 m (female)	6 min 28.4 sec	Sophie Balmary (FRA)
Fastest marathon (male)	2 hr 28 min 54 sec	Glen Goodman (UK)
Fastest marathon (female)	2 hr 53 min 16 sec	Anna Bailey (UK)
Fastest 1,000,000 m	128 hr 38 min 19 sec	Nigel Gower (UK)
Fastest time to "row the Equator" (40,075 km)	2 years 6 months 20 days	David Holby (UK)

TREADMILL

Fastest time to run 50 km	3 hr 55 min 28 sec	Gemma Carter (UK)
Fastest time to run 100 km (male)	6 hr 21 min 40 sec	Phil Anthony (UK)
Fastest time to run 100 km (female)	8 hr 35 min 5 sec	Edit Bérces (HUN)
Greatest distance in 12 hours (male)	131.35 km (81.62 mi)	David Staley (USA)
Greatest distance in 12 hours (female)	96.98 km (60.26 mi)	Dee Boland (IRL)
Greatest distance in 24 hours (male)	257.88 km (160.24 mi)	Suresh Joachim (CAN/LKA)
Greatest distance in 24 hours (female)	247.20 km (153.60 mi)	Edit Bérces (HUN)
Greatest distance in one week (male)	827.16 km (513.97 mi)	Marcio Villar (BRA)
Greatest distance in one week (female)	833.05 km (517.63 mi)	Sharon Gayter (UK)

DUMBBELLS

Most weight lifted with front raises in one minute	1,215 kg (2,678 lb)	Eamonn Keane (IRL)
Most weight lifted with front raises in one hour	18,830 kg (41,513 lb)	Eamonn Keane (IRL)
Most weight lifted by rows in one minute (one arm)	1,975.85 kg (4,356 lb)	Robert Natoli (USA)
Most weight lifted by rows in one hour	32,730 kg (72,157 lb)	Eamonn Keane (IRL)
Most weight lifted by standing press in one minute	910 kg (2,006 lb)	Kristin Rhodes (USA)
Most weight lifted by incline flyes in one minute	2,160 kg (4,761 lb)	Eamonn Keane (IRL)
Most weight lifted by incline flyes in one hour	40,600 kg (89,508 lb)	Eamonn Keane (IRL)

DATELINE

1770

First modern circus
Trick rider Philip Astley (UK) adds acrobats, rope dancers and clowns to his horse show in London, UK. In 1782, a former member of his company, Charles Hughes (UK), will found the first such show to call itself a circus.

EXERCISE BIKE

Greatest distance in one minute	3.06 km (1.90 mi)	Miguel Ángel Castro Rodríguez (ESP)
Greatest distance in three minutes	5.80 km (3.60 mi)	Miguel Ángel Castro Rodríguez (ESP)
Greatest distance in one hour (male)	122.00 km (75.80 mi)	Miguel Ángel Castro Rodríguez (ESP)
Greatest distance in one hour (female)	35.30 km (21.93 mi)	Tina Ternjak (SVN)
Greatest distance in eight hours	742.14 km (461.14 mi)	Philippe Vaz (FRA)
Greatest distance in 12 hours (male)	832.35 km (517.20 mi)	Miguel Ángel Castro Rodríguez (ESP)
Greatest distance in 12 hours (female)	348.00 km (216.23 mi)	Tina Ternjak (SVN)
Greatest distance in 24 hours	1,421.05 km (883.00 mi)	Philippe Vaz (FRA)
Longest marathon (duration)	268 hr 32 min 44 sec	Jamie McDonald (UK)

PUNCH BAG

Longest marathon punching	52 hr	Kaveh Fatemian (UK)

STEP BOARD

Most step-ups in one minute	105	Takahiro Morishita (JPN)
Most step-ups in one hour	4,135	Manjit Singh (UK)
Most step-ups in eight hours	8,898	Arran McLellan (CAN)
Most step-ups in 24 hours	25,061	Subhash Sasne (IND)
Most step-ups with a 40-lb pack in one minute	52	Robert Natoli (USA)
Most step-ups with a 60-lb pack in one minute	47	Robert Natoli (USA)
Most step-ups with an 80-lb pack in one minute	41	Robert Natoli (USA)
Most step-ups with a 100-lb pack in one minute	40	Paddy Doyle (UK)

MEDICINE BALL

Most push-ups on a medicine ball in one minute	68	Mohammad Hassaan Butt (PAK)
Longest control of a medicine ball	1 min 34 sec	Conny Strömberg (SWE)

KETTLEBELLS

Greatest weight lifted by kettlebell long cycle in one hour	33,184 kg (73,158 lb)	Anatoly Ezhov (BLR)
Greatest weight lifted by kettlebell snatch in one hour (male)	34,160 kg (75,309 lb)	Evgeny Nazarevich (BLR)
Greatest weight lifted by kettlebell snatch in one hour (female)	14,340 kg (31,614 lb)	Lyubov Cherepaha (UKR)
Greatest weight lifted by kettlebell jerk in one hour	53,424 kg (117,779 lb)	Anatoly Ezhov (BLR)
Greatest weight lifted by kettlebell swing in one hour	12,400 kg (27,337 lb)	James Saward-Anderson (UK)
Most weight lifted with kettlebells in one minute (alternating floor press)	4,347 kg (9,583 lb)	Anatoly Ezhov (BLR)

SWISS BALLS

Fastest time to jump across 10 Swiss balls	8.31 sec	Neil Whyte (AUS)
Greatest weight squat-lifted on a Swiss ball in one minute	1,979.6 kg (4,364 lb)	Stephen Buttler (UK)
Most knee bends on a Swiss ball in one hour	1,716	Stephen Buttler (UK)
Longest time standing on a Swiss ball	5 hr 25 min 36.98 sec	Garrett Lam (USA)
Most passes of a Swiss ball in five minutes (team)	198	Health & Diet Centres Ltd (UK)
Longest jump between two Swiss balls	2.3 m (7 ft 6 in)	Neil Whyte (AUS)

Oldest working steam engine
The Smethwick Engine, designed by James Watt and built by the Birmingham Canal Company (both UK), enters service on 27 May at Smethwick, West Midlands, UK. It is used to pump water back up a series of canal locks.

1779

DATELINE

DON'T TRY THIS AT HOME...

DID YOU KNOW?
Josef wore three layers of protective clothing for his full-body burn, as well as liberally covering his skin with heat-resistant stunt gel. Assistants constantly re-fuelled the flames, which must be kept alive to ensure the longest possible burn, while monitoring Josef's safety.

1783

First manned flight
On 15 Oct in France, Jean-François Pilâtre de Rozier rises 26 m (84 ft) in a hot-air balloon built by inventors Joseph and Jacques Montgolfier (all FRA). On 21 Nov, he and the Marquis d'Arlandes also make the **first free manned balloon flight**.

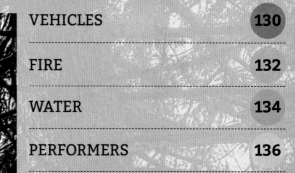

CONTENTS

Longest duration full-body burn (without oxygen)

The activities on the following pages are *strictly* for experts only, so please don't try any of these stunts at home – that's official! And who better to introduce a chapter about risky records than Austrian professional stuntman Josef Tödtling? He spent 5 min 41 sec aflame, without oxygen, in a full-body burn at Salzburg Fire Department in Austria on 23 Nov 2013. Needless to say, this record required very careful preparation. And he had to keep a cool head to concentrate on controlling his movements: one careless gesture might have fanned flames into his eyes or mouth.

Josef put himself in the hot spot again for this Guinness World Records photoshoot in Styria, Austria, on 17 Sep 2015, setting himself on fire five times, just so we could get the best shot! You'll find another of Josef's fiery new records on p.132.

First modern vaccination
To demonstrate the power of inoculation, Dr Edward Jenner (UK) deliberately infects a child with cowpox; a few weeks later, he injects him with smallpox, but the child proves immune to this otherwise deadly disease.

1796

Fastest speed in a monster truck

Driving the Ram Truck-sponsored *Raminator,* Mark Hall (USA) achieved a speed of 159.49 km/h (99.1 mph) at the Circuit of the Americas in Austin, Texas, USA, on 15 Dec 2014.

Fastest motorcycle wheelie

On 18 Apr 1999, Sweden's Patrik Fürstenhoff reached 191.30 mph (307.86 km/h) on the back wheel of a Honda Super Blackbird 1100 cc Turbo. The record run took place at Bruntingthorpe Proving Ground in Leicestershire, UK.

Longest time to restrain a car

On 26 Jul 2015, Gerald Gschiel (AUT) held back a Chevrolet Corvette Z06 for a duration of 22.33 sec on the set of *ZDF Fernsehgarten* in Mainz, Germany.

Most times to roll a car by hand in 5 minutes

Jean Caron (CAN) rolled a car 13 times in 5 min on the set of CCTV's *Guinness World Records Special* in Jiangyin, Jiangsu Province, China, on 11 Jan 2015.

Highest air on a motorcycle (quarterpipe)

Ronnie Renner (USA) pulled off a 35-ft 4-in (10.77-m) air on a motorcycle from a quarterpipe ramp during the Red Bull High Rise in Grant Park at Butler Field in Chicago, Illinois, USA, on 25 Jul 2009.

Longest wheelie on a UTV

Canada's Roger LeBlanc maintained a wheelie in a Utility Terrain Vehicle (UTV) for a distance of 3,741 ft 1.2 in (1.14 km) at Greater Moncton International Airport in New Brunswick, Canada, on 23 Aug 2014. Roger's record-breaking wheelie, partially uphill, was achieved in a Honda 700 Pioneer UTV, and he took along four fearless passengers for the ride: Jeff Gallant, Gilles Dupuis, Paul Arsenault and Martin Phinney.

Longest ramp jump in a monster truck

On 1 Sep 2013, Joe Sylvester (USA) propelled his 10,000-lb (4,536-kg) truck *Bad Habit* across 237 ft 7 in (72.42 m) at the Cornfield 500 in Columbus, Pennsylvania, USA. He had to take off at 85 mph (136.7 km/h) to cover the distance. Sylvester had held this record before, but it was broken in 2012 by Dan Runte (USA). So what drove him to reclaim his record? "The same thing that motivates me every day to push my limits. The rush of adrenaline."

Heaviest road vehicle pulled by teeth

Igor Zaripov (RUS) pulled a 13,713.6-kg (30,233-lb) bus with his teeth for 5 m (16 ft 5 in) on the set of CCTV's *Guinness World Records Special* in Jiangyin, Jiangsu Province, China, on 7 Jan 2015.

Fastest time to drive a car 1 mile on two wheels

Terry Grant (UK) drove 1 mi (1.6 km) in 2 min 55 sec on side wheels at the Goodwood Festival of Speed in West Sussex, UK, on 3 Jul 2011.

DID YOU KNOW?

On landing, *Bad Habit* began to nose forward, nearly tipping over. That would have brought back unwelcome memories. In 2010, while Sylvester was practising for his first ramp-jump record in *Bad Habit*, its front end caught on landing. The truck cartwheeled and crashed.

DATELINE

1800

Longest human horn
An 82-year-old French woman known as Madame Dimanche has an operation to remove a horn (technically a keratinous skin tumour) that has been growing out of her forehead for six years. It is 24.9 cm (9.8 in) long.

130 Don't Try This At Home...

FAST FACTS

Monster truck tyres are some 5 ft 3 in–5 ft 6 in (1.6–1.67 m) tall – about the height of the average woman • Evel Knievel (USA) pioneered motorcycle distance jumping – and suffered the **most bones broken in a lifetime**: 433

LONGEST...

Reverse ramp jump in a car
On 13 Feb 2014, Rob Dyrdek (USA) performed an 89-ft 3.25-in (27.2-m) reverse ramp jump for *Rob Dyrdek's Fantasy Factory* (MTV) at Six Flags Magic Mountain in Valencia, California, USA.

Wheelie in a car
On 12 Aug 2012, "Nitro" Mike Kunz (CAN) maintained a wheelie in a car for 763.4 m (2,504 ft 7 in) at the Temiskaming Drag'N'Fly Summer Classic in Earlton, Ontario, Canada.

Distance riding backwards on a motorcycle
India's Dipayan Choudhury rode a motorcycle in reverse for 202 km (125.52 mi) in Jabalpur, India, on 7 Oct 2014.

Fastest motorcycle wheelie on ice

Sweden's Robert Gull executed a wheelie at 206.09 km/h (128.06 mph) in Årsunda, Sweden, on 28 Feb 2015. He performed the stunt on a 2011 BMW S1000RR motorcycle – a standard model, apart from the addition of studded tyres.

Longest ramp jump in a truck cab

On 24 Jul 2015, Gregg Godfrey (USA) made a 166-ft (50.6-m) ramp jump in a truck cab at the Evel Knievel Days event in Butte, Montana, USA. In doing so, Godfrey went three times farther than the previous record of 50 ft 6 in (15.39 m), which he had set at Godfrey Trucking/Rocky Mountain Raceway in Salt Lake City, Utah, USA, on 17 Nov 2008.

LARGEST LOOP-THE-LOOP IN A CAR

Stunt driver Terry Grant and Jaguar (both UK) achieved a loop-the-loop measuring 19.08 m (62 ft 7.1 in) in diameter at the Niederrad Racecourse in Frankfurt, Germany, on 14 Sep 2015. The measurement was calculated from the flat of the track to the apex of the loop. Grant was driving a Jaguar F-PACE, and the record was achieved as part of the car's debut appearance in front of the world's motoring press.

DID YOU KNOW?

This stunt was months in the planning. At the apex of the loop-the-loop, the car's velocity fell to just 15 mph (24.1 km/h). The organizers used a precise mathematical formula to ensure the car didn't drop off at this point. They calculated that Grant must approach the loop at 53 mph (85.3 km/h) to maintain the car's grip.

First passenger car
On 24 Dec, inventor and mining engineer Richard Trevithick (UK) takes passengers for a ride through Camborne in Cornwall, UK, in the *Puffing Devil*, a steam-powered automobile.

1801

DATELINE

DON'T TRY THIS AT HOME...
FIRE

Longest quad bike ride through a tunnel of fire
On the set of *Lo Show dei Record* in Rome, Italy, Dan Serblin (ITA) rode through the flames for 25 m (82 ft) on 12 Apr 2012.

Farthest distance as a human arrow (full-body burn)
Fired from a giant crossbow, Brian Miser (USA) made a dazzling trajectory of 31.87 m (104 ft 7 in) for CCTV's *Guinness World Records Special* and *Lo Show dei Record* in Peru, Indiana, USA, on 14 Jun 2014.

Most people performing full-body burns
On 19 Oct 2013, a total of 21 people were set alight at the same time in Cleveland, Ohio, USA. Organized by stuntman Ted Batchelor and Hotcards.com (both USA), the event generated money for charities including the Cleveland Foodbank.

Longest motorcycle ride through a tunnel of fire
On 5 Sep 2014, South African daredevils Enrico Schoeman and André de Kock (pillion) rode a motorcycle with sidecar 395 ft (120.4 m) through a flaming tunnel in Parys, South Africa. It was difficult for Enrico to see properly but, thanks to his motorcycling experience, he and André emerged virtually unscathed.

Most fire wicks attached to the body simultaneously
Pyrophile Snake Fervor, aka Heidi Bradshaw (UK), became incandescent by attaching 31 flaming wicks to her body on 13 Dec 2013 in London, UK. All of the wicks had to burn at the same time – and continuously for 10 sec – and none could be held. Those on her hands were kept in place by special attachments fitted to her gloves.

LONGEST DISTANCE PULLED BY A HORSE (FULL-BODY BURN)
On 27 Jun 2015, while performing a full-body burn, professional stuntman Josef Tödtling (AUT) was pulled 500 m (1,640 ft) by a horse. Josef protected himself with several layers of clothing and cooling gel, as well as metal shin and elbow pads. The latter were a vital piece of equipment, as the specially trained stunt horse kept up a brisk canter for the whole attempt, dragging Josef along on his front at about 35 km/h (21 mph). The fearless daredevil was accompanied on his bumpy journey – in Teichalm-Fladnitz, Styria, Austria – by a quad-bike rider, who replenished the flames with lamp oil as needed.

Having made the full 500-m, pre-measured distance, Josef promptly outstripped it with another record: a 582-m (1,909-ft) haul, tied this time to the back of the quad bike – the **longest distance pulled by a vehicle (full-body burn)**!

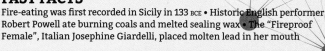

FAST FACTS

Fire-eating was first recorded in Sicily in 133 BCE • Historic English performer Robert Powell ate burning coals and melted sealing wax • The "Fireproof Female", Italian Josephine Giardelli, placed molten lead in her mouth

DID YOU KNOW?

Jamie grew up in Hawaii, USA, and began surfing at a young age. The idea of riding a wave while on fire came from an Instagram message he received. Pulling off such a challenge was a major feat, even though he spent a year preparing with a team led by Los Angeles stuntman Riley Harper.

First person to surf a wave while on fire

On 22 Jul 2015, professional surfer Jamie O'Brien (USA) rode one of the world's biggest waves – at Teahupo'o, in Tahiti, French Polynesia – having been set alight! He was engulfed in fire inside the "barrel" (hollow) of the wave, later calling it "the biggest adrenaline rush of my life".

Highest shallow dive into fire

On 21 Jun 2014, Professor Splash, aka Darren Taylor (USA), dropped 26 ft 3 in (8 m) into 10 in (25.4 cm) of flaming water on NBC's *Show Stopping Sunday Special* in Los Angeles, California, USA. The surface of the pool was ignited just before he jumped.

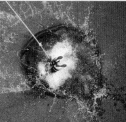

Highest bungee jump into water while on fire

Yoni Roch (FRA), his body ablaze, plunged 65.09 m (213 ft 6.6 in) from the Viaduc de la Souleuvre in Normandy, France, on 14 Sep 2012. The flames were extinguished when Yoni landed in the river below. The railway bridge, built by Gustave Eiffel, became a platform for bungee jumping in 1990.

Most fire clubs juggled while sword-swallowing

On 14 Sep 2012, at Wonderground in London, UK, The Great Gordo Gamsby (AUS) juggled three fire clubs for 10 sec while swallowing a sword at the same time.

On the same day, Pippa "The Ripper" Coram (AUS) matched this number for the **most fire hoops spun while in the splits position**.

Most flames blown in one minute (fire-breathing)

Zhu Jiangao (CHN) blew 189 flames on the set of CCTV's *Guinness World Records Special* in Jiangyin, China, on 9 Jan 2015.

Longest duration fire-torch teething

On 30 Aug 2015, Hector Alexander "Spitfire" Gonzalez (USA) spent 3 min 38.39 sec "teething" – holding the lit end of a torch in his teeth – in Newark, New Jersey, USA.

Most fire torches…

• **Extinguished in one minute:** On 7 Sep 2014, fire performer Bret Pasek (USA) put out 99 flaming torches with his mouth as they were "fed" to him by assistants in Shakopee, Minnesota, USA.

• **Lit and extinguished in 30 seconds** and **one minute:** Snake Fervor (see opposite page) lit and snuffed out 59 torches in her mouth in 30 sec at Electrowerkz in London, UK, on 4 Jul 2014. The following year, on 29 Sep, she upped her pace and set a second record, extinguishing 126 torches in 60 sec.

Deadliest volcanic eruption
On 5 Apr, the Tambora volcano on Sumbawa island in the Dutch East Indies (later Indonesia) begins to erupt for several days. An estimated 71,000 people will die – some from the after-effects, which include severe climatic changes.

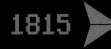

1815 ▸ DATELINE

DON'T TRY THIS AT HOME...
WATER

Largest human waterskiing pyramid formation

On 14 Sep 2013, Big Pull 2013 (USA) assembled 60 people into a mass water-borne human pyramid on Lake Wazeecha in Grand Rapids, Wisconsin, USA. Five different show ski teams (Aqua Ducks, Backwater Gamblers, Badgerland, Beaverland Must-Skis and Water Bugs) from Wisconsin and Illinois made up the multi-pyramid formation.

Most waterskiers towed behind a single boat
A total of 145 waterskiers from the Horsehead Water Ski Club (AUS) rode behind one boat for more than 1 nautical mi (1.1 mi; 1.8 km) in Strahan, Tasmania, Australia, on 27 Jan 2012.

Highest bungee jump dive into water
On 8 Jun 2015, Raymond Woodcock (UK) performed a bungee jump of 141.7 m (464 ft 11 in) – taller than the Great Pyramid of Giza – fully submerging himself into water, in Chepstow, UK.

Highest waterfall diving
Di Huanran (CHN) dived 12.1 m (39 ft 11 in) off the Diaoshuilou Waterfall at Jingpo Lake in Mudanjiang City, China, for *Zheng Da Zong Yi – Guinness World Records Special* on 5 Oct 2008.

Largest vessel to tow a waterskier

Galileo TV reporter Jan Schwiderek (DEU) successfully water-skied behind the *AIDAbella* for 6 min 25 sec, at a speed of 14 knots (26 km/h; 16 mph), off Alicante in Spain on 1 Oct 2010. The vessel has a 69,203 gross tonnage and was commanded by Captain Josef Husmann (DEU). The *AIDAbella* is 252 m (826 ft) long overall, with a breadth of 32.2 m (105 ft). It has 13 full decks and 1,025 passenger cabins.

DEEPEST UNDERWATER CYCLING
When it comes to submarine cycling, no one is as deeply committed as Vittorio Innocente (ITA, pictured). On 21 Jul 2008, he rode his bicycle at a depth of 66.5 m (218 ft 2 in) in Santa Margherita Ligure in Liguria, Italy.

The **farthest distance cycled underwater** is 6.7 km (4.1 mi), by Jens Stötzner (DEU) at Bibert Bad Zirndorf in Zirndorf, Germany, on 8 Sep 2013.

FASTEST SPEED...

Kite surfing (male)
Alexandre Caizergues (FRA) reached a speed of 56.6 knots (104.8 km/h; 65.1 mph) kite surfing in Port St Louis, France, on 11 Nov 2013.

The **fastest speed kite surfing by a woman** is 50.4 knots (93.3 km/h; 58 mph). The feat was achieved by France's Charlotte Consorti at the Lüderitz Speed Challenge held in Lüderitz, Namibia, on 28 Oct 2010.

DID YOU KNOW?
At the start of his submarine record, Vittorio Innocente was lowered into the water by scuba divers. He got on to his bike at a depth of 28 m (92 ft) and set off down an underwater slope until he reached his record-breaking depth. The ride took him about 9 min.

DATELINE

1826
Oldest zoo
Founded by British statesman Stamford Raffles, the Zoological Society of London is the earliest scientific zoo. Two years later, its first animal houses are erected at Regent's Park, marking the birth of London Zoo.

134 **Don't Try This At Home...**

FAST FACTS

"Scuba" is an acronym, standing for Self-Contained Underwater Breathing Apparatus • American Ralph Samuelson invented waterskiing in 1922; his initial efforts at fashioning skis included using wooden staves from barrels

Sailing (male)

On 24 Nov 2012, Paul Larsen (AUS) attained a speed of 65.4 knots (121.2 km/h; 75.3 mph) by sail over a timed 500-m (1,640-ft) run in Walvis Bay, Namibia. He rode a Vestas Sailrocket 2.

The **fastest speed under sail on water by any craft (female)** over a 500-m timed run was set by windsurfer Karin Jaggi (CHE). She sped to 46.3 knots (85.7 km/h; 53.2 mph) on board her customized Patrik speed board in Lüderitz, Namibia, on 2 Nov 2015.

LONGEST...

Open saltwater scuba dive (cold water)

Daniel Sammut (MLT) remained submerged for 13 hr 42 min in St Paul's Bay, Malta, on 19 Mar 2015.

Swim under ice with breath held (no fins, no diving suit)

Stig Åvall Severinsen (DNK) swam 250 ft (76 m) beneath the ice at Qordlortoq Lake (Lake 40) on Ammassalik Island, East Greenland, on 17 Apr 2013.

Underwater walk by an individual in 24 hours

On 17–18 Nov 2011, Joey Kelly (DEU) walked 16.3 km (10.1 mi)

Deepest dive under ice with breath held (female)

Wearing a diving suit and fins, but without breathing apparatus, Aurore Asso (FRA) dived to 57.9 m (189 ft 11 in) at Ikerasak in Uummannaq Bay, Greenland, on 3 May 2015. She descended on a rope to a tag that she retrieved to prove she had reached the intended depth. Her attempt was for "One Breath for Arctica", which raises awareness for the protection of the Arctic environment.

underwater on the set of *RTL-Spendenmarathon* at MMC studios in Hürth, Germany. His walk raised €115,000 (£99,498; $155,716) for a charity to support children in need.

Underwater walk with one breath

On 19 Apr 2015, Turkey's Sertan Aydın took a 79.9-m (262-ft 3-in) submarine stroll at Anafartalar Olympic Pool in Çanakkale, Turkey.

Stand-up surfing ride on a river bore

Steve King (UK) surfed the Severn bore on the River Severn in Gloucestershire, UK, for 12.2 km (7.6 mi) on 30 Mar 2006.

Highest shallow dive

Professor Splash, aka Darren Taylor (USA), jumped from 11.56 m (37 ft 11 in) into a paddling pool with just 30 cm (12 in) of water on 9 Sep 2014. The daring drop took place on the set of *CCTV – Guinness World Records Special* in Xiamen, Fujian, China. Like all the records on these pages, this one is strictly for professionals: Professor Splash is an experienced stuntman.

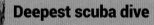

Deepest scuba dive

Ahmed Gabr (EGY, inset and right) dived to a depth of 332.35 m (1,090 ft 4.5 in) in the Red Sea, off the coast of Dahab in Egypt, on 18 Sep 2014. That's about the same as the height of the Chrysler Building in New York City, USA.

Verna van Schaik (ZAF) dived 221 m (725 ft) into the Boesmansgat cave in South Africa's Northern Cape province on 25 Oct 2004 – the **deepest scuba dive (female)**. Her dive lasted 5 hr 34 min, but only 12 min of that was spent descending. To avoid decompression sickness (aka "the bends"), she made a super-slow ascent that took 5 hr 15 min to complete.

First comic
Swiss cartoonist Rodolphe Töpffer creates the 30-page *Histoire de M. Vieux Bois* ("The Adventures of Mister Wooden Head"), although it is not published for another decade.

1827

DATELINE

guinnessworldrecords.com 135

Most apples held in the mouth and cut in half by chainsaw

Chainsaw-wielding Johnny Strange cut 12 apples in half – each held in the mouth of Daniella D'Ville, aka Danielle Martin (both UK) – in 1 min at the Tattoo Jam at Doncaster Racecourse in South Yorkshire, UK, on 12 Oct 2013. At the same event, Johnny set a new record (since broken) for the **most apples held in one's own mouth and cut by chainsaw in one minute**: eight.

Most beer bottles opened with the feet in one minute

Contortionist Zlata, aka Julia Günthel (DEU), removed the caps from eight beer bottles with her feet in 1 min on the set of *Rekorlar Dünyası* in Istanbul, Turkey, on 5 Jun 2013. That beat her own record of seven, set two years before. Zlata performed the feat in the contortionist elbow-stand position, seen right.

Farthest distance to throw and catch a running chainsaw

The Space Cowboy, aka Chayne Hultgren, hurled a running chainsaw 4 m (13 ft 1 in) to catcher The Great Gordo Gamsby (both AUS) at London Wonderground, UK, on 14 Sep 2012.

Fastest underwater escape from a straitjacket

Lucas Wilson (CAN) freed himself from a straitjacket underwater in 22.86 sec on the set of *Lo Show dei Record* in Milan, Italy, on 7 Jul 2014.

Heaviest weight lifted by both eye sockets

Manjit Singh (UK) raised a weight of 24 kg (52 lb 14.5 oz) using his eye sockets at Cossington Sports Hall in Leicester, UK, on 15 Nov 2012.

Highest blindfolded tightrope walk

Nik Wallenda (USA) crossed a tightrope while blindfolded 170.04 m (557 ft 10 in) above the ground in Chicago, Illinois, USA, on 2 Nov 2014.

Most mousetraps released on the tongue in one minute

Sweet Pepper Klopek (CAN) set off 58 mousetraps on his tongue in 60 sec in St John, New Brunswick, Canada, on 16 Jul 2015. That's five more than the previous record, set by Casey Severn (USA) in 2014.

The **highest tightrope crossing on a motorcycle** took place at a height of 130 m (426 ft 6 in) on a tightrope 666.1 m (2,185 ft 4.3 in) long. The feat was achieved by Mustafa Danger (MAR) in Benidorm, Spain, on 16 Oct 2010.

Longest duration balancing a chainsaw on the chin

Serial GWR record-breaker Ashrita Furman (USA) kept a chainsaw balanced on his chin for 1 min 42.47 sec in New York City, USA, on 15 Sep 2013. The chainsaw he used weighed 4.75 kg (10 lb 7 oz).

DID YOU KNOW?

After Zlata was profiled on a Discovery Channel show in 2010, a doctor performed an MRI scan to investigate her superlative flexibility. The ligaments of most of us harden over time, but the scan revealed that Zlata's ligaments have remained as soft and supple as those of a baby.

DATELINE 1838
First photograph of a human
Louis Daguerre (FRA) takes a test photo of a street scene showing a man having his shoes shined. The subject sits still for long enough to be visible in the long-exposure shot.

136 Don't Try This At Home...

Most spears caught underwater in one minute
On 13 Nov 2014, in a swimming pool in Armidale, Australia, Anthony Kelly (AUS) caught 10 bolts fired from a fisherman's spear gun at a range of just 2 m (6 ft 6 in). The event took place in celebration of Guinness World Records Day 2014.

Most swords swallowed on a unicycle

The Space Cowboy (see opposite page) swallowed three swords while atop a unicycle at Wonderground in London, UK, on 14 Sep 2012. Each sword measured 42 cm (1 ft 4.5 in) long, 3 mm (0.1 in) thick and 2 cm (0.78 in) wide. The extra-tall unicycle he used was 2.49 m (8 ft 2 in) high.

MOST BACKFLIPS PERFORMED WHILE SWALLOWING A SWORD IN ONE MINUTE

On 2 Jul 2014, in Milan, Italy, Aerial Manx, aka James Loughron (AUS), swallowed a 41-cm-long (1-ft 4-in) sword before carrying out an eye-watering 20 backflips against the clock. The sword prevented Aerial from breathing, so he had to hold his breath during the feat. He took two breaks during the one-minute attempt, removing the sword and then swallowing it again each time before continuing.

Most bowling balls caught on the forehead

Entertainer Matt Baker (USA) has a head for weights. He caught six bowling balls on his forehead in 30 sec in Coeur d'Alene, Idaho, USA, on 31 Jan 2014. Matt attempted the record before an audience of 300 people at the Kroc Center Theater.

Heaviest weight pulled by pierced ears

Britain's Johnny Strange tugged a Cessna 172P aircraft weighing 677.8 kg (1,494 lb 4 oz) over a distance of 6.22 m (20 ft 4 in) on 12 May 2014. Johnny pulled off the lobe-stretching challenge at North Weald Airfield in North Weald, Essex, UK.

First selfie
Robert Cornelius (USA) becomes the first person to take a self-portrait. He uses the daguerreotype process – an early photographic technique employing mercury vapour and an iodine-sensitized silvered plate.

1839 ➤ DATELINE

DID YOU KNOW?
In 2013, *Minecraft* was put on the curriculum of the Viktor Rydberg school in Stockholm, Sweden, with a view to boosting young teens' creativity. "They learn about city planning, environmental issues, getting things done and even how to plan for the future," explained teacher Monica Ekman.

DATELINE

1844 **Oldest subway tunnel**
The 767-m (2,517-ft) Atlantic Avenue Tunnel is completed. The tunnel runs beneath Brooklyn, New York, USA, and carries the trains of the Long Island Rail Road until its closure in 1861. It will lie undisturbed and forgotten until 1981.

CONTENTS

Most views for a *Minecraft* video channel

As of 24 Mar 2016, the YouTube channel "TheDiamondMinecart", hosted by DanTDM, aka Daniel Middleton (UK), had accumulated a total of 6,284,997,560 views from 1,811 videos since its launch on 14 Jul 2012. Astonishingly, Dan's videos register an estimated 70 million hits every month. He receives fan mail from around the world, too. "I like to think my niche is adding in stories, editing tricks [...] to enhance the game's creativity," he says.

In order for a video channel to be considered "dedicated", 85–90% of its content should relate to a specific videogame franchise.

Longest time to crack a code
British mathematician and computing pioneer Charles Babbage cracks the Vigenère cipher, a polyalphabetic encryption system that had been thought unbreakable since its invention in 1553.

1854 ➤

DATELINE

LEGO-OLOGY

The name LEGO® combines the Danish words "leg" and "godt", meaning "play well". The company began producing "Automatic Binding Bricks" back in 1949. And the design was built to last: you can open a brand-new LEGO box today and join any of the standard bricks with any LEGO brick made since 1958 (the picture to the right shows box set 700/5 from that year). Today, LEGO is found in almost every country on Earth – and even in outer space...

BUILDING A LEGEND, BRICK BY BRICK

All LEGO bricks start out as granules of plastic (below) – acrylonitrile butadiene styrene (ABS), to be precise. On arrival at a manufacturing plant, they are dispersed into silos, then transported via tubes to injection moulding machines. Here, they are subjected to temperatures up to 310°C (590°F) and pressures of 25–150 tonnes (27–165 US tons), which squeeze them into moulds. Seconds later, the bricks pop on to a conveyor belt, then into a bin. Next, robots take the bricks to an assembly room, where machines stamp them and put together multi-part toys, such as Minifigures.

PLENTY OF LEGO BRICKS TO GO ROUND...

According to LEGO Education, if you divided the total number of LEGO bricks among the planet's population, each person would have an average of 86 bricks. That's quite a claim, but understandable when you consider that in 2012, a total of 45.7 billion LEGO bricks were produced at a rate of 5.2 million LEGO bricks per hour! And they sell quickly, too: for most of the year, around seven LEGO sets are sold every second. But at Christmas time, that rate rockets to 28 sets per second!

LARGEST TYRE MANUFACTURER

Think of all the brands of tyre you know. Who would make the most tyres on an annual basis? Goodyear? Firestone? Pirelli? The answer is... the LEGO Group! In 2015 alone, the company produced in excess of 675 million tyres for its construction kits, easily beating all other manufacturers. What's more, the rubber compound used for these toy tyres wouldn't be out of place on a real car.

FARTHEST DISTANCE TRAVELLED BY A LEGO MINIFIGURE

Three specially made LEGO Minifigures have made the arduous trek to the planet Jupiter on board NASA's *Juno* space probe. They launched on 5 Aug 2011, travelling a total of 2.8 billion km (1.74 billion mi) from Earth. The figures take the form of the Roman god Jupiter, his wife Juno and the 17th-century Italian scientist Galileo (pictured right), who discovered Jupiter's four largest moons. (See also p.148.)

A GLOBAL PHENOMENON

On 28 Jan 1958, the LEGO Group patented the now-famous studded bricks with tubes inside. They have proved enduringly popular. Around 45 billion bricks are sold each year, on average. Laid end-to-end, they would stretch around the world an astonishing 18 times.

Stacked on top of each other, the same number of bricks would form a column that could extend from the surface of Earth to more than 30,000 mi (48,280 km) beyond the orbit of the Moon.

It's estimated that the children of the world spend 5 billion hr a year playing with LEGO bricks. If all these hours were arranged consecutively across time, it would work out at around 571,000 years in total – nearly three times the duration that modern human beings have lived on Earth.

THINK OF A NUMBER

A big part of the attraction of this construction toy is the way that it can be combined in as many ways as our imagination will allow. Bearing this in mind, how many possible combinations do you think you can make with just six two-by-four (eight-stud) LEGO bricks? The answer is below.

A: There are 915,103,765 possible combinations with six two-by-four LEGO bricks!

BENEATH THE SURFACE

Artist Jason Freeny (USA) has brought his own unique twist to conventional toys by suggesting what their interiors might look like. It was only a question of time before he applied his cutaway skills to the LEGO universe. Jason took three special 18-in (45.7-cm) LEGO figures, then created anatomical interiors from them out of sculpted foam, which he then painted. But these works are purely for entertainment, and Jason never pretends otherwise. "My anatomies are hypothetical," he told streetanatomy.com. "This is strictly art."

DID YOU KNOW?

Among his other novelty items, Jason has also produced cutaways of Barbie dolls and gingerbread men. He has also created similar anatomical dogs, and balloon and rubber ducks — both of which are available as a kit that you assemble yourself.

LARGEST LIFE-SIZE HOUSE MADE FROM LEGO BRICKS

Standing 4.69 m (15 ft 4 in) high, 9.39 m (30 ft 9 in) long and 5.75 m (18 ft 10 in) wide, and consisting of two floors with four rooms altogether, this life-size LEGO brick dwelling was built in Dorking, UK, on 17 Sep 2009. It was completed by 1,200 volunteers together with James May (UK) for *James May's Toy Stories* (BBC, UK). In all, 2.4 million LEGO bricks were used in the construction, which had an internal wooden support structure. By way of comparison, you would need approximately 9,000 standard-size building bricks to construct a conventional three-bedroomed house.

TOP 5 LARGEST LEGO SETS

The days of simple LEGO buildings and vehicles are long gone. Today, the company produces an impressive range of complex kits. In terms of pieces, the **largest LEGO set** is the Taj Mahal, which includes 5,922 separate parts. Next up is the 5,195-piece *Millennium Falcon*, followed by the 2016-released Ghostbusters Firehouse Headquarters, with 4,634 bricks. London's Tower Bridge is fourth with 4,287 parts. The fifth largest set is a second *Star Wars* entry: the *Death Star* (above) with 3,803 pieces.

LARGEST POPULATION GROUP ON EARTH

There are more than 4 billion LEGO Minifigures on the planet — and the number is growing all the time (725 million-plus were produced in 2015 alone). If they were real humans, they would form the largest nation on Earth. The figurines are hugely varied, from solid-gold collectables to customisable characters such as GWR adjudicators (see below). If you lined up all the LEGO Minifigures ever produced, side by side, they would stretch more than 2.5 times around the Equator!

The dawn of LEGO Minifigures

The introduction of LEGO Minifigures in 1978 — such as the red classic spaceman below — rejuvenated the LEGO universe. The full range of characters now takes in everyone from nurse, fireman and policeman to Santa Claus, Harry Potter and even film director Steven Spielberg! Initially, all characters had smiling or neutral faces, but in 1989 pirate LEGO Minifigures were among the first to sport scowls and grumpy expressions.

"Mr Gold"

Released in 2013, series 10 of LEGO Minifigures featured a golden figure with top hat, monocle and jewel-topped cane. Limited to a run of just 5,000, "Mr Gold" quickly became a collectors' item. Soon these figurines were being re-sold for up to $1,100 (£660) each, making them worth almost three times their weight in real gold.

Wheelchair user

Although buildable wheelchairs have previously been released, the LEGO Group revealed its first wheelchair moulded to Minifigure scale in Jan 2016. The beanie-wearing figure pleased disability campaigners, who have argued that children with disabilities are not fairly represented in the toy industry.

Business-card Minifigures

A few LEGO Group employees — such as Casey Blossom (right) — use Minifigures instead of business cards. In addition to the usual name, job title and contact information, the figurines are modelled to resemble the person they represent.

Casey Blossom

Largest collection of model cars

Rally-driving enthusiast Nabil "Billy" Karam (LBN) started collecting model cars in 1985, when he acquired a toy Porsche 911. His collection has since grown considerably; when counted in his purpose-built museum in Zouk, Lebanon, on 17 Nov 2011 for Guinness World Records Day, it contained 27,777 unique scaled-down cars.

Billy also holds another model-related world record – find out more on p.149.

Fastest time to solve a Rubik's Cube

On 21 Nov 2015, Lucas Etter (USA), aged 14 years old, became the first person to breach the 5-sec barrier, solving a 3x3 cube in an extraordinary 4.9 sec at the River Hill Fall 2015 at River Hill High School in Clarksville, Maryland, USA. This also beat the record of 5.09 sec set that same day by Keaton Ellis (USA).

Just over a month earlier, on 15 Oct 2015, a robot built by Zackary Gromko (USA) achieved the **fastest time to solve a Rubik's Cube by a robot** – 2.39 sec – at Saint Stephen's Episcopal School in Bradenton, Florida, USA.

Meanwhile, Feliks Zemdegs (AUS) created a new personal best time of 6.88 sec for the **fastest time to solve a Rubik's Cube one-handed**, on 10 May 2015 in Canberra, Australia. And on 4 Oct 2015, at the China Championship in Guangzhou, Kaijun Lin (CHN) achieved the **fastest time to solve a Rubik's Cube blindfolded**: 21.05 sec.

Fastest battery-powered, remote-controlled model car

The aptly named *Radio Controlled Bullet*, built by Nic Case (USA, right), achieved a speed of 325.12 km/h (202.02 mph) in St George, Utah, USA, on 25 Oct 2014 at the Radio Operated Scale Speed Association (ROSSA) World Championships.

Largest loop-the-loop by a remote-controlled (RC) model vehicle

A Venom VMX-450 RC Dirt Bike controlled by Jason Bradbury (UK) looped a loop 3.18 m (10 ft 5 in) high. The record was set on Channel 5's *The Gadget Show* in Birmingham, West Midlands, UK, on 15 Jun 2013.

Fastest RC jet-powered model aircraft

On 14 Sep 2013, a turbine-driven aeroplane built by Niels Herbrich (DEU) flew at 706.97 km/h (439.29 mph) at WLP Ballenstedt airfield in Saxony-Anhalt, Germany. To ensure accurate results, Niels had to guide the plane down a 200-m-long (656-ft), 20-m-wide (65-ft 7-in) "measurement corridor" via his remote-control device.

DID YOU KNOW?
Regular-size *Skylanders* figures are the **biggest-selling interactive gaming toys**, shifting more than 240 million units by Jan 2016. They connect to the videogame series of the same name using near-field communication (NFC), bringing the toys to life inside the game.

Largest Skylander

As of Jul 2013, the largest Skylander is a "life-sized" Tree Rex that tours the world and appears at exhibitions and trade fairs. Standing a tree-mendous 3.15 m (10 ft 4 in) tall, the statue was carved from polystyrene and coated with glass fibre by UK-based model company Sculpture Studios (pictured right is founder Aden Hynes with Tree Rex and another *Skylanders* character, Jet-Vac). Tree Rex is an exact scale duplicate of the *Skylanders Giants* figure, right down to eyes that light up.

1859 ⟩ **First tightrope walk over Niagara Falls**
Jean-François Gravelet (FRA), aka Charles Blondin, crosses the famous waterfalls between the USA and Canada on a 335-m-long (1,100-ft) rope.

FAST FACTS

The Ancient Egyptian board game Senet was depicted on the tomb of Hesy in around 2686 BCE • Engineer Richard T James invented the Slinky by accident while testing springs for hanging up instruments at sea

Largest rocking horse

A three-storey-tall rocking horse was built by Gao Ming (CHN) and unveiled on 7 Jul 2014 in Linyi, China. Created for the Children's Folklore & Folkgame Festival, it stands 8.20 m (26 ft 10 in) tall and 12.72 m (41 ft 9 in) long.

Largest collection of Slinkys

On 25 Oct 2014, Susan Suazo of Los Lunas in New Mexico, USA, was declared the proud owner of 1,054 different Slinkys – a collection so large that it has its own insurance policy.

Largest Monopoly board
On 6 September 2015, Hasbro created a 405.6-m² (4,365.9-sq-ft) Monopoly board – almost twice the size of a tennis court – to celebrate the 650th anniversary of the founding of Warsaw, Poland.

Six times larger than the mammoth Monopoly board was the **largest Twister game**, which was pieced together from 1,200 regular boards by country star Thomas Rhett and Big Machine Label Group (USA) in Arlington, Texas, USA, on 23 Sep 2015. This produced an overall playable surface area of 2,521 m² (27,135 sq ft).

Largest toy-pistol fight
A volley of suction darts and foam bullets secured a world record for 577 Drake University students wielding Nerf blasters in Des Moines, Iowa, USA. The "Dogtown After Hours" campus event saw the Red and Blue teams shoot it out on 28 Mar 2015. The final result? It was a draw.

Largest model vehicle brand

The hottest name in toy cars is currently Hot Wheels (USA), with a revenue in 2014 of $835,700,000 (£537,974,000). This helps to make Mattel (USA), the owner of Hot Wheels, the **largest model vehicle company**, with a 2014 revenue of $1,477,300,000 (£950,998,000).

Longest marathon playing foosball (doubles)
Between 29 Aug and 1 Sep 2012, Alexander Kuen, Manuel Larcher, Bernd Neururer and Dietmar Neururer (all AUT) played table football for 61 hr 17 min in Innsbruck, Austria. The feat made them record holders for the third time.

LONGEST FOOSBALL TABLE

On 25 Sep 2015, Marco Berry Onlus (ITA) occupied the Via Roma, the main street in Turin, Italy, with a table football (or foosball) game played on a 121.4-m-long (398-ft 3.5-in) table – in fact, a series of linked tables. The fast and furious action saw a total of 2,332 plastic players or *foos men* in red and blue jerseys pass, kick and shoot 101 balls – all operated by 424 pairs of hands. The event raised money for building and maintaining the Mohamed Aden Sheikh Children's Teaching Hospital in Hargeisa, Somaliland. Afterwards, the tables were divided up and given out to the participating teams to keep.

First man-made plastic
Parkesine, a plastic developed by Alexander Parkes (UK) and derived from plant cellulose, is publicly unveiled at the Great International Exhibition in London.

1862

DATELINE

CHESS

Youngest chess grandmaster (female)

Hou Yifan (CHN, b. 27 Feb 1994) qualified as a grandmaster on 29 Aug 2008, at the age of 14 years 184 days.

To date, the **youngest chess grandmaster** of all is Sergey Karjakin (UKR, b. 12 Jan 1990), who achieved the status on 12 Aug 2002 at the age of 12 years 212 days.

Youngest World Chess Champion

Hou Yifan (CHN, above) was 16 years 300 days old when she beat her compatriot Ruan Lufei to become world champion on 24 Dec 2010.

The Russian (formerly Soviet) grandmaster Garry Kasparov (b. Garik Kimovich Weinstein, 13 Apr 1963) is the **youngest World Chess Champion (male)**. He was aged 22 years 210 days when he gained the title in a match against his compatriot Anatoly Karpov on 9 Nov 1985.

First computer to beat a World Chess Champion under regular time controls

IBM chess-playing computer Deep Blue defeated World Chess Champion Garry Kasparov in a formal match on 11 May 1997. Deep Blue was capable of assessing 200 million board positions per sec. At the time, this was the fastest evaluation of board positions by a chess computer.

Largest networked chess computer

On 30 Jan 2004, Danish grandmaster Peter Heine Nielsen played ChessBrain: 2,070 computers operating together across 56 countries. The game, professionally refereed in Copenhagen, Denmark, ended in a draw after 34 moves.

Longest chess marathon

Magne Sagafos and Joachim Berg-Jensen (both NOR) played for 40 hr 42 min in Stavanger, Norway, on 22–24 Jun 2015.

Longest game of correspondence chess

Dr Reinhart Straszacker and Dr Hendrik Roelof van Huyssteen (both ZAF) played their first game of

Fastest time to arrange a large chess set

On 4 Oct 2015, Altynbek Bekmuratov (KGZ) arranged a large chess set in 1 min 44 sec. He achieved this at the GWR Live! event at the opening of the Kuntsevo Plaza shopping centre in Moscow, Russia, breaking the previous day's record by 14.6 sec.

correspondence chess in 1946. After 112 games, with both men having won half the games, their record marathon of more than 53 years ended with the death of Straszacker on 13 Oct 1999.

Slowest chess move (pre-clock)

Until the chess clock was adopted in the 1860s, players could take as long as they wanted to decide a move. In Nov 1857, in the First American Chess Congress final, Paul Morphy (USA) and Louis Paulsen (DEU) took more than 15 hr to play 56 moves. Paulsen, who decisively lost the match overall, caused most of the delay, taking as long as 1 hr 15 min to decide on a single move.

DID YOU KNOW?

The design students who made this king chose it as their record attempt because they play chess in their lunch break. To make it, they scaled up the proportions of a normal-size king and cut out sections of laminated MDF, recycling offcuts from their own projects.

LARGEST CHESS PIECE

On 4 Apr 2014, a chess king measuring 5.076 m (16 ft 7 in) tall and 2.04 m (6 ft 8 in) in diameter at its base was unveiled by the Gitok technical school (BEL) in Kalmthout, Belgium. The piece was made during lessons in which students learned artisanal skills such as woodworking. The attempt was also a team-building exercise, and helped to raise money and awareness for an orphanage and cancer charity.

DATELINE

1863

First detective novel
Opening with a murder, *The Notting Hill Mystery* by Charles Felix (UK) – first serialized in the magazine *Once a Week* between 1862 and 1863 – is published in its complete form, and establishes the classic detective genre.

144 Toys & Games

FAST FACTS
Russia's Anatoly Karpov won the 1975 World Chess Championship without playing a match, after reigning world champion Bobby Fischer (USA) resigned his title
• The term "checkmate" comes from the Persian *Shah mat* – "The king is dead"

DID YOU KNOW?
An extraordinary cache of 59 Norse chess pieces, beautifully carved from ivory, was found on the Isle of Lewis (UK) around two centuries ago. Two of the chess kings are thought to be possible likenesses of the 12th-century Norwegian kings Magnus V and Sverrir.

Largest collection of chess sets
As of 30 Jan 2012, Akın Gökyay (TUR) owned 412 chess sets, housed in Ankara, Turkey. Akın, a lawyer and businessman, started his collection in 1975. The decorative sets from around the world are made from diverse materials – including wood, metal, marble and fish bones – and cover popular themes such as Harry Potter and the French cartoon character Asterix.

Most simultaneous chess wins (blindfolded)
A blindfolded player has to memorize all their opponent's moves during a game. On 27 Nov 2011, the German master Marc Lang won 25 and drew 19 of 46 games in 21 hr.

Most simultaneous games of chess by an individual
On 8–9 Feb 2011, Ehsan Ghaem Maghami (IRN), a grandmaster and nine-time Iranian national champion, played 135 chess games concurrently in Tehran, Iran.
Anna-Maria Botsari (GRC) played the **most consecutive games of chess**, in Kalavryta, Greece, on 27–28 Feb 2001. Of her 1,102 games, seven were draws and the rest wins.

Smallest machine-made chess set
A chess board 435 microns (0.017 in) square – the diameter of four human hairs – was created by students at Texas Tech University, USA, in 2010. The playable chess set has "micro-pieces" engraved as traditional chess figures, each about 50 microns (0.002 in) square.
On 3 Mar 2008, Malla Siva (IND) presented the **smallest hand-made chess set** (right). It is 18 mm (0.7 in) square, with pieces ranging from 4 mm (0.16 in) to 6.5 mm (0.26 in) high, as verified in Bilaspur, Chhattisgarh, India.

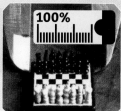

Most chess moves
On 17 Feb 1989, Ivan Nikolić and Goran Arsović (both SRB) made 269 moves in a game lasting 20 hr 15 min.

Longest time consecutively ranked chess world number one (female)
From 1 Feb 1989 to 1 Mar 2015, grandmaster Judit Polgár (HUN) dominated the women's rankings for 26 years 28 days, until overtaken by Hou Yifan (see above left). In 2005, Polgár achieved a peak rating of 2735: the **highest chess rating (female)**.

Highest chess rating
FIDE, the World Chess Federation, uses the Elo rating system for awarding points to rank players according to their performance in matches and tournaments. In May 2014, grandmaster Magnus Carlsen (NOR) attained the highest FIDE rating ever, of 2882. This resulted from an impressive performance the previous month at the Shamkir Chess tournament in Azerbaijan. Carlsen, who is World Chess Champion, scored five victories against grandmaster opponents and won the competition.

First road-traffic death
On 31 Aug, Mary Ward, an Irish scientist, becomes the first person to die in a road accident, after falling out of her cousin's experimental steam car.

1869

DATELINE

guinnessworldrecords.com   145

CHAIN REACTIONS

The "domino effect" made its Guinness World Records debut in 1977 after Bob Speca Jr (USA) toppled 22,222 dominoes at the University of Pennsylvania, USA, on 2 May 1976 – beating his own personal best of 11,111.

Most dominoes toppled
On 13 Nov 2009, a team of 89 builders toppled 4,491,863 dominoes in the WTC Expo center in Leeuwarden, Netherlands, for Domino Day 2009.

The **most dominoes toppled by an individual** is 321,197, achieved by Liu Yang (CHN) at Citic Guoan Grand Epoch City in Beijing, China, on 31 Dec 2011.

Largest toppling domino stone

Measuring 9.18 m (30 ft 1.5 in) tall, 4.57 m (15 ft) wide and 1.25 m (4 ft 1.5 in) thick, this outsized domino stone was produced by Prudential Financial Inc. (USA). It was the last of a series of dominoes to be toppled by members of the Prudential in Charlotte, North Carolina, USA, on 6 Aug 2014.

Largest Great Ball Contraption

A Great Ball Contraption (GBC) is a series of modules – designed from LEGO® Technic – arranged in a loop so that a small plastic ball can pass from module to module. The largest yet built comprised 100 modules, and was erected by Maico Arts and Ben Jonkman (both NLD) at the BRICK exhibition in London, UK, on 12 Dec 2015.

Longest time for continuous domino toppling
A team of 60 people kept a domino circle toppling continuously for 35 min 22 sec at the Domino Day 2008 event in Leeuwarden, Netherlands, on 7 Nov 2008.

Tallest domino structure
Students Michael Hörmann and Philipp Zimmermann (both DEU) erected and toppled a 9.17-m-high (30-ft 1-in) structure composed of 8,044 dominoes in Buchloe, Germany, on 21 Apr 2014.

Largest stickbomb

Weave a number of flat sticks into a spring-loaded grid and you've got yourself a stick bomb. Remove one, and you kickstart a shockwave that launches the sticks, one after the other, into the air. On 6 Jun 2015, the Natick High School Bomb Squad – comprising 15 students from Natick High School in Massachusetts, USA – successfully triggered a stick bomb made from 31,370 wooden tongue depressors.

Longest human domino line
On 12 Aug 2010, a group of 10,267 people formed a record-breaking human domino line at the Ordos International Nadam Fair in Ordos City, Inner Mongolia Autonomous Region, China.

Most dominoes stacked in 30 seconds
Serial record-breaker Silvio Sabba (ITA) built a column of 48 dominoes in 30 sec in Pioltello, Milan, Italy, on 28 Apr 2013.

The **most dominoes stacked on one domino piece** is 1,055, by Sinners Domino Entertainment at the Wilhelm-Lückert-Gymnasium in Büdingen, Germany, on 12 Aug 2014.

Most bricks toppled
A total of 165,384 house bricks were toppled in an unbroken line in and around the city of Bremerhaven in Germany on 17 Jan 2004. The event was arranged by Röben Tonbaustoffe (DEU) and involved 1,305 volunteers from the youth fire departments of Cuxhaven.

Most books toppled in a domino fashion

As part of the launch of the German edition of *Guinness World Records 2016*, Sinners Domino Entertainment (DEU) assembled 10,200 copies of the world's **best-selling annual** and set them sprawling sequentially. The event took place during the Frankfurt Book Fair in Germany on 14 Oct 2015. The team, who have toppled several other records (see right), consisted of 12 people. It took them at least 11 hr to set up the books, which fell in just over a minute.

First telephone call
In March, the first intelligible phone call takes place in Boston, Massachusetts, USA. Alexander Graham Bell (UK), who had filed his patent for the telephone on 14 Feb 1876, phones his assistant in a nearby room to say, "Mr Watson – come here – I want to see you."

FAST FACTS
Dominoes represent all of the possible throws of a pair of dice (plus blanks) • Domino spots are known as "pips" • The start of the domino-toppling craze can be traced back to a segment on *The Tonight Show* (USA) in 1976

Most dominoes toppled in a 3D pyramid
On 21 Jul 2014, Kevin Pöhls (DEU) knocked over 15,022 dominoes that had been assembled in a 3D pyramid at a Pizza Express in Waren (Müritz), Germany.

Most mousetraps triggered in a line
Synology Inc. (TPE) in Hualien, Chinese Taipei, set off a chain reaction involving 1,508 mousetraps on 13 Sep 2013. In fact, 1,509 traps were initially set but one failed to snap.

Fastest time to topple 10 portable toilets
Philipp Reiche (DEU) sent 10 portable loos toppling consecutively in 11.30 sec on the set of *Wir Holen Den Rekord Nach Deutschland* at Europa-Park in Rust, Germany, on 22 Jun 2013.

Largest Rube Goldberg
A 382-step Rube Goldberg machine (see definition below) was demonstrated in Székesfehérvár, Hungary, on 23 Apr 2015 by a team of 11 from the Budapest University of Technology and Economics. Its many processes included dissolving salt into water to change its conductivity and pushing balls down slopes by means of pneumatic pistons.

Longest domino wall
On 6 Jul 2012, Sinners Domino Entertainment constructed and then knocked down a wall of dominoes 30 m (98 ft 5 in) long, comprising 31,405 dominoes, at the Wilhelm-Lückert-Gymnasium in Büdingen, Germany.

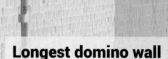

Most dominoes toppled in a spiral
Sinners Domino Entertainment toppled a 55,555-domino spiral for the *Officially Amazing* TV show in Büdingen, Germany, on 12 Jul 2013. On the same day, the same team set a new record for the **most mini dominoes toppled**: 2,000. These diminutive dominoes measure 1 x 0.5 x 0.2 cm (0.4 x 0.2 x 0.07 in).

DID YOU KNOW?
The term "Rube Goldberg" refers to any deliberately overcomplicated invention created to achieve very simple results. It's named after the American satirist (and graduate engineer) whose cartoons featured this kind of crazy contraption.

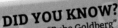

LARGEST RUBE GOLDBERG IN COMPETITION
The building of Rube Goldberg machines has become a competitive pastime, and the most complex yet seen in competition is the 300-step device built by the Purdue Society of Professional Engineers Rube Goldberg Team (USA). It was activated at the National Rube Goldberg Machine Contest at Purdue University in Lafayette, Indiana, USA, on 31 Mar 2012. Its objective was to blow up and pop a balloon!

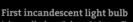

First incandescent light bulb
On 18 Dec, Joseph Wilson Swan (UK) reveals his incandescent light bulb (also called an "electric lamp") in a demonstration before a gathering at the Newcastle Chemical Society, UK. It burns out quickly.

1878 ▶ DATELINE

guinnessworldrecords.com 147

ACTION FIGURES & DOLLS

Most expensive doll sold at auction

A rare doll by Kämmer & Reinhardt (DEU), made in 1909–12, realized £242,500 ($395,750) at Bonhams in London, UK, on 24 Sep 2014. The life-like doll is a little girl dressed in white. She is thought to have been a design experiment that was abandoned.

Most valuable dolls' house

The 29-room Astolat Dollhouse Castle was constructed over a period of 13 years (1974–87) by US artist Elaine Diehl and valued at $8.5 m (£6 m). Modelled after the castle in Alfred Lord Tennyson's poem *The Lady of Shalott*, the 9-ft-tall (2.7-m) dolls' house contains 10,000 miniature items, including a grand piano ($7,000; £4,900), an ornate desk ($5,000; (£3,500) and a tiny portrait painted with a single-bristle brush ($1,840; £1,290). The dolls' house weighs 800 lb (363 kg) and boasts a total floor area of almost 30 sq ft (2.78 m²).

Largest action-figure brand

Based on retail figures from 19 Aug 2015, the current largest action-figure brand is Playmobil (DEU) with approximately $727.1 m (£468.064 m; €598.126 m) in revenue in 2014. Playmobil's classic toy, originally known as a "Klicky", is a 7.5-cm-tall (3-in) human figure that fits a huge array of scenarios – as an astronaut, knight, pirate, policeman and so on. The brand was developed by German inventor Hans Beck and has been sold worldwide since 1975. The detailed and inventive settings, limited editions, new introductions and discontinued lines, along with Playmobil TV series, films and real-size FunParks, have created a wide Playmobil community that includes adult collectors.

Most expensive collection of figurines (single auction)

A sale of Action Man and *Star Wars* figurines and accessories made £180,000 ($256,800) at Vectis Toy Auction House in Thornaby, North Yorkshire, UK, on 27 May 2015. Until then, they had languished in the garage of retired toy-sales rep Doug Carpenter. He had been allowed to keep them after manufacturer Palitoy ceased trading in the 1980s.

The **most expensive collection of *Star Wars* figurines (single auction)** was also sold at Vectis. On 28 Jan 2015, Craig Stevens (UK) – a former chairman of the UK *Star Wars* Fan Club – sold 70 figurines in their original packaging for £41,796 ($63,209).

Most valuable LEGO Minifigure

Two 14-carat solid gold reproductions of *Star Wars* bounty hunter Boba Fett were made by the LEGO® Group in 2010 as competition prizes. They are valued by the Minifigure Price Guide website at $11,495.95 (£8,115) apiece. Only the "priceless" Minifigures sent to Jupiter (see p.140) could be considered more valuable, on account of their inaccessibility!

Most expensive toy soldier

The first handcrafted 1963 G.I. Joe prototype was sold on 7 Aug 2003 by its creator Don Levine to Baltimore businessman Stephen A Geppi (both USA) for $200,000 (£124,309). The auction was conducted by Heritage Comics Auctions of Dallas, Texas, USA.

Largest collection of toy soldiers

Jonathan Perry Waters (USA) owns 1,020 different toy-soldier models, as verified in Macon, Georgia, USA, on 28 Feb 2016. The figurines are all 1:32-scale and sourced from around the world.

The world's **largest public collection of toy soldiers** can be found at the Museo de los Soldaditos de Plomo in Valencia, Spain. There are in excess of a million pieces in the collection, 85,000 of which are on display.

(see p.140)

DID YOU KNOW?

Barbie was created by Ruth Handler (USA), co-founder of Mattel. She named her after her daughter Barbara, whom she observed using paper dolls for adult role-play rather than baby dolls. And so the aspirational teenage doll was born.

MOST EXPENSIVE BARBIE DOLL SOLD AT AUCTION

On 10 Oct 2010, a glamorous, one-off Barbie sold at Christie's in New York City, USA, for $302,500 (£189,445). The 11.5-in (29.2-cm) doll wears a strapless black evening dress and a diamond choker showcasing a rare pink diamond. The doll, unveiled on 4 May 2010 during Australian Fashion Week, was designed by celebrated jeweller Stefano Canturi (AUS). He was enlisted by Barbie manufacturer Mattel to help promote the launch of the Barbie Basics range in Australia, which features dolls wearing commonly available clothing. All proceeds from the sale went to breast cancer research.

Most expensive *Star Wars* figure

A mint edition of *The Empire Strikes Back* 30B Boba Fett action figure, in its packaging, sold at auction for £15,000 ($22,684) on 28 Jan 2015. The **most valuable *Star Wars* action figure** is a prototype Boba Fett that was never produced. It was listed on eBay for $150,000 (£104,600) but had not sold as of 26 Feb 2016.

DATELINE **1883**

Loudest noise
On 27 Aug, the island-volcano Krakatoa in Indonesia explodes in an eruption. The sound is heard 5,000 km (3,100 mi) away. It is estimated to be audible over 8% of Earth's surface and have 26 times the power of the largest ever H-bomb test.

148 Toys & Games

FAST FACTS

The first LEGO Minifigures had no movable arms or legs • Barbie's full name is Barbara Millicent Roberts • Hans Beck based his Playmobil faces on children's drawings, showing a very large head with a smiley mouth and no nose

DID YOU KNOW?

In the UK, the earliest Action Man figures were Action Soldier, Action Sailor and Action Pilot, kitted out in US uniforms and accessories. These were gradually replaced by UK regalia, and the line-up extended to the non-military, such as explorers and sportsmen.

Largest collection of Barbie dolls

A devotee of Barbie since childhood, Bettina Dorfmann (DEU) was the owner and curator of at least 15,000 different dolls in original outfits, as of Oct 2011. Bettina has been collecting since 1993, and her treasures include numerous vintage editions. Most prized (and rare) of all is the very first Barbie, attired in a simple striped swimsuit, who debuted on 9 Mar 1959 – Barbie's official birthday.

Largest Transformers toy

Released in Aug 2013, the Titan-class Metroplex is billed by Hasbro (USA), the official maker of the long-running toy line, as the largest Transformers Autobot ever sold.

At 24 in (60.9 cm) tall, Metroplex surpassed the previous record holder, Fortress Maximus, released in 1987, by 2 in (5 cm). When not in robot form, Metroplex can be transformed into a battle station vehicle or even an entire city. Its rival and equivalent is Trypticon, of the villainous Decepticons.

Fastest-selling Playmobil figure

According to the toy manufacturer, a figure of 16th-century Protestant reformer Martin Luther sold out all 34,000 units within 72 hr of its release in Feb 2015. Luther founded the Protestant Church in Germany, where 95% of the sales occurred. The toy was issued ahead of the 500th anniversary of the Protestant Reformation in 2017.

The **largest private collection of dioramas** numbers 333 different items and belongs to Nabil Karam (LBN). They were counted in Zouk Mosbeh, Lebanon, on 17 Nov 2011 in celebration of GWR Day. A diorama is a model scene, typically of a famous battle, containing toy soldiers and vehicles as well as buildings, trees and other landscape features.

First action figure

Taken from a 1940s comic strip, G.I. Joe was launched by Hasbro in 1964. Two years later, it was licensed to British toymaker Palitoy as Action Man. More than 50 years on, G.I. Joe figures are still being produced. The original figure, with 19 articulated joints, was invented by Don Levine, Hasbro's Vice President, as a boys' alternative to Barbie dolls. G.I. Joe has since become a star of TV, film and videogames.

First skyscraper
The Home Insurance Building in Chicago, USA, is completed. The so-called "Father of the Skyscraper" towers 10 storeys high, with its peak at 42 m (138 ft). It will go on to be dwarfed by later builds, but is gargantuan for its day.

 1885 DATELINE

guinnessworldrecords.com 149

PUZZLES

100%

Smallest commercially available jigsaw puzzle (500–1,000 pieces)

Tomax of China produces a range of 500-piece jigsaws measuring 21 x 29.7 cm (8.27 x 11.69 in) – the size of an A4 sheet of paper. The puzzles depict famous works of art and world heritage landmarks; pictured above is the corner of a jigsaw showing the ancient Inca citadel of Machu Picchu in the Peruvian Andes. Each piece is about one-third of the size of a regular jigsaw piece.

Oldest unsolved number problem

A "perfect number" is a number that equals the sum of its factors excluding itself. The smallest is 6 – its factors (the whole numbers that divide into 6 exactly) are 1, 2 and 3, and the sum of these factors also comes to 6. The next three perfect numbers are 28, 496 and 8,128. All the perfect numbers discovered so far are even – but could a perfect number ever be odd? This puzzle perplexed the ancient Greeks, back to Nicomachus of Gerasa in the 1st century AD,

and, according to some historians, right back to Euclid, 500 years earlier. Over the centuries other mathematicians, including Pierre de Fermat and René Descartes, have attempted a solution, without success.

Highest score in a Scrabble tournament

On 21 Jan 2012, Toh Weibin (SGP) scored 850 points in a tournament match against Rik Kennedy (UK) at the Northern Ireland Scrabble Championship in Belfast, UK. The game was conducted under World English-language

Scrabble Players' Association (WESPA) rules and used the Collins Scrabble Wordlist.

The **highest opening score in a Scrabble tournament** is 126, for MUZJIKS (with a blank for the U). It was played by Jesse Inman (USA) on 26 July 2008 at the National Scrabble Championship in Orlando, Florida, USA.

Most wins of the World Puzzle Championship by an individual

Ulrich Voigt (DEU) has won the World Puzzle Championship 10 times. He took the gold medal in 2000–01, 2003, 2005–06, 2008–09 and 2012–14. Voigt's last win came in London, UK, on 17 Aug 2014 at the 23rd annual championships.

Largest commercially available jigsaw puzzle

Made by Ravensburger (DEU), the largest puzzle measures 5.4 x 1.9 m (17 ft 8.6 in x 6 ft 2.8 in). First sold in Sep 2014, the jigsaw is called "New York Window" and depicts an ultra-detailed view of the city skyline.

The **largest commercially available jigsaw puzzle by number of pieces** is "Wildlife", an African panorama made by Educa (ESP) in 2014, featuring 33,600 pieces.

Largest jigsaw puzzle

This gigantic jigsaw puzzle measured 5,428.8 m² (58,435 sq ft) – larger than a soccer pitch – and consisted of 21,600 pieces. Devised by Great East Asia Surveyors & Consultants Co., it was assembled by 777 people at the former Kai Tak Airport in Hong Kong, China, on 3 Nov 2002. Each piece measured a maximum of 0.5 x 0.5 m (1 ft 7.6 in x 1 ft 7.6 in).

Largest mechanical puzzle

A "mechanical" puzzle is an interlocking puzzle created from separate pieces (typically wooden), one of which holds the whole structure together. Swiss construction company Foffa Conrad created the largest such puzzle – a six-piece challenge known as a "Devil's Knot" – in Valchava, Switzerland, on 16 Apr 2013. Each piece measured 6 m (19 ft 8 in) long, 40 cm (1 ft 3 in) wide and 40 cm thick.

LARGEST WORD SEARCH PUZZLE

Pictured below, and as a background to these pages, is part of a word search containing 10,500 words hidden among 129,600 letters. The puzzle was created by Ashish Dutt Sharma (IND) in Rajasthan, India, and verified on 18 Oct 2015. Prof Sharma, Principal of the Apex Institute of Engineering & Technology in Jaipur, worked on the word search for 10 years. He filled it with technical words – and also the names of various scientists and inventors – to teach these terms to his engineering students.

DID YOU KNOW?

Given the size of *The World's Largest Word Search Puzzle*, and the vast number of potential letter combinations it offers, it is impossible to have a definitive list of searchable words. The words that were put in deliberately are joined by hundreds more that formed by chance.

Largest multi-sudoku puzzle

Beijing Sudoku Association (CHN) created a multi-sudoku puzzle of 200 standard grids in Beijing, China, on 25 Jul 2015. The event was part of the 2015 World Junior Sudoku Championship.

FIRST...

Crossword puzzle
On 21 Dec 1913, a crossword puzzle appeared in the Sunday "Fun" section of the US newspaper *New York World*. Created by Arthur Wynne (UK), it

DATELINE

1886

First newspaper with a print run of 1 million
Ushering in a new era for mass media, French daily *Le Petit Journal* surpasses the 1-million circulation mark. Its popularity is likely a result of its small format and low price.

150 Toys & Games

CROSSWORD CHAMPIONSHIPS

When it comes to solving cryptic crosswords, these record-breaking wordsmiths have all the right answers.

THE TIMES NATIONAL CROSSWORD CHAMPIONSHIP

Title	Holder	Record	Date(s) of win
Most wins	John Sykes (UK)	10	1972–75, 1977, 1980, 1983, 1985, 1989 and 1990
Most consecutive wins	Mark Goodliffe (UK, pictured above)	8	2008–15

AMERICAN CROSSWORD PUZZLE TOURNAMENT

Title	Holder	Record	Date(s) of win
Most wins	Jon Delfin (USA)	7	1989–91, 1995, 1999 and 2002–03
Most consecutive wins	Dan Feyer (USA)	6	2010–15
Youngest winner	Tyler Hinman (USA, b. 5 Nov 1984)	20 years 128 days	13 Mar 2005
Oldest winner	Doug "The Iceman" Hoylman (USA, 2 Jul 1943–2 Nov 2015)	56 years 254 days	12 Mar 2000

Longest-running puzzle world championship

The World Puzzle Federation, currently based in the Czech Republic, has organized an international puzzle contest since 1992. All of the challenges contested at the World Puzzle Championship are simple, logic-based puzzles that can be understood irrespective of your language. Pictured above is a puzzle from the 2015 Puzzle Grand Prix. Two of these images are identical, and all you have to do is find them. See how long it takes you! For the answer, see Stop Press.

was based on a diamond-shaped grid, had simple, non-cryptic clues and no blacked-out squares.

Needless to say, the **first crossword clue** appeared in the same puzzle. The crossword had no 1-across, so the first clue was placed at 2-across. The clue was "What bargain hunters enjoy." The answer? "Sales."

The **first crossword made up entirely of cryptic clues** appeared in 1925 in a Saturday edition of the British newspaper *Westminster Gazette*. Although cryptic elements had appeared within crosswords before, Edward Powys Mathers (UK) – who later set crosswords under the name "Torquemada" – used only cryptic clues. He is often called the inventor of the cryptic crossword.

The **first crossword book** appeared in the USA in 1924. *The Cross Word Puzzle Book* was the first publication by Dick Simon and Lincoln Schuster (both USA); a compilation of crosswords from US newspaper *New York World*, it was an instant success and helped establish Simon & Schuster, who continue to produce crossword books.

Sudoku World Championship
The first World Sudoku Championship was staged by the World Puzzle Federation in Lucca, Italy, on 10–11 Mar 2006. Accountant Jana Tylová (CZE) beat 85 players from 22 countries, and was the only woman in the top 18.

Videogame to improve brain function
In 1991, Richard Haier of the University of California at Irvine (USA) scanned the brains of *Tetris* players. Haier discovered that, in new players, cerebral glucose metabolic rates soared; after playing daily for up to eight weeks, brain functioning and efficiency significantly improved, and success rates at the game rose sevenfold!

Most people playing sudoku simultaneously

On 3 May 2013, a total of 3,452 students, parents, teachers and alumni from Yan Chai Hospital Lim Por Yen Secondary School in Tsuen Wan, Hong Kong, China, took part in a mass session of sudoku at the nearby Shing Mun Valley Sports Ground.

Oldest surviving film
Using a single-lens camera and paper film, French inventor Louis Le Prince records a two-second, silent "home movie" of his family and friends in Roundhay Garden, Leeds, UK.

1888 ▶ DATELINE

CONSTRUCTION TOYS

Fastest Jenga tower (30 levels)

Brothers Tyler and Ryan Measel (both USA) stacked up a 30-level Jenga tower – following the rules of the game – in 2 min 51.04 sec in Pilesgrove, New Jersey, USA, on 7 Jun 2014.

Tallest LEGO® brick zigzag structure in 30 seconds (one hand)

On 1 Nov 2015 – the final day of the BRICK event staged at the NEC in Birmingham, UK – Leon Ip (UK) single-handedly assembled 28 levels of bricks in a zigzag shape.

Most LEGO brick castles built in one minute

On 30 Oct 2015, the second day of BRICK 2015, Ed Diment (UK) built 15 castles in 60 sec – an average construction time of 4 sec per castle. His record was equalled two days later at the same event by Jack Clarke (UK).

Most contributors to an interlocking plastic-brick sculpture

A total of 19,274 volunteers from 22 locations in Hong Kong, China, helped to build a sculpture from Mega Bloks between 12 Jul and 9 Aug 2015. The event was sponsored by Mead Johnson Nutrition and Mattel East Asia (both HKG), and the bricks were later donated to charity.

Longest LEGO brick structure

Organized by Consorzio Esercenti C C Shopville Le Gru, a millipede as long as 32 Olympic swimming pools walked off with this record in Turin, Italy, on 13 Feb 2005. It was 1,578.81 m (5,179 ft 10 in) long and made from 2,901,760 bricks.

Largest modelling-balloon sculpture by an individual

On 25 Jul 2015, at Thanksgiving Point in Lehi, Utah, USA, Jeremy Telford (USA) unveiled a magnificent (resting) balloon dog, made from 8,867 balloons and measuring 20.09 x 9.93 m (65 ft 11 in x 32 ft 7 in).

Most prolific videogame series based on a toy

Since the launch of *LEGO Island* (Mindscape, 1997), the series has produced 67 games inspired by the famous brick, as of 1 Feb 2016. As well as recent games *LEGO Dimensions* and *Marvel's Avengers*, this total includes titles for the LEGO Group's BIONICLE franchise, numerous entertainment licences, mobile games, educational games and sporty spin-offs.

Largest commercially available LEGO set

Designed for "experienced builders", the 5,922-piece Taj Mahal (also see p.140) measures 51 x 41 cm (1 ft 8 in x 1 ft 4 in) when completed. Features from the iconic Indian temple include minarets, domes, finials and arches.

The **largest commercially available LEGO Technic set** is the 1:12.5-scale Mercedes-Benz Unimog U 400 truck, which comprises 2,048 pieces. The vehicle features a pneumatically

LARGEST K'NEX SCULPTURE

This full-sized replica of the *Bloodhound SSC* (supersonic car) – 3.87 m (12 ft 8.3 in) high, 2.44 m (8 ft) wide and 13.38 m (43 ft 10.7 in) long – comprises more than 350,000 K'Nex pieces. It took 1,280 hr of assembly time by the BLOODHOUND SSC RBLI K'NEX Build Team (UK) and was measured at the Royal British Legion Industry HQ in Aylesford, Kent, UK, on 26 Aug 2014. The supersonic car itself – which is jet-powered and designed to reach more than 1,600 km/h (1,000 mph) – is aiming to beat the land-speed record in 2016.

DATELINE

1889

First production car factory
René Panhard and Émile Levassor (both FRA) build the Panhard-Levassor factory in France. Their first production car is ready by the following year.

152 Toys & Games

FAST FACTS

Meccano was patented in 1901 by Frank Hornby (UK) as "Mechanics Made Easy" • As of 2015, there were 3,600 different types of LEGO element • Jenga's inventor, Leslie Scott, took the name from the Swahili for "build"

Largest LEGO brick caravan

This full-sized caravan was built from 215,158 LEGO bricks by NCC (National Caravan Council) Events and ratified in Bordon, East Hampshire, UK, on 8 Oct 2015. The 3.6-m-long (11-ft 9-in) caravan took 12 weeks to assemble and features a fitted kitchen, a bed, running water and electricity.

Largest Meccano structure

On 1 Jul 2015, the School of Architecture at Queen's University Belfast, UK, presented a bridge constructed from 10,000 pieces of Meccano. The structure – built over Belfast's Clarendon Dock by third-year engineering students and local schoolchildren – measured 28.76 m (94 ft 4 in) long. It was officially opened by the Head of School, Prof. Trevor Whittaker, and Meccano's Meccanoid G15 KS robot (inset).

powered crane with working grabber, and a recovery winch on the front. It also has working steering, four-wheel drive and suspension, a gear block for ground clearance, and an engine with moving pistons.

Largest modelling-balloon sculpture made in the shape of a LEGO Minifigure

Larry Moss and his team (all USA) took three days and 1,985 balloons to make a 6-m (19-ft 8-in) sculpture in the likeness of a LEGO Minifigure, presented on 30 Nov 2014 in London, UK.

Most modelling-balloon sculptures made in an hour

John Cassidy (USA) twisted 747 balloon shapes in one hour at Bucks County Community College in Newtown, Pennsylvania, USA, on 14 Nov 2007.

The **most modelling balloon sculptures made in 24 hours** is 6,176 – more than four per minute – by Tim Thurmond (USA) in Northville, Michigan, USA, on 16–17 Apr 2004.

Largest LEGO brick mammoth

On 1 Nov 2015, at the BRICK event in Birmingham, UK, Bright Bricks (UK) unveiled their rugged Ice Age giant, which was a mighty 2.47 m (8 ft 1.2 in) tall, 3.8 m (12 ft 5.6 in) long and 1.3 m (4 ft 3.1 in) wide. On the same day, Bright Bricks presented the **largest LEGO brick moa**, a leggy bird 3.17 m (10 ft 4 in) tall, 1.47 m (4 ft 9.8 in) long and 0.8 m (2 ft 7.4 in) wide.

First radio patent
On 2 Jun, a patent for a system of communication by means of electromagnetic waves is granted to the Italian-Irish inventor Guglielmo Marconi.

1896

DATELINE

VIDEOGAMES
GALLERY

Now in its 10th year, our *Gamer's Edition* is going from strength to strength. You'll find it jam-packed with breath-taking gameplay, larger-than-life vloggers and eSports pros, and even a few affectionate nods to vintage arcade gaming. Here we present a selection of some of the amazing pictures we've taken of our record-breaking gamers.

DID YOU KNOW?
Kat Gunn has been an avid gamer since early childhood. Her introduction to large-scale competitive gaming came in 2002, when she was selected as one of the beta testers for Microsoft's Xbox Live online gaming service.

1

2

3

1
HIGHEST-EARNING PRO GAMER (FEMALE)
Kat "Mystik" Gunn (USA) has earned $122,000 (£77,094) in prize money since she turned pro in 2007. She started out in the fighting-game scene, scoring top-three finishes in two *Dead or Alive 4* tournaments, but the biggest prize win of her career was $100,000 for first place in the televised competition *WCG Ultimate Gamer*. This 2010 contest challenged eSports pros to compete in games as diverse as *Mario Kart*, *Rock Band* and *Halo: Reach*.

2
TALLEST ARCADE CABINET
At an astonishing 14 ft 5 in (4.4 m) high, 6 ft 4 in (1.93 m) wide and 3 ft 5 in (1.06 m) deep, Jason Camberis' (USA) Arcade Deluxe is almost three times the size of a classic arcade cabinet. The scaled-up machine would be just the right height for Sultan Kösen (the **tallest man living**), but everyone else has to stand on a chair or fetch a ladder in order to reach the 4-in-wide (10.2-cm) buttons. The cabinet is fully functional and can play a variety of classic arcade games.

3
LONGEST *FIFA* MARATHON
On 5–7 Nov 2014, Christopher Cook (UK), a committed gamer and soccer fan, combined his two obsessions to set a new record for the longest *FIFA* marathon, playing the game continuously for 48 hr 49 min. He played more than 120 matches, both online and offline, during his attempt. Christopher's exhausting gaming session was organized to raise money for the charity Special Effect, which creates adaptive controllers that allow people with disabilities to play videogames.

4
FASTEST COMPLETION OF *THE LEGEND OF ZELDA: OCARINA OF TIME*
On 16 Mar 2015, Joel "Jodenstone" Ekman (pictured) stormed through Nintendo's 1998 epic in a mind-blowing 17 min 55 sec. His record only stood until 10 Jul, however, when it was beaten by an American gamer known only as "Skater82297", who saved Hyrule in 17 min 45 sec. Both players used glitches and tricks to skip huge portions of the game, which takes most players about 30 hr.

FASTEST COMPLETION OF *ASSASSIN'S CREED II* **5**

On 26 Mar 2011, François "Fed981" Federspiel dashed through *Assassin's Creed II* in 5 hr 42 min, mowing down hundreds of guards and knocking over a whole city's worth of bystanders to reach his targets. François is a prolific speed-runner with a love of the *Assassin's Creed* series – he also set records for the **fastest completion of *Assassin's Creed: Brotherhood*** and ***Assassin's Creed: Revelations***, in 2 hr 23 min and 2 hr 48 min respectively.

LONGEST JOURNEY IN *MINECRAFT* **6**

YouTuber Kurt J Mac (USA) set out for *Minecraft*'s fabled Far Lands in Mar 2011, and had covered 2,723,612 blocks (2,723 km; 1,692 mi) by 28 Mar 2016. The Far Lands lie beyond the normal gameplay area where errors in the game's code start producing landscapes that look like colossal termite mounds. They have never been reached on foot before, and even after five years of travel, Kurt was less than 22% of the way there.

MOST KOs ON *SUPER SMASH BROS. BRAWL* **7**

Klayton Schaufler (USA) recorded an amazing 51-knockout game for the GWR Challengers website on 8 Feb 2013. Playing as Zero-Suit Samus, Klayton dispatched his opponents by standing at the edge of the map on Flat Zone 2 and launching them into the off-screen "blast line". Klayton also set the record for the **longest hammer throw on *Mario & Sonic at the Olympic Games***. He threw the hammer 97.1 m (318 ft 6 in) using Vector the Crocodile.

GAMER'S EDITION

These record holders were all photographed for our dedicated *Gamer's Edition*. Fully updated and illustrated, it is packed with speed-runs, high scores and other amazing achievements.

First land-speed record set with an internal combustion engine
On 5 Aug, millionaire playboy William K Vanderbilt, driving a Mors racing car, achieves a speed of 76.08 mph (122.43 km/h) in Ablis, France.

1902

DATELINE

ENGINEERING & ARCHITECTURE

DATELINE ▶ **1903**

First power-driven flight
At 10:35 a.m. on 17 Dec, Orville Wright (USA) flies the 9-kW (12-hp) chain-driven *Flyer I*, built with his brother Wilbur, for 120 ft (36.5 m) near Kitty Hawk in North Carolina, USA. The flight lasts for about 12 sec, at an altitude of 8–12 ft (2.4–3.6 m).

CONTENTS

Fastest monowheel

On 20 Sep 2015, driver Kevin Scott (pictured) and the UK Monowheel Team (all UK) achieved a speed of 98.464 km/h (61.182 mph) with *WarHorse*, a monowheel motorcycle, at Elvington airfield in North Yorkshire, UK. Scott broke the previous speed record for single-wheel motorcycling – 91.7 km/h (57 mph), set by Kerry McLean (USA) at Irwindale Speedway in California, USA, on 10 Jan 2001. The team spent two years building *WarHorse,* which includes a carbon-fibre frame and custom-made parts, but the result more than justified all that effort. The other members of the record-breaking team included Peter Orton, Peter Kay and Tim Mann.

One major challenge to monowheel riders is avoiding a "gerbil incident" – in which the driver accidentally loops around with the outer wheel instead of remaining seated at the base. Happily, Kevin achieved the record speed without "gerbilizing".

Largest diamond

On 26 Jan, a 3,106-carat diamond is found at the Premier Diamond Mine, near Pretoria in South Africa. It is later named "The Cullinan" and presented to the reigning British monarch, Edward VII.

1905

ENGINEERING

For thousands of years, buildings were created from natural substances such as mud, ice, clay, stone and wood. Over time, however, humanity has amassed ever-more-inventive ways of developing innovative materials and techniques that have redefined the possibilities of architecture. Incredibly, eight of the top 10 tallest buildings in the world have been completed since the turn of the century – and virtuoso engineering is constantly rewriting the record books. Below, we present a snapshot of the 10 tallest buildings as of 2016 – with some classic older structures alongside, for comparison. The heights are calculated to the tallest "architectural" point of the building, discounting fixtures such as antennae or flagpoles. This is the approach adopted by the Council on Tall Buildings and Urban Habitat (CTBUH) when measuring the world's tallest buildings.

BURJ KHALIFA
Location: Dubai, UAE
Completed: 2010
Height: 828 m (2,717 ft)
Floors: 163 (plus one below ground)
Number of steps: 2,909
Elevator top speed: 10 m per sec (32 ft 9 in per sec)
Additional information:
• The fastest time to climb the Burj Khalifa is 6 hr 13 min 55 sec, by Alain Robert (FRA) on 29 Mar 2011.
• The fastest time to climb the Burj Khalifa on a bicycle is 2 hr 20 min 38 sec, by Vittorio Brumotti (ITA) on 18 Oct 2012.

ABRAJ AL-BAIT TOWERS (AKA MAKKAH ROYAL CLOCK TOWER)
Location: Mecca, Saudi Arabia
Completed: 2012
Height: 601 m (1,972 ft)
Floors: 120 (plus three below ground)
Elevator top speed: 6 m per sec (19 ft 8 in per sec)
Additional information:
• The Dokaae clock face is 43 m (141 ft) in diameter – the largest clock face.
• The spire at the top of the building is capped with a gold mosaic crescent that weighs 35 tonnes (77,160 lb).

TAIPEI 101
Location: Taipei, Chinese Taipei
Completed: 2004
Height: 508 m (1,667 ft)
Floors: 101 (plus five below ground)
Number of steps: 2,046
Elevator top speed: 16.83 m per sec (55 ft 2 in per sec)
Additional information:
• The most steps climbed on a bicycle is 3,139, by Krystian Herba (POL) at the Taipei 101, in 2 hr 12 min on 22 Mar 2015. He went from the first floor to the 52nd floor, then took an elevator back down before climbing again, this time to the 91st floor.

INTERNATIONAL COMMERCE CENTRE
Location: Hong Kong, China
Completed: 2010
Height: 484 m (1,588 ft)
Floors: 108 (plus four below ground)
Number of steps: 2,120
Elevator top speed: 9 m per sec (29 ft 6 in per sec)
Additional information:
• Highly energy-efficient for a building of such a size.

ZIFENG TOWER
Location: Nanjing, China
Completed: 2010
Height: 450 m (1,476 ft)
Floors: 66 (plus five below ground)
Elevator top speed: 7 m per sec (23 ft per sec)
Additional information:
• The design of the tower incorporates sky gardens that wind their way up the façade.

DID YOU KNOW?
Originally 146.5 m (481 ft) tall, the Great Pyramid at Giza in Egypt is more than five times smaller than today's tallest building, the Burj Khalifa. But for this 3rd-century-BCE building, this 3rd-century-BCE edifice remained the tallest building on Earth.

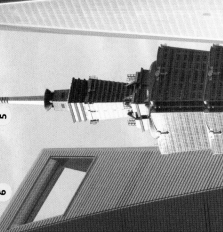

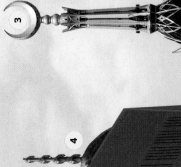

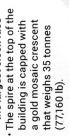

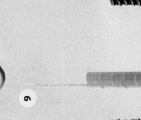

SHANGHAI TOWER
2
Location: Shanghai, China
Completed: 2015
Height: 632 m (2,073 ft)
Floors: 128 (plus five below ground)
Elevator top speed: 18 m per sec (59 ft per sec)
Additional information:
• The twisting shape of the tower is designed to make it more wind resistant.

ONE WORLD TRADE CENTER
4
Location: New York City, USA
Completed: 2014
Height: 541.3 m (1,776 ft)
Floors: 94 (plus five below ground)
Elevator top speed: 10.16 m per sec (33 ft 4 in per sec)
Number of steps: 1,970 (to 90th floor)
Additional information:
• Its height in feet is a reference to 1776 – the year of the US Declaration of Independence.

SHANGHAI WORLD FINANCIAL CENTER
6
Location: Shanghai, China
Completed: 2008
Height: 492 m (1,614 ft)
Floors: 101 (plus three below ground)
Elevator top speed: 10 m per sec (32 ft 9 in per sec)
Additional information:
• Its trapezoid top has seen it dubbed the "Bottle Opener".

PETRONAS TWIN TOWERS
8
Location: Kuala Lumpur, Malaysia
Completed: 1998
Height: 451.9 m (1,483 ft)
Floors: 88 (plus five below ground)
Elevator top speed: 7 m per sec (23 ft per sec)
Additional information:
• A "sky bridge" links the two towers at the level of the 41st and 42nd storeys.

WILLIS TOWER
10
Location: Chicago, USA
Completed: 1974
Height: 442.1 m (1,451 ft)
Floors: 108 (plus three below ground)
Elevator top speed: 8.1 m per sec (26 ft 6 in per sec)
Additional information:
• Completed in 1974, and formerly the Sears Tower, it was the tallest building in the world for 25 years.

Empire State Building
Height: 381 m (1,250 ft)
Completed: 1931

Eiffel Tower
Height: 300 m (984 ft)
Completed: 1889

Statue of Liberty
Height: 92.99 m (305 ft 1 in)
Completed: 1886

Leaning Tower of Pisa
Height: 56.67 m (185 ft 11 in) "high" side
Completed: 1372

DID YOU KNOW?
From 2004 to 2008, the Empire State Building's 24th storey was given over to take "nap pods" for workers to take a rest. Officially, but there is a less well-known a private has 102 storeys, but there is 103rd storey offering observation deck to a select few.

All measurements and unit conversions are sourced from the CTBUH.

DOMES
GALLERY

The noble hemispheres gracing cathedrals, temples, mosques and mausoleums worldwide had humble beginnings as a simple way of roofing where timber was not available. Graduated mud bricks were used instead to cover small huts and tombs in the ancient Middle East, India and the Mediterranean. The Romans were the first to turn the dome into a monumental construction, since when architects have reinvented it in many forms and beautified the sweeping space inside – often simply by letting in pure light from a central roof lantern.

3

2

1

FIRST GEODESIC DOME **1**

A geodesic dome is a shell structure made from tessellated geometric shapes. The Zeiss-Planetarium built by Walther Bauersfeld (DEU) on top of the Carl Zeiss optics factory in Jena, Germany, opened on 18 Jul 1926. Starting with an icosahedron or symmetrical 20-faced structure that stood 8.5 m (27 ft 10 in) tall, each face was subdivided into smaller triangles and lozenges using 3,500 thin iron rods to form the shell. The dome's interior displays the planets and fixed stars.

LARGEST CAST-IRON DOME **2**

The iron-framed dome of the Devonshire Royal Hospital in Buxton, UK, is 145 ft (44.2 m) in diameter and dates from 1881. Slightly larger than that of the famous Pantheon in Rome, at the time it was the **largest dome** overall (see No.5). Inside, light filters down from a circular lantern topped by a small cupola. Originally part of a large 18th-century hotel, the dome was added when the hospital was converted, and the building now belongs to the University of Derby.

MOST NORTHERLY GLASS DOME ROOMS **3**

In a forested, mountainous landscape in Finnish Lapland, more than 250 km (155 mi) north of the Arctic Circle, Kakslauttanen Arctic Resort offers luxuriously heated "igloo" hotel rooms. The thermal glass domes accommodate four guests each and provide encompassing views of clear starry nights and – from August to April – the region's approximately 200 annual appearances of the spectacular Northern Lights.

LARGEST WOODEN DOME HOUSE **4**

Kevin Shea's (USA) "Green Dome" is 70 ft (21.33 m) wide and 44 ft (13.41 m) high – a timber-framed, eco-friendly geodesic house on Long Island in New York, USA. All of the property's electricity is derived from solar and wind power, while a green roof captures rainwater, as well as providing insulation and a home for wildlife. Kevin's self-styled "hippy's Moon base station" could have been yours, as of 2015, for $1 million (£663,500).

4

5

6

7

LARGEST DOME **5**

The $1.3-billion (£862.7-million) Sports Hub national stadium in Singapore is the largest true dome (i.e., it is completely self-supporting). Designed by Arup and DP Architects, it spans 312 m (1,023 ft) – almost big enough to house four A380 airbuses wing to wing. The lightweight plastic roof has a retractable middle section that doubles as a giant projector screen, while mechanized seating can be reconfigured in 48 hours for different sports, concerts and cultural events.

LARGEST UNDERWATER VIEWING DOME **6**

Inaugurated on 28 Jan 2014, the Whale Shark Exhibit tank at Chimelong Ocean Kingdom in Hengqin, Zhuhai, China, has a viewing dome with an external diameter of 12 m (39 ft 4 in). The acrylic cupola and its supporting cylinder reach 6 m (19 ft 8 in) high and are accessed via two tunnels. Visitors enjoy 360° and overhead views of the aquatic environment, which hosts marine giants such as manta rays and whale sharks – the **largest fish**.

TALLEST THEATRE DOME **7**

(See also main picture.) The National Centre for the Performing Arts in Beijing, China, is 46.68 m (153 ft) tall – as tall as the Statue of Liberty – and covers an area of 30,500 m² (328,600 sq ft). Owing to its ellipsoidal steel shell, clad with titanium and glass, the building is often called "The Giant Egg". Cradled within the $325-m (£215.7-m) egg-on-a-lake are an opera house (2,398 seats), concert hall (2,019 seats) and two theatres (1,035 and 556 seats).

DID YOU KNOW?
Beijing's National Centre for the Performing Arts descends 32.5 m (106 ft 7 in) underground, equivalent to a 10-storey building. Noise-elimination technology ensures that no sound is heard if anyone has to leave their seat during a performance.

Greatest recorded impact on Earth
Energy released from the disintegration of a meteoroid over the basin of the Podkamennaya Tunguska River in Russia on 30 Jun is equivalent to 10–15 megatons of explosive. It devastates an area of 3,900 km² (1,505 sq mi)

1908

 TELINE

WALLS

Longest war memorial wall

Completed in 1982, the 150.42-m (493-ft 6-in) Vietnam Veterans Memorial in Washington, DC, USA, was designed by Maya Ying Lin (USA). It comprises two 75.21-m-long (246-ft 9-in) walls made of dark gabbro granite, on which the names of 58,307 servicemen and women are inscribed, listed in chronological order of death.

Longest ancient city wall

The city wall of Nanjing in China's Jiangsu Province was 35.2 km (21.8 mi) long when first built in the Ming Dynasty (1368–1644). It took 200,000 labourers 21 years to build the wall, which has an average height of 12 m (39 ft) and contains 13 gates. Some two-thirds of it remains.

Longest sea wall

South Korea's 33.89-km-long (21.06-mi) Saemangeum Seawall was completed on 27 Apr 2010. It is the country's largest-ever engineering project, costing $2.6 bn (£1.6 bn). The wall encloses 160 sq mi (414 km²) of seawater and mudflats – about two-thirds the size of the South Korean capital city Seoul.

Thickest wall

The city walls of Ur (now Tell al-Muqayyar in Iraq) were 27 m (88 ft) thick – similar to the length of a blue whale – and made of mud bricks. Despite this impressive fortification, the walls were razed in 2006 BCE by Elamite forces hailing from what is now south-west Iran.

First cavity-wall insulation

Built in 1860, Overstone Hall in Northampton, UK, was the first building to boast double walls (two skins of masonry, separated by an air gap). It was designed by architect William Milford Teulon for Lord and Lady Overstone as a distinctly "modern" residence. Behind the Grade II-listed historical façade lie a central heating system, gas lighting and a butler's lift.

First curtain-wall office building

A "curtain wall" is a non-structural barrier around the outside of a building. Oriel Chambers on Water Street in Liverpool, UK, is the oldest surviving metal-framed, glass curtain-walled building, completed in 1864. It was designed by architect Peter Ellis for its owner, the Reverend Thomas Anderson.

Longest fort walls

Built during the 15th century by Rana Kumbha (IND), the walls at Kumbhalgarh Fort in Rajasthan, India, are 22.4 mi (36 km) long and around 5 m (16 ft) thick. They divided the competing Mewar and Marwar kingdoms; the fort within was used by Mewar rulers as a last refuge.

Most walls covered by a mural

In 2014–15, art collective the Germen Crew painted 209 building walls in the Mexican city of Pachuca with a single, brightly coloured pattern. Entitled *El Macro Mural Barrio de Palmitas*, the mural measured 20,000 m² (215,278 sq ft). The finished design used more than 20,000 litres (5,280 US gal) of paint and took 14 months to complete with the help of local residents. Seen from afar it appears as a vibrant, swirled rainbow, with stripes running across houses.

LONGEST WALL

The Great Wall of China has a main-line length of 3,460 km (2,150 mi) – nearly three times the length of Great Britain – plus 3,530 km (2,193 mi) of branches and spurs. Construction of the wall – which was erected to help keep out marauding nomadic tribes from the north, such as the Mongols – began during the reign of Qin Shi Huang (221–210 BCE). Its height varies from 4.5 to 12 m (15–39 ft) and it is up to 9.8 m (32 ft) thick. The wall runs from Shanhaiguan, on the Gulf of Bohai, to Yumenguan and Yangguan. Although it was extended and rebuilt over the course of two millennia, most of the wall was constructed during the Ming Dynasty (1368–1644). Some 51.5 km (32 mi) of the structure has been destroyed since 1966, and in Jul 1979, part of it was blown up in order to make way for a dam.

DATELINE

1909
First people to reach the North Pole
On 6 Apr, Robert Peary and Matt Henson (both USA) reach the North Pole, having trekked from Ellesmere Island in Canada. Historians are unsure if they reached the exact pole, but they certainly came much closer than their rivals.

FAST FACTS
In 1979, Germany's Eija-Riitta Eklöf-Berliner-Mauer "married" the Berlin Wall (her surname means "Berlin Wall"!) • In 2011, competitive wallpapering was contested at the UK's National Painting and Decorating Show

Longest ancient Roman wall (surviving)

Running for 118 km (73 mi), Hadrian's Wall was built as a defensive and customs barrier in the Roman province of Britannia (now the UK). Much of it still runs from the Solway Firth in the west to the River Tyne in the east. The wall was likely begun in 122 CE, under the orders of Emperor Hadrian. Mostly made from stone, by Roman legionnaires, it was 2.5–3 m (8–10 ft) wide and 4.5–6 m (15–20 ft) tall.

Longest wall of fire
On 14 Mar 2009, Marine Corps Community Services (USA) marked the 50th anniversary of Marine Corps Air Station Yuma – located in Arizona, USA – by setting off a spectacular 10,178-ft-long (3,102-m) wall of fire at the base's annual air show.

Tallest free-standing artificial climbing wall
The climbing wall located at Historic Banning Mills in Whitesburg, Georgia, USA, was measured at 41.89 m (137 ft 5 in) – equal to 14 storeys – on 9 Dec 2011. See right for another record-breaking climbing wall.

Largest vertical garden (green wall)

Cleanaway Company Ltd and Shine Green Energy Enterprise Co., Ltd (both TPE) unveiled a green wall measuring 2,593.77 m² (27,919.1 sq ft) in Kaohsiung, Chinese Taipei, on 29 Jun 2015. More than 100,000 plants of various species have been used to create the wall's "sunset" design.

Tallest artificial climbing wall

Part of the BaseCamp sports venue, this vertigo-inducing artificial wall offers 49.85 m (163 ft 6.5 in) of climbing experience. It is attached to the side of the 16-storey Whitney Peak Hotel in Reno, Nevada, USA, and opened on 1 Oct 2011. The top is 57.3 m (188 ft) above Reno – higher than the famous Horseshoe Falls at Niagara.

DID YOU KNOW?

The myth that the Great Wall of China is the only man-made structure visible from space (or from the Moon) predates space flight by more than 200 years. When Chinese astronaut (or "taikonaut") Yang Liwei went into space in 2003, he admitted that he couldn't see it.

Most valuable object stolen
On 21 Aug, Leonardo da Vinci's priceless painting *Mona Lisa* disappears from the Louvre in Paris, France. It is returned in 1913, and Vincenzo Peruggia (ITA) is charged with its theft.

1911 ▶ DATELINE

guinnessworldrecords.com **163**

MAZES

Oldest hedge maze

The maze at Hampton Court Palace in Surrey, UK, was built for King William III and Mary II of England. It was designed by George London and Henry Wise, and planted in 1690 using hornbeam (*Carpinus betulus*). It covers an area of 0.2 ha (0.5 acres).

Most identical doorways in a maze

The Bhul Bhulaiya maze at the Bara Imambara in Lucknow, India, contains 489 identical doorways. It includes several staircases and around 1,000 narrow passages, some with dead ends and others with precipitous drops. This bewildering three-storey construction was intended to keep intruders away from a large central chamber containing the tomb of Asaf-ud-Daula, Nawab of Awadh. It dates from 1791.

TRIVIA

Strictly defined, a maze (below left) has multiple routes, while a labyrinth (right) has just one path (with no dead ends or branches) from entrance to exit. In practice, many variants exist and the terms are frequently interchanged.

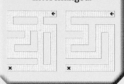

Largest hand-drawn maze

David A Book Jr (USA) drew a maze measuring 15.2 m (49 ft 10.4 in) long and 1.12 m (3 ft 8 in) wide at Covington Library in Washington, USA, on 11 Aug 2014. But as you can see (right), it didn't take GWR adjudicator Shantha Chinniah long to get to the middle of it...

Most books in a labyrinth

Created in Aug 2012 by Marcos Saboya and Gualter Pupo (both BRA) with production company HungryMan, the aMAZEme labyrinth at the Royal Festival Hall in the Southbank Centre, London, UK, had walls built from 250,000 books. The 500-m² (5,382-sq-ft) installation was inspired by writer Jorge Luis Borges' love of labyrinths and took the shape of the Argentinian author's fingerprints.

LARGEST...

Maze

The Labirinto Della Masone in Fontanellato, near Parma, Italy, covers 17 acres (6.8 ha) – more than 10 times the size of a US football field – and has 1.86 mi (2.9 km) of pathways. Fast-growing bamboo from more than 30 subspecies forms tall hedges reaching 5 m (16 ft 4 in) high. The maze has a Roman-style pattern, with right-angled paths in four interconnected quadrants. Created by former art publisher Franco Maria Ricci with architects Pier Carlo Bontempi and Davide Dutto (all ITA), the maze cost $11 m (£7.2 m) and opened on 1 Jun 2015.

Ancient Egyptian labyrinth

The temple precinct built by Amenemhet III at Hawara in 1844–1797 BCE was a complex architectural puzzle. Ancient Greek historian Herodotus, who visited the site, described it as a labyrinth of identical courtyards connected by twisting corridors lined with false doors. The labyrinth probably acted as a cult centre and meeting place for Egyptian rulers as well as Amenemhet's tomb.

Buddhist prayer maze

The square prayer maze at the 15th-century Buddhist temple of Haeinsa in Gyeongsangnam-do, South Korea, measures some 18 x 18 m (59 x 59 ft). With four quadrants decorated by coloured markers, the right-angled path maze promotes meditation and focused inward reflection, and takes about 30 min to walk around. It is a UNESCO World Heritage Site.

Largest temporary corn (maize) maze

Cool Patch Pumpkins (USA) crafted this amazing maize maze at their premises in Dixon, California, USA. It covered an area of 60 acres (24.28 ha) when measured on 3 Oct 2014 – a "footprint" equivalent to the base of the Great Pyramid at Giza *four* times over!

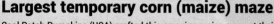

DID YOU KNOW?

If you are looking for a fail-safe method of reaching the end of a maze, keep your right hand on the wall as you move around. It might take you a while, and you may find that you are going back on yourself, but you will eventually find your way out.

DATELINE 1912

First parachute jump from a moving aircraft
On 1 Mar, Captain Albert Berry (USA) leaps from a biplane flying some 15,000 ft (460 m) above St Louis in Missouri, USA, and makes a safe landing on the grounds of Jefferson Barracks.

164 Engineering & Architecture

FAST FACTS
The word "maze" derives from an old English word meaning "delusion" or "bewilderment" • The **largest temporary corn maze** (below left) was so big that some visitors got lost in it and had to call 911 for assistance

Largest 3D wood-panel maze
Labyrinthia at Silkeborg in Denmark measures 1,300 m² (14,000 sq ft) and comprises larch wood panels slotted into concrete posts. Built in 1998, and rebuilt in 2005, it has 1 km (0.62 mi) of paths. Most visitors take about 30–45 min to reach the four corners marked with coloured flags and then find the centrally placed exit. Those who complete the maze are awarded a certificate.

Largest permanent tree maze
Built on an old plantation of Nordmann fir trees, Samsø Labyrinten on the Danish island of Samsø covers 60,000 m² (645,835 sq ft), with a 5,130-m (16,830-ft) path. Designed by Erik and Karen Poulsen, it was created in Sep 1999 and opened on 6 May 2000.

Glass-block labyrinth
Made in 2007 by British labyrinth historian Jeff Saward, Glass Labyrinth is found in the Chianti Sculpture Park in Siena, Italy. At 9 m (29 ft 6 in) across and comprising 3,600 blocks, this octagonal labyrinth is a reconstruction of a stone design found in the Val Camonica valley in eastern Lombardy, Italy, from 800–700 BCE. At the centre, visitors find an orange cube stool and a mirror with the word "self" set above their reflection.

PAC-Man maze
A real-life *PAC-Man* maze covering 580.86 m² (6,252 sq ft) – about the size of a basketball court – was built in Los Angeles, California, USA, for a Bud Light Super Bowl advertising spot on 7 Jan 2015. Created by Anheuser-Busch, Energy BBDO, Bandai Namco Games America and Mosaic (all USA), the maze included four Power Pellets and 242 Pac-dots, all individually programmed to turn off when a player ran over them, as per the famous videogame.

LARGEST VERTICAL MAZE
The front façade of the Al Rostamani Maze Tower, completed in Jan 2012 in Dubai, UAE, has an area of 3,947 m² (42,485 sq ft) – the size of 15 tennis courts. The lines of the balconies on the front and rear façades form real mazes by acclaimed puzzle designer Adrian Fisher (UK). Pictured right is Hassan Abdulla Al Rostamani, Vice Chairman of the Al Rostamani Group.

First industrial moving assembly line
On 7 Oct, the Ford Motor Company (USA) opens its factory in Highland Park, Michigan. Here, the car moves on a conveyor through the factory, passing workstations where specific parts are fitted until it is complete.

1913 DATELINE

guinnessworldrecords.com **165**

WATER PARKS

Longest water coaster

Opened on 11 May 2012, *Mammoth* at Holiday World & Splashin' Safari in Santa Claus, Indiana, USA, has a total track length of 1,763 ft (537 m). It has the capacity for 11 round boats, each designed to carry six people. The ride includes seven drops and passes through enclosed tunnels, plunging riders into total darkness.

Longest body slide

The *Jungle Slide* – also known as the *Eco Slide* – at Buena Vista Eco Lodge & Adventure Center in Rincón de la Vieja, Guanacaste, Costa Rica, is 425 m (1,394 ft 4 in) long. Riders experience a thrilling journey as they weave through the natural jungle environs wearing a rubber ring for safety.

Tallest body slide
The drop on the *Kilimanjaro* water slide at Águas Quentes Country Club in Barra do Piraí in Rio de Janeiro, Brazil, measures 49.9 m (163 ft 9 in).

Constructed in 2002, the slide cleverly makes use of the local topography to achieve its record-breaking height. It was built on top of a hill that was adapted to accommodate it.

Largest wave pool
According to the World Waterpark Association, the largest wave pool – often referred to

as an artificial sea – covers 13,600 m², or 1.36 ha (146,389 sq ft, or 3.36 acres), and is located in Siam Park, Bangkok, Thailand.

LONGEST...

Inflatable water slide
Live More Awesome (NZ) created a 1,975-ft-long (601.98-m) inflatable

water slide at Action Park in Vernon, New Jersey, USA, as verified on 10 Jul 2015.

Slip and slide
At 611.7 m (2,006 ft 10 in), the longest slip and slide was constructed by

Orange Jordan, Ziyad Mazzawi Corporation and Monaco Business Development (all JOR) in Amman, Jordan, on 16 Oct 2015. Water was sprayed along the length of the run to ensure slipperiness.

Largest indoor water park

Originally an airship hangar, Tropical Islands in Krausnick, Germany, has a 66,000-m² (710,400-sq-ft) main hall – technically an arch-supported membrane structure. It is constructed from 14,000 tonnes (15,430 US tons) of steel and stands 107 m (351 ft) tall. The interior space is large enough to contain eight soccer pitches, hold the Statue of Liberty standing upright or the Eiffel Tower on its side. Opened in 2004, Tropical Islands is fitted out with a mangrove jungle, 50,000-plant rainforest, lagoon, spa, saunas (including one within an Angkor Wat-style "temple") and themed accommodation venues. It's even possible to go for a balloon ride inside the dome.

1916

Most powerful steam locomotive
Baldwin Locomotive Works (USA) builds *No. 700* – a triple-articulated six-cylinder 2–8–8–8–4 tank engine. It has a tractive force (the force exerted at the rim of the driving wheel) of 166,300 lb (75,432 kg) working compound and 199,560 lb (90,519 kg) working simple.

DID YOU KNOW?
Flowriding combines aspects of different sports, including surfing, skateboarding, wakeboarding and snowboarding. Participants employ techniques from all these activities to maintain balance, and sometimes perform tricks, on an artificial wave.

Tallest flowriding wave

A flowriding wave is produced by directing a high-pressure sheet of water over a curved surface. It is used in flowriding (or flowboarding), a board sport that resembles surfing or wakeboarding. On 24 Sep 2015, the surf simulator *Da Wave* produced a flowriding wave measuring 3.5 m (11 ft 5 in) tall at Splashworld in Monteux, France.

Tube/mat water slide
Magic Eye at Galaxy Erding, in Erding, Germany, is 356.32 m (1,169 ft) long, as confirmed on 18 Nov 2010 on Guinness World Records Day. The slippery slide opened in May 2007 and was constructed by Klarer Freizeitanlagen AG (CHE). *Magic Eye* stands 22 m (72 ft 2.14 in) tall.

MOST...

Water slides in a water park
There are 59 water slides in Yinji Kaifeng Waterpark in Zhengzhou, Henan, China, which opened on 1 Jul 2015.

Water slides in a single tower
Designed and constructed by WhiteWater West Industries Ltd (CAN) in 1991, the tower located at Splash Garden on Rokkō Island in Kobe, Japan, had 50 slides departing from either the upper (16 m; 52 ft 6 in) or lower (12.4 m; 40 ft 8 in) level. Each slide swirled visitors down a different winding route, ending in one of seven pools.

People to travel down a water slide in one hour
Beerze Bulten (NLD) held an event in which 396 people descended on a water slide in an hour in Overijssel, Netherlands, on 30 Jul 2014.
   The **most people down a water slide in four hours** is 620, by Swiss youth group Jugendwerk in Münchenbuchsee, Switzerland, on 21 Jun 2014.

Water slides ridden in six months
Between 1 May and 31 Oct 2013, Sebastian Smith (UK) rode 186 water slides in Europe and North Africa, as a tester for the First Choice holiday company.

Most visited water park
Chimelong Water Park in Guangzhou, Guangdong, China, attracted 2,259,000 visitors in 2014, according to the Global Attractions Attendance Report for the year produced by industry monitors AECOM and the Themed Entertainment Association (TEA).

TALLEST WATER SLIDE
Verrückt at Schlitterbahn Waterpark in Kansas City, Kansas, USA, measured 51.38 m (168 ft 7 in) tall as of 18 Apr 2014. That makes it almost as tall as Niagara Falls. It took more than two years to create the ride.

168 FEET 7 INCHES

VERRÜCKT

168 FEET 7 INCHES

First non-stop flight across the Atlantic Ocean
On 14 Jun, John William Alcock and Arthur Whitten Brown (both UK) take off from St John's in Newfoundland, Canada, in a Vickers Vimy biplane. The pair land near Clifden in Ireland some 16 hr 12 min later.

1919

DATELINE

guinnessworldrecords.com   **167**

EPIC ENGINEERING

Longest tunnel-to-tunnel bridge

The Aizhai Bridge, near Jishou in Hunan, China, has a tower-to-tower main span of 1,176 m (3,858 ft) and a total length of 1,534 m (5,033 ft). The suspension bridge has a deck height of 336 m (1,102 ft) above the Dehang Canyon, making it also the **highest tunnel-to-tunnel bridge**. It opened in 2012 as part of the Jishou-to-Chadong expressway.

What makes this structure unusual is that it is approached by two tunnels that are carved into the mountainous terrain, so the bridge is hidden until drivers are already on it.

Longest suspension bridge

Opened in 1998, the Akashi-Kaikyō road bridge linking Honshu and Shikoku in Japan has an overall suspended length, with two side spans, of 3,911.1 m (12,831 ft 8 in). Almost half of this consists of its main span of 1,990.8 m (6,531 ft) – the **longest bridge span**.

Longest rail tunnel

On 15 Oct 2010, engineers completed drilling for the 57-km (35-mi) Gotthard Base Tunnel, 2,000 m (6,560 ft) beneath the Swiss Alps. It took 14 years to build and will carry 300 trains a day when it opens in 2016.

Largest artificial island

The Flevopolder is an island in the Netherlands that was created by a vast land-reclamation project between 1955 and 1968. It covers some 969.95 km^2 (374.5 sq mi) of what was once part of a shallow bay called the Zuiderzee and is separated from the mainland by a chain of lakes.

Largest gasification and carbon-capture power station

As of 2016, the 582-MW Kemper Project in eastern Mississippi, USA, burns around 4,000,000 tonnes (4,409,000 US tons) of local lignite coal annually. In a major innovation, the power station strips out most of the dust, 90% of the toxic mercury, 99% of the hydrogen sulphide and 65% of the carbon dioxide emissions. The diverted CO_2 is then used in enhanced oil recovery. Kemper is heralded as the first "clean coal" facility in the USA.

Highest concrete dam

Grande Dixence, on the river Dixence in Switzerland, rises 285 m (935 ft) high – almost twice the height of the Great Pyramid at Giza in Egypt – and has a crest length of 700 m (2,297 ft). It required 5,960,000 m^3 (210,475,000 cu ft) of concrete, enough to build a wall 1.5 m (5 ft) high and 10 cm (4 in) wide all around the Equator. Its triangular cross-section defines it as a "gravity" dam – wide at the base, narrow at the top – making it also the **highest gravity dam**. This design, and the dam's 15,000,000-tonne (16,535,000-US-ton) weight – 45 times as heavy as the Empire State Building – enables the Grande Dixence to withstand the pressure of 400 million m^3 (14 billion cu ft) of water.

HIGHEST CANTILEVERED GLASS-BOTTOMED SKYWALK

Opened on 28 Mar 2007, the Grand Canyon Skywalk in Arizona, USA, has a maximum vertical drop of 250 m (820 ft). Located at Grand Canyon West on the Hualapai Indian Reservation, the structure consists of a 20-m-wide (65-ft) U-shaped and cantilevered glass-bottomed observation deck jutting out past the rim of the Grand Canyon. Conceived by Las Vegas businessman David Jin and realized by Lochsa Engineering, the Skywalk can resist an 8.0-magnitude earthquake and 160-km/h (100-mph) winds. It can hold 120 people at any one time.

Most expensive ground-based telescope

The Atacama Large Millimeter/submillimeter Array (ALMA) comprises 66 high-precision antennae spread over distances up to 16 km (10 mi) and cost $1.3 bn (£890 m) to set up. Sited on the 5,050-m-high (16,560-ft) Chajnantor plateau in the Chilean Andes, ALMA studies light from some of the universe's coldest objects. Its main array of 50 antennae, each 12 m (39 ft) in diameter, acts as a single telescope – an interferometer. The near-perfect surfaces of the radio dish arrays enable maximum cosmic light to be captured.

DATELINE

1921

Longest home run hit
On 18 Jul, baseball legend George Herman "Babe" Ruth (USA) smashes a 175-m (574-ft) home run for the New York Yankees against the Detroit Tigers at Navin Field in Detroit, Michigan, USA.

168 Engineering & Architecture

FAST FACTS

The first pyramid structures are thought to date from 5,000 years ago in Mesopotamia • The Proserpina gravity dam in Spain, built by the Romans around the 2nd century CE, is thought to be the **oldest operational dam**

First artificial fog building

Designed by architects Diller Scofidio + Renfro (USA) as a pavilion for the 2002 Swiss Expo in Yverdon-les-Bains, the Blur Building was a steel platform (inset) enclosed in an artificial cloud above Lake Neuchâtel in Switzerland. Some 31,400 high-pressure jets sprayed out water in a constant, shape-shifting mist to create the effect.

Largest clock face

The Dokaae clock face at the top of the 120-storey Makkah Royal Clock Tower Hotel (aka the Abraj al-Bait Hotel Tower) in Mecca, Saudi Arabia, is 43 m (141 ft) wide. It is some six times larger than the clock face on the Elizabeth Tower (often wrongly called Big Ben, which is the bell inside the tower) in London, UK.

Largest...
• **Ancient stadium:** Until 550 CE, audiences of 255,000 watched chariot races, athletics and other spectacles at the 2,000-ft-long (610-m) Circus Maximus in Rome, Italy.

• **Amphitheatre:** Completed in 80 CE, the Flavian amphitheatre or Colosseum in Rome, Italy, covers 2 ha (5 acres) — equivalent to three international soccer pitches. Up to 87,000 people would flock here to see gladiators and wild beasts in mortal combat.
• **Pyramid:** The Quetzalcoatl Pyramid at Cholula de Rivadavia, south-east of Mexico City,

is 54 m (177 ft) tall and its base covers around 18.2 ha (45 acres). The Aztec structure is also the **largest monument ever built**.

DID YOU KNOW?
The granite blocks of the bridge section of the Segovia aqueduct are laid without mortar, probably owing to a lack of local limestone for cement. This makes it flexible enough to survive small earthquakes and buffeting winds.

Largest Roman aqueduct

Still in use after 19 centuries, the aqueduct at Segovia in Spain transports water more than 32.6 km (20.3 mi), from the Fuente Fría river to Segovia. At its tallest, the 683-m-long (2,240-ft) bridge section reaches 28 m (92 ft) high above two rows of 166 arches supported on 120 pillars, each with a different design. Probably dating from the 1st century CE, the system features many settlement tanks, cleansing basins, channels and bends.

Highest-grossing silent movie
The Big Parade (USA) makes $22 m (£4.96 m). The record will stand until the release of *The Artist* (FRA, 2011), which closely follows the traditions of silent-era movies and will gross in excess of $133 m (£91 m) by Jan 2016.

1925 ▶ DATELINE

guinnessworldrecords.com 169

ARTS & MEDIA

DATELINE

1927

First land-speed record run to exceed 200 mph
On 29 Mar, British racing driver Henry Segrave drives his Sunbeam 1000 HP – a twin-V12-engined monster known as *Mystery* – to a speed of 203.79 mph (327.97 km/h) at Daytona Beach in Florida, USA.

CONTENTS

Fastest movie to gross $500 million at the US box office

Sci-fi blockbuster *Star Wars VII: The Force Awakens* (USA, 2015) took $540,058,914 (£361,877,000) within 10 days of its US release on 18 Dec 2015, adding yet another box-office record to its collection. This equated to a staggering average daily gross of $54,005,891 (£36,188,700) and meant that the much-anticipated sequel stormed ahead of *Jurassic World* (USA, 2015), which took 17 days to reach the $500-m milestone.

Not surprisingly, *Star Wars VII* also claimed the US box-office records for **fastest movie to gross $100 million** and **fastest movie to gross $200 million**. Clearly, the Force is strong with this one...

First flight over Mount Everest
Squadron Leader Douglas Douglas-Hamilton (UK) leads a flight of two open-cockpit biplanes over the summit of Mount Everest. Fighting the thin air and high winds, they clear the peak by only 100 ft (30 m).

1933

DATELINE

MOVIE MONEY

To enter a movie theatre is to arrive in a magical realm where delights are played out daily for our entertainment. But just beyond the on-screen magic, in a land not very far away at all, dwells a business every bit as competitive and cut-throat as the crew of a pirate ship. Join us as we journey outside the enchanted kingdom and explore the gritty reality behind the fantasy.

DID YOU KNOW?

Seen right are the films with the highest domestic gross in the territories of Bollywood, Nollywood and Hollywood. From left: *PK* (IND, 2014), *30 Days in Atlanta* (NGA, 2014) and *Star Wars: The Force Awakens* (USA, 2015).

MOVIE TICKETS: WHO GETS WHAT

Illustrated above and right is the breakdown of costs associated with your movie ticket, and how ticket income is apportioned between the studio and the theatre itself. Figures are based on a generic $10-ticket model averaged over a four-week run. In the first week, the studio often takes as much as 90% (and sometimes even 100%) after the theatre's deduction for basic costs such as rent and heating. This figure drops week on week. The theatre covers any first-week losses with the income from concession stands.

Advertising and marketing	$2.00	20%
Production costs: costumes, sets, insurance, permits, rights, etc.	$1.70	17%
Distribution: manufacture and shipping of multiple copies of the movie	$1.00	10%
Actors' fees	$0.80	8%
Theatre staff costs, further investment and profit	$3.00	30%
Standing charge, aka "theatre nut": automatic deduction to cover basic theatre operating costs	$1.50	15%

ASTRONOMICAL COSTS

India's first Mars mission (right), launched in 2013, cost less than the movie *Gravity* (USA/ UK, 2013). At "just" $75 m (£52.7 m), putting *Mangalyaan* in orbit around Mars cost $25 m (£17.5 m) less than putting George Clooney (USA) in green-screen orbit around Earth.

SHOWBUSINE$$

Once the world's movie capital, Hollywood now lies third behind India, the home of Bollywood, in terms of annual output. India is the **most prolific producer of movies**, with 1,724 feature films produced in 2013, according to UNESCO and India's Central Board of Film Certification. Fast-rising Nigeria, often dubbed Nollywood, is not far behind, with around 1,000 movies released annually.

While the USA usually produces far fewer films – most recently around 738 a year, according to UNESCO – Hollywood's 150 or so biggest releases gross nearly five times as much in revenue as Bollywood and Nollywood combined. According to The Numbers, in 2015 there were 1.3 billion cinema tickets sold in the USA and Canada (compared with c.3–4 billion in India annually), earning $11.3 bn (£7.8 bn) and making the USA and Canada the largest domestic film market by box-office receipts.

WORDS ARE NOT CHEAP

Arnold Schwarzenegger (AUT/USA) was paid $15 m (£10.5 m) for his role as the back-from-the-future Terminator with a heart of gold (and other as-yet-undreamed-of metals) in *Terminator 2: Judgment Day* (USA, 1991). With only 700 words to say, this works out at $21,428 (£15,055) per word. In the time it took Arnie to utter "Hasta la vista, baby", he earned $85,712 (£60,222) – more than 10 times the average annual income in several Latin American countries.

At this rate, how would other classic movie catch-phrases compare? "Frankly, my dear, I don't give a damn" from *Gone with the Wind* (USA, 1939) would have earned Arnie $171,242 (£120,317), while "I'm gonna make him an offer he can't refuse", uttered in *The Godfather* (USA, 1972), would've netted him $192,852 (£135,501)!

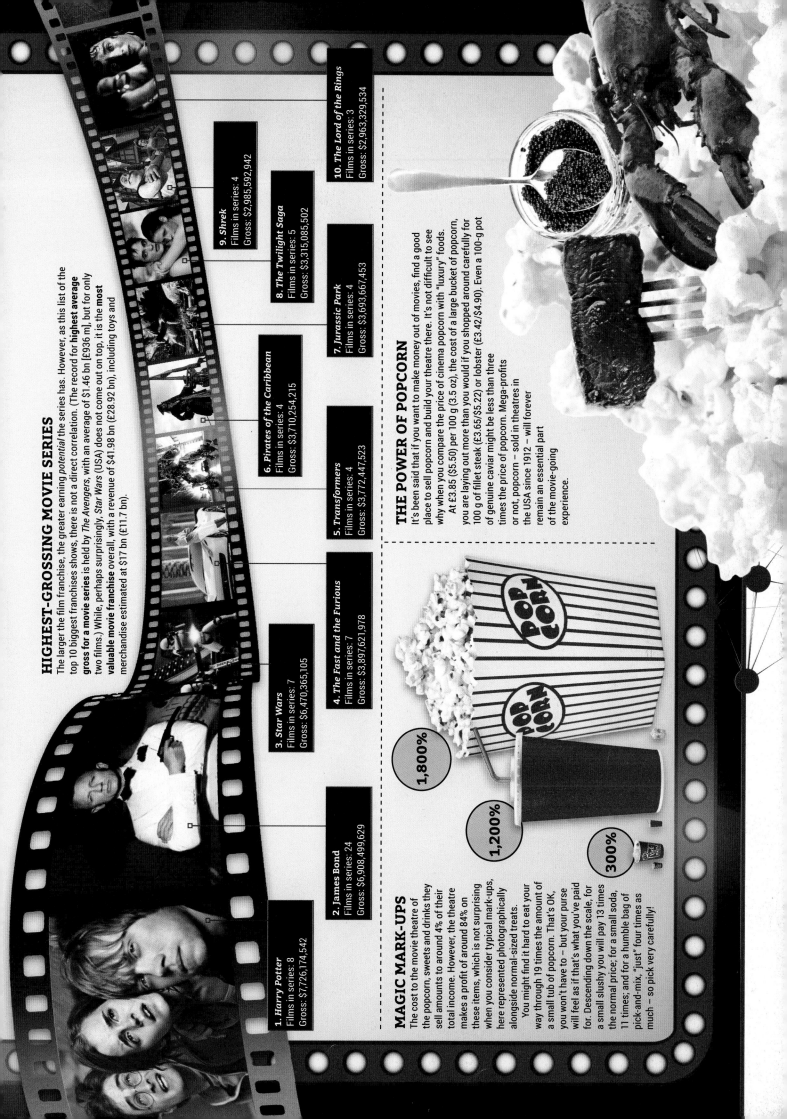

HIGHEST-GROSSING MOVIE SERIES

The larger the film franchise, the greater earning *potential* the series has. However, as this list of the top 10 biggest franchises shows, there is not a direct correlation. (The record for **highest average gross for a movie series** is held by *The Avengers*, with an average of $1.46 bn [£936 ml], but for only two films.) While, perhaps surprisingly, *Star Wars* (USA) does not come out on top, it is the **most valuable movie franchise** overall, with a revenue of £41.98 bn (£28.92 bn), including toys and merchandise estimated at $17 bn (£11.7 bn).

1. *Harry Potter*
Films in series: 8
Gross: $7,726,174,542

2. James Bond
Films in series: 24
Gross: $6,908,499,629

3. *Star Wars*
Films in series: 7
Gross: $6,470,365,105

4. *The Fast and the Furious*
Films in series: 7
Gross: $3,897,621,978

5. *Transformers*
Films in series: 4
Gross: $3,772,447,523

6. *Pirates of the Caribbean*
Films in series: 4
Gross: $3,710,254,215

7. *Jurassic Park*
Films in series: 4
Gross: $3,693,667,453

8. *The Twilight Saga*
Films in series: 5
Gross: $3,315,085,502

9. *Shrek*
Films in series: 4
Gross: $2,985,592,942

10. *The Lord of the Rings*
Films in series: 3
Gross: $2,963,329,534

MAGIC MARK-UPS

The cost to the movie theatre of the popcorn, sweets and drinks they sell amounts to around 4% of their total income. However, the theatre makes a profit of around 84% on these items, which is not surprising when you consider typical mark-ups, here represented photographically alongside normal-sized treats.

You might find it hard to eat your way through 19 times the amount of a small tub of popcorn. That's OK, you won't have to – but your purse will feel as if that's what you've paid for. Descending down the scale, for a small slushy you will pay 13 times the normal price; for a small soda, 11 times; and for a humble bag of pick-and-mix, "just" four times as much – so pick very carefully!

1,800%

1,200%

300%

THE POWER OF POPCORN

It's been said that if you want to make money out of movies, find a good place to sell popcorn and build your theatre there. It's not difficult to see why when you compare the price of cinema popcorn with "luxury" foods.

At £3.85 ($5.50) per 100 g (3.5 oz), the cost of a large bucket of popcorn, you are laying out more than you would if you shopped around carefully for 100 g of fillet steak (£3.65/$5.22) or lobster (£3.42/$4.90). Even a 100-g pot of genuine caviar might be less than three times the price of popcorn. Mega-profits or not, popcorn – sold in theatres in the USA since 1912 – will forever remain an essential part of the movie-going experience.

ART SALES

Most expensive painting by a living artist

Flag (1958), one of a series of paintings on this theme by US artist Jasper Johns, was sold privately to the hedge-fund billionaire Steven A Cohen (USA) in 2010 for a reported $110 m (£73 m).

Highest total from a single art auction

An evening auction of *Post-War and Contemporary Art* held by Christie's in New York City, USA, on 12 Nov 2014 raised $852,887,000 (£598,244,000). The auction featured works by artists such as Andy Warhol, Roy Lichtenstein, Jeff Koons (all USA) and Willem de Kooning (USA, b. NLD).

Most money made at auction by a single artist

Damien Hirst (UK) made £111 m ($200.8 m) from the sale of 167 of his works on 15–16 Sep 2008 at Sotheby's in London, UK.

MOST EXPENSIVE SOLD AT AUCTION

Painting

On 11 May 2015, at Christie's in New York City, USA, *Les Femmes d'Alger (Version O)* by Pablo Picasso (ESP), dated 14 Feb 1955, sold for $179.3 m (£115 m), with a commission of just over 12%. The buyer, who bid by telephone, chose to remain anonymous. For the **most expensive painting sold at a private sale**, see below.

Most expensive moonscape painting

Now a best-selling artist, US astronaut Alan Bean was lunar module pilot on *Apollo 12* (14–24 Nov 1969) and commander of the Skylab 3 mission (28 Jul–25 Sep 1973). *If We Could Do It All Over Again – Are You Ready for Some Football?* (below) depicts Bean chasing an American football on the Moon. It was sold to an unnamed buyer in 2004 for $182,369 (£98,415).

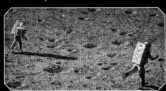

Painting sold online

October on Cape Cod (1946) by Edward Hopper (USA) typifies the isolation and solitude common to much of his work. It fetched $9.6 m (£6.7 m) in an internet auction by Christie's on 28 Nov 2012.

TRIVIA

Leonardo da Vinci's *Mona Lisa* once hung in the bedroom of French emperor Napoleon. The name is more correctly spelled *Monna Lisa* ("My Lady Lisa") in Italian.

DID YOU KNOW?

For decades, *Nafea Faa Ipoipo* was on loan to the Kunstmuseum Basel, in Switzerland, before Rudolf Staechelin decided to sell it. The previous most expensive painting was *The Card Players* (1890s), by Paul Cézanne (FRA), which sold to Qatar's royal family in 2011 for $250 m (£158.3 m).

MOST EXPENSIVE PAINTING

Produced in 1892, *Nafea Faa Ipoipo* ("When Will You Marry?", above) by French Post-Impressionist painter Paul Gauguin reputedly sold for around $300 m (£197 m) in Feb 2015. It was a private sale from the collection of a retired Sotheby's executive to an unnamed buyer.

Seven months later, US tycoon Ken Griffin reportedly paid $300 m for Willem de Kooning's *Interchange* (1955). He bought it alongside a $200-m (£129.8-m) piece by Jackson Pollock (USA), *Number 17A* (1948).

DATELINE **1935**

First land-speed record to exceed 300 mph
On 3 Sep, Sir Malcolm Campbell (UK) achieves a speed of 301.129 mph (484.62 km/h) at Bonneville in Utah, USA, driving the Campbell-Railton *Blue Bird*. It is powered by a Rolls-Royce R V12 engine.

174 Arts & Media

FAST FACTS

For 46 days in 1961, New York's Museum of Modern Art hung Henri Matisse's work *Le Bateau* upside down by mistake • Alan Bean has used real dust from the Moon in his paintings • From 1912 to 1948, the Olympic Games included art competitions

Most expensive work by a living artist sold at auction

Balloon Dog (Orange) – a 12-ft-high (3.6-m), orange-tinted, stainless-steel sculpture by Jeff Koons (USA, right) – sold at Christie's in New York City, USA, on 12 Nov 2013 for $58.4 m (£41 m). The sale was made to an anonymous telephone bidder. It is one of five "Balloon Dog" sculptures, each a different colour, created by Koons in the 1990s.

Print

On 20 Mar 2013, at Christie's on King Street in London, UK, the print *Young Woman on the Beach* (1896) by Edvard Munch (NOR) sold for £2.1 m ($3 m). That's three times the pre-sale estimate of £700,000 ($1 m). It is believed that Munch made 11 copies of the print altogether.

Drawing by an Old Master

Head of a Muse, by the Renaissance artist Raphael (ITA), sold for £29,200,000 ($47,788,400) on 9 Dec 2009 at Christie's in London, UK.

Private collection of paintings

In all, $377 m (£264.4 m) was raised at Sotheby's in New York City, USA, on 4 Nov 2015 from the sale of 69 artworks once owned by a billionaire real-estate developer. *Portrait de Paulette Jourdain* (1919), by Amedeo Modigliani (ITA), sold for $42.8 m (£27.7 m).

Painting by Rembrandt

Portrait of a Man, Half-length, With His Arms Akimbo (1658) sold by telephone to an anonymous bidder for £20 m ($28.5 m) at Christie's in London, UK, on 8 Dec 2009.

Sculpture by Rodin

A cast of the French sculptor's work *The Thinker* realized $15.3 m (£10.7 m) at Sotheby's in New York City, USA, on 7 May 2013.

DID YOU KNOW?

Created at short notice for a show in New York City in 1947, *L'homme au doigt* (right) was reportedly made in a single night between midnight and 9 a.m. It is thought that the left arm of the sculpture was originally curled around a second figure, which the artist then removed.

MOST EXPENSIVE PAINTINGS SOLD PRIVATELY

Few artists make a fortune during their lifetime. But once they die, the value of their work can rise to dizzy heights. Below, we list the 10 most expensive paintings ever sold privately. As the precise prices for private sales are not often made public, all values are approximate.

	TITLE / DATE PAINTED	ARTIST	PRICE	DATE SOLD
=1	*Nafea Faa Ipoipo* (1892)	Paul Gauguin (FRA)	$300 m (£197 m)	Feb 2015
=1	*Interchange* (1955)*	Willem de Kooning (USA, b. NLD)	$300 m (£194.7 m)	Sep 2015
3	*The Card Players* (1890s)	Paul Cézanne (FRA)	$250 m (£158.3 m)	2011
4	*Number 17A* (1948)*	Jackson Pollock (USA)	$200 m (£129.8 m)	Sep 2015
5	*No. 6 (Violet, Green and Red)* (1951)	Mark Rothko (USA)	$186 m (£112 m)	Aug 2014
6	Pendant portraits of Maerten Soolmans and Oopjen Coppit (1634)	Rembrandt Harmenszoon van Rijn (NLD)	$180 m (£118.6 m)	Sep 2015
7	*Le Rêve* (1932)	Pablo Picasso (ESP)	$155 m (£101.8 m)	26 Mar 2013
8	*No. 5, 1948* (1948)	Jackson Pollock (USA)	$140 m (£73.3 m)	2 Nov 2006
9	*Woman III* (1953)	Willem de Kooning (USA, b. NLD)	$137.5 m (£72.8 m)	18 Nov 2006
10	*Portrait of Adele Bloch-Bauer I* (1907)	Gustav Klimt (AUT)	$135 m (£72.9 m)	18 Jun 2006

* Joint sale

Most expensive sculpture sold at auction

Swiss sculptor Alberto Giacometti's 1947 work *L'homme au doigt* ("Pointing Man") sold for $141 m (£98.9 m) at Christie's in New York City, USA, on 11 May 2015. Standing 180 cm (70.8 in) tall, it is also the **most expensive bronze statue sold at auction**.

Largest airship

The 213.9-tonne (471,569-lb) German *Hindenburg* (LZ 129) has her maiden flight. Two years later, the *Graf Zeppelin II* (LZ 130) takes to the air. Each is 245 m (803 ft 10 in) long with a gas capacity of 200,000 m³ (7,062,933 cu ft).

1936 ▶ DATELINE

guinnessworldrecords.com 175

SHAKESPEARE

Longest-running Shakespeare show in the West End

Surprisingly, William Shakespeare has never made it big in London's West End theatres in his own right. However, the Reduced Shakespeare Company's tongue-in-cheek production *The Complete Works of William Shakespeare (Abridged)* notched up 3,744 performances from its opening night on 7 Mar 1996 until it closed on 3 Apr 2005.

Best-selling playwright
The plays and poetry of England's William Shakespeare (1564–1616) are believed to have sold in excess of 4 billion copies in the 400 years since his death.

Longest-running Shakespeare on Broadway
Directed by Margaret Webster, a production of *Othello* that opened on Broadway in Oct 1943 ran for 296 performances. The play starred Paul Robeson in the title role, making him the first African-American actor to play Othello on Broadway.

Youngest professional actor to play King Lear

Shakespeare's King Lear is an old man who gives up his kingdom to two of his daughters and disowns the other. For most actors, the part is the capstone of a long career, but UK actor Nonso Anozie (b. 28 May 1979) played the part in a production for the Royal Shakespeare Company in 2002 when he was only 23.

Longest speech in a Shakespeare play
In *Romeo and Juliet*, Romeo's friend Mercutio is given 43 lines to say on the subject of dreams in Act I, scene iv (lines 57–99).

In the play, she is just 13 years old when she meets Romeo. Usually, Juliet is played by a young actress who is older than 13, but in 2010 the 76-year-old Siân Phillips (UK) was cast in the role at the Bristol Old Vic, UK. This makes her the **oldest professional actor to play Juliet**.

Most expensive literature by Shakespeare sold at auction

The earliest collected edition of Shakespeare's plays is known as the "First Folio", printed by Isaac Jaggard and Edward Blount in 1623. One of only five copies of the work sold at Christie's in New York City, USA, on 8 Oct 2001 for $6,166,000 (£4,156,947) – the highest price ever paid for a 17th-century book.

FASTEST RECITAL OF HAMLET'S SOLILOQUY

Sean Shannon (CAN) recited Hamlet's 260-word soliloquy "To be or not to be" in 23.8 sec in Edinburgh, UK, on 30 Aug 1995 – a rate of 655 words per minute. The monologue, from Act III, scene i of *Hamlet*, reflects on death. Hamlet speculates about whether it is better to endure life's hardships stoically or to end them by killing oneself – although he fears that the "undiscover'd country" beyond death may hold supernatural terrors of its own.

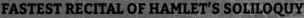

DATELINE 1938

Fastest steam locomotive
The London and North Eastern Railway "Class A4" No. 4468 *Mallard* reaches a speed of 125 mph (201 km/h) at Stoke Bank, near Essendine in Rutland, UK, on 3 Jul.

Most Laurence Olivier Awards won by an individual

As of 3 Apr 2016, Dame Judi Dench (UK) had won eight Olivier Awards. Her latest win came for Best Actress in a Supporting Role for her portrayal of Paulina in Shakespeare's *The Winter's Tale* (2015, above). She has also won Olivier Awards for appearances in *Macbeth* (1977) and *Antony and Cleopatra* (1987).

Most deaths in a Shakespeare play

The Bard wrote 74 death scenes in his plays. The goriest of his works is *Titus Andronicus*, which stages 14 deaths – including decapitations and suicides – alongside cannibalism.

TRIVIA

In 1890, Shakespeare fanatic Eugene Schieffelin began to try to introduce all the bird species mentioned in the Bard's plays into North America. Alas, the starlings he released had a devastating effect on native birds and are widely seen as a menace.

FAST FACTS

No one knows Shakespeare's date of birth, although traditionally it is regarded as 23 Apr 1564 – St George's Day • Shakespeare's name is spelled differently in each of the six surviving versions of his signature

Highest-grossing Shakespeare movie

William Shakespeare's Romeo + Juliet (USA, 1996), directed by Baz Luhrmann (AUS), took $147,542,381 (£91,030,600) on general release between 1 Nov 1996 and 14 Feb 1997. The big-budget, high-octane adaptation starred Leonardo DiCaprio and Claire Danes as the "star-cross'd lovers".

Shakespeare has 1,121 writing credits on film and TV productions, making him the **most filmed author**, as of Feb 2016. These include 106 versions of *Hamlet*, 98 versions of *Macbeth* and 64 versions of *Romeo and Juliet*. The most recent adaptations include the feature films *Macbeth* (UK/FRA/USA, 2015), starring Michael Fassbender and Marion Cotillard, and *Romeo and Juliet in Harlem* (USA, 2015), and *The Hollow Crown* (2012), the BBC's serial of Shakespeare's history plays.

Most lines by one character in a Shakespeare play

Hamlet delivers 1,495 lines of rumination on mortality and the human condition. Seen above is David Tennant (UK), who played the part in a 2008–09 production. At 4,042 lines and 29,551 words, *Hamlet* is the **longest Shakespeare play**.

Fastest time to watch every Shakespeare play

It took Dan Wilson (UK) just 328 days – between 27 Nov 2014 and 21 Oct 2015 – to see live performances of all 37 of Shakespeare's plays.

DID YOU KNOW?

Built in 1587, The Rose (below) was the fifth purpose-built playhouse in London. It staged works by some of the Elizabethan era's best-known playwrights, such as Christopher Marlowe and Shakespeare. By 1605, however, it was no longer a working theatre.

First documented reference to a Shakespeare play

There are no records of when any of Shakespeare's works were first performed, but his three *Henry VI* plays were certainly the first to be written about. On 3 Mar 1592, "harej the vi" was staged at The Rose, a playhouse in Southwark, London, UK. That same year, playwright Robert Greene quoted a line from one of the *Henry VI* plays in a pamphlet and Thomas Nashe wrote about a performance relating to the soldier John Talbot, a main character in the first of the *Henry VI* trilogy.

There is much debate about the authenticity of Shakespeare's portraits. It is widely believed, however, that the "Chandos portrait" (below), which dates from c. 1600–10, was painted from life.

First man-made object in space
On 3 Oct, Germany's V-2 rocket has its third and most successful test launch to date, from Peenemünde on the country's Baltic coast. The V-2 climbs to an altitude of 50 mi (80.4 km) above Earth's surface.

1942

DATELINE

guinnessworldrecords.com   177

MUSIC

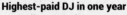

Most comments on a Weibo post

When pop star Luhan, aka Lu Han (CHN), posted a video about his favourite soccer team, Manchester United, on 10 Sep 2012, little could he have predicted the reaction it would spark. By 19 Apr 2016, the post had received 100,899,012 comments on the Weibo social network.

Highest-paid DJ in one year

According to Forbes, Scottish DJ Calvin Harris (b. Adam Wiles) earned $66 m (£43.12 m) in the 12 months to 1 Jun 2015.

In Mar 2015, Harris began dating US singer Taylor Swift. They are the **highest-paid celebrity couple**, with annual earnings of $146 m (£94.2 m), as announced by Forbes in Jun 2015.

Best-selling digital single

"Call Me Maybe" by Carly Rae Jepsen (CAN) has sold an estimated 18 million copies worldwide since its release in 2011. The Grammy-nominated single topped charts in 19 countries.

Best-selling download single in the USA in one week

"Hello" by Adele (UK, b. Adele Adkins) had approximately 1,112,000 downloads in its first week of release, from 23 Oct to 29 Oct 2015.

Most expensive vinyl record sold at auction

A mono copy of *The Beatles* (aka the *White Album*) sold by ex-band member Ringo Starr (UK) fetched $790,000 (£522,438) at Julien's Auctions in Los Angeles, California, USA, on 5 Dec 2015. Numbered 0000001, it was a first pressing of The Beatles' 1968 chart-topper.

First male artist to achieve three 10-million-selling singles

Three singles that feature Bruno Mars (USA, b. Peter Hernandez) have all sold in excess of 10 million copies worldwide: "Just the Way You Are" (2010), "Grenade" (2010) and "Uptown Funk!" (2014).

SPOTIFY

- **Most streamed track in 24 hours**: On 31 Jul 2015, "Drag Me Down" by One Direction (UK/IRL) was streamed 4.75 million times.
- **Most streamed track in one week**: "What Do You Mean?" by Justin Bieber (CAN) was streamed 30,723,708 times between 28 Aug and 3 Sep 2015.
- **Most streamed album in one week**: Justin Bieber's chart-topping album *Purpose* was streamed 205 million times on Spotify worldwide in the week after its release on 13 Nov 2015.
- **Most streams in one year**: In 2015, Canadian rapper Drake (b. Aubrey Drake Graham) attracted 1.8 billion streams from 46 million listeners.

THE RETURN OF ADELE

In 2011, Adele became the **first female to have the biggest-selling album and single in the USA and UK in the same year**. Released in 2015, her third LP, *25*, soon became the **fastest-selling pop album in the USA**, shifting 2,433,000 units in four days from its release on 20 Nov. Only 24 hr after its release, more than 900,000 copies of *25* had been downloaded on Apple's iTunes store, according to *Billboard*, making it the **fastest-selling album on iTunes**. And on 30 Nov 2015, it reached the million-selling mark on the UK albums chart, the **fastest time for an album to sell 1 million copies in the UK**.

Largest battleship
The Japanese battleships *Yamato* and *Musashi* have a full-load displacement of 71,111 tonnes (78,386 US tons), an overall length of 263 m (863 ft), a beam of 38.7 m (127 ft) and a full-load draught of 10.8 m (35 ft 5.1 in).

FAST FACTS

Shakira speaks Spanish, Portuguese, Italian and English • In 2015, superstar DJ Calvin Harris became the new "face" of Giorgio Armani underwear • At its peak, Adele's *25* was selling more than double the rest of *Billboard*'s top 100

YOUTUBE & VEVO

Fastest time for a video to reach 1 billion views on YouTube
Adele's "Hello", which was uploaded to YouTube on 22 Oct 2015, reached 1 billion views a mere 88 days later on 18 Jan 2016. It was the 18th YouTube video to attract 1 billion views since 21 Dec 2012, when PSY's (KOR) "Gangnam Style" became the **first video to receive 1 billion views** (after a period of 159 days).

• **Most viewed music channel on YouTube (individual)**: JustinBieberVEVO had 10,478,651,389 views logged by 19 Apr 2016, for the 120 videos uploaded to the channel since 25 Sep 2009.

• **Most views for an act on VEVO in 24 hours**: Recordings by David Bowie (UK, b. David Jones) attracted 51 million views on the video-hosting platform VEVO on 11 Jan 2016, the day after his death at the age of 69.

Most liked female on Facebook

The Facebook page of singer Shakira (COL, b. Shakira Isabel Mebarak Ripoll) had been liked by 104,537,619 fans as of 19 Apr 2016. The "Hips Don't Lie" star was the **first person on Facebook to attract 100 million likes** (on 18 Jul 2014) and is the second most popular celebrity on the social media network behind soccer player Cristiano Ronaldo (with 111,047,562 likes).

Most streamed album on Spotify in one year

Released on 28 Aug 2015, *Beauty Behind the Madness*, by Canadian R&B musician The Weeknd (b. Abel Tesfaye), was the most streamed album on Spotify between 1 Dec 2014 and 1 Dec 2015. It attracted a total of 60 million listeners in 2015.

• **Most streams in one year (female)**: Rihanna's (BRB, b. Robyn Rihanna Fenty) songs were streamed more than 1 billion times in 2015.

• **Most streamed act**: Singer Ed Sheeran's (UK) tracks had been streamed more than 3 billion times on Spotify as of 1 Dec 2015.

Most followers on Twitter

As of 19 Apr 2016, Katy Perry (USA, b. Katheryn Hudson; @katyperry) had an audience of 86,944,886 on Twitter. In second and third places were fellow pop stars Justin Bieber (@justinbieber) – the **most followers on Twitter (male)** – and Taylor Swift (@taylorswift), with 79,737,002 and 75,517,216 followers respectively. As of the same date, One Direction (@onedirection) remained the **most popular music group on Twitter**, with 28,092,141 followers.

Highest annual earnings ever for a female pop star

Katy Perry earned $135 m (£85.87 m) in the 12 months to Jun 2015, according to Forbes. The singer was ranked third on the list of the "World's Highest-Paid Celebrities", behind boxers Floyd Mayweather Jr (USA, $300 m; £190.83 m) and Manny Pacquiao (PHL, $160 m; £101.77 m). After Perry, the highest-earning musicians on Forbes' 2015 rich list were: One Direction (No.4, $130 m; £82.69 m), country singer Garth Brooks (USA, No.6, $90 m; £57.25 m) and Taylor Swift (No.8, $80 m; £50.88 m).

First general-purpose electronic computer
The US Army's Electronic Numerical Integrator And Computer (ENIAC) machine is built. It weighs 27 tonnes (59,525 lb), measures 2.6 x 0.9 x 24 m (8 ft 6 in x 2 ft 11 in x 78 ft 9 in) and is used to calculate artillery trajectories.

1946

DATELINE

MUSIC

Most weeks at No.1 on the US Digital Songs chart

Two singles have spent a total of 13 weeks at No.1 on *Billboard*'s Digital Songs chart. "Low" by Flo Rida (right) featuring T-Pain (both USA) achieved the feat between 15 Dec 2007 and 8 Mar 2008. "Uptown Funk!" by Mark Ronson (UK) featuring Bruno Mars (USA) matched that record in three separate runs between 3 Jan and 11 Apr 2015. Ronson is shown above (far left), along with Mars (third from left) and his backing band The Hooligans.

Most simultaneous entries on the UK albums chart

On the Official Albums Chart dated 21 Jan 2016, David Bowie (UK, b. David Jones) placed 19 albums in the Top 100. The ground-breaking musician, who succumbed to cancer on 10 Jan 2016, owned a quarter of the UK Top 40. His 25th studio album, *Blackstar*, debuted at No.1 with sales of 146,168 – enough to give "The Thin White Duke" a 10th chart-topper in the UK.

FIRST ACT TO HOLD ALL TOP 3 PLACES ON THE UK SINGLES CHART

In the 65 years of the UK's Official Singles Chart (1952–present), no act had held the top three positions in the same week until Justin Bieber (CAN) did so with "Love Yourself" (No.1), "Sorry" (No.2) and "What Do You Mean?" (No.3) on the chart dated 14 Jan 2016.

On the *Billboard* Hot 100 dated 5 Dec 2015, Bieber had 17 tracks, the **most simultaneous tracks on the US singles chart**. The highest placed was "Sorry", at No.2. Of these, 13 tracks were new entries, the **most simultaneous new entries in the Hot 100 by a solo act.**

DID YOU KNOW?
Elvis Presley, The Shadows, The Beatles, John Lennon and Frankie Goes to Hollywood have all occupied No.1 and No.2 simultaneously on the UK chart. But nobody had locked down the entire Top 3 until Justin Bieber came along.

First act with 100 million RIAA single certifications
The Recording Industry Association of America (RIAA) issues gold records for sales of 500,000 units; platinum records reflect sales of 1 million units. In Jul 2015, the RIAA announced that Rihanna (BRB, b. Robyn Rihanna Fenty) was the first act to reach 100 million gold and platinum single sales certifications in the USA.

Most songs on a digital album
The Pocket Gods (UK) packed 100 songs, all a little over 30 sec long, on to their Dec 2015 album *100x30*. The band made the eclectic album to protest against the small royalties offered by the digital music industry for tracks longer than 30 sec.

Largest attendance at a music festival (one location)
Austria's free, open-air Donauinselfest ("Danube Island Festival") drew 3.3 million revellers to Vienna on 26–28 Jun 2015.

CHARTS

Youngest male solo artist to debut at No.1 on the *Billboard* Hot 100
Justin Bieber (b. 1 Mar 1994) was 21 years 202 days old when "What Do You Mean?" debuted at No.1 on the *Billboard* Hot 100 on 19 Sep 2015.

Most *Billboard* Hot 100 entries by a solo artist
As of 30 Apr 2016, US rapper Lil Wayne had placed 129 different songs on the *Billboard* Hot 100. His debut was "Back that Thang Up" in 1999.

DATELINE

1947

Largest aircraft
On 2 Nov, the Hughes H-4 Hercules, better known as the "Spruce Goose", makes its first – and only – flight, off the coast of California, USA. This colossal flying boat has a wing-span of 319 ft 11 in (97.51 m) and is 218 ft 8 in (66.65 m) long.

180 Arts & Media

Most consecutive weeks in the Top 10 of the *Billboard* Hot 100 (male)

The Weeknd (CAN, b. Abel Tesfaye) spent 45 weeks in the Top 10 of *Billboard*'s Hot 100 between 7 Mar 2015 and 9 Jan 2016 – the longest ever Top 10 streak by a solo male. The historic run comprised three singles: "Earned It" (7 Mar to 4 Jul 2015), "Can't Feel My Face" (11 Jul to 14 Nov 2015) and "The Hills" (1 Aug and 29 Aug 2015 to 9 Jan 2016).

Most consecutive weeks in the UK Top 40 (one single)

Ed Sheeran's (UK) "Thinking Out Loud" debuted on the UK's Official Singles Chart on 5 Jul 2014 and spent its 54th consecutive week in the Top 40 on 11 Jul 2015. The ballad was No.1 for two weeks and spent 20 weeks inside the Top 10.

Most viewed music video online (female)

Taylor Swift's (USA) "Blank Space" had racked up a viewer count of 1,566,138,812 on the video-hosting platform VEVO as of 19 Apr 2016.

DID YOU KNOW?
The "Blank Space" video was shot in two days, mostly at Oheka Castle in Long Island, New York, USA, which appears in the classic 1941 movie *Citizen Kane*. Swift really did stand on a white horse for the video, but she *didn't* actually wreck the Shelby AC Cobra car that she attacks with a golf club.

Most weeks at No.1 on *Billboard*'s Artist 100 chart

As of 30 Apr 2016, Taylor Swift (USA) had topped *Billboard*'s Artist 100 chart for a record-breaking total of 31 weeks. That's 20 weeks more than the second most successful act on the countdown, Justin Bieber (CAN). Swift's dominance of the fledgling chart included 12 successive weeks at the top, from 8 Nov 2014 to 24 Jan 2015.

Most successive weeks in the UK Top 10 for a debut album

On the Official Albums Chart for 26 Sep 2015, *In the Lonely Hour* (2014), by Sam Smith (UK), spent a 69th straight week in the Top 10. Its UK sales exceed 1.75 million copies.

Most words in a hit single

"Rap God", by Eminem (USA), packs 1,560 words into 6 min 4 sec – averaging 4.28 words per sec! In one 15-sec burst, Eminem spits out 97 words – 6.46 words per sec. "Rap God" debuted at No.5 on the UK singles chart on 26 Oct 2013 and No.7 on the US *Billboard* Hot 100 on 2 Nov 2013.

Inspired by "Rap God", "Animal", by the Harry Shotta Show (UK), contains 1,771 words in 6 min 9 sec, or 4.79 words per sec – the **most words in a single**. "This is purely about pushing our art and having some fun," MC Shotta told website UKF. "Animal" premiered on BBC Radio 1Xtra on 4 Jun 2015.

Loudest siren

In March, American car maker Chrysler begins making a V8-engined air-raid siren, designed to warn the public in case of a nuclear attack. It emits a 138-decibel wail that can be heard up to 25 mi (40 km) away.

1952 ▶ DATELINE

guinnessworldrecords.com **181**

MOVIES

Most valuable vehicles in a movie car chase

In one of the central action set-pieces of the 24th official James Bond film *Spectre* (UK/USA, 2015), Bond (played by Daniel Craig) drives through the streets of Rome at speeds of up to 100 mph (160 km/h) in a prototype Aston Martin DB10. This non-production model, of which only 10 were made – all exclusively for this film – is valued at $4.6 m (£3.17 m). Bond is pursued by the villain Mr Hinx (played by Dave Bautista), who drives a Jaguar C-X75 – another specially produced super-car, with an estimated value of $1 m (£689,000). Overall, the two vehicles used in the chase represent a total market value of $5.6 m (£3.86 m).

Highest annual earnings for a film actress and actor

According to the Forbes list of the "World's Highest-Paid Celebrities", *Hunger Games* star Jennifer Lawrence (USA) took home $52 m (£33 m) for the year ending 30 Jun 2015. She is the second-highest-earning actor on the list, surpassed only by Robert Downey Jr (USA), who earned $80 m (£50.8 m) from Jun 2014 to Jun 2015. This includes his fee for playing Iron Man in the Avengers movie *Age of Ultron*.

DID YOU KNOW?
Joe Simon and Jack Kirby created Captain America, who debuted in his own comic in Mar 1941. Back then, he had a triangular shield rather than the familiar round one. Cap first hit the big screen in 1944, played by Dick Purcell, in a black-and-white serial – with no shield.

Highest box-office film gross
As of 22 Sep 2015, *Avatar* (US/UK, 2009) had grossed $2,783,918,982 (£1.79 bn) worldwide, according to The-Numbers.com.

Highest-grossing female action movie star
As of 8 Feb 2016, Jennifer Lawrence was history's most successful female action movie star. According to The-Numbers.com, the *Hunger Games* series (in which she plays Katniss Everdeen) and her two *X-Men* movies (in which she plays Raven/Mystique) have grossed $4,005,735,448 (£2.76 bn) worldwide.

Highest opening weekend gross for an R-rated film
Deadpool (USA, 2016) grossed $260 m (£179.4 m) worldwide over its three-day opening weekend of 12–14 Feb 2016. The risqué superhero movie went on to become the **highest-grossing R-rated movie** ever, making $758,987,687 (£537.1 m) by 13 Apr 2016.

Largest IMAX opening
On 3 Apr 2015, the global opening of *Furious 7* (USA), the seventh film in the *Fast & Furious* franchise, saw screenings in a total of 810 IMAX locations. The previous record of 760 IMAX screens was set in Nov 2014 by *Interstellar* (USA). With a global gross of $1,516,246,709 (£965.8 m) as of 18 Jun 2015, *Furious 7* is also the **highest-grossing car-chase movie**.

Longest movie trailer
In Jul 2014, Anders Weberg (SWE) unveiled a 72-min trailer for his forthcoming 720-hr film *Ambiancé*, which will be released in 2020.

TRIVIA
British comedy actor Simon Pegg appears in two sci-fi institutions. He plays Montgomery "Scotty" Scott (above) in the *Star Trek* franchise, and Unkar Plutt (below) in the latest *Star Wars* episode.

MOST PROFITABLE ACTOR FOR A HOLLYWOOD STUDIO (CURRENT)
In the year up to Jun 2015, no other Hollywood actor has returned more profit relative to what they were paid than Captain America star Chris Evans (USA), according to Forbes. In his last three major films of this period – which include *Avengers: Age of Ultron* (USA, 2015) and *Captain America: The Winter Soldier* (USA, 2014) – Evans grossed $181.80 (£118) for every $1 (£0.65) that he was paid.

DATELINE

1953 — **First ascent of Everest**
Edmund Percival Hillary (NZ) and Indo-Tibetan Tenzing Norgay reach the 8,848-m-high (29,029-ft) summit of the world's **highest mountain** at 11:30 a.m. on 29 May.

182 Arts & Media

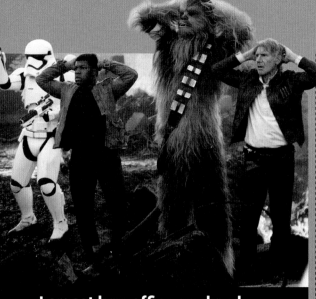

FAST FACTS
Daniel Craig has starred in the three longest Bond films: *Casino Royale* (2006), *Skyfall* (2012) and *Spectre* (2015) • Robert Downey Jr's Iron Man suit has around 450 parts • *The Force Awakens* is the first *Star Wars* movie not released in May

Largest box-office weekend

As well as being the **fastest movie to gross $500 million at the domestic box office** (see p.170), the seventh *Star Wars* instalment *The Force Awakens* (USA, 2015) enjoyed the biggest domestic weekend – and **opening weekend** – on its launch over the weekend of 18–20 Dec 2015, grossing $247.9 m (£166.3 m).

Most visual effects shots in a film

The number of digital visual effects (VFX) shots in blockbuster movies continues to multiply. In this respect, India's film industry has raced ahead of Hollywood in recent years. Effects supervisors for S S Rajamouli's medieval fantasy epic *Baahubali: The Beginning* (IND, 2015) confirm that the film contains around 4,500 separate VFX shots. They were created by more than 600 VFX staff working for 16 different effects studios across five countries.

Most connected living actor
The University of Virginia's (USA) "Oracle of Bacon" is software – named after American actor Kevin Bacon – that maps the working ties between 2.9 million actors and actresses, as well as 1.9 million movies/TV shows, in the Internet Movie Database. As of 4 Dec 2015, the most connected living movie star – that is, the person at the "Centre of the Hollywood Universe" – is Eric Roberts (USA), who has the lowest score of 2.83285.

Longest James Bond movie
At 148 min, *Spectre* outruns all other movies in the Bond franchise. The **shortest Bond film** is *Quantum of Solace* (2008) at 106 min.
   Spectre's basic production budget has been estimated at $245 m (£169 m), making it the **most expensive Bond movie**. *Spectre* isn't the **highest-grossing Bond movie**, however. That honour goes to *Skyfall* (UK/USA, 2012). It grossed $1,110,526,981 (£743.8 m).
   Jesper Christensen (DNK) has made the **most appearances as a Bond villain**. As Mr White, he appears in *Casino Royale* (2006), *Quantum of Solace* and *Spectre*.
   The record for the **most appearances as James Bond** is shared by Sean Connery and Roger Moore (both UK), with 007 outings each. Connery appeared in the first Bond movie, *Dr No* (UK, 1962), and Moore made his debut in *Live and Let Die* (UK, 1973).

Dressed to kill: Bond and *Spectre*

Daniel Craig is the **highest-paid actor to have played James Bond**. His salary for portraying agent 007 in *Spectre* is estimated to have totalled $39 m (£25.4 m).
   In the movie, Craig is seen on-screen wearing clothes and accessories with a total retail value of at least $56,220 (£39,060), making his Bond the **most expensively dressed movie character**.
   According to information provided by Gary Powell, chief stunt coordinator on *Spectre*, vehicles worth $48 m (£33 m) were demolished during the making of the film, the **highest value of vehicles destroyed in the making of a movie**. This figure includes seven of the 10 Aston Martin DB10 prototypes created for the film.
   Sam Smith's (UK) "Writing's on the Wall", taken from *Spectre*, became the **first Bond theme to reach No.1 in the UK chart** when it debuted at the top on 10 Oct 2015.

DID YOU KNOW?
Spectre also featured the **largest film stunt explosion** (pictured). A total yield of 68.47 tonnes (75.4 US tons) of TNT equivalent were ignited for the scene in Erfoud, Morocco: the result of detonating 8,418 litres (2,224 US gal) of kerosene with 33 kg (72 lb 12 oz) of powder explosives.

First person to run a mile in under four minutes
On 6 May, in front of a 3,000-strong crowd at Oxford University, UK, 25-year-old Roger Bannister (UK) runs one mile in 3 min 59.4 sec. Up to this point, many people had believed that this feat was impossible.

1954

DATELINE

guinnessworldrecords.com **183**

DISNEY
GALLERY

Walter (Walt) Elias Disney (USA, 1901–66) is arguably the most celebrated movie-maker of all time. The films bearing his name offer a roll-call of records – the highlights of which are listed here – but the man himself earned a few of his own, too, including: **most Oscars won in a lifetime** (26), **most Oscars won in a year** (four, in 1954) and **most consecutive Oscar wins** (eight, from 1932 to 1940).

1 | HIGHEST BOX-OFFICE GROSS FOR AN ANIMATION (INFLATION-ADJUSTED)
Disney's first full-length feature film, *Snow White and the Seven Dwarfs* (1937), took $184.9 m (then £37.3 m) at the box office worldwide, equivalent to $1.6 bn (£1.02 bn) today. On 10 Mar 1938, the picture was granted a "special" Academy Award – of one regular-sized award and seven smaller versions! *Snow White* was also the **first movie with an official soundtrack**.

2 | FIRST ANIMATION NOMINATED FOR BEST PICTURE OSCAR
In 1992, *Beauty and the Beast* achieved an animated movie first by making the shortlist for Best Picture Oscar. It lost to *Silence of the Lambs* at the awards ceremony on 30 Mar 1992, but the song "Beauty and the Beast" was voted Best Original Song, and Alan Menken's music won Best Original Score. In Apr 1994, the movie became the **first Disney film adapted into a stage musical**.

3 | BEST-SELLING ANIMATION SOUNDTRACK
The soundtrack of *The Lion King* (1994) has achieved 7.7 million confirmed sales in the USA, and an estimated 10 million units worldwide. The movie itself also holds the record for the **best-selling home video**, with more than 55 million copies sold worldwide, and in musical form it is the **highest-grossing Broadway show**. Since opening in Oct 1997, it has taken $1.12 bn (£742.8 m) – up to Jan 2015 – and sold a total of 12,091,055 seats.

4 | MOST POSITIVELY REVIEWED FILM
As of Jan 2016, around 410 movies had a 100% rating on review-aggregation website Rotten Tomatoes. The most widely celebrated is *Toy Story 2* (1999), accruing 163 published reviews, all deemed positive. On 18 Jun 2010, *Toy Story 3* enjoyed what was then the most successful opening weekend for a 3D animation, taking $110,307,189 (£71,692,765). Earning $1.063 bn (£681 m) globally to 2 Dec 2010, it was the **first animated movie to gross $1 bn**.

DATELINE 1956
First transatlantic telephone cable
On 25 Sep, the telephone cable Transatlantic Number One (TAT-1) between Scotland, UK, and Clarenville in Newfoundland, Canada, opens for business. It carries 588 UK–USA calls and 119 UK–Canada calls in the first 24 hr.

5

6

7

DID YOU KNOW?
Disney's Magic Kingdom in Florida, USA, boasts the **tallest castle in a theme park**. Cinderella Castle, as it's known, towers a magical 189 ft (57.6 m) tall and was inspired by various real castles, châteaux and palaces in Europe. It opened in 1971, and its image now forms part of Disney's logo.

8

HIGHEST-GROSSING PUPPET MOVIE **5**	**HIGHEST-GROSSING COMPUTER ANIMATION** **6**	**MOST VES AWARDS WON BY AN ANIMATION** **7**	**HIGHEST-GROSSING OPENING WEEKEND FOR AN ORIGINAL MOVIE** **8**

HIGHEST-GROSSING PUPPET MOVIE — **5**

Debuting on television in the 1950s, Kermit the Frog, Miss Piggy and the rest of the Muppets have had a long and successful career. This has included eight theatrical releases and two TV movies. The most successful to date in terms of box-office sales is the 2011 Disney revamp *The Muppets*. By 30 Mar 2012, the film had grossed $160,971,922 (£101,206,000), according to The-Numbers.com.

HIGHEST-GROSSING COMPUTER ANIMATION — **6**

According to The-Numbers.com, *Frozen* (2013), and its 2014 re-release as a singalong version, had global box-office receipts of $1,274,234,980 (£829,688,000) by 5 Jun 2015. This means it is also the **highest-grossing Disney movie**. In a less official compliment, *Frozen* had 29.919 million illegal downloads in 2014, according to German piracy-monitoring company Excipio, making it the **most pirated animated movie** that year.

MOST VES AWARDS WON BY AN ANIMATION — **7**

Big Hero 6 (2014), starring inflatable robot Baymax and his human companion Hiro, received five awards at the Visual Effects Society Awards ceremony on 4 Feb 2015. To build the film's ground-breaking digital world, Disney Studios assembled a cluster of 4,600 computers split over four separate locations, which could run 400,000 rendering (animation) jobs in 24 hr – the **most computing power used in making a movie**.

HIGHEST-GROSSING OPENING WEEKEND FOR AN ORIGINAL MOVIE — **8**

Inside Out, a brand-new "first" from the Disney-owned Pixar Studios, grossed a total of $90,440,272 (£56,923,600) when it opened in 3,946 US theatres on the weekend of 19–21 Jun 2015. The previous record, held by *Avatar* (2009), had stood for almost six years. *Inside Out* was also a hit with the critics, winning the Oscar for Best Animated Feature at the 2016 ceremony.

First artificial satellite in orbit
On 4 Oct, *Sputnik 1* is launched by an inter-continental ballistic missile from the Baikonur Cosmodrome at Tyuratam in Kazakhstan, USSR. Its lifetime is believed to be 92 days.

1957 DATELINE

TV

Highest-rated TV series (current)

Season 2 of crime drama *Fargo* (FX, USA) achieved a metascore of 96/100 on Metacritic (representing "universal acclaim"), from 33 reviews. As of 26 Apr 2016, it had a user rating of 9.4/10.

Highest-earning comedian (current)

According to Forbes, Jerry Seinfeld (USA) earned $36 m (£25.57 m) between Jun 2014 and Jun 2015, primarily from giving live performances, but also from syndicating his eponymous TV comedy series.

Richest TV creator

The "Queen of all Media", Oprah Winfrey (USA), best known for the talk show she created and hosted in 1986–2011, had a net worth of $3.1 bn (£2.15 bn) in the Forbes 400 list of Apr 2016.

Forbes put John de Mol's (NLD) net worth at $1.49 bn (£1.03 bn), making him the **richest TV creator (male)** as of Apr 2016. De Mol took the reality TV concept global with *Big Brother*, and launched *The Voice of Holland,* which became the international hit *The Voice.*

Most scripted TV shows released in one year

According to TV channel FX (USA), networks and streaming services broadcast a record 409 dramas, comedies and limited series in 2015.

Most followers on Twitter for a TV personality

Ellen DeGeneres (USA, above left, @TheEllenShow) was the most popular TV personality on Twitter as of 18 Apr 2016, with 57,988,099 followers. The former stand-up comedian has hosted *The Ellen DeGeneres Show* since 2003.

As of the same date, the **most followers on Twitter for a TV personality (male)** was 39,173,743 for Jimmy Fallon (USA, above right @JimmyFallon).

HIGHEST-EARNING TV STAR, CURRENT (MALE AND FEMALE)

According to Forbes, Kaley Cuoco (USA, right), star of *The Big Bang Theory* (CBS, USA), earned around $28.5 m (£18.1 m) in the year from Jun 2014 – as did Sofía Vergara (COL) of *Modern Family* (ABC, USA). Meanwhile, *The Big Bang Theory* lead, Jim Parsons (USA, second right), earned an estimated $29 m (£18.4 m). The show's "Opening Night Excitation" episode (inset) scored Nielsen's **largest live+7 audience for a TV show**: a total of 24.38 million.

TRIVIA

In 2015, the *Big Bang Theory* LEGO® set was launched to amuse fans of both the show and plastic brick-building. It recreates Sheldon and Leonard's living room in detail, with minifigures of the seven characters, each dressed in their own style. Created by two LEGO fan designers, the concept originated from LEGO's Ideas crowdsourcing community.

DATELINE

1960

Deepest manned descent
On 23 Jan, Dr Jacques Piccard (CHE) and Lt Donald Walsh (USA) pilot the Swiss-built US Navy bathyscaphe *Trieste* to a depth of 10,911 m (35,797 ft) in the Challenger "Deep section of the Mariana Trench, thought to be the **deepest point on Earth**.

186 Arts & Media

FAST FACTS
SpongeBob SquarePants was created by bona fide marine biologist Stephen Hillenburg • The *Bazinga rieki* jellyfish was named after Sheldon's catchphrase "bazinga!" in *The Big Bang Theory* • *The Walking Dead* started life as a comic book

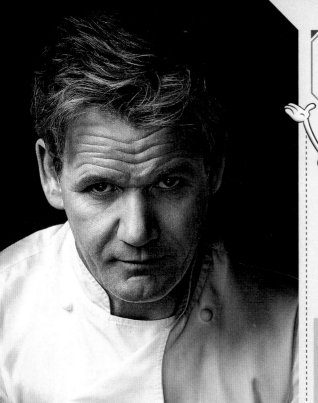

Highest annual earnings for a TV chef

British chef Gordon Ramsay earned an estimated $60 m (£38.1 m) between Jun 2014 and Jun 2015, according to Forbes' Celebrity 100 list. He is best known for his culinary TV shows, such as *Hell's Kitchen*, *Masterchef USA* and *Ramsay's Kitchen Nightmares*. Ramsay currently owns or manages more than 20 premises around the world, and his restaurants have been awarded 16 Michelin stars across his career to date.

Longest-running TV sketch comedy show (current)
As of 20 Feb 2016, Colombia's *Sábados Felices* ("Happy Saturdays"), originally titled *Campeones de la Risa* ("Laughter Champions"), had run on the Caracol TV channel for a record 44 years 15 days.

The **longest-running TV music talent show** is *Nodo Jiman* ("Proud of My Voice"), which is created by NHK (JPN). First broadcast on 15 Mar 1953, the Asia-wide karaoke-based show was still running as of 29 Feb 2016 – 63 years later.

Most Nickelodeon Kids' Choice Awards won by a cartoon

No other animated series has won the "Favorite Cartoon" category more often than *SpongeBob SquarePants*, with 13 wins since 2003. The last eight, since 2009, have been consecutive. Its run was interrupted in 2008 by *Avatar: The Last Airbender*.

Most watched show worldwide (current)
Eurodata TV Worldwide surveys the best-performing episodes of TV shows across a number of countries. According to their reports, crime drama *NCIS* (CBS, USA) was sold into more than 200 markets and seen by 55 million viewers in 2014, far in excess of *Game of Thrones* and *The Walking Dead*.

Largest series premiere on cable TV

The 90-min debut of the horror/drama spin-off *Fear the Walking Dead* (AMC, USA) on 23 Aug 2015 drew 10.1 million viewers and an incredible 6.3 rating among adults aged 18–49, according to the Entertainment Weekly website. Its first season won higher ratings than the hugely popular original, *The Walking Dead*.

DID YOU KNOW?
Peter Dinklage (USA, below right) has won Emmy and Golden Globe awards for his portrayal of Tyrion Lannister. He was the first choice of George R R Martin, author of the books on which the *Game of Thrones* TV series is based.

Game of Thrones

As of 2 Feb 2016, HBO's smash-hit fantasy series had received 16 awards from the Visual Effects Society since 2012 – the **most VES awards won by a TV series**.

On 20 Sep 2015, *Game of Thrones* gained the **most Emmy awards won by a TV series in a season** – 12, for its fifth season.

In 2015, the series was the **most pirated TV show** for the fourth consecutive year, according to download-monitoring website TorrentFreak. From Apr to Jun 2015, there were about 14,400,000 illegal downloads per episode.

The Season 5 finale also saw the **most viewers sharing a single torrent file simultaneously**: 258,131. And for around 7,997,000 bona fide viewers in the USA, it was *Thrones*' most successful season to date.

First manned spaceflight
At 6:07 a.m. GMT on 12 Apr, Cosmonaut Flight Major Yuri Gagarin (USSR) takes off in *Vostok 1* from Baikonur Cosmodrome in Kazakhstan. He lands 118 min later, after a flight of 40,868.6 km (25,394.6 mi).

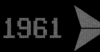 1961

DATELINE

guinnessworldrecords.com **187**

VIDEO

Most subscribers for a band on YouTube

One Direction (UK/IRL) are on a break, but their VEVO channel is still going strong – they had 19,842,367 subscribers as of 11 Apr 2016. The group's account was set up on 4 Dec 2010 while they were competing in the UK talent show *The X Factor*.

MOST SUBSCRIBERS ON YOUTUBE (AS OF 11 APR 2016)

TV show
TheEllenShow, featuring clips, interviews and behind-the-scenes footage from the eponymous chat show, has 15,650,054 subscribers. Its videos have been viewed more than 5.9 billion times.

Comedy channel
Published by Chilean comedian/entertainer Germán Alejandro Garmendia Aranis, the channel "HolaSoyGerman" has 27,210,540 subscribers.

"Fail video" channel
FailArmy by Jukin Media (USA) has a total of 10,264,097 subscribers.

Fashion/beauty channel
Yuya, aka Mariand Castrejón Castañeda (MEX), has amassed a total of 14,069,841 subscribers. She began her vlog in 2009.

Musician (male)
The VEVO channel for Canadian pop star Justin Bieber has garnered 20,711,202 subscribers.

Most subscribers for an "unboxing" channel on YouTube

Leading the way in the field of "unboxing" (online videos of toys or other products being unpacked, assembled and demonstrated) is "DisneyCollectorBR", aka "FunToyzCollector", an anonymous female YouTuber from Brazil. As of 11 Apr 2016, she had a fan base of 6,936,644 subscribers. YouTube stats expert Social Blade estimated that DisneyCollectorBR may have earned as much as $23.4 m (£15.7 m) in 2015, making her the **highest-earning YouTube contributor**.

Most subscribers for a musician on YouTube (female)

As of 11 Apr 2016, Rihanna (BRB, b. Robyn Rihanna Fenty) had 20,204,099 subscribers to her VEVO channel.

First person to reach a million followers on Twitch

British YouTuber and vlogger Tom Cassell, aka "Syndicate" (UK), achieved an unprecedented 1 million followers on Twitch on 17 Aug 2014.

Most viewed app trailer

As of 11 Apr 2016, the trailer for the *My Talking Tom* app had been viewed 163,266,308 times on YouTube. The app is based on a kitten called Tom, whom users can nurture to adulthood, and features a variety of mini-games.

Most followers on Vine

As of 11 Apr 2016, King Bach, aka Andrew Bachelor (USA, b. CAN, above left), had 15,464,061 followers on the Twitter-owned video-sharing network Vine. A trained actor, this online sensation's 6-sec clips for Vine had amassed more than 5.8 billion loops as of the same date.

Lele Pons, aka Eleonora Pons Maronese (USA, b. VEN, above right), is the **female with the most followers on Vine**, with 10,842,047 as of 11 Apr 2016. Most of her videos are humorous, including practical jokes on herself, her friends or her family. She was chosen as one of *TIME*'s 30 most influential teens in 2015.

FAST FACTS

There are approximately 4 billion video views on YouTube each day
- The name of the video-sharing service Vine is short for "vignette"
- Every day, around 1.5 billion 6-sec loops are played on Vine

Most popular female videogames broadcaster on YouTube

Describing herself as a "true geek at heart" who loves to "make people smile", YouTuber Tiffany "iHasCupquake" Herrera (USA) had 4,396,662 subscribers as of 11 Apr 2016. Her channel features a wide range of creative and "geek culture" content, with a huge emphasis on her gaming adventures, especially in *Minecraft*. She also features "geek baking" and DIY videos.

DID YOU KNOW?
The multi-talented PewDiePie is a multi-platform star. Aside from his YouTube channel, he has his own videogame (*Legend of the Brofist*) and, in 2015, became an author. *This Book Loves You* is a tongue-in-cheek parody of "inspirational" self-help books.

MOST VIEWS ON YOUTUBE

Educational video
"Wheels On The Bus | Plus Lots More Nursery Rhymes | 54 Minutes Compilation from LittleBabyBum!" had attracted 1,334,622,451 views as of 11 Apr 2016. Aimed at young children, the 54-min movie features popular nursery rhymes and animated characters. Created by app developers and animators Derek and Cannis Holder (both UK), it was posted on their "LittleBabyBum" channel on 9 Aug 2014.

Movie trailer (official)
Posted on 19 Oct 2015, the trailer for the seventh instalment in the *Star Wars* series, *The Force Awakens*, had amassed 91,512,152 views as of 11 Apr 2016.

As of the same date, the **most viewed superhero movie trailer** was for Marvel's *Avengers: Age of Ultron* (USA, 2015), which had garnered a total of 78,849,269 views.

Gaming video
A video created in *Minecraft* and uploaded by Jordan "CaptainSparklez" Maron (USA) had 160,312,315 views as of 21 Feb 2016. Originally titled "Revenge – A Minecraft Parody of Usher's DJ Got Us Fallin' in Love", its soundtrack was altered in 2016 (presumably for legal reasons). Now featuring "TryHardNinja" (USA), it was renamed "Revenge – A Minecraft Original Music Video".

Video
Posted to YouTube on 15 Jul 2012, the video for pop song "Gangnam Style" by PSY (aka Park Jae-sang, KOR) had 2,554,380,660 views as of 11 Apr 2016.

Characterized by its zany dance moves, "Gangnam Style" is also the **most liked video**, with 10,721,274 likes.

First music video filmed on a reduced-gravity aircraft

The video for "Upside Down & Inside Out" by OK Go (USA), published on YouTube on 13 Feb 2016, was filmed in one take on a reduced-gravity aircraft. GWR spoke to frontman Damian Kulash about the challenges involved in this unique project.

What inspired the idea to film on a reduced-gravity aeroplane?
I learned about parabolic flight – aka "the vomit comet" – around 2007 or 2008, when new private ventures [SpaceX and Virgin Galactic] ignited public interest in civilians going to space. I couldn't find any music videos that had been shot in weightlessness, and among the several art and advertising projects that existed, none were very carefully choreographed or planned. Everything I found showed the filmed subjects improvising [...] and collecting the most interesting pieces later as a montage. The aim with our project was to plan an event that relies on the unusual context and reveals the moments of joy and wonder intentionally.

How complex was this video compared with the others that you've done? Was this the most challenging yet?
This was certainly the most physically demanding video we've ever made, because the alternating periods of zero gravity and double gravity were very hard on us.

Were you fans of *Guinness World Records* when you were younger?
Yes, I remember spending hours in my school library poring over the book, fascinated in particular by the pictures. Everyone remembers that guy with the fingernails. It's a big honour to be included.

MOST SUBSCRIBERS ON YOUTUBE

As of 11 Apr 2016, the all-time most subscribed YouTube channel was "PewDiePie", with 43,248,969 subscribers. "PewDiePie" – aka Felix Arvid Ulf Kjellberg (SWE) – is a games reviewer who posts over-the-top commentaries of games as he plays. As of the same date, his videos had received 11,766,793,379 views. In Feb 2016, a new web series called *Scare PewDiePie* launched on pay-for service YouTube Red, in which Kjellberg walks around sets inspired by horror videogames that he has played.

Land-speed record: first to exceed 400 mph
Driving the jet-engine-powered *Spirit of America*, Craig Breedlove (USA) reaches a speed of 407.518 mph (655.836 km/h) in Bonneville, Utah, USA, on 5 Aug.

1963

DATELINE

guinnessworldrecords.com 189

SCIENCE & TECHNOLOGY

1964

First civilian in space
Konstantin Feoktistov (RUS) makes his sole space flight, in *Voskhod 1*, on 12–13 Oct. As an engineer, he helps design the *Sputnik* satellites as well as the Vostok, Voshhod and Soyuz capsules, but is not a member of the military.

CONTENTS

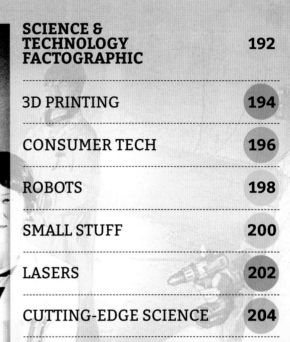

Largest robot snake

Built between 2011 and 2015, mighty "Titanoboa" is 50 ft (15.2 m) long, 2 ft (60.9 cm) wide and weighs 1,750 lb (794 kg). It was modelled as a life-size replica of the extinct *Titanoboa* snake that exists in fossil evidence. The robot slithers along at 4 km/h (2.5 mph), powered by lithium batteries that drive a hydraulic system guided by eight microcontrollers. It has 34 aluminium vertebrae, slick, "all-terrain" belly scales and hydraulic oil "blood". Created at the eatART lab in Vancouver, Canada, by a team of scientists, engineers, artists and technicians, Titanoboa is regularly displayed at design fairs in North America (inset). It also promotes climate-change events and causes a dance-floor sensation at festivals.

First car to exceed 600 mph
Driving the jet-powered *Spirit of America Sonic I*, Craig Breedlove (USA) achieves a new land-speed record of 600.6 mph (966.5 km/h) in Bonneville, Utah, USA, on 15 Nov.

1965

SCI-FI vs SCIENCE

Science fiction has a habit of predicting science fact. Space travel is the main theme of Jules Verne's novel *From the Earth to the Moon* (1865), *2001: A Space Odyssey* (USA/UK, 1968) features a voice-controlled computer – HAL 9000 – and automatic doors are mentioned in H G Wells' novel *The Sleeper Awakes* (1910). Check out these other examples of futuristic concepts and technology from sci-fi culture and see how close we've come to making them a reality.

REVIVING EXTINCT SPECIES

• **FICTION:** Based on the novel by Michael Crichton, *Jurassic Park* (USA, 1993, near right) imagines a world in which scientists clone dinosaurs from prehistoric DNA.

• **FACT:** The Pyrenean ibex (*Capra pyrenaica pyrenaica*), commonly known as the bucardo, became extinct in 2000. Scientists preserved cells from the last known species and, in Jul 2003, injected nuclei from these specimens into goat eggs, from which the DNA had been extracted. They then implanted these into surrogate mothers (far right). Only seven of the animals became pregnant, and of these only one gave birth. Sadly, the 2-kg (4-lb 8-oz) baby goat lived for only a very short time.

ALONE IN SPACE

• **FICTION:** In *The Martian* (USA, 2015), Matt Damon plays Mark Watney (above left), an astronaut who is separated from his crew on Mars in a raging storm. Presuming him dead, his fellow astronauts leave the planet. Can Watney find a way of signalling that he is still alive and survive until he is rescued?

• **FACT:** During the Apollo 15 mission (26 Jul–7 Aug 1971), Alfred M Worden (USA, above right) was orbiting the Moon in command module *Endeavour* while fellow astronauts David Scott and James Irwin (both USA) were at the Hadley base on the Moon's surface. On the far side of the Moon, Worden was 3,596.4 km (2,234.69 mi) away from the nearest living person, making him history's **most isolated human**. For some, being separated from your companions might be an unsettling prospect – but not Al Worden. "First off, you wish them luck: 'I hope you land okay!'" he recounted to the BBC in 2014. "The second thought is: 'Gee I'm glad they've gone because I've got this place all to myself.'"

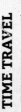

KILLER ROBOTS

• **FICTION:** *The Terminator* (USA, 1984) introduced a terrifying cyborg killer played by Arnold Schwarzenegger (above left), sent from the future to assassinate a woman who will otherwise give birth to a legendary freedom fighter.

• **FACT:** On 25 Jan 1979, Robert Williams (USA) became the **first human killed by a robot** when he was accidentally struck in the head by the arm of a production-line robot at a Ford Motor Company casting plant in Flat Rock, Michigan, USA. The robot belonged to a system that moved parts around the factory. It began running slowly, so Williams reportedly climbed inside to retrieve parts. Hit in the head, he died instantly.

TIME TRAVEL

• **FICTION:** In *Doctor Who*, the Doctor (played in his latest incarnation by British actor Peter Capaldi, above) travels effortlessly through space, and from the past to the future, by means of his time machine the *TARDIS* (*Time And Relative Dimension In Space*).

• **FACT:** Cosmonaut Gennady Padalka (RUS, above right) touched down on 12 Sep 2015 after a 168-day-long mission in space. Added to his previous four missions, Padalka has spent 879 days beyond Earth's atmosphere – the **longest cumulative time in space**. Consistent with Albert Einstein's theories of relativity, Padalka has also genuinely travelled through time, as his internal body clock will have slowed down marginally in comparison to clocks back on Earth. From his perspective, he has returned to an Earth that has moved forward in time by around 0.02 sec.

HAND-HELD COMMUNICATORS

• **FICTION:** The 1960s TV series of *Star Trek* featured mobile communicators. Flipped open, they enabled personnel on alien planets to contact the crew on board the Starship *Enterprise*.

• **FACT:** Martin Cooper (USA) of Motorola was inspired by sci-fi comic books to invent the **first cellular phone**, an 800-g (1-lb 12-oz) behemoth dubbed "the Brick". His first call was to his rival, Joel Engel (head of research at Bell Labs), on 3 Apr 1973. Today, mobile phones such as the iPhone 6s (above right) make long-distance communication on the go commonplace, along with online access, app downloads and super-sharp photos.

DID YOU KNOW?

In *Prometheus*, android David 8 is fascinated by the movie *Lawrence of Arabia* (UK, 1962), which he watches while the crew are in hypersleep. He quotes lines from the film and even adopts the same hairstyle as lead actor Peter O'Toole.

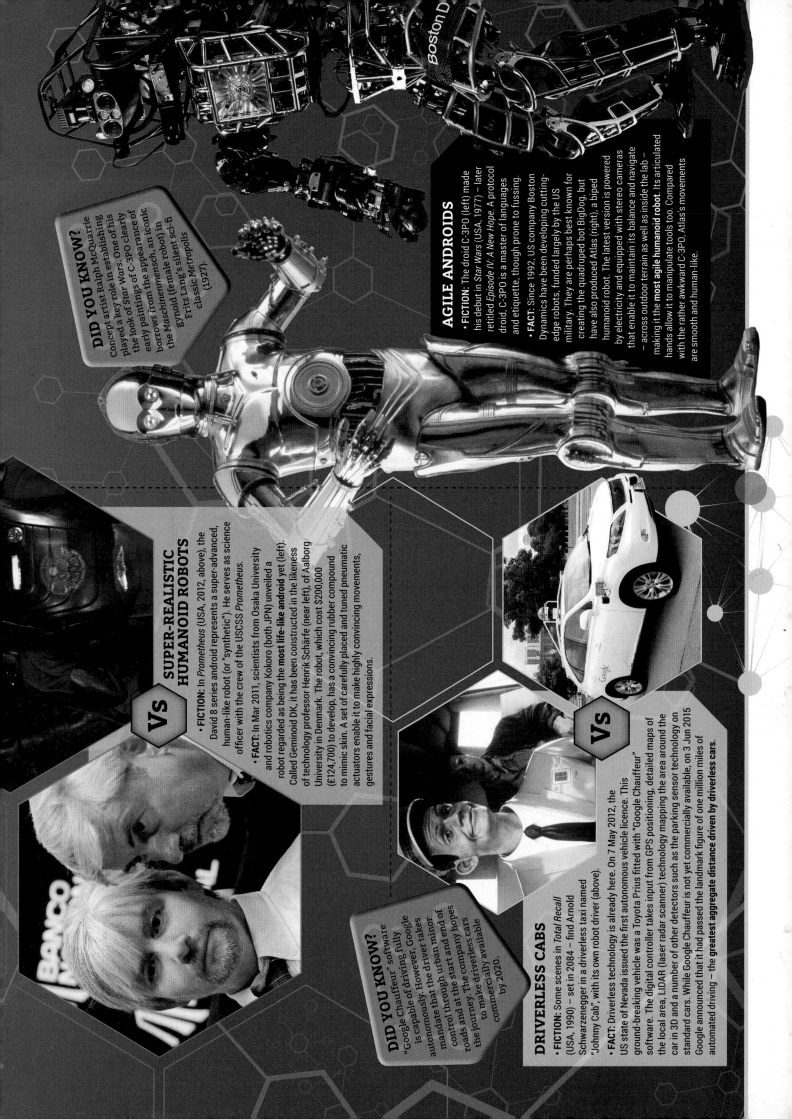

DID YOU KNOW?
Concept artist Ralph McQuarrie played a key role in establishing the look of C-3PO clearly borrows from the appearance of early paintings from the *Star Wars*. One of his the *Maschinenmensch*, an iconic gynoid (female robot) in Fritz Lang's silent sci-fi classic *Metropolis* (1927).

AGILE ANDROIDS

- **FICTION**: The droid C-3PO (left) made his debut in *Star Wars* (USA, 1977) – later retitled *Episode IV: A New Hope*. A protocol droid, C-3PO is a master of languages and etiquette, though prone to fussing.

- **FACT**: Since 1992, US company Boston Dynamics have been developing cutting-edge robots, funded largely by the US military. They are perhaps best known for creating the quadruped bot BigDog, but have also produced Atlas (right), a biped humanoid robot. The latest version is powered by electricity and equipped with stereo cameras that enable it to maintain its balance and navigate – across outdoor terrain as well as inside the lab – making it the **most agile humanoid robot**. Its articulated hands allow it to manipulate tools too. Compared with the rather awkward C-3PO, Atlas's movements are smooth and human-like.

SUPER-REALISTIC HUMANOID ROBOTS

Vs

- **FICTION**: In *Prometheus* (USA, 2012, above), the David 8 series android represents a super-advanced, human-like robot (or "synthetic"). He serves as science officer with the crew of the USCSS *Prometheus*.

- **FACT**: In Mar 2011, scientists from Osaka University and robotics company Kokoro (both JPN) unveiled a robot regarded as being the **most life-like android yet** (left). Called Geminoid DK, it has been constructed in the likeness of technology professor Henrik Schärfe (near left), of Aalborg University in Denmark. The robot, which cost $200,000 (£124,700) to develop, has a convincing rubber compound to mimic skin. A set of carefully placed and tuned pneumatic actuators enable it to make highly convincing movements, gestures and facial expressions.

DID YOU KNOW?
"Google Chauffeur" software is capable of driving fully autonomously. However, Google takes mandate that the driver takes control through urban minor roads and at the start and end of the journey. The company hopes to make driverless cars commercially available by 2020.

DRIVERLESS CABS

Vs

- **FICTION**: Some scenes in *Total Recall* (USA, 1990) – set in 2084 – find Arnold Schwarzenegger in a driverless taxi named "Johnny Cab" with its own robot driver (above).

- **FACT**: Driverless technology is already here. On 7 May 2012, the US state of Nevada issued the first autonomous vehicle licence. This ground-breaking vehicle was a Toyota Prius fitted with "Google Chauffeur" software. The digital controller takes input from GPS positioning, detailed maps of the local area, LIDAR (laser radar scanner) technology mapping the area around the car in 3D and a number of other detectors such as the parking sensor technology on standard cars. While Google Chauffeur is not yet commercially available, on 3 Jun 2015 Google announced that it had passed the landmark figure of one million miles of automated driving – the **greatest aggregate distance driven by driverless cars**.

3D PRINTING

First village to 3D-print all of its residents

Spanish company Grupo Sicnova scanned all 318 residents of the small village of Torrequebradilla in the south of Spain in just one day. The company used its new Clonescan 3D machine, a 7-ft-tall (2.1-m) 3D colour scanner, to complete 15-sec-long scans of each person. Colour 3D models of them were then uploaded to cloud-accessible storage in all popular 3D-printer file formats. Each of the scanned residents received their own miniature clone within a week of the scanning event (see inset).

Most 3D-printed 3D printer

It's now possible to 3D-print everything from car parts to medical devices. What's more surprising, perhaps, is that you can even 3D-print a 3D printer. The open-source RepRap Snappy 1.1c printer was made using 2.4 kg (5 lb 4.6 oz) of plastic filament to print 86 of its 110 pieces. The design was created by Garth Minette (USA), who – along with Adrian Bowyer (UK), the designer of the original RepRap – encourages people to freely share or modify the design so that they can 3D-print their own 3D printer.

Largest 3D-printed boat

Seattle's Seafair festival holds an annual contest for the best paddle boat made of recycled milk containers. In Jun 2012, a team from the Washington Open Object Fabricators (WOOF) group entered the competition with a 3D-printed boat that was 2 m (6 ft 6.7 in) long and weighed 18 kg (39 lb 10 oz). The plastic used came from ground-up milk containers.

Fastest 3D-printed robot

In May 2015, engineers at UC Berkeley (USA) built a robotic cockroach using 3D-printed components. Because these parts bend and stretch without breaking, the X2-VelociRoACH can zip around at 4.9 m/s (16 ft/s) – that's comparable to a speed between jogging and running for an average adult human.

Not far behind is the commercially available Ollie from Orbotix (now Sphero); it rolls around at 4.26 m/s (13 ft 11 in/s) and is also made from 3D-printed parts.

Most commonly 3D-printed medical device

More than 10 million of the world's 16 million hearing aids are made using 3D printing. The technology allows for hearing aids to be tailored to an individual without extra expense. The result is cheaper hearing aids that fit the wearer better than mass-produced models. US hearing-aid manufacturers were so taken with 3D printing that 100% of them now use it.

Medical researchers are always interested in pain-free alternatives to administering medicine. One example is the 3D-printed micro-needle, comprising an array of needles that measures 1 mm (0.03 in) across, making it the **smallest 3D-printed medical device**. Each of the 25 needles in the instrument is only 20 micrometres wide – a fifth the diameter of a human hair.

First 3D-printed pills

In Jul 2015, a pharmaceutical drug was 3D-printed for the first time. Spritam is made by Aprecia from New Jersey, USA, and is intended to relieve symptoms associated with seizures. With 3D printing, different doses can be

First 3D-printed car

The "Strati", designed by Michele Anoè (ITA), was printed in five days in Sep 2014 at the International Manufacturing Technology Show in Chicago, Illinois, USA. Only 44 hr in the making, it is the first fully drivable car with a 3D-printed chassis and body (pictured inset is a detail of the printed layers). It was the brainchild of crowd-funded Local Motors (USA), who completed the car's detailed design with help from Oak Ridge National Lab and manufacturing company SABIC.

DATELINE

1966

Longest survival without food
On 12 Jul, Angus Barbieri (UK) eats his first meal in 382 days, having lost around 293 lb (132.9 kg) by living on tea and water. The formerly obese man had been taking part in an experiment looking at the health effects of starvation.

Largest object 3D-printed in metal

In mid-2015, Rolls-Royce began testing jet engines using 3D-printed metal parts. The Trent XWB-97 engine uses the largest metal component made by 3D printing: the front bearing housing of the jet that holds 48 aerofoils. It is 1.5 m (4 ft 11 in) across and 0.5 m (1 ft 7 in) deep, and is made from nickel using an electron-beam melting process developed by Swedish-based company Arcam.

FAST FACTS

Chuck Hull (USA) invented "stereolithography" (a technique of building up 3D objects in thin layers) in 1983 • Three 3D-printed models of an Aston Martin DB5 were made by Voxeljet (DEU) for the 2012 James Bond movie *Skyfall*

cryogenic hydrogen per minute by spinning at a rate of more than 90,000 rpm. During the test, the rocket generated almost 90 kilonewtons of thrust.

First dress made from 3D-printed material

In Jun 2000, Dutch industrial engineer Jiri Evenhuis led a team to produce the "Drape Dress" from 3D-printed fabric. The material was made from nylon particles and was comprised of interlocking rings like plastic chain mail.

First 3D-printing conviction

Yoshitomo Imura (JPN) was imprisoned for two years on 21 Oct 2014 for 3D-printing plastic guns. He also posted clips of himself test-firing the weapons on video website YouTube.

First 3D-printed laptop

Created in Dec 2014 by Jesse Lozano and Ryan Dunwoody (both UK), the "Pi-Top" is a 3D-printed laptop built around the Raspberry Pi 2 microcomputer. It is available as a kit of parts (including screen, battery and controller board) and design files that allow anyone with a conventional 3D printer to print their own laptop.

created for different needs, instead of creating one size of pill for all. The pill's porous 3D structure allows it to dissolve in around 4 sec – far faster than standard over-the-counter medicines.

In Jul 2015, Spritam was recognized by the US Food and Drug Administration (FDA) – the **first 3D-printed medicine to be approved for commercial release**.

Most powerful rocket with 3D-printed parts

In Aug 2013, NASA test-fired a rocket engine with a fuel injector that had been 3D-printed from nickel-chromium alloy powder. The injector provides liquid hydrogen for the rocket to burn, and can supply almost 5,500 litres (1,450 US gal) of

DID YOU KNOW?

It may be a world-beating first, but this Harley-Davidson replica does have its limitations – including a top speed of only 15 mph (24 km/h). It's unlikely that anyone will be using one of these 3D-printed motorcycles to go on a road trip any time soon...

FIRST 3D-PRINTED MOTORCYCLE

After 3D-printed cars, it was only a matter of time before motorcycle enthusiasts printed a two-wheeled wonder. At 2015's RAPID show, in Long Beach, California, USA, TE Connectivity (USA) unveiled the world's first 3D-printed motorcycle. Of the orange-and-blue bike's 100 components, a total of 76 were 3D-printed, using 4.32 mi (6.95 km) of ABS plastic filament as well as bronze and steel components. Multiple printers worked together for 1,700 hr of total print time to create the parts. The electric motor, tyres and mirrors could not be printed, however, as that technology doesn't yet exist.

First heart transplant
On 3 Dec, South African surgeon Christiaan Barnard completes the first successful heart transplant. The patient dies of pneumonia soon after, but for 18 days his new heart functions without external aid.

1967 ▶ DATELINE

guinnessworldrecords.com **195**

CONSUMER TECH

Most valuable brand name
According to Interbrand's annual "Best Brands" ranking, the world's most valuable brand is currently tech giant Apple (USA), which grew 43% in 2015 to be worth an extraordinary $170.276 bn (£112.1 bn). This places it far ahead of second-placed Google on $120.314 bn (£79.2 bn). It's the third consecutive year that Apple and Google have taken first and second places, respectively, in the Interbrand report.

Most money pledged for a Kickstarter project
On 18 May 2012, a funding proposal for the Pebble: E-Paper Watch for iPhone and Android closed on the crowdfunding site Kickstarter, having secured $10,266,845 (£6,468,610) from 68,929 backers.

Best-selling remote/radio-control toy brand
Air Hogs is a range of radio-controlled toys including

DID YOU KNOW?
Dr Andrej Karpathy, a computer science graduate from Stanford University (USA), data-mined social media sites to determine the "perfect selfie". His top findings? 1. Be a woman with long flowing hair. 2. Your face should fill one third of the frame. 3. Use filters. 4. Add a border.

cars, rockets and free-flying helicopters produced by Spin Master (CAN). In 2014, the brand earned a record $239,600,000 (£154,240,000).

Most buttons on a videogame controller
With 113 different buttons representing every possible finger position on a 17-fret guitar, the wireless Fender Mustang PRO-Guitar controller released with *Rock Band 3* (Harmonix/MTV Games/EA, 2010) has more individual inputs than any peripheral in console history – even more than a standard PC keyboard.

Longest relay chain of selfies

On 10 Jan 2016, a total of 586 participants lined up to photograph themselves in an event organized by Meizu Technology Co. (CHN) in Zhuhai, Guangdong, China. The selfies were snapped during the course of a technology fair, at which products by Meizu were exhibited.

Best-selling eighth-gen videogame console
With 39,810,000 units sold as of 6 Apr 2016, the PlayStation 4 (Sony Interactive Entertainment) is not only the **fastest-** selling PlayStation to date but also the biggest-selling of the eighth-generation consoles. By the same date, the PS4's closest rival – the Xbox One (Microsoft) – had sold 18.06 million units.

The **best-selling hand-held videogame console** is the Nintendo DS (released 2004), with total worldwide sales of 154.88 million units as of 13 Apr 2016.

BEST-SELLING BRANDS

We are surrounded by consumer electronics and gadgetry – from the ubiquitous smartphones we carry with us to the printers and monitors at work and laptops and TVs at home. Electronics is big business. And the brands shown here did the biggest business of all in 2014 – the latest year for which full sales figures are available – as confirmed by market-research company Euromonitor.

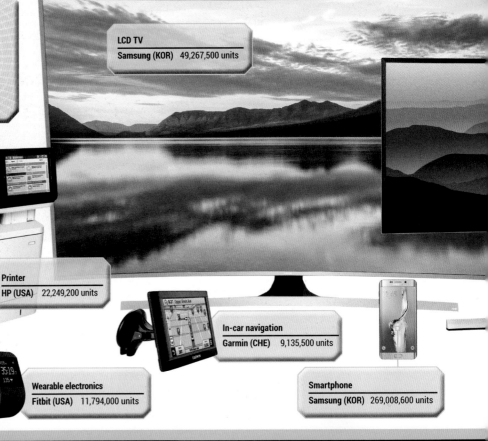

LCD TV
Samsung (KOR)   49,267,500 units

Tablet
iPad (USA)   65,167,900 units

Printer
HP (USA)   22,249,200 units

In-car navigation
Garmin (CHE)   9,135,500 units

Wearable electronics
Fitbit (USA)   11,794,000 units

Smartphone
Samsung (KOR)   269,008,600 units

DATELINE **1969** **First men on the Moon**
During the Apollo 11 mission, Neil Alden Armstrong becomes the first man to set foot on the Moon, at 2:56 a.m. and 15 sec GMT on 21 Jul 1969. He is followed out of the lunar module *Eagle* by Buzz Aldrin (both USA).

FAST FACTS

Plasma displays employ minute gas cells set between two glass sheets. Each cell acts like a tiny fluorescent tube • In 2015, Disney banned selfie sticks from its theme parks • "Nomophobia" is the fear of being without your mobile phone

Most money pledged for a haptic device on Kickstarter

The word "haptic" – from the Greek "to touch" – describes technology that artificially recreates the sense of touch via vibrations or pressure. To date, no other haptic technology project on Kickstarter has raised more money than the KOR-FX gaming vest, manufactured by Immerz (USA). By 24 Jul 2014, it had received $183,449 (£107,567) in funding from 1,202 backers. The jacket is designed to create a more immersive experience for gamers, reproducing the shocks of explosions, bullets, sword attacks and the like to make the virtual feel more real.

Longest selfie stick

At the premiere of *Zoolander 2* in London, UK, on 4 Feb 2016, the film's star, Ben Stiller (USA), pulled his best "Blue Steel" pose and took a photograph with a selfie stick measuring 8.56 m (28 ft 1 in) long – taller than a giraffe or a three-storey building! The blue-carpet photo featured Stiller and the other stars of the comedy movie, including Owen Wilson, Penélope Cruz and Will Ferrell. Pictured inset is Stiller receiving his official certificate from Guinness World Records adjudicator Mark McKinley.

DID YOU KNOW?

The abbreviation LED stands for "light-emitting diode". These supply the backlight for the display screen. By contrast, OLED screens are lit by organic light-emitting diodes. "Organic" refers to a thin layer of carbon film behind the screen, which provides superior image quality.

OLED TV
LG (KOR)   65,800 units

Computer monitor
Samsung (KOR)   9,005,100 units

Portable tablet (eReader)
Kindle (USA)   9,508,000 units

Portable player
iPod (USA)   26,740,900 units

Laptop
Lenovo (CHN)   20,698,100 units

Farthest distance from Earth reached by humans
At 00:21 a.m. GMT on 15 Apr 1970, the crew of *Apollo 13* were 254 km (158 mi) from the lunar surface, on the far side of the Moon, putting them 400,171 km (248,655 mi) away from Earth.

1970

DATELINE

ROBOTS

Farthest distance by a quadruped robot

Xingzhe No.1 is a four-legged robot that walked 134.03 km (83.28 mi) unaided on 24–27 Oct 2015. Xingzhe (which means "walker") was built by Li Qingdu and his team at Chongqing University of Posts and Telecommunications (CHN), where the robot made 1,405 laps of an athletics track.

First robot to be "arrested"

On 18 Aug 1982, the Beverly Hills Police Department took into custody a robot called DC-2 for "illegally distributing business cards and generally causing a commotion" on North Beverly Drive in Los Angeles, USA. The operators turned out to be the two teenage sons of the owner of the company that had made the robot, who had taken the $30,000 (£17,350) machine on an unauthorized joyride.

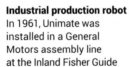

FIRST...

Documented robot

The philosopher Archytas (b. 428 BCE in Tarentum, Magna Graecia, now southern Italy) built an artificial pigeon from wood and an animal's bladder. Using steam to power its movements, Archytas launched the bird from a pivot bar; according to contemporary reports, it flew about 200 m (656 ft) before running out of steam.

Industrial production robot

In 1961, Unimate was installed in a General Motors assembly line at the Inland Fisher Guide Plant in Ewing Township,

First domestic robot chef

At the 2015 Hannover Messe trade fair for industrial technology, held annually in Germany, Moley Robotics (UK) demonstrated the first consumer-targeted robot chef, which prepared a lobster bisque for exhibition attendees. The robot comprises a pair of dextrous arms and hands that are integrated in a worktop/cooker/sink unit. It is able to download recipes created by a professional chef via an online database that operates like a cookery equivalent of iTunes. Once a recipe has been stored, the robot is capable of repeating it as often as necessary.

MOST CROWDFUNDED SOCIAL ROBOT

In 2014, a venture was launched on funding platform Indiegogo to finance production of a robot called JIBO. When the campaign started in July, it attracted huge interest, with funding soaring past the initial goal of $100,000 in less than four hours. The final total raised was $3,714,505 (£2,415,985) from 7,422 supporters.

JIBO is a social robot that has the capability to recognize owners' faces, read emails and perform social-media interaction via voice commands and apps. It also has the ability to identify its owner's moods by recognizing smiles and frowns, and it can interact using a series of complex artificial intelligence (AI) routines. JIBO stands 11 in (28 cm) tall and weighs in at 6 lb (2.7 kg). It is pictured here with Cynthia Breazeal (USA), who is the founder of the creative team behind the robot.

First email
Computer engineer Ray Tomlinson (USA, 1941–2016) sends the landmark electronic message in Cambridge, Massachusetts, USA. The text was not preserved, but "it was something like 'QWERTYUIOP'," said Tomlinson.

FAST FACTS

Leonardo da Vinci devised a "robotic knight" c. 1495; Mark Rosheim built it in 2002, then applied some of its features to robots he designed for NASA • The word "robot" comes from the Czech *robota* ("forced labour" or "work")

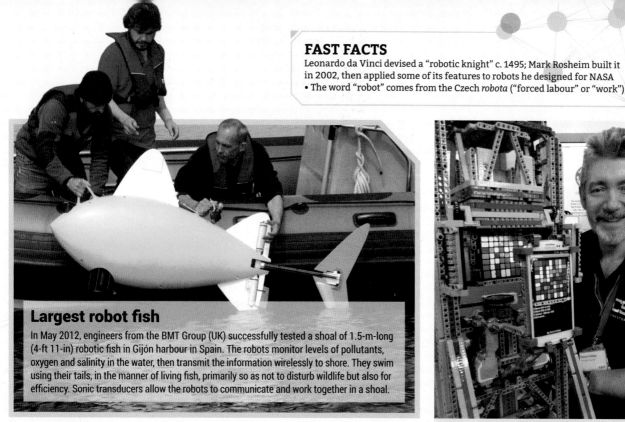

Largest robot fish

In May 2012, engineers from the BMT Group (UK) successfully tested a shoal of 1.5-m-long (4-ft 11-in) robotic fish in Gijón harbour in Spain. The robots monitor levels of pollutants, oxygen and salinity in the water, then transmit the information wirelessly to shore. They swim using their tails, in the manner of living fish, primarily so as not to disturb wildlife but also for efficiency. Sonic transducers allow the robots to communicate and work together in a shoal.

Largest Rubik's Cube solved by a robot

MultiCuber 999 successfully tackled a 9x9x9 Rubik's Cube at the Big Bang Fair in the Birmingham NEC, UK, on 15 Mar 2014. Built by David Gilday (UK, above), the robot is made from LEGO® Mindstorms NXT robotic kits and powered by ARM processor technology. It solved the puzzle in 34 min 25.89 sec.

New Jersey, USA. Invented by George Devol (USA), Unimate was used to transport die castings from an assembly line and weld them on to car bodies. It weighed 4,000 lb (1,814 kg) and cost $25,000 (£8,928).

"Sweating" robot

Following the H1N1 swine flu scare in 2009, engineers in Japan created a robot that could exhibit the symptoms of the virus. The robot has a life-sized body and is coated in a human-like skin that "perspires". It uses animatronics to moan, cry and convulse like a person infected with H1N1. Without effective treatment, the symptoms worsen and the robot "dies". It was launched as a training aid for doctors in Oct 2009.

Robot basketball contest

The first Rebound Rumble was staged on 7 Jan 2012 at the Edward Jones Dome in St Louis, Missouri, USA. At either end of the "court" were stations for human drivers and a range of basketball hoops comprising a low hoop, two middle hoops and one high hoop. The knock-out stages and the final both took the form of 135-sec matches. For the first part of the match, the robots would be autonomous ("Hybrid" mode), while in the second part they were controlled by their human operators ("Teleop" mode).

DID YOU KNOW?
The table tennis tutor's software is capable of assessing all aspects of a ball's motion. With timing precision down to a thousandth of a second, the robot is programmed to keep the rally going, tackling shots that would be impossible for a human to achieve in order to help its pupil improve.

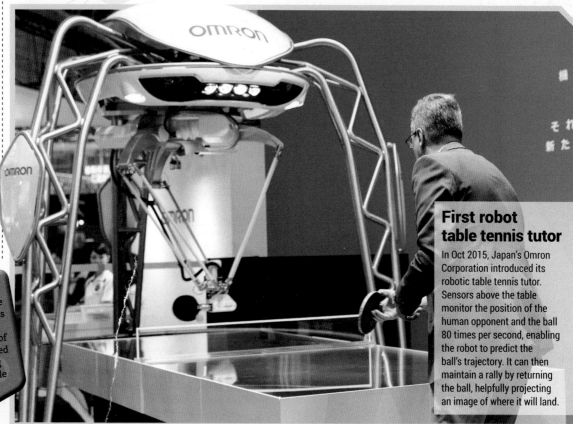

First robot table tennis tutor

In Oct 2015, Japan's Omron Corporation introduced its robotic table tennis tutor. Sensors above the table monitor the position of the human opponent and the ball 80 times per second, enabling the robot to predict the ball's trajectory. It can then maintain a rally by returning the ball, helpfully projecting an image of where it will land.

First all-in-one desktop computer
Hewlett-Packard launches the HP 9830, which includes a display, keyboard, hard drive and processor all in one unit. It uses the BASIC programming language.

1972

DATELINE

SMALL STUFF

Smallest working power tool

In 2015, Lance Abernethy (NZ) produced a fully functioning 3D-printed cordless drill measuring just 17 mm (0.67 in) high. It uses an 11.75-mm-long (0.46-in) twist drill and is powered by a hearing-aid battery. Lance also built a matching power saw measuring a minuscule 18.9 mm (0.74 in) in length.

100%

Fastest nanotech DNA diagnostic machine
On 7 Oct 2015, an international team of scientists revealed their design for a nanometre-scale DNA analysis machine. It uses synthetic DNA tuned to respond to antibodies that indicate diseases such as arthritis and HIV, giving a result in just 5 min.

Most powerful MRI machine
Magnetic Resonance Imaging (MRI) detects disease by scanning inside the body. A French-German project, the INUMAC (Imaging of Neuro disease Using high-field MR and Contrastophores) has a magnetic-field strength of 11.7 Tesla (compared to conventional 3- or 7-Tesla machines). This enables it to image at a cube size of 0.1 mm (0.003 in), one-tenth of current imaging size. It can also take a picture every 0.1 sec, 10 times faster than average. Due to be installed in 2016 in France's NeuroSpin centre, it will help in studying and diagnosing brain conditions.

SMALLEST...

Thermometer
On 9 Aug 2007, researchers from McMaster University in Hamilton, Ontario, Canada, published a paper on a thermometer made from green fluorescent protein – the substance that makes jellyfish glow. The thermometer emitted "flashes" of light in direct relationship to its temperature. The protein is approximately 4.2 nanometres (0.0000042 mm; 0.00000016 in) long – the size

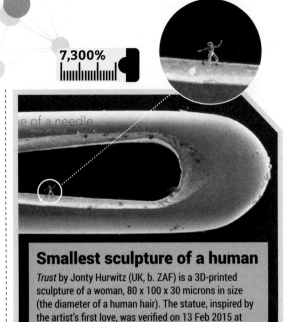

7,300%

Smallest sculpture of a human

Trust by Jonty Hurwitz (UK, b. ZAF) is a 3D-printed sculpture of a woman, 80 x 100 x 30 microns in size (the diameter of a human hair). The statue, inspired by the artist's first love, was verified on 13 Feb 2015 at the Karlsruhe Nano Micro Facility in Germany.

Smallest engineering truss framework

Professor of materials science and mechanics Julia Greer (USA) has invented a fractal nanotruss with a wall thickness of 5 nanometres (0.000005 mm; 0.00000019 in). The trusses form nanostructures in a lattice framework, like that used in France's Eiffel Tower. They can be built in various patterns that are up to 99% air, but as strong as steel. If scaled up, they might be used to create tough but lightweight vehicles and buildings.

Smallest printed book

Shiki no Kusabana (Flowers of the Four Seasons) was printed in a run of 250 copies by Toppan Printing Co. in Bunkyō, Tokyo, Japan, in 2012 and is a mere 0.74 x 0.75 mm (0.0291 x 0.0295 in) when closed. Its 22 pages – each of which can fit through the eye of a needle – carry drawings of Japanese flowers, with names given in *hiragana* and *katakana*, the two main Japanese scripts, as well as with an English transliteration. The book, printed using technology usually reserved for anti-forgery features on bank notes, was sold as a set with an enlarged version and a magnifying glass for 29,400 Yen (£211; $307).

100%

MICROBOOK

of a cell – and is safe for use in humans. It could be used in micro-surgical monitoring.

Battery
In 2011, engineers at Rice University in Houston, Texas, USA, unveiled a battery 0.5 microns (0.0005 mm; 0.000019 in) high and an almost-invisible 150 nanometres (0.00015 mm; 0.0000059 in) thick – 60,000 times smaller than an AAA. The battery is formed by nanowires, one half being the cathode and one half being the anode.

DATELINE

1973

First cellular phone
On 3 Apr, American engineer Martin Cooper makes the first ever call on his prototype Motorola DynaTAC cellular phone. Using a base station on the roof of his office, he phoned his rival, Joel Engel of AT&T, while standing in the street.

200 Science & Technology

Smallest scissors

Created by Chen Yu Pei (CHN) in 2003, these working scissors are made from stainless steel and measure 1.75 mm (0.068 in) long and 1.38 mm (0.054 in) wide.

Chen also holds the record for the **smallest china teapot**, which measures 6.8 mm (0.26 in) wide including spout and handle.

540%

of the USS *Enterprise* (NCC-1701-D) was created by Takayuki Hoshino and Shinji Matsui (both JPN) of the Himeji Institute of Technology in Hyōgo, Japan. They used a 30-kV focused ion beam to etch the replica of the iconic *Star Trek* ship, creating a sculpture that was just 8.8 microns (0.0088 mm; 0.0003 in) long – more than 1,000 to the centimetre (or nearly 3,000 to the inch)! It won the Best Ion Micrograph prize at the 2003 conference on Electron, Ion and Photon Beam Technology and Nanofabrication in Tampa, Florida, USA.

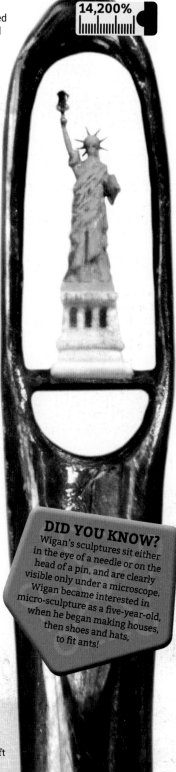

14,200%

Motorized model car
In 2003, a team of engineers from the Denso Corporation (JPN) created a motorized model of a 1936 Toyota AA sedan that was only 4.785 mm (0.0681 in) long. It contained a tiny electric motor that propelled the car at a top speed of 0.018 km/h (0.011 mph).

The **smallest model car** was made in 2005 by scientists at Rice University (USA) from a cluster of carbon atoms less than 4 nanometres (0.00000015 in) across. This "nanocar" had a chassis, two independent axles and four wheels made from buckminsterfullerene (a type of spherical carbon molecule).

3D map of Earth
In 2010, scientists at IBM made a detailed 3D map of Earth so small that 1,000 of them could fit on a grain of salt. Patterns of Earth's continents were created with a silicon cutting tip 100,000 times finer than a sharpened pencil. It carved out geographical features as small as 15 nanometres high (0.000015 mm; 0.00000059 in).

Starship *Enterprise*
Aptly named *Nano Trek*, a 1-billionth-scale model

Animal sculpture
In 2015, Jonty Hurwitz (see opposite page) created *Fragile Giant* – a life-like elephant that measured a mere 0.157 mm (0.006 in) tall. He first made a computer model from photographs of a real elephant, then rendered it in 3D using a technique called multiphoton lithography. This sets fluid "plastic" in a process similar to 3D printing, but on a micro scale. The sculpture, which has features just a few thousandths of a millimetre across, can perch on one ridge of a human fingerprint.

DID YOU KNOW?
Wigan's sculptures sit either in the eye of a needle or on the head of a pin, and are clearly visible only under a microscope. Wigan became interested in micro-sculpture as a five-year-old, when he began making houses, then shoes and hats, to fit ants!

Smallest working cannon
Fired in Melbourne, Australia, on 4 Jul 2015, this minuscule heavy weapon was hand-made by Marcus Hull (AUS) and measures 6.88 mm (0.27 in) long, 4.34 mm (0.17 in) wide and 2.8 mm (0.11 in) high. It fires a steel ball 0.25 mm (0.0098 in) in diameter and uses red phosphorus as propellant.

SMALLEST STATUE OF LIBERTY
There are a few Statues of Liberty around the world, including the most famous one on Liberty Island in New York, USA. While that statue is an imposing 93.1 m (305 ft 5 in) high, the world's smallest version of "Lady Liberty", by UK artist Willard Wigan, fits within the eye of a needle. At c. 0.5 mm (0.02 in) in height, it is the smallest Statue of Liberty that exactly conforms to the dimensions of the New York original. The sculpture is crafted from a tiny speck of gold painstakingly hand-carved using tools made by Wigan himself. He applies his sculpting tools in between heartbeats to reduce the effects of hand tremor.

First aircraft to fly on solar power
The *AstroFlight Sunrise*, an unmanned electric aircraft, takes off on the morning of 4 Nov using the power from solar panels in its wings. It will make another 27 flights before breaking up in heavy turbulence.

1974

DATELINE

LASERS

Highest Earth–Moon bandwidth

In Oct 2013, a team from NASA and the Massachusetts Institute of Technology sent signals to the *Lunar Atmosphere and Dust Environment Explorer* (*LADEE*) spacecraft orbiting the Moon. They achieved a download data rate of 622 megabits per sec. Engineers were able to download the spacecraft's 1-GB science data in less than 5 min. Using conventional radio waves, it would have taken three days.

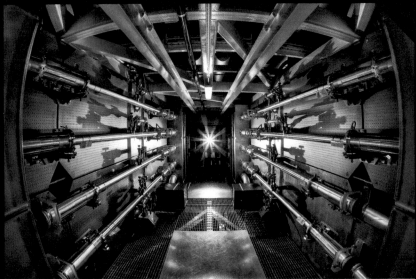

Highest laser energy shone on to a single target

In Jun 2009, scientists at the National Ignition Facility at Lawrence Livermore National Laboratory in California, USA, began operating an array of 192 powerful lasers designed to research nuclear fusion. The lasers are focused on to a fingernail-sized container known as a hohlraum holding a pellet of hydrogen fuel for fusion experiments. On 27 Jan 2010, researchers fired the laser array for a few billionths of a second and delivered one megajoule of energy on to the hohlraum target. This is equivalent to the explosion caused by 0.2 kg (7.05 oz) of TNT.

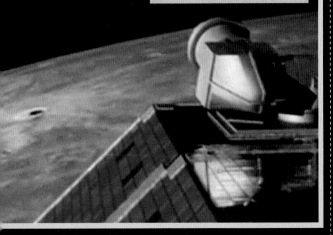

Longest flight powered by transmitted laser light
In Jul 2012, LaserMotive and Lockheed Martin (both USA) flew a Stalker UAV for more than 48 hr using a ground-based laser and a receiver that converted the laser light into electricity.

Highest altitude achieved by laser power
On 2 Oct 2000, Lightcraft Technologies (USA)

flew a 12.2-cm-diameter (4.8-in) craft to a height of 71 m (233 ft), powered only by light. They used a US Army 10-kW pulsed carbon-dioxide laser on the ground, fired upwards at the 51-g (1.8-oz) craft, which reflected the light backwards to a point just beneath it. The resulting expansion of the superheated air provided the thrust. These test flights

occurred at the White Sands Missile Range in New Mexico, USA.

Longest laser communications link
In May 2005, NASA's *Messenger* spacecraft communicated with Earth using a laser beam from a distance of 24 million km (15 million mi). This experimental form of

long-distance space communication is designed to allow a higher rate of data return from interplanetary space than current methods of microwave communication.

Shortest laser wavelength
Lasers operate across a range of wavelengths, typically between 200 and 700 nanometres. In 2009,

the Linac Coherent Light Source at the Stanford Linear Accelerator in California, USA, achieved a 0.15-nanometre wavelength – the first free-electron laser to emit hard X-rays.

On 26 Aug 2015, however, scientists at The University of Electro-Communications in Tokyo, Japan, revealed that they had created an atomic X-ray laser also

MOST BALLOONS BURST IN ONE MINUTE USING A LASER

On 22 Sep 2014, Daniel Black (UK) popped 55 balloons in 60 sec with a self-built laser at the Institute of Making at UCL in London, UK. His laser had a wavelength of 445 nanometres. The balloons were black, to absorb as much incident energy (the energy hitting the surface) as possible.

First hand-held electronic videogame
Mattel (USA) release *Auto Race*, the first gaming toy with no moving parts. Players have to navigate their car – represented by a large red dot on a tiny LED display – past their slower-moving competitors (smaller dots) to win the race.

FAST FACTS

The word "laser" stands for Light Amplification by Stimulated Emission of Radiation • In 1969, the *Apollo 11* astronauts used a laser to measure the distance from the Moon to Earth; the result was accurate to within the width of a finger

First artificial guide star

On 1 Jun 1992, scientists at Lick Observatory and Lawrence Livermore National Labs (both in California, USA) shot a laser beam into the sky to create an artificial "star" of glowing atmospheric sodium ions. Astronomers used this star to observe how much "distortion" Earth's atmosphere introduced into a telescope's image. They could then compensate for this distortion when viewing other objects in space, creating much more accurate images.

cavity made from silicon, which traps light energy and dissipates it as heat. This prototype can absorb 99.4% of the laser light for a specific frequency. Anti-lasers may have uses in the fields of optical computing and medical imaging.

Living laser
In Jun 2011, scientists at the Wellman Center for Photomedicine at Massachusetts General Hospital, USA, announced that they had used cells from a human kidney to create the first laser light emitted by a living cell. The kidney cell was injected with DNA from luminous jellyfish, which made it glow green when bombarded with blue light. By using mirrors, the scientists were able to make the cell emit green laser light.

with a wavelength of just 0.15 nanometres. The team are now seeking to make such lasers more stable and coherent, with potential applications in medicine and particle physics.

FIRST...

Maser
The maser (Microwave Amplification by Stimulation Emission of Radiation) was the precursor to the laser. Charles Hard Townes (USA) first conceived of it in 1951, before putting the process into practice in 1954. Townes shared the 1964 Nobel Prize in Physics, both for inventing the maser and for his later work on developing the first lasers.

Anti-laser
In Feb 2011, scientists from Yale University, USA, unveiled their anti-laser, the first device capable of cancelling out a laser beam. It uses an optical

Cooling of liquid by laser
On 26 Nov 2015, scientists at the University of Washington, USA, revealed that they had used a laser to refrigerate liquid water by around 20°C (68°F).

Most powerful laser by output

On 27 Jul 2015, researchers at Osaka University in Japan fired the Laser for Fast Ignition Experiment (LFEX) for one-trillionth of a second at a power of 2 petawatts. For reference, 2 petawatts is 2,000,000,000,000,000 watts.

DID YOU KNOW?
The Nd:YAG laser used to burst 200 balloons (see right) is named after the neodymium-doped yttrium aluminium garnet crystal that it incorporates. The laser was first demonstrated at Bell Laboratories in New Jersey, USA, in 1964.

Longest line of balloons popped using a laser

The three presenters of ITV's science and technology show *It's Not Rocket Science* (UK) burst a line of 200 balloons by means of an Nd:YAG laser in Borehamwood, UK, on 23 Jan 2016. Pictured above, from left to right, are the trio Rachel Riley, Romesh Ranganathan and Ben Miller (all UK), with GWR adjudicator Sam Mason, who oversaw the record attempt.

Highest box-office gross by a science-fiction film series
Star Wars (USA) – later retitled *Star Wars Episode IV: A New Hope* – is released. It is the first movie in a franchise that will go on to gross $6,452,324,357 (£4,513,190,000) worldwide as of Feb 2016.

1977

DATELINE

CUTTING-EDGE SCIENCE

First rocket-landing on Earth after deploying a payload in orbit

On 22 Dec 2015, SpaceX successfully landed the first stage of its *Falcon 9* rocket at Cape Canaveral Air Force Station in Florida, USA. The rocket had been launched the day before and had deployed 11 satellites into Earth orbit. The *Falcon 9* reached an altitude of 200 km (124 mi), after which the rocket's second stage took its payload of satellites into orbit. The first stage, which is 47 m (154 ft) tall, returned under its own power and landed vertically. The full journey is illustrated in this time-lapse photo.

First effective Ebola vaccine

The experimental vaccine VSV-EBOV has been trialled in Guinea with a success rate of at least 75% and possibly far higher. The results of the vaccine trials were published in the journal *The Lancet* on 31 Jul 2015. The first recipient of the vaccine was Mohamed Soumah of Guinea (above); he was given the all-clear three months later.

Most atoms quantum-entangled

On 26 Mar 2015, scientists from the Massachusetts Institute of Technology (USA) and the University of Belgrade (SRB) announced that they had quantum-entangled 2,910 atoms of rubidium (give or take 190 atoms). They achieved this by trapping the super-cooled particles between two slightly transparent mirrors and bombarding them with weak laser pulses.

Quantum entanglement occurs when particles are so fundamentally connected that they can theoretically influence each other – even across vast distances.

Shortest pulse of visible light

Scientists have created a light pulse lasting for just 380 attoseconds. One attosecond is a quintillionth (10^{-18}) of a second. The feat was achieved by Eleftherios Goulielmakis (GRC/DEU) and his team of researchers at the Max Planck Institute of Quantum Optics in Garching, Germany, and published on 4 Feb 2016.

Largest known prime number

On 7 Jan 2016, a computer volunteered by Dr Curtis Cooper (USA) at the University of Central Missouri, USA, discovered the Mersenne prime number $2^{74,207,281}-1$. The number has a designation M74207281. Reading two digits per second, it would take more than 100 days to read out the 22,338,618-digit number.

FIRST DETECTION OF GRAVITATIONAL WAVES

Albert Einstein proposed the existence of gravitational waves in 1916, but they were not detected until 11 Feb 2016. They are made when huge objects in space speed up or slow down. By mapping the movements of these waves, scientists have a new way of analysing signals from the universe. The detection was made by the LIGO Scientific Collaboration and the Virgo Collaboration using the Laser Interferometer Gravitational-Wave Observatory (LIGO).

LIGO is the **largest gravitational-wave detector**. It is located at two sites in the USA: Hanford in Washington and Livingston in Louisiana (below). Each houses two L-shaped, 4-km (2.5-mi) steel vacuum tubes, down which lasers are fired. The lasers interfere with each other in detectors, allowing tiny fluctuations in space-time to be studied, a process called interferometry.

DATELINE 1978

Most Tour de France stage wins
Eddie Merckx (BEL) celebrates his 34th stage win in the Tour de France. His first had come in 1969. Along with three other riders, Merckx also shares the record for the **most Tour de France wins** (5), with victories in 1969–72 and 1974.

204 Science & Technology

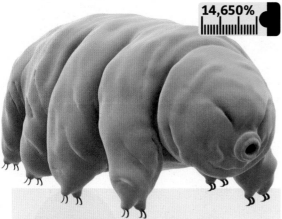

14,650%

Longest time for tardigrades to survive frozen in ice

A tardigrade is a highly resilient, microscopic, eight-legged aquatic invertebrate. On 25 Dec 2015, scientists from Japan's National Institute of Polar Research announced that they had revived two adult tardigrades that had been frozen in water ice since Nov 1983. Also known as "water bears" owing to their appearance (above), the creatures were thawed in Mar 2014. Nicknamed SB-1 and SB-2 (short for "Sleeping Beauty"), they began moving after they defrosted. Only SB-1 fully recovered, but went on to give birth to young (above).

Most durable digital storage medium

According to results published on 23 Jan 2014, nanostructured glass made by researchers from the University of Southampton's Optoelectronics Research Centre, UK, can remain stable at room temperature for 300 quintillion years. At 188.8°C (371.9°F), it has an estimated lifetime of 13.8 billion years (roughly the current age of the universe). Data is written to the glass as three layers of nanostructured dots using an ultrafast femtosecond laser, giving a storage capacity of 360 TB (terabytes) per disc. For comparison, the text content of the entire Library of Congress is equivalent to 20 TB.

DID YOU KNOW?
Incredibly, one nanostructured glass disc has had the entire Universal Declaration of Human Rights etched on to it (inset left) using an ultra-fast laser. No other existing storage medium can so reliably ensure that data will be accessible by future generations.

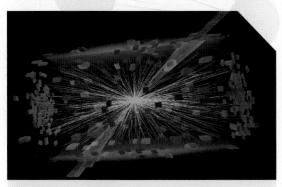

Highest-energy ion collisions in a particle collider

On 25 Nov 2015, scientists using the Large Hadron Collider at CERN in Geneva, Switzerland, announced that they had collided two beams of lead ions together at 1,045 teraelectronvolts (TeV). This measurement is the energy equivalent to that of a bumblebee striking your face.

First spacecraft to orbit a comet
On 6 Aug 2014, the European Space Agency's *Rosetta* spacecraft entered orbit around comet 67P/ Churyumov-Gerasimenko (67P). On 12 Nov 2014, it released *Philae*, a lander designed to analyse the comet's surface. As of 27 Jan 2016, *Rosetta* had been orbiting 67P for 539 days, and is the **longest orbital survey of a comet**.

Most distant object in the universe
Using data from the Wide Field Camera 3 on the *Hubble Space Telescope*, a team of astronomers announced on 3 Mar 2016 their discovery of a galaxy in the Ursa Major constellation. The light detected by *Hubble* from this galaxy, GN-z11, dates back 13.4 billion years, around 400 million years after the Big Bang. In that time, the expansion of the universe means that GN-z11 is now some 32 billion light years from Earth.

Longest X-ray free-electron laser
Located in Germany, the European XFEL stretches 3.4 km (2.1 mi) and across three research sites. This X-ray free-electron laser (XFEL) incorporates high-speed electrons moving through magnets. The laser itself measures 2 km (1.2 mi) long, with an acceleration length of 1.7 km (1.06 mi). It requires 17.5 billion electron volts and operates at a temperature of -271°C (-455.8°F).

First object 3D-printed from extraterrestrial material

On 8 Jan 2016, at the Consumer Electronics Show in Las Vegas, Nevada, USA, Planetary Resources and 3D Systems (both USA) revealed a 3D-printed model of a spacecraft part made from meteorite metals. The feat is a successful proof of concept that should allow future missions into the Solar System to create equipment and parts from asteroids.

Oldest person to get divorced
On 21 Nov, after nine years of marriage, 101-year-old Harry Bidwell of East Sussex, UK, divorces his 65-year-old wife, Lucy. He feels that she "wasn't domesticated enough" and is soon seeking a new partner.

1980

DATELINE

SPORTS

> **1981** { **First car to sell 20 million units**
> On 15 May, the 20-millionth Volkswagen Beetle rolls off the assembly line, at Volkswagen de
> México's factory in Puebla. Production of the car in Germany had ceased three years previously.

CONTENTS

Highest annual earnings for an athlete ever

When it comes to financial muscle, one sportsman remains undisputed champion. Floyd Mayweather Jr (USA, far left) earned a knockout $300 m (£190.8 m) from Jun 2014 to Jun 2015, according to Forbes. And in the inset picture above left, he proudly holds aloft his GWR certificate to confirm it.

Mayweather also enjoys the **highest career pay-per-view sales for a boxer**, a reported $1.311 bn (£843.7 m) from 19.53 million PPV buys, for 15 fights between 25 Jun 2005 and 12 Sep 2015. His welterweight title fight against Manny Pacquiao (PHL, left) at the MGM Grand in Las Vegas, Nevada, USA, on 2 May 2015 grossed a reported $425 m (£275.8 m) from 4,400,000 purchases, making it the **highest-selling pay-per-view boxing match**.

Youngest player in a FIFA World Cup
On 17 Jun, Norman Whiteside appears for Northern Ireland vs Yugoslavia at La Romareda stadium in Zaragoza, Spain, aged 17 years 41 days. The game finishes goalless.

{ 1982 ▶

SPORT'S BIG HITTERS

Sport is big business – and getting bigger all the time. Alongside their salary and match winnings, players make a lucrative living from endorsements with blue-chip companies or payments for personal appearances. Meet the world's most bankable sports stars.

All values are in US dollars ($1 = £0.70, as of 15 Apr 2016).

HIGHEST-PAID ATHLETES 2015

When it comes to money-making, sport's biggest hitters are in a different league – although for some, such as Roger Federer, endorsements provide a much larger slice of the pie than for others (e.g., Floyd Mayweather Jr). The colour-coding refers to the split between the two (see artwork, right).

	NAME/NATIONALITY	SPORT	Pay	Salary/Winnings	Endorsements
1	Floyd Mayweather Jr (USA)	Boxing	$300 m	$285 m	$15 m
2	Manny Pacquiao (PHL)	Boxing	$160 m	$148 m	$12 m
3	Cristiano Ronaldo (PRT)	Soccer	$79.6 m	$52.6 m	$27 m
4	Lionel Messi (ARG)	Soccer	$73.8 m	$51.8 m	$22 m
5	Roger Federer (CHE)	Tennis	$67 m	$9 m	$58 m
6	LeBron James (USA)	Basketball	$64.8 m	$20.8 m	$44 m
7	Kevin Durant (USA)	Basketball	$54.2 m	$19.1 m	$35 m
8	Phil Mickelson (USA)	Golf	$50.8 m	$2.8 m	$48 m
9	Tiger Woods (USA)	Golf	$50.6 m	$0.6 m	$50 m
10	Kobe Bryant (USA)	Basketball	$49.5 m	$23.5 m	$26 m

Source: Forbes

KEY FOR EARNINGS INFOGRAPHIC

= $7,000,000

Endorsements | Salary/Winnings

DID YOU KNOW?

In Feb 2004, Lionel Messi began his youth contract just over with Barcelona, earning £1 over his nearest fast-forward to more than Ballon d'Or $1,800 per week. And the five-time 2016, and is taking home winner is taking $362,500 per week.

FLOYD MAYWEATHER JR: $300 m

Mayweather Jr's pay for 2015 is almost double that of his nearest rival. And it's more than four times the estimated total of $69 m earned by boxing legend Muhammad "The Greatest" Ali during his 20-year career.

MANNY PACQUIAO: $160 m

Pacquiao's money-spinning fight with Floyd Mayweather Jr in May 2015 earned him a knockout $125 m alone – four times his previous highest payment. And that's what he got for *losing*…

LIONEL MESSI: $73.8 m

In Mar 2016, smartphone manufacturer Huawei announced it had struck a two-year endorsement deal with Messi worth more than $13 m.

CRISTIANO RONALDO: $79.6 m

Any team wishing to poach Ronaldo from Real Madrid must pay a guaranteed €1 bn to the Spanish side in return for his services (and a share of his image rights).

ROGER FEDERER: $67 m

Federer has a string of records to his name, including the highest ever annual earnings **for a tennis player** – $71.5 m from Jun 2012 to Jun 2013.

LEBRON JAMES: $64.8 m

In 2015, James signed a sponsorship deal with Nike thought to be worth up to $1 bn. However, it will tie him to Nike for the rest of his life – not just for the rest of his playing career.

KEVIN DURANT: $54.2 m

Durant's salary in 2015 was just over $19 m, but he added a cool $35 m to that figure in sponsorship deals.

PHIL MICKELSON: $50.8 m

Around 80% of Mickelson's hefty 2015 income came from endorsements and appearances. His endorsement partners include ExxonMobil, Rolex and Barclays.

TIGER WOODS: $50.6 m

Forbes put Woods' net worth at $700 m in 2015. His most loyal sponsor, Nike, pays him $20-m-plus annually.

KOBE BRYANT: $49.5 m

Life-long LA Lakers player Bryant enjoyed a salary of around $25 m in his final NBA season. As of the start of 2016, he had a net worth of some $366 m.

HOLY COW!

With a net worth believed to be in the region of $320 m, tennis ace Roger Federer is among the wealthiest sportsmen in the world. Of the many prizes he has picked up over the years, perhaps the most unusual is Juliette, a cow he was gifted after winning his first Wimbledon title back in 2003.

RICHEST RETIRED ATHLETES 2015

They say you have to be in it to win it, but that isn't necessarily the case for sportsmen. A fortunate – and highly talented – few are able to carry on earning long after retirement courtesy of endorsements, licensing and personal appearances.

	NAME/NATIONALITY	SPORT	INCOME
1	Michael Jordan (USA, right)	Basketball	$110 m
2	David Beckham (UK)	Soccer	$65 m
3	Arnold Palmer (USA)	Golf	$40 m
4	Junior Bridgeman (USA)	Basketball	$32 m
5	Jerry Richardson (USA)	American football	$30 m
6	Jack Nicklaus (USA)	Golf	$26 m
7	Shaquille O'Neal (USA)	Basketball	$22 m
8	Roger Penske (USA)	Motorsport	$20 m
9	Gary Player (ZAF)	Golf	$19 m
10	Ervin "Magic" Johnson (USA)	Basketball	$18 m

Source: Forbes

NBA EARNINGS

Per game, National Basketball Association (NBA) players earn on average nearly 600 times the salary of an NBA cheerleader.

Cheerleader: $100

Player: $59,756

Lakers: $2.6 bn

NBA average: $1.25 bn

NBA VALUE

In Jan 2015, the value of the average NBA team topped $1 bn for the first time ever. The Los Angeles Lakers were valued at around 2.5 times this average in Forbes' 2015 list. Above, Lakers legend Kobe Bryant, who played his final game on 13 Apr 2016.

TIGER WOODS' EARNINGS

When it comes to golf, there's way more money made off the green than on it. In 20 years as a professional golfer, Woods has won $156 m in prize money. Not bad, but it's dwarfed compared to the $1-bn-plus he's earned in sponsorship deals during the same period.

Prize winnings

Endorsements

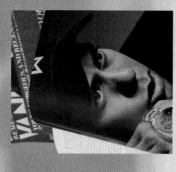

TOP 10 RICHEST TEAMS

Every year, Forbes publishes its list of the 50 wealthiest teams. This is the Top 10 from their last official list, published in Jul 2015.

Real Madrid earned $608 m in gate receipts in 2015, but $1,091 bn from broadcasting.

1. Real Madrid (ESP)
Soccer
$3.26 bn

=2. Dallas Cowboys (USA)
American football
$3.2 bn

=2. New York Yankees (USA)
Baseball
$3.2 bn

4. FC Barcelona (ESP)
Soccer
$3.16 bn

5. Manchester United (UK)
Soccer
$3.1 bn

=6. Los Angeles Lakers (USA)
Basketball
$2.6 bn

=6. New England Patriots (USA)
American football
$2.6 bn

8. New York Knicks (USA)
Basketball
$2.5 bn

=9. Los Angeles Dodgers (USA)
Baseball
$2.4 bn

=9. Washington Redskins (USA)
American football
$2.4 bn

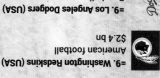

Source: Forbes

AMERICAN FOOTBALL

Most consecutive pass completions

Miami Dolphins quarterback Ryan Tannehill made 25 pass completions over two NFL games: seven straight against the Tennessee Titans on 18 Oct 2015, and 18 against the Houston Texans on 25 Oct 2015.

First quarterback to win the Super Bowl with two different teams

Peyton Manning led the Indianapolis Colts to a 29–17 victory over the Chicago Bears in Super Bowl XLI on 4 Feb 2007, and nine years later guided the Denver Broncos to a 24–10 win over the Carolina Panthers in Super Bowl 50 on 7 Feb 2016. The latter victory made Manning, at the age of 39, the **oldest quarterback to win a Super Bowl**. See below for more Manning records.

All teams and players are USA.

Youngest NFL player to reach 1,000 receptions
At 32 years 97 days old, Larry Fitzgerald (b. 31 Aug 1983) of the Arizona Cardinals caught his 1,000th pass on 6 Dec 2015.

Most passing yards in an NFL career
On 15 Nov 2015, Peyton Manning of the Denver Broncos gained 35 yards

passing in a game against the Miami Dolphins to reach 71,871 passing yards – the NFL's all-time record.

Manning is also the **first player to win 200 games as NFL starting quarterback** (including

postseason). He won 186 regular season games and 14 postseason games, playing for the Indianapolis Colts and Denver Broncos between 1998 and 2015.

Most games gaining 200 yards rushing in an NFL career
Adrian Peterson gained 203 yards rushing while playing for the

Minnesota Vikings in a 30–14 win over the Oakland Raiders on 15 Nov 2015. It was Peterson's sixth 200-yard game, equalling the mark set by O J Simpson.

Shortest regular season overtime game
On 4 Oct 2015, New Orleans Saints' Drew Brees (below), playing the Dallas Cowboys, threw a touchdown pass to C J Spiller for a 26–20 win in 13 sec of overtime.

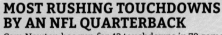

MOST RUSHING TOUCHDOWNS BY AN NFL QUARTERBACK

Cam Newton has run for 43 touchdowns in 78 games for the Carolina Panthers since 2011. This equals the record set by Steve Young in 169 games over 15 seasons, playing for the Tampa Bay Buccaneers and San Francisco 49ers from 1985 to 1999.

Newton also threw two touchdown passes and ran for two touchdowns in a 38–10 victory over the Tampa Bay Buccaneers on 3 Jan 2016. This represents the **most times passing and running for touchdowns in the same NFL game** – a record 31.

Most combined touchdown passes in an NFL game

A total of 13 touchdown passes were thrown during New Orleans' 52–49 victory over the New York Giants on 1 Nov 2015. Seven were by Drew Brees (above) of the New Orleans Saints and six were by Eli Manning of the New York Giants. The previous mark of 12 touchdown passes had stood for 46 years.

DATELINE

1983

Deepest penetration into Earth's crust
Excavation ceases on a geological exploratory borehole near Zapolyarny, on the Kola Peninsula of Arctic Russia. The depth reached is 12,261 m (40,226 ft) when work stops owing to a lack of funds.

210 Sports

BASEBALL

Longest Major League Baseball (MLB) World Series game (innings)

On 27 Oct 2015, the Kansas City Royals defeated the New York Mets 5–4 in 14 innings. Their record equalled that of the Chicago White Sox vs Houston Astros in Oct 2005, and the Boston Red Sox vs Brooklyn Dodgers in Oct 1916.

All teams and individuals are USA, unless otherwise stated.

Most runs batted in by a pitcher in his first game

On 28 Jun 2015, Steven Matz, the winning pitcher for the New York Mets against the Cincinnati Reds, batted in four runs.

Most at-bats without recording a hit to start a career

Playing for the Boston Red Sox, Oakland Athletics and Chicago Cubs from 16 Jun 2006 to 6 Jul 2015, Jon Lester had the longest hitless drought: 66 official regular season at-bats.

Most grand slam home runs in an MLB career

A grand slam home run is one hit when all the bases are occupied. Playing for the Seattle Mariners, Texas Rangers and New York Yankees, Alex Rodriguez has recorded 25 since 1994.

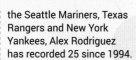

Most consecutive postseason games hitting a home run (individual)

Playing for the New York Mets, Daniel Murphy hit a home run in six successive playoff games in the 2015 postseason. In Jan 2016, Murphy signed with the Washington Nationals.

Most home runs in one postseason game by a team

On 12 Oct 2015, in Game Three of the National League Division Series, the Chicago Cubs hit six home runs in an 8–6 victory over the St Louis Cardinals. The Cardinals hit two home runs in the same game for a combined total of eight – the **most home runs hit in one postseason game by both teams**. Chicago's home-run hitters were Starlin Castro (DOM), Anthony Rizzo, Dexter Fowler, Kris Bryant, Jorge Soler (CUB) and Kyle Schwarber. Jason Heyward and Stephen Piscotty each connected for the Cardinals.

Most consecutive matches in MLB without an error in the outfield

Outfielder Nick Markakis went 398 games without an error while playing for the Baltimore Orioles and Atlanta Braves from 10 Aug 2012 to 25 Jun 2015. He has twice won the American League Gold Glove Award for fielding, in 2011 and 2014.

Highest National Baseball Hall of Fame vote percentage

Ken Griffey Jr was elected to the National Baseball Hall of Fame in 2016 with the highest ever percentage of votes. He appeared on 437 (or 99.3%) of the 440 ballots cast. Griffey, of the Seattle Mariners, commented, "To get the call is unbelievable."

DID YOU KNOW?

Adrián Beltré (b. 7 Apr 1979) was 36 years old when he hit for the cycle (pictured) for the third time. Playing against the Houston Astros, he hit a triple in the first innings, a double in the second, a single in the third and a home run in the fifth.

MOST TIMES HITTING FOR THE CYCLE

The cycle is a rare baseball feat in which a batter hits a single, double, triple and home run (in any order) in the same game. The greatest number of times this has been done in a career is three: by John Reilly from 1883 to 1890 (including twice in seven days); Bob Meusel from 1921 to 1928; "Babe" Herman from 1931 to 1933; and Adrián Beltré (DOM; pictured) from 2008 to 3 Aug 2015. Beltré, of the Texas Rangers, secured his third cycle in a 12–9 victory against the Houston Astros.

Most games to feature a right- and left-handed home run by the same player

Two players have each hit a home run left-handed and another right-handed in the same game on 14 occasions. They are Mark Teixeira (since 2003, for the Texas Rangers, Atlanta Braves, Los Angeles Angels and New York Yankees) and Nick Swisher (since 2004, for the Oakland Athletics, Chicago White Sox, New York Yankees, Cleveland Indians and Atlanta Braves).

Most valuable shipwreck found
Treasure-hunter Mel Fisher (USA, 1922–98) finds the *Nuestra Señora de Atocha* off the Florida coast on 20 Jul. The ship sank in 1622, with a cargo of 40 US tons (36.2 tonnes) of gold and silver and some 70 lb (32 kg) of emeralds.

1985

DATELINE

guinnessworldrecords.com 211

BASKETBALL

Most three-point field goals in a postseason by an individual

Stephen Curry converted 98 three-point field goals for the Golden State Warriors during the 2015 NBA playoffs. The Warriors set a new record for the **best season start** in NBA history with 24 consecutive victories to begin the 2015/16 season.

All records relate to the National Basketball Association (NBA). All teams and individuals are USA.

Most points scored by a team in an All-Star Game

The West All-Stars scored 196 points in the All-Star Game held on 14 Feb 2016.

The **most points scored by a player in an All-Star Game** is 42, by Wilt Chamberlain in 1962. The same year, he recorded the **most points scored by an individual in an NBA game**: 100.

The **most points scored in NBA All-Star games** is 291 by LeBron James (USA), playing in 11 All-Star games from 2005 to 2016.

Most points scored by a team in the first quarter of a postseason match

The Houston Rockets scored 45 points in the first quarter of their postseason match against the Golden State Warriors on 25 May 2015. This matched the total set by the Los Angeles Lakers on 18 Apr 1985 and Dallas Mavericks on 4 May 1986.

Highest-scoring All-Star Game

On 14 Feb 2016, the two All-Stars sides scored a combined 369 points. The West All-Stars beat the East squad 196–173.

First father-son player-coach tandem

For 11 min on 16 Jan 2015, Austin Rivers played under Los Angeles Clippers coach Doc Rivers against the Cleveland Cavaliers.

Most consecutive losses

The Philadelphia 76ers lost 28 games in a row from 27 Mar 2015 to 29 Nov 2015. They also share the record for **most consecutive losses to start a season** (18) with the New Jersey Nets.

Kobe Bryant

The 2015/16 season sees the end of a remarkable NBA career. Among his many records, the Los Angeles Lakers' Kobe Bryant is the **youngest player to start a game** (at 18 years 158 days) and **youngest player to score 25,000 points** (at 31 years 151 days). He also shares the record for the **most field goals made in NBA All-Star games** (119) with LeBron James. Bryant is the only NBA player with more than 30,000 points, 6,000 assists and 6,000 rebounds.

DID YOU KNOW?

James Harden's prodigious performances during the 2011/12 season saw him become the second-youngest winner of the prestigious NBA Sixth Man of the Year Award. Not bad for someone who has suffered from asthma attacks since childhood...

MOST THREE-POINT FIELD GOALS BY A TEAM IN A SEASON

The Houston Rockets set an NBA record by scoring 933 three-point field goals during the 2014/15 season. In the course of achieving that milestone, the Rockets also registered the **most three-point field goals attempted by a team in a season**: 2,680. James Harden (right) performed the **most turnovers in a postseason game by an individual** – 13 – while playing for the Rockets in a 104–90 loss to the Golden State Warriors. He set the record on 27 May 2015, during Game 5 of the team's playoff series.

DATELINE

1986

Largest monster truck
Over the summer, Bob Chandler (USA) builds the monstrous *Bigfoot 5*, which stands 15 ft 6 in (4.7 m) tall and tips the scales at 38,000 lb (17,235 kg). Each of its tyres measures 10 ft (3 m) off the ground.

212 Sports

ICE HOCKEY

Most career game-winning goals

Jaromír Jágr (CZE) had scored 132 game-winning career goals as of 30 Jan 2016, outstripping the 121-goal record set by the legendary Canadian right wing Gordie Howe.

Longest shootout

The Florida Panthers took 20 rounds to defeat the Washington Capitals (both USA) 2–1, on 16 Dec 2014. Other records set during the game include the **most shootout goals by both teams** (11) and the **most shootout goals by a team** (six, by Florida).

All records relate to the National Hockey League (NHL) contested in the USA and Canada.

Fastest ice hockey shot
Zdeno Chára (SVK) delivered a 108.8-mph (175.09-km/h) slap shot for the Boston Bruins (USA) during the All-Star Game's Skills Competition in Ottawa, Ontario, Canada, on 29 Jan 2012.

Highest-scoring All-Star Game
In total, 29 goals were scored in the 2015 NHL All-Star Game at Columbus in Ohio, USA. Team Toews beat Team Foligno 17–12.

Most shots blocked in a season
Kris Russell blocked 283 shots for the Calgary Flames

(both CAN) in 2014/15. His feat surpassed the record of 273 blocks by Anton Volchenkov (RUS) of the Ottawa Senators (CAN) in 2006/07.

Most saves in a shutout
In a shutout, a goalie stops the opposing team from

scoring for the whole game. The Edmonton Oilers' Ben Scrivens (both CAN) made 59 saves in a 3–0 win over the San Jose Sharks (USA) on 29 Jan 2014.

Most points by a team without reaching the playoffs
The Boston Bruins earned 96 points in the standings during the 2014/15 season, yet still failed to qualify for the postseason. The Bruins finished with 41–27–14 for their points.

Most shootout goals in a career

A shootout takes place in a game that is tied after an overtime period. By the end of the 2014/15 season, Jonathan Toews (CAN, above left) had netted 40 shootout goals for the Chicago Blackhawks (USA). He is seen here competing for the puck with Shane Doan (CAN) of the Arizona Coyotes (USA) on 9 Feb 2015.

LONGEST ROAD WINNING STREAK BY A TEAM

The longest unbroken run of wins away from home is 12 games, first accomplished by the Detroit Red Wings during the 2005/06 season and matched by the Minnesota Wild (both USA) in 2014/15. Pictured, Zach Parise (USA, far left) and Mikko Koivu (FIN, left) celebrate as the Wild tie the score at 1–1 against the Los Angeles Kings on 16 Oct 2015.

The Detroit Red Wings recorded the **longest home winning streak by a team**, with 23 consecutive home wins during the 2011/12 season. The **longest winning streak overall by a team** is 17 games, set by the Pittsburgh Penguins (USA) between 9 Mar and 10 Apr 1993.

Greatest collapse of global stock markets
On 19 Oct – "Black Monday" – stocks begin a dramatic worldwide decline. By the end of the month, the US stock market has dropped by 22.68%, the Canadian stock market by 22.5% and the UK stock market by 26.4%.

1987

DATELINE

guinnessworldrecords.com **213**

BOXING

Most gold medals won in the AIBA World Boxing Championships (light heavyweight)

Julio César La Cruz (CUB) won three consecutive AIBA titles, in 2011, 2013 and 2015. La Cruz is pictured above, in blue, defeating Ireland's Joe Ward in the 2015 finals in Doha, Qatar.

HIGHEST REVENUE FROM TICKET SALES FOR A BOXING MATCH

A welterweight title fight between Floyd Mayweather Jr (USA) and Manny Pacquiao (PHL) earned $72,198,500 (£46,843,387) from the sale of 16,219 tickets. The fight took place at the MGM Grand in Las Vegas, Nevada, USA, on 2 May 2015. Mayweather won on points.

Most expensive boxing championship belt

The World Boxing Council (WBC) Emerald Belt awarded to Floyd Mayweather Jr (USA) on 2 May 2015 cost $1,000,000 (£657,251) to produce. Mayweather received the belt following his defeat of the Philippines' Manny Pacquiao (see below).

Most bouts undefeated by a world champion boxer in a career

Legendary heavyweight champion Rocky Marciano, aka Rocco Francis Marchegiano (USA), won every fight of his professional career, with 49 victories between 17 Mar 1947 and 21 Sep 1955 (he announced his retirement on 27 Apr 1956). In all, 43 of his 49 fights were by knockouts or stoppages. This feat was equalled by Floyd Mayweather Jr (USA), a champion across five weight divisions, who also retired with a 49–0 record, which he set between 11 Oct 1996 and 12 Sep 2015. He won 26 fights by knockout.

Oldest boxing world champion (female)

Bettering her own record set in 2013,

Most world heavyweight title bouts

Wladimir Klitschko (UKR, above) was crowned WBO champion on 14 Oct 2000. With his world title fight on 28 Nov 2015, he set a new record of 28 for the most world heavyweight title bouts. Until then, Klitschko had matched the record set by Joe Louis (USA), who became champion on 22 Jun 1937 and had his 27th and final shot at the title on 27 Sep 1950.

Jamaican-American boxer Alicia Ashley (b. 23 Aug 1967) defeated Christina McMahon (IRL) to regain the WBC Female Super Bantamweight title, in New York, USA, on 29 Oct 2015, aged 48 years 67 days.

DID YOU KNOW?

There was an unfortunate epilogue to Mayweather's victory against Pacquiao. His title was taken from him just two months later by the World Boxing Organization (WBO) for failing to pay a set $200,000 (£130,931) fee that was to have come out of his winner's purse.

DATELINE ▶ **1990** Most distant image of Earth
On 14 Feb, NASA's *Voyager 1* takes a picture of Earth from a distance of almost 6.5 billion km (4 billion mi). (For more on the *Voyager* spacecraft's incredible – and still ongoing – journey, see pp.24–25.)

214 Sports

MARTIAL ARTS

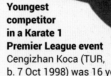

First athlete to win boxing and MMA world titles

The first athlete, male or female, to be both boxing world champion and an MMA (mixed martial arts) world champion is Holly Holm (USA, right), who became WBA (World Boxing Association) welterweight champion in 2006 and held world titles until 2013. She became UFC (Ultimate Fighting Championship) bantamweight champion by defeating Ronda Rousey (USA, left) by way of second-round knockout in Melbourne, Australia, on 14 Nov 2015. Earlier in the year, Rousey had set her own world record, however, achieving the **fastest UFC title fight victory by submission** in just 14 sec when she defeated Cat Zingano at UFC 184, staged at the Staples Center in Los Angeles, California, USA, on 28 Feb.

Most top-division sumo bouts

Kyokutenhō Masaru (MNG) contested 1,470 top-division (*makuuchi*) sumo wrestling bouts from 1998 to 27 Jul 2015. He took the record from Kaiō Hiroyuki on 14 May 2015, when he fought his 1,445th bout. He is second only to Ōshio, aka Kenji Hatano (JPN), in terms of the **most sumo wrestling career bouts**; Ōshio fought 1,891 bouts to Kyokutenhō's 1,870.

Most top-division sumo championships won

As of 26 Jul 2015, Hakuhō Shō, aka Mönkhbatyn Davaajargal (MNG), had won 35 top-division sumo championships. In 2009, and again in 2010, he won 86 bouts out of the 90 regulation fights that top *rikishi* (sumo wrestlers) contest annually – the **most wins in a calendar year**.

Most wins of the World Judo Championships team competition (female)

The Japanese women's team has taken the top spot at the World Judo Championships five times, in 2002, 2008, 2012, 2013 and 2015.

Most wins of the World Judo Championships (male)

Guadeloupe-born Teddy Riner (FRA) has won eight titles at the World Judo Championships – seven in the +100 kg (heavyweight) division (2007, 2009–11, 2013–15) and one as a member of the French men's team in 2011.

LONGEST TOTAL FIGHT TIME IN A UFC CAREER

The greatest aggregate time spent in the octagon (the eight-sided enclosure where UFC bouts take place) by a UFC fighter is 5 hr 37 min 51 sec by Frankie Edgar (USA), between 3 Feb 2003 and 11 Dec 2015.

Edgar attained his feat in 18 UFC fights, breaking the record set by Georges St-Pierre (CAN), who had achieved a time of 5 hr 28 min 12 sec across 21 bouts in 2013.

A UFC lightweight champion in 2010, Edgar defended the title three times before losing to Benson Henderson in 2012. Edgar is shown below (left) during his defeat of fellow American Urijah Faber on 16 May 2015 in the Philippine capital of Manila.

Most medals won in the Karate 1 Premier League

Alisa Buchinger and Bettina Plank (both AUT) each won 14 Karate 1 Premier League medals from 2013 to 2015.

Youngest competitor in a Karate 1 Premier League event

Cengizhan Koca (TUR, b. 7 Oct 1998) was 16 years 333 days old when he fought at the Karate 1 Istanbul 2015 event on 5 Sep 2015.

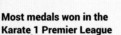

First website
On 6 Aug in Geneva, Switzerland, computer scientist Tim Berners-Lee (UK) launches the website he has built to demonstrate the World Wide Web: http://info.cern.ch/.

1991

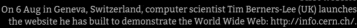

DATELINE

CRICKET

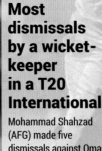

Highest partnership in a Twenty20 (T20) International

On 17 Jan 2016, New Zealand openers Martin Guptill (left) and Kane Williamson achieved an unbroken stand of 171 runs in a T20 International against Pakistan at Seddon Park in New Zealand. Guptill (87 not out off 58 balls) and Williamson (72 not out off 48 balls) saw the hosts home in 17.4 overs with 14 balls to spare.

First day–night Test match
On 27–29 Nov 2015, Australia and New Zealand contested a day–night Test, with a pink ball (to increase visibility), at the Adelaide Oval in Australia. With this experiment in starting and finishing the match later, the International Cricket Council (ICC) hoped to enable more people to watch Test cricket.

Fastest Test match hundred
On 20 Feb 2016, playing against Australia in his final Test match, New

Zealand captain Brendon McCullum smashed a 54-ball hundred, featuring 16 fours and four sixes. The feat took 79 min at Hagley Oval in Christchurch, New Zealand. McCullum has also hit the **most sixes in a Test match career**: 107 in 176 innings.

Fastest fifty in a T20 match
Chris Gayle (JAM) recorded a 12-ball fifty for the Melbourne Renegades

against the Adelaide Strikers in Australia on 18 Jan 2016. This equalled the record set in 2007 by Yuvraj Singh (IND), playing against England in the ICC World Twenty20 tournament.

Most runs scored by teams in an ODI series
England (1,617) and New Zealand (1,534) together scored 3,151 runs in their One-Day International (ODI) series in England in Jun 2015, including tons from England's Jos Buttler, Joe Root (2) and Eoin Morgan, and New Zealand's Ross Taylor (2) and Kane Williamson. England, who scored the **most runs by a team in a five-match ODI series**, won the series 3–2.

Most dismissals by a wicket-keeper in a T20 International

Mohammad Shahzad (AFG) made five dismissals against Oman at Sheikh Zayed Stadium in Abu Dhabi, UAE, on 29 Nov 2015. He took three catches and made two stumpings to help his team win by 27 runs.

Fastest five-wicket haul in a Test match (balls bowled)

On 6 Aug 2015, England's Stuart Broad (above right) took 19 balls and 40 min to dismiss five of Australia's top order in the Fourth Ashes Test at Trent Bridge, UK. He equalled the record by Ernie Toshack (AUS), who took five wickets for two runs in 2.3 eight-ball overs against India at Brisbane Cricket Ground, Australia, on 4 Dec 1947.

FASTEST BALL BOWLED IN A TEST MATCH

160.4 km/h

Australia's Mitchell Starc delivered a ball at 160.4 km/h (99.66 mph) during a Test match between Australia and New Zealand at the WACA in Perth, Australia, on 15 Nov 2015. The left-armer's yorker was defended by New Zealand batsman Ross Taylor, who weathered the storm and went on to make 290 – the highest Test score by a visiting batsman in Australia. Starc is only the fourth bowler – after Shoaib Akhtar (PAK, 2003), Brett Lee (AUS, 2005) and Shaun Tait (AUS, 2010) – to achieve a bowling speed of 160 km/h (99.41 mph) or more in the history of international cricket.

First ODI series win for an associate ICC member against a full member
Afghanistan won the first ODI series against a Test-playing nation, beating Zimbabwe 3–2 in Oct 2015.

▲ Highest score in a limited-overs match (minor cricket)
On 3 Nov 2014, in Ooty (Ootacamund), India, 15-year-old Sankruth Sriram (IND) smashed 486 not out playing for JSS International School against Hebron School.

Most runs in Test matches between dismissals
From 10 Dec 2015 to 14 Feb 2016, Adam Voges (AUS) scored 614 runs.

DID YOU KNOW?
There are 10 full ICC members (Test-playing nations). Associate ICC members with ODI status are Afghanistan, Hong Kong, Ireland, Papua New Guinea, Scotland and the UAE. As of 24 Oct 2015, Afghanistan had won six of their first 20 ODIs against Test-playing nations.

1996 **First animal cloned from an adult cell**
On 5 Jul, Dolly the Sheep is born in the UK to a surrogate mother. Dolly is successfully cloned from the cell of an adult Finnish Dorset sheep. She will give birth to lambs by natural means and reach the age of six.

GOLF

Most wins of the Presidents Cup by a team

The USA has won the biennial tournament nine times: in 1994, 1996, 2000, 2005, 2007, 2009, 2011, 2013 and 2015. The Presidents Cup is contested by the USA and an international team made up of players who are ineligible to play in the Ryder Cup – that is, the rest of the world less Europe. In 2015, it was held in Incheon, South Korea, and the USA won by 15½ to 14½ points.

Lowest score to par in a men's golf major

On 13–16 Aug 2015, Jason Day (AUS) achieved -20 at the 97th Professional Golfers' Association (PGA) Championship, on the Straits Course of Whistling Straits near Kohler, Wisconsin, USA. Day's performance secured him his first major. He finished with 268 (68–67–66–67).

Largest comeback in the Solheim Cup
On 20 Sep 2015, at the start of the third and final day of play at the Golf Club St Leon-Rot in Baden-Württemberg, Germany, the USA trailed 6–10 to Europe. Making a spectacular comeback of four points, the USA stormed to victory by 14½ to 13½ – the **smallest winning margin in the Solheim Cup.**

Lowest score to par in a women's golf major
Five golfers in three different majors have recorded -19. It was first achieved by Dottie Pepper (USA) at the 1999 Kraft Nabisco Championship. This was matched by Karen Stupples (UK) at the 2004 British Open, and by Cristie Kerr (USA) and Yani Tseng (TPE) at the 2010 and 2011 LPGA championships. Most recently it was achieved by Inbee Park (KOR, right) at the LPGA Championship in Harrison, New York, USA, on 11–14 Jun 2015. For Kerr, Tseng and Park, these records also marked the **lowest score under par in the LPGA Championship.**

Youngest golfer to win a women's major golf championship
Lydia Ko (NZ, b. KOR, 24 Apr 1997) was aged 18 years 142 days when she won the 2015 Evian Championships in Évian-les-Bains, France, on 13 Sep 2015. At the time of setting this record, Ko was already the **youngest golfer ranked number one** (aged 17 years 283 days on 1 Feb 2015). She was also the **youngest LPGA Tour event winner** – of the CN Canadian Women's Open in Vancouver, Canada, on 26 Aug 2012, at the age of 15 years 124 days.

Highest annual earnings for a golfer (current year)
In Jun 2014–Jun 2015, Phil Mickelson (USA) earned an estimated $51 m (£32.4 m), surpassing Tiger Woods by one place in the Forbes list.

DID YOU KNOW?
Mickey Wright (USA) was the first to win the LPGA Championship back-to-back (1960–61) and achieved the **most wins of the LPGA Championship:** four. She also shares the record for the **most US Women's Open titles** (four) with Betsy Rawls (UK).

Most consecutive wins of the LPGA Championship

In 2013–15, Inbee Park (KOR) won the Ladies Professional Golf Association Championship three times, twice by play-off and once by five strokes. She equalled the record set by Annika Sörenstam (SWE) in 2003–05. See left for another of Park's records.

HIGHEST EARNINGS IN A PGA SEASON
Jordan Spieth (USA, b. 27 Jul 1993) dominated the 2015 PGA Tour and received $12,030,465 (£7,851,960) in earnings. No one had ever won more than $11 m prior to Spieth's lucrative season. Other than the standard PGA earnings, he also picked up a $10-m (£7.18-m) bonus by winning the Tour's finale, the FedEx Cup. In so doing, he became the **youngest player to win the FedEx Cup**, aged 22 years 62 days. Clinching this and the Tour Championship returned Spieth to his position as world No.1.

Land-speed record
On 15 Oct, Andy Green (UK) pilots the jet-powered *Thrust SSC* to a speed of 1,227.985 km/h (763.035 mph; Mach 1.020) in the Black Rock Desert, Nevada, USA. It is the **first car to break the sound barrier**.

1997 — DATELINE

guinnessworldrecords.com 217

EXTREME SPORTS

The aviation records on this page were either sourced from the Fédération Aéronautique Internationale (FAI) or set at FAI-accredited events.

Farthest flight by a paraglider (male)
Three paraglider pilots covered a straight distance of 514 km (319.3 mi) in the same trip. Frank Brown, Marcelo Prieto and Donizete Lemos (all BRA) flew from Tacima to Monsenhor Tabosa in Paraíba, Brazil, on 9 Oct 2015.

Seiko Fukuoka-Naville (FRA, b. JPN) achieved the **farthest flight by a paraglider (female)** when she flew 402 km (249.7 mi) from Deniliquin, Australia, on 9 Dec 2015.

Farthest out-and-return distance hang-gliding (female)
Britain's Kathleen Rigg flew an out-and-return distance of 229.8 km (142.7 mi) by hang-glider in Bischling, Austria, on 5 Jul 2015.

The **farthest out-and-return hang-gliding (male)** title is jointly held by Carlos Puñet Pellisé (ESP) and Ralf Miederhoff (DEU). They both covered 410 km (254.7 mi) with flights that started and ended in Bugsdorf, Namibia, on 18 Dec 2015.

Most wins of the Red Bull Air Race Championship
Paul Bonhomme (UK) has won the Red Bull Air Race championship three times, in 2009, 2010 and 2015. Bonhomme took part in all 66 races between the championship's founding in 2003 and 2015, but after winning his third title he announced his retirement from air-racing.

Most wins of the Red Bull Cliff Diving World Series (female)
Rachelle Simpson (USA) has won the Red Bull Cliff Diving World Series twice, in 2014 and 2015. Britain's Gary Hunt has five wins overall, in 2010–12 and 2014–15, the **most wins of the Red Bull Cliff Diving World Series (male)**. The competition began in 2009.

Fastest 1 km ice swim (male)
On 20 Mar 2015, Christof Wandratsch (DEU) swam 1 km (0.6 mi) in 13 min exactly at the International Ice Swimming Association (IISA) World Championships. The 2015 event was held in the near-freezing waters of Lake Semenovskoye in Murmansk, Russia.

On the same day, and at the same event, Renata Nováková (CZE) recorded the **fastest 1 km ice swim by a female swimmer**, in a time of 14 min 21 sec.

Fastest 5 km barefoot on ice or snow
Latvia's Edgars Rencis took just 21 min 28.48 sec to cover 5 km (3.1 mi) in the deep snow of the Latvian winter. His toe-numbing record was achieved on the race track of the Daugava Stadium in Riga, Latvia, on 24 Jan 2015.

Highest cliff jump
On 4 Aug 2015, canyoner and cliff-jumper par excellence Laso Schaller (CHE, b. BRA) performed a heart-stopping 58.8-m (192-ft 11-in) leap from the Cascata del Salto in Maggia, Switzerland. That's a drop several metres greater than the height of the Leaning Tower of Pisa in Italy. As the frame-by-frame photo above shows, the jump ended in a plunge pool, which was some 8 m (26 ft 3 in) deep.

FASTEST 15 M SPEED CLIMB
Ukraine's Danylo Boldyrev (right) took just 5.6 sec to scale 15 m (49 ft 2 in) at the International Federation of Sport Climbing (IFSC) World Championships in Gijón, Spain, on 12 Sep 2014. He beat Russian rival Stanislav Kokorin to win the World Championships title and break the record just weeks after Libor Hroza (CZE) had established a new world mark of 5.73 sec.

The **fastest 15 m speed climb (female)** is 7.53 sec, by Iuliia Kaplina (RUS, above) at the IFSC World Cup in Chamonix, France, on 11 Jul 2015. Kaplina had also set a world record two months earlier with a 7.74-sec climb, breaking the previous record – which she had also set – by 0.11 sec.

DATELINE **2000**

Largest change in share price (24 hr)
On 27 Mar, after months of optimistic valuations and exuberant investment, the share price of Yahoo! Japan goes into freefall, losing 54% of its value in 24 hr. A similar fate awaits many other companies as the dot-com technology bubble bursts.

STREET SPORTS

DID YOU KNOW?
World Cup Skateboarding (WCS) is the only organization that assembles and monitors a ranking system for pro skaters. The federation has been active since 1994 and oversees the largest international skateboarding contests in the disciplines of vert and street.

Most wins of the World Cup Skateboarding street world rankings

Between 2010 and 2014, Brazil's Kelvin Hoefler topped the World Cup Skateboarding world rankings in the street discipline an unprecedented five times.

Most wins of the French City Pro Tour
Eric Malavergne (FRA) has won the French City Pro Tour – France's long-running annual urban street-golf competition – twice. He represented the Los Golfos team in 2012 and 2015.

X Games

Most Summer X Games medals won
From 1997 to 5 Jun 2015, skateboarder Bob Burnquist (BRA) secured 29 medals.
The **most skateboarding street gold medals won at the Summer X Games** is six, by Nyjah Huston (USA) in 2011–15.

Most wins of the World Cup Skateboarding street world rankings (female)

Leticia Bufoni (BRA) finished No.1 in the World Cup Skateboarding world rankings for street skating a total of four times between 2010 and 2013. She is a three-time X Games champion.

Youngest X Games participant in a motorized sport
Aged just 14 years 292 days, Gavin Harlien (USA, b. 20 Aug 1999) took part in the Off-Road Truck Racing event in Austin, Texas, USA, on 8 Jun 2014. He finished in ninth place.

Most BMX one-handed time machines in 30 seconds
Takahiro Ikeda (JPN) performed 45 one-handed time machines at Oasis Park in Kakamigahara, Gifu, Japan, on 10 Oct 2015.

Most backflips on a bicycle (single leap)
Jed Mildon (NZ) completed a total of four backflips at Pastranaland in Davidsonville, Maryland, USA, on 12 Jul 2015.

Highest air on a skateboard (quarterpipe)

After several terrifying failed attempts, Danny Way (USA) performed a 7.772-m (25-ft 6-in) air on a quarterpipe in Alpine, California, USA, on 18 Jul 2015.

MOST CONSECUTIVE GOLD MEDALS AT THE SUMMER X GAMES

Jamie Bestwick (UK) picked up nine consecutive gold medals at the Summer X Games from 2007 to 2014. All his golds came in the BMX Vert event, which also earned him the record for the **most consecutive BMX Vert gold medals won at the Summer X Games**. There were two X Games held in 2013, hence the reason Bestwick's nine consecutive gold medals came in an eight-year span. His incredible run finally came to an end in Jun 2015, when he finished second to Vince Byron (AUS) – by one point.

Most individuals killed in a terrorist act
Two aircraft are deliberately flown into the twin towers of the World Trade Center in New York City, USA, on 11 Sep. The official death toll stands at 2,753 fatalities, including those who died from subsequent health complications.

2001 ▶ DATELINE

AUTO SPORTS

Most consecutive F1 races led
Lewis Hamilton (UK) led 18 Formula 1 (F1) races in a row from 27 Jul 2014 to 5 Jul 2015. Hamilton broke the record set in 1970 by Jackie Stewart (UK), who led 17 straight races for at least one full lap. Hamilton's run ended at the Hungarian Grand Prix; despite being in pole position, he was overtaken on the first lap by eventual race winner Sebastian Vettel.

Most consecutive NASCAR starts
Jeff Gordon (USA) made 797 NASCAR (National Association for Stock Car Auto Racing) starts for Hendrick Motorsports over 23 Sprint Cup Series seasons from 15 Nov 1992 to 22 Nov 2015. Gordon retired in 2015, having never missed a race over 23 years in his Sprint Cup Series career. In Sep 2015, he broke Ricky Rudd's (USA) "Ironman" record of 788 consecutive starts.

Most consecutive F1 Grand Prix starts from debut
Nico Rosberg (DEU) made 189 F1 Grand Prix starts racing for Williams and Mercedes, from 12 Mar 2006 to 1 May 2016.

Most pole positions by a constructor in an F1 season
In 2011, Red Bull Racing (AUT) became the first constructor to achieve 18 pole positions in an F1 season. This was equalled by Mercedes (DEU) during the 2014 season and again during the 2015 season. Mercedes has also registered the **most one-two finishes by a constructor in an F1 season**, with 12 from 15 Mar to 29 Nov 2015.

Fastest lap in the Le Mans 24-hour race
Driving an Audi R18 e-tron Quattro, Germany's André Lotterer recorded a 3-min 17.475-sec lap in the famous 24-hour race in Le Mans, France, on 14 Jun 2015.

Three days earlier saw the **fastest practice lap for the Le Mans 24-hour race**. Neel Jani (CHE) lapped the course in 3 min 16.887 sec in a Porsche 919 Hybrid.

Fastest average speed at a World Rally Championship event
Jari-Matti Latvala (FIN) averaged 125.44 km/h (77.94 mph) at the Neste Rally Finland in Jyväskylä, Finland, on 2 Aug 2015.

MOST WORLD CHAMPIONSHIP CAREER RACE WINS IN MOTOGP (500 CC)
Italy's Valentino Rossi has secured 86 World Motorcycle Championship race wins in the MotoGP (500 cc) class. He has ridden for Honda, Ducati and Yamaha. Rossi's first 500 cc championship win came at the British Grand Prix in 2001, riding for Honda. He won 12 more times in the 500 cc class before it was rebranded as MotoGP in 2002. Since then he has won 73 Grand Prix races – including four in the 2015 season. Giacomo Agostini (ITA) has 122 wins overall compared to Rossi's 112, but "only" 68 came in the 500 cc class.

Longest time between Indianapolis 500 wins
The greatest lapse of time between wins of the Indianapolis 500 is 14 years 361 days by Juan Pablo Montoya (COL). He won his first Indianapolis 500 on 28 May 2000 but did not score a second victory in the iconic IndyCar race until 24 May 2015.

DATELINE

2002

First aerial battle involving a drone
In December, an American MQ-1 Predator is attacked by an Iraqi MiG-25 while on a surveillance mission. Both planes fire missiles at each other, but the drone's is diverted by the Iraqi jet's own missile. The MiG-25 eventually wins the dogfight.

220 Sports

CYCLING

Pauline Ferrand-Prévot

The **first cyclist to hold the UCI Road, Cyclo-cross and Mountain Bike World Championships at once** is Pauline Ferrand-Prévot (FRA). She won the UCI Road World Championships in Spain on 27 Sep 2014 and the Cyclo-cross World Championships in the Czech Republic on 1 Feb 2015. Finally, she secured the Mountain Bike World Championships Cross-Country Elite title in Andorra on 6 Sep 2015.

DID YOU KNOW?

Pauline Ferrand-Prévot's (left) sport of cyclo-cross presents unique challenges. Competitors ride and carry their bicycle over both road and cross-country sections. They must also complete multiple laps of the courses while negotiating sand pits, hurdles and other obstacles.

Fastest speed on a human-powered vehicle (HPV) by a single rider

Team Aerovelo's Todd Reichert (CAN) reached 86.65 mph (139.45 km/h) at the World Human Powered Speed Challenge in Nevada, USA, on 19 Sep 2015. In fact, he broke the record three times, hitting 85.71 mph (137.93 km/h) on 17 Sep and 86.5 mph (139.2 km/h) on 18 Sep.

Most stage wins of the Tour de Suisse cycling event

The Tour de Suisse has run annually (bar a hiatus in World War II) since 1933. The greatest number of stage wins in the event is 11, a feat first achieved by Switzerland's Ferdinand Kübler between 1940 and 1951 and equalled by fellow Swiss Hugo Koblet from 1950 to 1955. The achievement was most recently matched by Peter Sagan (SVK, above), between 2011 and 2015.

Fastest average speed in a stage of the Tour de France

Rohan Dennis (AUS) averaged 55.446 km/h (34.453 mph) in the first stage of the Tour in Utrecht, Netherlands, on 4 Jul 2015.

Most consecutive Grand Tour finishes

The Grand Tours in cycling are the Tour de France, Giro d'Italia and Vuelta a España. Adam Hansen (AUS) achieved 13 Grand Tour finishes in a row from 11 Sep 2011 to 13 Sep 2015, bettering a record unbroken since 1958.

FARTHEST DISTANCE IN A ONE-HOUR UNPACED STANDING START (MALE)

On 7 Jun 2015, Sir Bradley Wiggins (UK, right) cycled an aggregate distance of 54.526 km (33.881 mi) in one hour at the Olympic velodrome in London, UK. In doing so, he bettered Alex Dowsett's (UK) 52.937 km (32.893 mi), set only one month before.

Bridie O'Donnell (AUS) claimed the **female** record on 22 Jan 2016, covering 46.882 km (29.131 mi) in one hour at the Adelaide Super-Drome in Australia.

Most wins on the UCI World Tour by a team

The Union Cycliste Internationale (UCI) World Tour is the leading road tour race for elite male riders. Movistar Team (ESP) won the tour three times, in 2013–15.

Most successful country at the UCI Track World Championships

France has won a total of 365 medals at the World Championships: 138 gold, 107 silver and 120 bronze. The wins were recorded between the first event, held for amateurs in 1893, and Feb 2015.

Greatest bank heist
On 6–7 Aug, robbers steal some $69.8 m (£38.6 m) from the Banco Central in Fortaleza, Brazil. To date, the authorities have only recovered in the region of $9 m (£5 m) of the haul.

2005

DATELINE

guinnessworldrecords.com 221

RUGBY

Most tries by a player in a league Challenge Cup final

On 29 Aug 2015, Tom Briscoe (UK, left) of the Leeds Rhinos scored five tries against Hull Kingston Rovers at Wembley Stadium in London, UK. The previous record of four, by the Rhinos' Leroy Rivett, had stood since 1999.

Most rugby union World Cup wins

New Zealand have won the World Cup three times, in 1987, 2011 and 2015. They beat Australia 34–17 in the 2015 final, both teams having won the tournament twice before. This was also the **highest-scoring final in terms of aggregate score**.

First father and son to play together in a Pro12 rugby union match
Regan King and Jacob Cowley (both NZ) played for the Scarlets against the Newport Gwent Dragons at Parc y Scarlets in Llanelli, Wales, UK, on 30 Oct 2015. Cowley, aged 18, was making his Pro12 debut as a winger.

First National Rugby League (NRL) Grand Final decided by a golden point
On 4 Oct 2015, in an all-Queensland final, the North Queensland Cowboys beat the Brisbane Broncos 17–16 at the ANZ Stadium in Sydney, Australia.

Largest comeback in a rugby union World Cup match
On 6 Oct 2015, Romania made up 15 points after half-time to beat Canada 17–15 in their pool match at Leicester City Stadium, UK.

Largest margin of victory in a league Challenge Cup final
Leeds Rhinos defeated Hull Kingston Rovers 50–0 in the final at Wembley Stadium in London, UK, on 29 Aug 2015 (see above).

Longest time between wins in the rugby union World Cup
After a barren 24 years 340 days, Japan beat South Africa in a thrilling last-minute victory at the Brighton Community Stadium in Brighton, UK, on 19 Sep 2015.

Largest attendance at a rugby union World Cup match
A crowd of 89,267 watched the Ireland vs Romania pool match in London, UK, on 27 Sep 2015.

On 10 Oct 2015, at Old Trafford in Manchester, UK, 73,512 people witnessed Leeds Rhinos' victory over Wigan Warriors – the **largest attendance at a Super League Grand Final**.

MOST TRIES BY A PLAYER IN A WORLD CUP TOURNAMENT
The All Blacks' Julian Savea scored eight tries in the 2015 rugby union World Cup: two against Namibia, three against Georgia and three against France. He equalled the record first set in 1999 by fellow New Zealander Jonah Lomu (1975–2015), who scored his eight tries in five games: against Tonga (two), England, Italy (two), Scotland and France (two). Bryan Habana (ZAF) also shares the title, scoring against Samoa (four), USA (two) and Argentina (two) in 2007.

Youngest player in a rugby union World Cup
Scrum-half Vasil Lobzhanidze (b. 14 Oct 1996) was aged 18 years 340 days when he played for Georgia against Tonga at Kingsholm in Gloucester, UK, on 19 Sep 2015. Georgia's 17–10 victory marked their third ever win in the World Cup.

DATELINE

2006

First tweet
Twitter founder Jack Dorsey (USA) creates the first tweet at 9:50 p.m. PST on 21 Mar. It reads "Just setting up my twttr." His microblogging and social-networking tool allows users to post text messages of up to 140 characters via the world wide web or SMS.

222 Sports

TENNIS

Most consecutive years to win an ATP title

Roger Federer (CHE) has won at least one title on the Association of Tennis Professionals (ATP) World Tour for 15 consecutive years (2001–15). The 17-time Grand Slam champion surpassed Ivan Lendl's (USA, b. CZE) achievement of 14 consecutive years with an ATP title (1980–93) when he won six more tour titles in 2015.

Longest span of Grand Slam singles titles (open era)

Serena Williams (USA) won her very first Grand Slam singles title at the US Open on 11 Sep 1999. Her 21st and most recent Slam came at the Wimbledon Championships in London, UK, on 11 Jul 2015 – 15 years 303 days later. That also makes Serena (b. 26 Sep 1981) the **oldest Grand Slam singles winner (female)**, claiming her latest victory at the age of 33 years 288 days.

Oldest player to win a maiden Grand Slam singles title (female)

On her 49th attempt to net a Grand Slam, Flavia Pennetta (ITA, b. 25 Feb 1982), aged 33 years 199 days, won the US Open at Flushing Meadows in New York City, USA, on 12 Sep 2015. She announced her retirement after the match.

Most Grand Slam meetings (singles)

As of the 2016 Australian Open, Novak Djokovic (SRB) and Roger Federer had met 15 times in Grand Slam tournaments. Djokovic has won nine matches.

Most Australian Open singles titles won (open era)

On 31 Jan 2016, Novak Djokovic won his sixth singles title at the Australian Open.

Most aces in an ATP career

Ivo Karlović (HRV) had served up an incredible 10,519 aces in 567 singles matches on the ATP World Tour as of 20 Apr 2016.

First mid-match interview at a Grand Slam match

Coco Vandeweghe answered two questions from Pam Shriver for ESPN at the end of the first set of her first-round match against fellow American Sloane Stephens at the US Open in Flushing Meadows, New York City, on 31 Aug 2015. Vandeweghe won 6–4, 6–3, but said afterwards of the 35-sec interview: "I don't remember a thing I said. Dead serious. I don't even remember what she [Shriver] asked."

Highest annual earnings for a tennis player

Forbes' annual earnings (versus seasonal earnings – see below) factor in both match winnings and sponsorship/endorsement.
- **Male (ever):** $71.5 m (£46.6 m), by Roger Federer in 2012–13.
- **Male (current):** $67 m (£42.6 m), earned by Roger Federer in 2014–15.
- **Female (current and ever):** $29.5 m (£18.7 m), amassed by Maria Sharapova (RUS) in 2014–15.

Most aces served in a WTA match

Sabine Lisicki (DEU) struck 27 aces in 10 service games during a second-round match against Belinda Bencic at the Aegon Classic in Birmingham, UK, on 17 Jun 2015.

It's no surprise that Lisicki also holds the female record for **fastest serve**: 131 mph (210.8 km/h), hit on 29 Jul 2014.

MOST PRIZE MONEY WON IN A TENNIS SEASON (MALE)

World No.1 Novak Djokovic earned $21,646,145 (£14,600,200) in the 2015 season, which included Grand Slam titles (Australian Open, Wimbledon, US Open), the **most ATP Masters 1000 titles won in a season** (six) and the **most ATP Masters 1000 finals in a season** (eight).

The **most prize money won in a tennis season (female)** is $12,385,572 (£7,510,410), recorded by Serena Williams in 2013.

Largest points fall on the Dow Jones Industrial Average
On 29 Sep, as Congress votes on the US government's "bail-out bill" to protect taxpayers and the financial markets, the Dow Jones stock-market index suffers a record drop of 777.68 points.

2008

DATELINE

guinnessworldrecords.com   223

CLUB SOCCER

Most goals by a substitute in a Bundesliga match

Robert Lewandowski (POL) scored five goals for Bayern Munich against Wolfsburg at the Allianz Arena in Munich, Germany, on 22 Sep 2015. He netted all his goals within 8 min 59 sec – the **fastest five goals scored in a Bundesliga match by an individual**. Lewandowski's first three goals came within a period of just 3 min 22 sec – the **fastest hat-trick in a Bundesliga match by an individual**.

Most Premier League clean sheets

Petr Čech (CZE) kept the ball out of his net in 174 games between 15 Aug 2004 and 7 Feb 2016, while playing for two clubs: Chelsea (2004–15) and Arsenal (2015–).

Most goals scored in a Premier League match by an individual

Five players have scored five goals in a Premier League match: Andy Cole (UK) for Manchester United vs Ipswich on 4 Mar 1995; Alan Shearer (UK) for Newcastle United vs Sheffield Wednesday on 19 Sep 1999; Jermain Defoe (UK) for Tottenham Hotspur vs Wigan Athletic on 22 Nov 2009; Dimitar Berbatov (BGR) for Manchester United vs Blackburn Rovers on 27 Nov 2010; and Sergio Agüero (ARG) for Manchester City vs Newcastle United on 3 Oct 2015.

Highest margin of victory in the UEFA Champions League

Two teams share this record of 8–0 wins: Liverpool (UK) beat Beşiktaş (TUR) in Liverpool, UK, on 6 Nov 2007, and Real Madrid (ESP) beat Malmö (SWE) in Madrid, Spain, on 8 Dec 2015.

Most Women's Champions League wins

FFC Frankfurt (DEU) have four wins: 2001/02, 2005/06, 2007/08 and 2014/15.

Most expensive player (combined transfer fees)

The fees for Ángel Di María's (ARG) four transfers from Jul 2007 to Aug 2015 total £132.6 m ($197.53 m).

FASTEST GOALS

- **Premier League**: 9.7 sec, by Ledley King (UK) for Tottenham Hotspur vs Bradford City on 9 Dec 2000.
- **Serie A**: 8.2 sec, by Paolo Poggi (ITA) for Piacenza vs Fiorentina on 2 Dec 2001.
- **Bundesliga**: 9 sec, by Karim Bellarabi (DEU) for Bayer Leverkusen vs Borussia Dortmund on 23 Aug 2014. Equalled by Kevin Volland (DEU) for TSG 1899 Hoffenheim vs Bayern Munich on 22 Aug 2015.
- **La Liga**: 7.8 sec, by Joseba Llorente (ESP) for Real Valladolid vs Espanyol on 20 Jan 2008.
- **Ligue 1**: 8 sec, by Michel Rio (FRA) for Caen vs Cannes on 15 Feb 1992.
- **Major League Soccer (MLS)**: 7 sec, by Mike Grella (USA) for New York Red Bulls vs Philadelphia Union on 18 Oct 2015.
- **UEFA Europa League**: 13.21 sec, by Vitolo (ESP) for Sevilla vs Villarreal on 12 Mar 2015.

MOST CONSECUTIVE PREMIER LEAGUE GAMES TO SCORE

Jamie Vardy (UK) scored in 11 successive games for Leicester City from 29 Aug 2015 to 28 Nov 2015. His run finished with his 14th goal of the season in a match against Manchester United at the King Power Stadium in Leicester, UK.

Most goals scored at the same Premier League club

On 2 Feb 2016, Wayne Rooney (UK) scored his 177th goal in the English Premier League for Manchester United during a 3–0 home win over Stoke. He scored his first goal for the team when playing against Arsenal on 24 Oct 2004. Inset, Rooney accepts a GWR certificate, having set the record with 176 goals on 17 Jan 2016.

DATELINE

2009

Fastest 100 m
Usain Bolt (JAM) crosses the finish line in a time of 9.58 sec in Berlin, Germany, on 16 Aug. This breaks his own record in the 100 m sprint, which he set exactly one year previously at the Beijing Olympics in China, with a time of 9.69 sec.

224 Sports

INTERNATIONAL SOCCER

Most goals in a FIFA Women's World Cup final by an individual

Carli Lloyd (b. 16 Jul 1982) scored three goals for the USA vs Japan in the 2015 final in Vancouver, Canada, on 5 Jul 2015. Her first, after 3 min, was the **fastest goal in a FIFA Women's World Cup final** and also made Lloyd the **oldest goal-scorer in a FIFA Women's World Cup final**: 32 years 354 days. The USA have the **most Women's World Cup wins**: three, in 1991, 1999 and 2015.

Most goals scored in a FIFA Club World Cup game by an individual
Luis Suárez (URY) scored three goals for Barcelona (ESP) against Guangzhou Evergrande (CHN) in the 2015 semi-final at the International Stadium Yokohama in Yokohama, Japan, on 17 Dec 2015.

Oldest goal-scorer in a FIFA Women's World Cup
Miraildes Maciel Mota, aka Formiga (BRA, b. 3 Mar 1978), scored Brazil's opening goal of the 2015 Women's World Cup against South Korea aged 37 years 98 days in Montreal, Canada, on 9 Jun 2015.

Most wins of the CONCACAF Gold Cup
Mexico has won the Confederation of North, Central America and Caribbean Association Football (CONCACAF) Gold Cup seven times. The wins came in 1993, 1996, 1998, 2003, 2009, 2011 and 2015.

Most consecutive Copa América soccer tournaments as top scorer
Pedro Petrone (URY) was top scorer in the Copa América of 1923 and 1924. Paolo Guerrero (PER) top-scored in 2011 and 2015.

Most clean sheets kept in international soccer
From 7 Jun 2000 to 13 Nov 2015, Iker Casillas (ESP) kept a clean sheet for 100 international games.

Smallest country to qualify for the UEFA European Championships
On 6 Sep 2015, Iceland (population 331,918) drew 0–0 with Kazakhstan in Reykjavík, Iceland, to qualify for the 2016 UEFA European Championships in France.

Most goals scored in a FIFA Beach Soccer World Cup career by an individual
João Victor Saraiva, aka Madjer (PRT), scored 87 goals in Beach Soccer World Cups from 8 May 2005 to 19 Jul 2015.

Most goals in FIFA Women's World Cup finals
Marta Vieira da Silva (BRA) found the back of the net 15 times during Women's World Cup finals matches while playing for the Brazilian women's national team between 21 Sep 2003 and 9 Jun 2015.

Most Africa Cup of Nations titles won with different countries (coach)
Hervé Renard (FRA) has won two Africa Cup of Nations titles with different countries. In 2012, he guided Zambia to a win over Ivory Coast on penalties. Three years later, he repeated the feat with Ivory Coast (above), who beat Ghana in a penalty shoot-out.

MOST GOALS SCORED IN UEFA CHAMPIONSHIPS QUALIFIERS
Robbie Keane (IRL, left) netted 23 goals from 14 Oct 1998 to 4 Sep 2015. He has scored in every qualifying campaign since Euro 2000, with his best tally in a tournament being seven in Euro 2012. The **most goals scored in a single UEFA Championships qualifying tournament** is 13. David Healy first achieved this feat, for Northern Ireland, from 6 Sep 2006 to 17 Nov 2007. Robert Lewandowski equalled it between 7 Sep 2014 and 11 Oct 2015.

DID YOU KNOW?
David Healy scored 13 out of his side's 17 goals during Northern Ireland's unsuccessful qualifying campaign for Euro 2008. Lewandowski opened his account with four goals in Poland's 7–0 thrashing of Gibraltar and scored a 4-min hat-trick against Georgia in 2015.

Tallest building
The Burj Khalifa (Khalifa Tower) officially opens in Dubai, UAE, on 4 Jan. It is 828 m (2,716 ft 6 in) tall and was developed by Emaar Properties and the architects Skidmore, Owings & Merrill LLP.

2010

DATELINE

TRACK

Most IAAF Athletics World Championships 400 m medals (men)

LaShawn Merritt (USA) has won five medals in the men's 400 m at the International Association of Athletics Federations (IAAF) World Athletics Championships, in 2007, 2009, 2011, 2013 and 2015. He is a double world champion, taking gold in 2009 and 2013.

Most IAAF Athletics World Championships 100 m wins (female)

Shelly-Ann Fraser-Pryce (JAM) has won the women's 100 m at the Athletics World Championships three times, in 2009, 2013 and 2015.

Most consecutive Athletics World Championships 4 x 400 m relay wins (male)

LaShawn Merritt (left) has enjoyed six 4 x 400 m final wins at the IAAF World Championships (2005, 2007, 2009, 2011, 2013 and 2015).

Most consecutive wins of the IAAF World Cross Country Championships by a country (female)

Kenya won the IAAF World Cross Country Championships five times, in 2009–15.

Fastest T44 100 m (male)

The 2015 International Paralympic Committee (IPC) Athletics World Championships in Doha, Qatar, saw a wealth of new records. The speediest 100 m in the T44 class (single below-knee amputation or equivalent impairment) is 10.61 sec, by Richard Browne (USA) on 29 Oct 2015.

Six days earlier, Omara Durand (CUB) ran the **fastest T12 400 m (female)** in 53.05 sec. T12 denotes athletes with visual impairment.

At the IPC Grand Prix in Canberra, Australia, on 7 Feb 2016, Isis Holt (AUS) ran the **fastest T35 200 m (female)**, in 28.38 sec. T35-class athletes have issues with dynamic balance.

Fastest 20 km road walk (female)

China's Liu Hong completed a 20-km road walk in a time of 1 hr 24 min 38 sec at the Gran Premio Cantones de Marcha in La Coruña, Spain, on 6 Jun 2015.

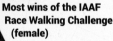

Most wins of the IAAF Race Walking Challenge (female)

Liu Hong (CHN) has won the IAAF Race Walking Challenge three times, in 2012, 2014 and 2015.

MOST IAAF ATHLETICS WORLD CHAMPIONSHIPS 100 M WINS (MEN)

Three athletes have each won three men's 100 m races at the IAAF World Athletics Championships. They are Carl Lewis (USA) in 1983, 1987 and 1991; Maurice Greene (USA) in 1997, 1999 and 2001; and, most recently, Usain Bolt (JAM, right) in 2009, 2013 and 2015.

Bolt also recorded the **most gold medals at the IAAF Athletics World Championships (male)**, with 11 wins from 2009 to 2015. His 13 medals (11 golds and two silvers) in the competition from 2007 to 2015 represent the **most medals won at the IAAF Athletics World Championships (male)**.

Finally, Bolt is the **first athlete to win the 100 m and 200 m sprints at successive Olympic Games** – Beijing in 2008 and London in 2012.

Fastest T42 200 m (male)

The T42 classification is for athletes with an impairment that affects their arms or legs, and includes amputees. The speediest 200 m in the T42 class is 24.10 sec, by Richard Whitehead (UK) in both the semi-final *and* final of the IPC World Championships on 27–28 Oct 2015.

Costliest natural disaster
An earthquake strikes off the Pacific coast of Tōhoku, Japan, on 11 Mar. *The Economist* estimates the financial loss to the country at $210 bn (£130 bn), of which only $35 bn (£21.6 bn) is insured.

FIELD

Farthest hammer throw (female)

Anita Włodarczyk (POL) hurled her hammer 81.08 m (266 ft 1 in) at the Kamila Skolimowska Memorial Throws Festival in Cetniewo, Poland, on 1 Aug 2015. She beat her own record of 79.58 m (261 ft 1 in) set in Berlin, Germany, on 31 Aug 2014.

Farthest hammer throw
Anita Włodarczyk's hammer throw record (see above) is relatively recent, but the male (and overall) record goes way back. Yuriy Sedykh (USSR, now RUS) produced a throw of 86.74 m (284 ft 7 in) on 30 Aug 1986 in Stuttgart, Germany.

Most wins of the IAAF hammer throw challenge (female)
Betty Heidler (DEU) achieved three wins in the IAAF hammer throw challenge from 2010 to 2012. Her feat was then equalled by Anita Włodarczyk between 2013 and 2015.

Most Diamond Race athletics titles won (male)
The Diamond League was inaugurated in 2010 to replace the Golden League as the premier annual athletics event. It is held in 14 different locations, from May to September, with 32 disciplines in total (16 for men and 16 for women). France's Renaud Lavillenie won six Diamond Race titles in the pole vault from 2010 to 2015.

Lavillenie shares the record for **most wins in Diamond Race athletics events by an individual** with Sandra Perković (HRV, right). Both athletes had 27 wins from 2010 to 11 Sep 2015.

Lavillenie has also scored the **most points in the Diamond League (male)**. By the end of the 2015 season, he had 135 points.

Overall, however, the **most points scored in a Diamond League career** is 138, by Perković in the discus in 2010–15.

The **youngest person to score points at a Diamond League athletics meeting** is Lázaro Martínez (CUB, b. 3 Nov 1997), who placed second in the triple jump event aged 16 years 196 days in Shanghai, China, on 18 May 2014.

Hicham El Guerrouj (MAR) is **the most successful IAAF Golden League athlete** in terms of having won the jackpot (or a share of the jackpot) the most times: four, in 1998 and 2000–02, which is one more than both Marion Jones and Sanya Richards (both USA). The Golden League was replaced by the Diamond League in 2010.

Most Diamond Race titles (female)

No female athlete has won more than four Diamond Race titles. Milcah Chemos Cheywa (KEN) first achieved the feat, in the 3,000 m steeplechase in 2010–13. In 2014, she was matched by Valerie Adams (NZ), in the shot put, and Kaliese Spencer (JAM), in the 400 m hurdles. In 2015, five more athletes won their fourth title: Dawn Harper-Nelson (USA), Shelly-Ann Fraser-Pryce (JAM), Allyson Felix (USA), Barbora Špotáková (CZE) and Sandra Perković (CRO, above).

MOST POINTS SCORED IN A DECATHLON (MALE)

Since taking an Olympic gold in 2012, decathlete Ashton Eaton (USA) has gone from strength to strength. At the 15th IAAF World Championships held in Beijing, China, on 29 Aug 2015, Eaton scored a total 9,045 points across the 10 disciplines (javelin and long jump pictured). In doing so, he bettered his own record, set in 2012, by six points to win gold at the World Championships for the second time.

Fastest speed in freefall
Felix Baumgartner (AUT) falls at 1,357.6 km/h (843.6 mph), from 39 km (24 mi) – the **highest freefall parachute jump** at the time. His stratospheric drop also makes him the **first person to break the sound barrier in freefall**.

2012

DATELINE

guinnessworldrecords.com   **227**

SWIMMING

Youngest participant in the FINA World Swimming Championships (female)

Alzain Tareq (BHR, b. 14 Apr 2005) competed in the 50 m butterfly event aged 10 years 115 days at the 16th FINA World Swimming Championships in Kazan, Russia, on 7 Aug 2015. Ironically, although she could compete in the senior contest, she was too young to take part in the Junior Swimming World Championships, which has a minimum entry age of 14.

FASTEST LONG COURSE 800 M FREESTYLE (FEMALE)

Katie Ledecky (USA) won the 800 m freestyle in 8 min 6.68 sec at the Arena Pro Swim Series in Austin, Texas, USA, on 17 Jan 2016. At the FINA World Swimming Championships in Kazan, Russia, on 8 Aug 2015, she had recorded the **fastest long course 1,500 m freestyle (female)**, in 15 min 25.48 sec.

On 3 Aug 2012, at the London Olympics, Ledecky (b. 17 Mar 1997) became the **youngest Olympic 800 m freestyle gold medallist (female)**, aged 15 years 139 days. She won in 8 min 14.63 sec.

Fastest long course 50 m breaststroke (male)

Adam Peaty (UK) swam the 50 m breaststroke in a time of just 26.42 sec at the 16th Fédération Internationale de Natation (FINA) World Swimming Championships in Kazan, Russia, on 4 Aug 2015. And he's just as good at double the distance: at the British Swimming Championships in London, UK, on 17 Apr 2015, Peaty achieved the **fastest long course 100 m breaststroke (male)**, finishing in 57.92 sec.

Most gold medals won in the FINA Swimming World Cup (female)

Hungary's Katinka Hosszú won 152 golds in the World Cup from 2012 to 2015.

Hosszú also recorded the **fastest long course 200 m medley (female)**, in 2 min 6.12 sec, at the 16th FINA World Swimming Championships in Kazan, Russia, on 3 Aug 2015.

The **most gold medals won in the FINA Swimming World Cup (male)** is 85, by Chad le Clos (ZAF) from 2009 to 2015.

Fastest long course relay 4 x 100 m freestyle (mixed)

The USA (comprising Ryan Lochte, Nathan Adrian, Simone Manuel and Missy Franklin) completed the long course 4 x 100 m freestyle in a time of 3 min 23.05 sec at the 16th FINA World Swimming Championships on 8 Aug 2015.

Fastest long course 100 m butterfly (female)

Sarah Sjöström (SWE) won the women's long course 100 m butterfly event in a time of 55.64 sec at the 16th FINA World Swimming Championships on 3 Aug 2015.

In 2014, she swam the **fastest long course 50 m butterfly (female)**, in a time of 24.43 sec in Borås, Sweden.

DID YOU KNOW?

Notably, Ledecky's feat at the London 2012 Olympics (see left) also marked the second-fastest women's 800 m freestyle swim in sporting history. At the time, only the UK's Rebecca Adlington had swum faster in the event, winning gold at the 2008 Olympics in Beijing in 8 min 14.10 sec.

First proof of the existence of the Higgs boson
On 14 Mar, two experiments at the Large Hadron Collider at the European Organization for Nuclear Research (CERN) in Geneva, Switzerland, confirm the existence of the (hitherto only theorized) Higgs boson particle.

WATER SPORTS

Most gold medals in the FINA World Championships 10 m platform diving event (male)

Greg Louganis (USA) was the first male diver to achieve three gold medals in the FINA World Championships 10 m platform diving event, with wins in 1978, 1982 and 1986. His feat was later equalled by Qiu Bo (CHN, above), in 2011, 2013 and 2015.

Most gold medals in the same FINA World Championships diving event (male)

Qin Kai (CHN) won five golds in the 3 m synchronized springboard event, in 2007, 2009, 2011, 2013 and 2015. He was partnered by Cao Yuan in 2015, but had previously won gold with Wang Feng (2007, 2009), Luo Yutong (2011) and He Chong (2013).

Most FINA Water Polo World League wins (men)

Serbia's water polo team has won the World League nine times, in 2005–08, 2010–11 and 2013–15. Serbia won the Water Polo World League 2015 Super Final against Croatia, 9–6, to complete their third successive win of the tournament. Since 2005, Serbia, Montenegro and Croatia have won all of the men's tournaments.

Youngest winner of a surfing World Qualifying Series event

On 12 Jul 2009, Brazil's Gabriel Medina (b. 22 Dec 1993) won the 2009 Maresia Surf International, aged 15 years 202 days in Florianópolis, Brazil. In 2014, he became the second-youngest world champion ever, at 20 years 362 days.

Fastest row double sculls lightweight class (female)

On 20 Jun 2015, Great Britain (Charlotte Taylor and Katherine Copeland) recorded a time of 6 min 48.38 sec at Varese in Italy. The British pair set the record in the semi-finals of the World Rowing Cup.

Most ICF Canoe Slalom World Championships gold medals in the same event (male)

The International Canoe Federation (ICF) Slalom World Championships are held annually except in Olympic years. Michal Martikán (SVK) has won eight golds in the C1 Team event, in 1997, 2003, 2009–11 and 2013–15.

Most ICF Canoe Sprint World Championships medals in the women's K1 5,000 m event

Maryna Litvinchuk (BLR) took gold in 2015, adding to two silver medals (2011, 2014) and a bronze (2010).

Most points scored in a WSL Surfing World Championship season (female)

In 2015, Hawaiian Carissa Moore (above) won her third world title and scored 66,200 points, breaking the record set by Stephanie Gilmore (AUS), who earned 64,200 points in 2014.

MOST CONSECUTIVE SYNCHRONIZED SWIMMING WORLD CHAMPIONSHIPS GOLD MEDALS

Russia won 19 gold medals in in a row in synchronized swimming FINA World Championships between 23 Jul 2009 and 26 Jul 2015. Pictured here is Natalia Ishchenko (RUS) at the World Championships in Kazan, Russia, in 2015. Ishchenko won the **most synchronized swimming FINA World Championships gold medals by an individual** – 19 – between 2005 and 2015.

Largest Ebola outbreak
The deadly Ebola virus disease (EVD) spreads across the African nations of Guinea, Liberia and Sierra Leone. It will claim more than 11,300 lives by Jan 2016.

2014

DATELINE

guinnessworldrecords.com   229

SPORTS ROUND-UP

Highest dressage freestyle score

Riding Valegro, Charlotte Dujardin (UK) scored 94.3% in dressage freestyle in the London Fédération Équestre Internationale (FEI) World Cup at Olympia, London, UK, on 17 Dec 2014. On the previous day, she recorded the **highest dressage Grand Prix score** – 87.46% – at the same event.

Most FIS Alpine Ski World Cup Super G race wins

From 3 Mar 2006 to 24 Jan 2016, Lindsey Vonn (USA) won the Fédération Internationale de Ski (FIS) World Cup Super G race 27 times. As well as the **most FIS Alpine Ski World Cup race wins** – 71 – achieved between 3 Dec 2004 and 12 Dec 2015, Vonn also claimed the **most FIS Alpine Ski World Cup women's downhill wins** with a 38th victory on 6 Feb 2016 at Cortina d'Ampezzo in Italy.

Oldest sports trophy
The Antient Scorton Silver Arrow is 342 years old and is still competed for to this day. It has been the prize in the Antient Silver Arrow Competition – an archery tournament held in the village of Scorton in Lancashire, UK – 307 times between 14 May 1673 and 16 May 2015.

Longest frame in a professional snooker match
The sixth frame of a match between Barry Pinches and Alan McManus (both UK) at the Ruhr Open in Mülheim, Germany, on 10 Oct 2015 lasted 100 min 24 sec.

Most career points in Major League Lacrosse
Casey Powell (USA) scored 504 points from 7 Jun 2001 to 25 Jul 2015.

MOST WINS OF THE...

All-Ireland Hurling finals
Kilkenny (IRL) has won the All-Ireland Senior Hurling Championship 36 times: 1904–05, 1907, 1909, 1911–13, 1922, 1932–33, 1935, 1939, 1947, 1957, 1963, 1967, 1969, 1972, 1974–75, 1979, 1982–83, 1992–93, 2000, 2002–03, 2006–09, 2011–12 and 2014–15.

ANZ Championship
Three teams have won netball's Australia and New Zealand (ANZ) Championship twice. They are: Adelaide Thunderbirds in 2010 and 2013; Melbourne Vixens in 2009 and 2014; and Queensland Firebirds (all AUS) in 2011 and 2015.

British Open Croquet Championships
The British Open Croquet Championships were instituted at Evesham, UK, in 1867. Robert Fulford (UK) has won 11 times, in 1991–92, 1996, 1998, 2003–04, 2006–08 and 2014–15.

DID YOU KNOW?
He originally called himself "Dreamboy", but today Gary Anderson is better known by the nickname "The Flying Scotsman". He is the first Scot to win the Professional Darts Corporation World Championship.

MOST 180s IN A DARTS PDC WORLD CHAMPIONSHIP BY A PLAYER
The greatest number of maximums scored by a player in a Professional Darts Corporation (PDC) World Championship is 64, by Gary Anderson (UK) at Alexandra Palace in London, UK, between 18 Dec 2014 and 4 Jan 2015. Anderson won the World Championship, beating 16-time champ Phil Taylor 7–6 in the final. He threw 19 maximums to surpass the previous tournament record of 60, set by Adrian Lewis in 2011.

EHF Handball Champions League
FC Barcelona Handbol (ESP) have won the European Handball Federation (EHF) Champions League nine times, in 1991, 1996–2000, 2005, 2011 and 2015.

DATELINE **2015**

Warmest year on record
According to the World Meteorological Organization (WMO), the global average temperature in 2015 was 0.76°C (+/ 0.1), or 1.3°F, above that for 1961–90, and 1°C (1.8°F) above the worldwide mean for the pre-Industrial Age.

230 Sports

Most Women's Hockey Champions Trophy wins by a team

Three teams have each won the Women's Hockey Champions Trophy six times. The feat was first achieved by Australia, with wins in 1991, 1993, 1995, 1997, 1999 and 2003. It was equalled by the Netherlands, who won in 1987, 2000, 2004–05, 2007 and 2011. Most recently, this record was matched by Argentina (above), who were champions in 2001, 2008–10, 2012 and 2014.

Highest total score in figure skating (male)

Japan's Yuzuru Hanyu scored 330.43 points at the International Skating Union (ISU) Grand Prix Final 2015–16 in Barcelona, Spain, on 12 Dec 2015. This combines points for the short and long programmes. Hanyu broke records in both, achieving the **highest score in figure skating – short programme (male)**, with 110.95 points, and **long programme (male)**, with 219.48 points.

Men's Hockey Champions Trophy by a team
Australia have won the Hockey Champions Trophy 13 times: 1983–85, 1989–90, 1993, 1999, 2005, 2008–12. Germany are second, with 10 wins.

Women's Hockey Champions Trophy by an individual
Argentina's Luciana Aymar (above left) has been on the winning side in all six of her team's record-equalling wins of the Women's Hockey Champions Trophy.

Most FIVB Beach Volleyball World Tour gold medals

• **Female**: Larissa França (BRA) won 57 Fédération Internationale de Volleyball (FIVB) golds on the Beach Volleyball World Tour from 10 Jul 2004 to 4 Oct 2015.
• **Male**: Emanuel Rego (BRA) won 77 Beach Volleyball World Tour golds between 25 Jun 1995 and 14 Jul 2012.

Most goals scored in an ANZ Championship match by an individual

Jhaniele Fowler-Reid (JAM, below left) has scored 65 goals in an ANZ Championship netball match on two occasions, for Southern Steel vs Canterbury Tactix (both NZ) in the "Southern Derby". The first time was in Christchurch, New Zealand, on 30 Mar 2013; the second was in Dunedin, New Zealand, on 9 Jun 2013.

First gravitational waves detected
Proving right a prediction made by physicist Albert Einstein 100 years earlier, the LIGO Scientific Collaboration and the Virgo Collaboration confirm that they have recorded gravitational waves at two sites in the USA.

2016 ▶

DATELINE

ATHLETICS: TRACK/ULTRA

An asterisk (*) denotes that a record is still awaiting ratification by the sport's governing body at the time of going to press

ATHLETICS – OUTDOOR TRACK EVENTS

MEN	TIME/DISTANCE	NAME & NATIONALITY	LOCATION	DATE
100 m	9.58	Usain Bolt (JAM)	Berlin, Germany	16 Aug 2009
200 m	19.19	Usain Bolt (JAM)	Berlin, Germany	20 Aug 2009
400 m	43.18	Michael Johnson (USA)	Seville, Spain	26 Aug 1999
800 m	1:40.91	David Lekuta Rudisha (KEN)	London, UK	9 Aug 2012
1,000 m	2:11.96	Noah Ngeny (KEN)	Rieti, Italy	5 Sep 1999
1,500 m	3:26.00	Hicham El Guerrouj (MAR)	Rome, Italy	14 Jul 1998
1 mile	3:43.13	Hicham El Guerrouj (MAR)	Rome, Italy	7 Jul 1999
2,000 m	4:44.79	Hicham El Guerrouj (MAR)	Berlin, Germany	7 Sep 1999
3,000 m	7:20.67	Daniel Komen (KEN)	Rieti, Italy	1 Sep 1996
5,000 m	12:37.35	Kenenisa Bekele (ETH)	Hengelo, Netherlands	31 May 2004
10,000 m	26:17.53	Kenenisa Bekele (ETH)	Brussels, Belgium	26 Aug 2005
20,000 m	56:26.00	Haile Gebrselassie (ETH)	Ostrava, Czech Republic	27 Jun 2007
1 hour	21,285 metres	Haile Gebrselassie (ETH)	Ostrava, Czech Republic	27 Jun 2007
25,000 m	1:12:25.40	Moses Cheruiyot Mosop (KEN)	Eugene, USA	3 Jun 2011
30,000 m	1:26:47.40	Moses Cheruiyot Mosop (KEN)	Eugene, USA	3 Jun 2011
3,000 m steeplechase	7:53.63	Saif Saaeed Shaheen (QAT)	Brussels, Belgium	3 Sep 2004
110 m hurdles	12.80	Aries Merritt (USA)	Brussels, Belgium	7 Sep 2012
400 m hurdles	46.78	Kevin Young (USA)	Barcelona, Spain	6 Aug 1992
4 x 100 m relay	36.84	Jamaica (Yohan Blake, Usain Bolt, Michael Frater, Nesta Carter)	London, UK	11 Aug 2012
4 x 200 m relay	1:18.63	Jamaica (Yohan Blake, Nickel Ashmeade, Warren Weir, Jermaine Brown)	Nassau, Bahamas	24 May 2014
4 x 400 m relay	2:54.29	USA (Andrew Valmon, Quincy Watts, Harry Reynolds, Michael Johnson)	Stuttgart, Germany	22 Aug 1993
4 x 800 m relay	7:02.43	Kenya (Joseph Mutua, William Yiampoy, Ismael Kombich, Wilfred Bungei)	Brussels, Belgium	25 Aug 2006
4 x 1,500 m relay	14:22.22	Kenya (Collins Cheboi, Silas Kiplagat, James Kiplagat Magut, Asbel Kiprop)	Nassau, Bahamas	25 May 2014

Fastest 100 m

Usain Bolt (JAM) sped to a new world record in Berlin, Germany, on 16 Aug 2009, running the men's 100 m in 9.58 sec. This broke his own record of 9.69 sec, set at the Beijing Olympics in China a year previously to the day. On 20 Aug 2009, Bolt proved he's a world-beater at double the distance too. He ran the **fastest 200 m** in 19.19 sec – again, breaking his own record (of 19.30 sec) set in Beijing exactly a year before to the day.

WOMEN	TIME/DISTANCE	NAME & NATIONALITY	LOCATION	DATE
100 m	10.49	Florence Griffith-Joyner (USA)	Indianapolis, USA	16 Jul 1988
200 m	21.34	Florence Griffith-Joyner (USA)	Seoul, South Korea	29 Sep 1988
400 m	47.60	Marita Koch (GDR)	Canberra, Australia	6 Oct 1985
800 m	1:53.28	Jarmila Kratochvílová (CZE)	Munich, Germany	26 Jul 1983
1,000 m	2:28.98	Svetlana Masterkova (RUS)	Brussels, Belgium	23 Aug 1996
1,500 m	3:50.07	Genzebe Dibaba (ETH)	Fontvieille, Monaco	17 Jul 2015
1 mile	4:12.56	Svetlana Masterkova (RUS)	Zurich, Switzerland	14 Aug 1996
2,000 m	5:25.36	Sonia O'Sullivan (IRL)	Edinburgh, UK	8 Jul 1994
3,000 m	8:06.11	Wang Junxia (CHN)	Beijing, China	13 Sep 1993
5,000 m	14:11.15	Tirunesh Dibaba (ETH)	Oslo, Norway	6 Jun 2008
10,000 m	29:31.78	Wang Junxia (CHN)	Beijing, China	8 Sep 1993
20,000 m	1:05:26.60	Tegla Loroupe (KEN)	Borgholzhausen, Germany	3 Sep 2000
1 hour	18,517 m	Dire Tune (ETH)	Ostrava, Czech Republic	12 Jun 2008
25,000 m	1:27:05.90	Tegla Loroupe (KEN)	Mengerskirchen, Germany	21 Sep 2002
30,000 m	1:45:50.00	Tegla Loroupe (KEN)	Warstein, Germany	6 Jun 2003
3,000 m steeplechase	8:58.81	Gulnara Samitova-Galkina (RUS)	Beijing, China	17 Aug 2008
100 m hurdles	12.21	Yordanka Donkova (BGR)	Stara Zagora, Bulgaria	20 Aug 1988
400 m hurdles	52.34	Yuliya Pechonkina (RUS)	Tula, Russia	8 Aug 2003
4 x 100 m relay	40.82	United States (Tianna Madison, Allyson Felix, Bianca Knight, Carmelita Jeter)	London, UK	10 Aug 2012
4 x 200 m relay	1:27.46	United States "Blue" (LaTasha Jenkins, LaTasha Colander-Richardson, Nanceen Perry, Marion Jones)	Philadelphia, USA	29 Apr 2000
4 x 400 m relay	3:15.17	USSR (Tatyana Ledovskaya, Olga Nazarova, Maria Pinigina, Olga Bryzgina)	Seoul, South Korea	1 Oct 1988
4 x 800 m relay	7:50.17	USSR (Nadezhda Olizarenko, Lyubov Gurina, Lyudmila Borisova, Irina Podyalovskaya)	Moscow, Russia	5 Aug 1984
4 x 1,500 m relay	16:33.58	Kenya (Mercy Cherono, Irene Jelagat, Faith Kipyegon, Hellen Oribi)	Nassau, Bahamas	24 May 2014

Fastest 4 x 1,500 m relay (female)

Mercy Cherono, Irene Jelagat, Faith Kipyegon and Hellen Oribi (all KEN) proved uncatchable in the women's 4 x 1,500 m relay taking place at the T Robinson Stadium in Nassau, Bahamas, on 24 May 2014. Their time of 16:33.58 was some 32 sec faster than the previous record, which was also set by a team from Kenya, in Apr 2014.

ATHLETICS – INDOOR TRACK EVENTS

MEN	TIME	NAME & NATIONALITY	LOCATION	DATE
50 m	5.56	Donovan Bailey (CAN)	Reno, USA	9 Feb 1996
60 m	6.39	Maurice Greene (USA)	Madrid, Spain	3 Feb 1998
			Atlanta, USA	3 Mar 2001
200 m	19.92	Frankie Fredericks (NAM)	Liévin, France	18 Feb 1996
400 m	44.57	Kerron Clement (USA)	Fayetteville, USA	12 Mar 2005
800 m	1:42.67	Wilson Kipketer (DNK)	Paris, France	9 Mar 1997
1,000 m	2:14.20	Ayanleh Souleiman (DJI)	Stockholm, Sweden	17 Feb 2016
1,500 m	3:31.18	Hicham El Guerrouj (MAR)	Stuttgart, Germany	2 Feb 1997
1 mile	3:48.45	Hicham El Guerrouj (MAR)	Ghent, Belgium	12 Feb 1997
3,000 m	7:24.90	Daniel Komen (KEN)	Budapest, Hungary	6 Feb 1998
5,000 m	12:49.60	Kenenisa Bekele (ETH)	Birmingham, UK	20 Feb 2004
50 m hurdles	6.25	Mark McKoy (CAN)	Kobe, Japan	5 Mar 1986
60 m hurdles	7.30	Colin Jackson (GBR†)	Sindelfingen, Germany	6 Mar 1994
4 x 200 m relay	1:22.11	Great Britain & Northern Ireland (Linford Christie, Darren Braithwaite, Ade Mafe, John Regis)	Glasgow, UK	3 Mar 1991
4 x 400 m relay	3:02.13	USA (Kyle Clemons, David Verburg, Kind Butler III, Calvin Smith)	Sopot, Poland	9 Mar 2014
4 x 800 m relay	7:13.11	USA All Stars (Richard Jones, David Torrence, Duane Solomon, Erik Sowinski)	Boston, USA	8 Feb 2014
5,000 m walk	18:07.08	Mikhail Shchennikov (RUS)	Moscow, Russia	14 Feb 1995

†GBR = Great Britain, as per IAAF listings

WOMEN	TIME	NAME & NATIONALITY	LOCATION	DATE
50 m	5.96	Irina Privalova (RUS)	Madrid, Spain	9 Feb 1995
60 m	6.92	Irina Privalova (RUS)	Madrid, Spain	11 Feb 1993
				9 Feb 1995
200 m	21.87	Merlene Ottey (JAM)	Liévin, France	13 Feb 1993
400 m	49.59	Jarmila Kratochvílová (CZE)	Milan, Italy	7 Mar 1982
800 m	1:55.82	Jolanda Batagelj (SVN)	Vienna, Austria	3 Mar 2002
1,000 m	2:30.94	Maria de Lurdes Mutola (MOZ)	Stockholm, Sweden	25 Feb 1999
1,500 m	3:55.17	Genzebe Dibaba (ETH)	Karlsruhe, Germany	1 Feb 2014
1 mile	4:13.31	Genzebe Dibaba (ETH)	Stockholm, Sweden	17 Feb 2016
3,000 m	8:16.60	Genzebe Dibaba (ETH)	Stockholm, Sweden	6 Feb 2014
5,000 m	14:18.86	Genzebe Dibaba (ETH)	Stockholm, Sweden	19 Feb 2015
50 m hurdles	6.58	Cornelia Oschkenat (GDR)	Berlin, Germany	20 Feb 1988
60 m hurdles	7.68	Susanna Kallur (SWE)	Karlsruhe, Germany	10 Feb 2008
4 x 200 m relay	1:32.41	Russia (Yekaterina Kondratyeva, Irina Khabarova, Yuliya Pechonkina, Yulia Gushchina)	Glasgow, UK	29 Jan 2005
4 x 400 m relay	3:23.37	Russia (Yulia Gushchina, Olga Kotlyarova, Olga Zaytseva, Olesya Krasnomovets)	Glasgow, UK	28 Jan 2006
4 x 800 m relay	8:06.24	Team Moscow (Aleksandra Bulanova, Yekaterina Martynova, Elena Kofanova, Anna Balakshina)	Moscow, Russia	18 Feb 2011
3,000 m walk	11:40.33	Claudia Stef (ROM)	Bucharest, Romania	30 Jan 1999

Fastest indoor mile (female)

Ethiopia's Genzebe Dibaba ran the indoor mile in 4:13.31 at the Globe Arena in the Swedish capital of Stockholm on 17 Feb 2016.

ATHLETICS – ULTRA LONG DISTANCE

MEN	TIME/DISTANCE	NAME & NATIONALITY	LOCATION	DATE
50 km	02:48:06	Jeff Norman (GBR)	Timperley, UK	7 Jun 1980
100 km	06:10:20	Donald Ritchie (GBR)	London, UK	28 Oct 1978
100 miles	11:28:03	Oleg Kharitonov (RUS)	London, UK	20 Oct 2002
1,000 km	5 days 16:17:00	Yiannis Kouros (GRC)	Colac, Australia	26 Nov–1 Dec 1984
1,000 miles	11 days 13:54:58	Peter Silkinas (LTU)	Nanango, Australia	11–23 Mar 1998
6 hours	97.2 km (60.39 mi)	Donald Ritchie (GBR)	London, UK	28 Oct 1978
12 hours	163.785 km (101.77 mi)	Zach Bitter (USA)	Phoenix, USA	14 Dec 2013
24 hours	303.506 km (188.59 mi)	Yiannis Kouros (GRC)	Adelaide, Australia	4–5 Oct 1997
48 hours	473.495 km (294.21 mi)	Yiannis Kouros (GRC)	Surgères, France	3–5 May 1996
6 days	1,038.851 km (645.51 mi)	Yiannis Kouros (GRC)	Colac, Australia	20–26 Nov 2005

WOMEN	TIME/DISTANCE	NAME & NATIONALITY	LOCATION	DATE
50 km	03:18:52	Carolyn Hunter-Rowe (GBR)	Barry, UK	3 Mar 1996
100 km	07:14:06	Norimi Sakurai (JPN)	Verona, Italy	27 Sep 2003
100 miles	13:52:07	Mami Kudo (JPN)	Chinese Taipei	10 Dec 2011
1,000 km	7 days 1:28:29	Eleanor Robinson (GBR)	Nanango, Australia	11–18 Mar 1998
1,000 miles	13 days 1:54:02	Eleanor Robinson (GBR)	Nanango, Australia	11–23 Mar 1998
6 hours	83.2 km (57.69 mi)	Norimi Sakurai (JPN)	Verona, Italy	27 Sep 2003
12 hours	147.6 km (91.71 mi)	Ann Trason (USA)	Hayward, USA	3–4 Aug 1991
24 hours	255.303 km (158.63 mi)	Mami Kudo (JPN)	Chinese Taipei	10–11 Dec 2011
48 hours	397.103 km (246.75 mi)	Inagiki Sumie (JPN)	Surgères, France	21–23 May 2010
6 days	883.631 km (549.06 mi)	Sandra Barwick (NZ)	Campbelltown, Australia	18–24 Nov 1990

ATHLETICS & CYCLING

Fastest 30 km road race

While running the 2016 Dubai Marathon on 22 Jan, Amos Choge Kipruto, Edwin Kibet Koech (both KEN) and Sisay Lemma (ETH, above) all reached the 30-km point in a record time of 1 hr 27 min 20 sec.

ATHLETICS – ROAD RACE

MEN	TIME	NAME & NATIONALITY	LOCATION	DATE
10 km	26:44	Leonard Patrick Komon (KEN)	Utrecht, Netherlands	26 Sep 2010
15 km	41:13	Leonard Patrick Komon (KEN)	Nijmegen, Netherlands	21 Nov 2010
20 km	55:21	Zersenay Tadese (ERI)	Lisbon, Portugal	21 Mar 2010
Half marathon	58:23	Zersenay Tadese (ERI)	Lisbon, Portugal	21 Mar 2010
25 km	1:11:18	Dennis Kipruto Kimetto (KEN)	Berlin, Germany	6 May 2012
30 km*	1:27:20	Amos Choge Kipruto (KEN) Edwin Kibet Koech (KEN) Sisay Lemma (ETH)	Dubai, UAE	22 Jan 2016
Marathon	2:02:57	Dennis Kipruto Kimetto (KEN)	Berlin, Germany	28 Sep 2014
100 km	6:13:33	Takahiro Sunada (JPN)	Tokoro, Japan	21 Jun 1998
Road relay	1:57:06	Kenya (Josephat Ndambiri, Martin Mathathi, Daniel Mwangi, Mekubo Mogusu, Onesmus Nyerere, John Kariuki)	Chiba, Japan	23 Nov 2005
WOMEN	**TIME**	**NAME & NATIONALITY**	**LOCATION**	**DATE**
10 km	30:21	Paula Radcliffe (GBR)	San Juan, Puerto Rico	23 Feb 2003
15 km	46:14	Florence Jebet Kiplagat (KEN)	Barcelona, Spain	15 Feb 2015
20 km	1:01:54	Florence Jebet Kiplagat (KEN)	Barcelona, Spain	15 Feb 2015
Half marathon	1:05:09	Florence Jebet Kiplagat (KEN)	Barcelona, Spain	15 Feb 2015
25 km	1:19:53	Mary Jepkosgei Keitany (KEN)	Berlin, Germany	9 May 2010
30 km	1:38:49	Mizuki Noguchi (JPN)	Berlin, Germany	25 Sep 2005
Marathon	2:15:25	Paula Radcliffe (GBR)	London, UK	13 Apr 2003
100 km	6:33:11	Tomoe Abe (JPN)	Tokoro, Japan	25 Jun 2000
Road relay	2:11:41	China (Jiang Bo, Dong Yanmei, Zhao Fengting, Ma Zaijie, Lan Lixin, Li Na)	Beijing, China	28 Feb 1998

*Still awaiting ratification at the time of going to press

Highest pole vault (female, indoors)

Jennifer Suhr (USA) is only the second woman in history, after Russia's Yelena Isinbayeva, to vault over 5 m (16 ft 4.8 in). She did so first in 2013 with a vault of 5.02 m (16 ft 5.6 in). Three years later, she improved her personal best by 1 cm (0.4 in) at the Golden Eagle Multi and Invitational in Brockport, New York, USA. As of Apr 2016, Suhr is also the reigning Olympic champion, having won gold at London 2012. She won a silver medal at the 2008 Olympics staged in Beijing, China.

ATHLETICS – RACE WALKING

MEN	TIME	NAME & NATIONALITY	LOCATION	DATE
20,000 m	1:17:25.60	Bernardo Segura (MEX)	Bergen, Norway	7 May 1994
20 km (road)	1:16:36.00	Yusuke Suzuki (JPN)	Nomi, Japan	15 Mar 2015
30,000 m	2:01:44.10	Maurizio Damilano (ITA)	Cuneo, Italy	3 Oct 1992
50,000 m	3:35:27.20	Yohann Diniz (FRA)	Reims, France	12 Mar 2011
50 km (road)	3:32:33.00	Yohann Diniz (FRA)	Zurich, Switzerland	15 Aug 2014
WOMEN	**TIME**	**NAME & NATIONALITY**	**LOCATION**	**DATE**
10,000 m	41:56.23	Nadezhda Ryashkina (USSR)	Seattle, USA	24 Jul 1990
20,000 m	1:26:52.30	Olimpiada Ivanova (RUS)	Brisbane, Australia	6 Sep 2001
20 km (road)	1:24:38.00	Liu Hong (CHN)	La Coruña, Spain	6 Jun 2015

ATHLETICS – INDOOR FIELD EVENTS

MEN	DISTANCE/POINTS	NAME & NATIONALITY	LOCATION	DATE	
High jump	2.43 m (7 ft 11.66 in)	Javier Sotomayor (CUB)	Budapest, Hungary	4 Mar 1989	† 60 m, 6.79 sec; long jump, 8.16 m; shot, 14.56 m; high jump, 2.03 m; 60 m hurdles, 7.68 sec; pole vault, 5.20 m; 1,000 m, 2 min 32.78 sec
Pole vault	6.16 m (20 ft 2.51 in)	Renaud Lavillenie (FRA)	Donetsk, Ukraine	15 Feb 2014	
Long jump	8.79 m (28 ft 10.06 in)	Carl Lewis (USA)	New York City, USA	27 Jan 1984	
Triple jump	17.92 m (58 ft 9.51 in)	Teddy Tamgho (FRA)	Paris, France	6 Mar 2011	
Shot	22.66 m (74 ft 4.12 in)	Randy Barnes (USA)	Los Angeles, USA	20 Jan 1989	
Heptathlon†	6,645 points	Ashton Eaton (USA)	Istanbul, Turkey	10 Mar 2012	
WOMEN	**DISTANCE/POINTS**	**NAME & NATIONALITY**	**LOCATION**	**DATE**	
High jump	2.08 m (6 ft 9.88 in)	Kajsa Bergqvist (SWE)	Arnstadt, Germany	4 Feb 2006	†† 60 m hurdles, 8.38 sec; high jump, 1.84 m; shot, 16.51 m; long jump, 6.57 m; 800 m, 2 min 11.15 sec
Pole vault*	5.03 m (16 ft 6.03 in)	Jennifer Suhr (USA)	Brockport, USA	30 Jan 2016	
Long jump	7.37 m (24 ft 2.15 in)	Heike Drechsler (GDR)	Vienna, Austria	13 Feb 1988	
Triple jump	15.36 m (50 ft 4.72 in)	Tatyana Lebedeva (RUS)	Budapest, Hungary	6 Mar 2004	
Shot	22.50 m (73 ft 9.82 in)	Helena Fibingerová (CZE)	Jablonec, Czechoslovakia	19 Feb 1977	
Pentathlon††	5,013 points	Natalia Dobrynska (UKR)	Istanbul, Turkey	9 Mar 2012	

*Still awaiting ratification at the time of going to press

ATHLETICS – OUTDOOR FIELD EVENTS

MEN	DISTANCE/POINTS	NAME & NATIONALITY	LOCATION	DATE
High jump	2.45 m (8 ft 0.45 in)	Javier Sotomayor (CUB)	Salamanca, Spain	27 Jul 1993
Pole vault	6.14 m (20 ft 1.73 in)	Sergei Bubka (UKR)	Sestriere, Italy	31 Jul 1994
Long jump	8.95 m (29 ft 4.36 in)	Mike Powell (USA)	Tokyo, Japan	30 Aug 1991
Triple jump	18.29 m (60 ft 0.07 in)	Jonathan Edwards (GBR)	Gothenburg, Sweden	7 Aug 1995
Shot	23.12 m (75 ft 10.23 in)	Randy Barnes (USA)	Los Angeles, USA	20 May 1990
Discus	74.08 m (243 ft 0.52 in)	Jürgen Schult (GDR)	Neubrandenburg, Germany	6 Jun 1986
Hammer	86.74 m (284 ft 6.95 in)	Yuriy Sedykh (USSR)	Stuttgart, Germany	30 Aug 1986
Javelin	98.48 m (323 ft 1.15 in)	Jan Železný (CZE)	Jena, Germany	25 May 1996
Decathlon†	9,045 points	Ashton Eaton (USA)	Beijing, China	29 Aug 2015
WOMEN	**DISTANCE/POINTS**	**NAME & NATIONALITY**	**LOCATION**	**DATE**
High jump	2.09 m (6 ft 10.28 in)	Stefka Kostadinova (BGR)	Rome, Italy	30 Aug 1987
Pole vault	5.06 m (16 ft 7.21 in)	Yelena Isinbayeva (RUS)	Zurich, Switzerland	28 Aug 2009
Long jump	7.52 m (24 ft 8.06 in)	Galina Chistyakova (USSR)	Leningrad, Russia	11 Jun 1988
Triple jump	15.50 m (50 ft 10.23 in)	Inessa Kravets (UKR)	Gothenburg, Sweden	10 Aug 1995
Shot	22.63 m (74 ft 2.94 in)	Natalya Lisovskaya (USSR)	Moscow, Russia	7 Jun 1987
Discus	76.80 m (251 ft 11.61 in)	Gabriele Reinsch (GDR)	Neubrandenburg, Germany	9 Jul 1988
Hammer	81.08 m (266 ft 0.11 in)	Anita Włodarczyk (POL)	Cetniewo, Poland	1 Aug 2015
Javelin	72.28 m (237 ft 1.66 in)	Barbora Špotáková (CZE)	Stuttgart, Germany	13 Sep 2008
Heptathlon††	7,291 points	Jacqueline Joyner-Kersee (USA)	Seoul, South Korea	24 Sep 1988
Decathlon†††	8,358 points	Austra Skujytė (LTU)	Columbia, USA	15 Apr 2005

† 100 m, 10.23 sec; long jump, 7.88 m; shot, 14.52 m; high jump, 2.01 m; 400 m, 45.00 sec; 110 m hurdles, 13.69 sec; discus, 43.34 m; pole vault, 5.20 m; javelin, 63.63 m; 1,500 m, 4 min 17.52 sec

†† 100 m hurdles, 12.69 sec; high jump, 1.86 m; shot, 15.80 m; 200 m, 22.56 sec; long jump, 7.27 m; javelin, 45.66 m; 800 m, 2 min 8.51 sec

††† 100 m, 12.49 sec; long jump, 6.12 m; shot, 16.42 m; high jump, 1.78 m; 400 m, 57.19 sec; 100 m hurdles, 14.22 sec; discus, 46.19 m; pole vault, 3.10 m; javelin, 48.78 m; 1,500 m, 5 min 15.86 sec

Most points in a decathlon

In 2015, Ashton Eaton (USA) scored 9,045 points to take the gold medal at the IAAF World Championships for the second time. He bettered his own record by six points in a stunning performance.

CYCLING – ABSOLUTE TRACK

MEN	TIME/DISTANCE	NAME & NATIONALITY	LOCATION	DATE
200 m (flying start)	9.347	François Pervis (FRA)	Aguascalientes, Mexico	6 Dec 2013
500 m (flying start)	24.758	Chris Hoy (GBR)	La Paz, Bolivia	13 May 2007
Team 750 m (standing start)	41.871	Germany (Joachim Eilers, René Enders, Robert Förstemann)	Aguascalientes, Mexico	5 Dec 2013
1 km (standing start)	56.303	François Pervis (FRA)	Aguascalientes, Mexico	7 Dec 2013
4 km (standing start)	4:10.534	Jack Bobridge (AUS)	Sydney, Australia	2 Feb 2011
Team 4 km (standing start)	3:51.659	Great Britain (Edward Clancy, Peter Kennaugh, Geraint Thomas, Steven Burke)	London, UK	3 Aug 2012
1 hour	54.526 km	Bradley Wiggins (GBR)	London, UK	7 Jun 2015
WOMEN	**TIME/DISTANCE**	**NAME & NATIONALITY**	**LOCATION**	**DATE**
200 m (flying start)	10.384	Kristina Vogel (DEU)	Aguascalientes, Mexico	7 Dec 2013
500 m (flying start)	29.234	Olga Streltsova (RUS)	Moscow, Russia	30 May 2014
500 m (standing start)	32.836	Anna Meares (AUS)	Aguascalientes, Mexico	6 Dec 2013
Team 500 m (standing start)	32.034	China (Jinjie Gong, Tianshi Zhong)	Saint-Quentin-en-Yvelines, France	18 Feb 2015
3 km (standing start)	3:22.269	Sarah Hammer (USA)	Aguascalientes, Mexico	11 May 2010
Team 4 km (standing start)	4:13.683	Australia (Amy Cure, Annette Edmondson, Ashlee Ankudinoff, Melissa Hoskins)	Saint-Quentin-en-Yvelines, France	19 Feb 2015
1 hour	47.980 km	Evelyn Stevens (USA)	Colorado Springs, USA	27 Feb 2016

Farthest 1 hr unpaced standing start

Sir Bradley Wiggins (GBR) cycled 54.526 km (33.881 mi) at the Olympic velodrome in London, UK, on 7 Jun 2015. It is a mark of the advances in both athletic fitness and cycling technology that when the record was first established – on 11 May 1893, by Henri Desgrange (FRA) – the distance achieved was "only" 35.325 km (21.949 mi).

Fastest 4 km team pursuit (women)

The Australian team of Amy Cure, Annette Edmondson, Ashlee Ankudinoff and Melissa Hoskins completed the 4 km team pursuit in 4 min 13.683 sec during the UCI Track Cycling World Cup meet in Saint-Quentin-en-Yvelines, France, on 19 Feb 2015.

DIVING & ICE SKATING

Longest freedive (dynamic apnea, no fins)

In this event, the diver has to swim the greatest distance underwater without fins or breathing aids. Mateusz Malina (POL) swam 226 m (741 ft 5 in) in Brno, Czech Republic, on 9 Nov 2014.

FREEDIVING

MEN'S DEPTH DISCIPLINES	DEPTH	NAME & NATIONALITY	LOCATION	DATE
Constant weight with fins	128 m (419 ft 11 in)	Alexey Molchanov (RUS)	Kalamata, Greece	19 Sep 2013
Constant weight without fins	101 m (331 ft 4 in)	William Trubridge (NZ)	The Bahamas	16 Dec 2010
Variable weight	146 m (479 ft)	Stavros Kastrinakis (GRC)	Kalamata, Greece	1 Nov 2015
No limit	214 m (702 ft 1 in)	Herbert Nitsch (AUT)	Spetses, Greece	14 Jun 2007
Free immersion	121 m (396 ft 11 in)	William Trubridge (NZ)	The Bahamas	17 Apr 2011
MEN'S DYNAMIC APNEA	DISTANCE	NAME & NATIONALITY	LOCATION	DATE
With fins	281 m (921 ft 10 in)	Goran Čolak (HRV)	Belgrade, Serbia	21 Jun 2013
Without fins	226 m (741 ft 5 in)	Mateusz Malina (POL)	Brno, Czech Republic	9 Nov 2014
MEN'S STATIC APNEA	TIME	NAME & NATIONALITY	LOCATION	DATE
Duration	11 min 54 sec	Branko Petrovic (SRB)	Dubai, UAE	7 Oct 2014
WOMEN'S DEPTH DISCIPLINES	DEPTH	NAME & NATIONALITY	LOCATION	DATE
Constant weight with fins	101 m (331 ft 4 in)	Natalia Molchanova (RUS)	Kalamata, Greece	15 Sep 2011
Constant weight without fins	70 m (229 ft 7 in)	Natalia Molchanova (RUS)	Dahab, Egypt	15 May 2014
Variable weight	130 m (426 ft 6 in)	Nanja van den Broek (NLD)	Sharm el-Sheikh, Egypt	18 Oct 2015
No limit	160 m (524 ft 11 in)	Tanya Streeter (USA)	Turks and Caicos Islands	17 Aug 2002
Free immersion	91 m (298 ft 6 in)	Natalia Molchanova (RUS)	Kalamata, Greece	15 Sep 2013
WOMEN'S DYNAMIC APNEA	DISTANCE	NAME & NATIONALITY	LOCATION	DATE
With fins	237 m (777 ft 6 in)	Natalia Molchanova (RUS)	Cagliari, Italy	19 Sep 2014
Without fins	182 m (597 ft 1 in)	Natalia Molchanova (RUS)	Belgrade, Serbia	21 Jun 2013
WOMEN'S STATIC APNEA	TIME	NAME & NATIONALITY	LOCATION	DATE
Duration	9 min 2 sec	Natalia Molchanova (RUS)	Belgrade, Serbia	21 Jun 2013

Fastest row in the single sculls lightweight class (female)

Zoe McBride (NZ) completed the women's single sculls lightweight class row in 7 min 24.46 sec at the World Rowing Cup regatta in Varese, Italy, on 20 Jun 2015. Aged just 19 at the time, McBride broke a record that was set before she was born during the semi-final of the regatta. Later on in 2015, she won the gold medal at the World Rowing Championships in Aiguebelette-le-Lac, France.

ROWING *(All events take place over a 2,000-m course)*

MEN	TIME	NAME & NATIONALITY	LOCATION	DATE
Single sculls	6:33.35	Mahé Drysdale (NZ)	Poznań, Poland	29 Aug 2009
Double sculls	5:59.72	Croatia (Valent Sinković, Martin Sinković)	Amsterdam, Netherlands	29 Aug 2014
Quadruple sculls	5:32.26	Ukraine (Morozov, Dovgodko, Nadtoka, Mikhay)	Amsterdam, Netherlands	30 Aug 2014
Coxless pairs	6:08.50	New Zealand (Eric Murray, Hamish Bond)	London, UK	28 Jul 2012
Coxless fours	5:37.86	Great Britain (Reed, James, Triggs-Hodge, Gregory)	Lucerne, Switzerland	25 May 2012
Coxed pairs**	6:33.26	New Zealand (Caleb Shepherd, Eric Murray, Hamish Bond)	Amsterdam, Netherlands	29 Aug 2014
Coxed fours**	5:58.96	Germany (Ungemach, Eichholz, Weyrauch, Rabe, Dederding)	Vienna, Austria	24 Aug 1991
Eights	5:19.35	Canada (Brown, Bergen, McCabe, Csima, Price, Gibson, Byrnes, Crothers, Howard)	Lucerne, Switzerland	25 May 2012
LIGHTWEIGHT	TIME	NAME & NATIONALITY	LOCATION	DATE
Single sculls**	6:43.37	Marcello Miani (ITA)	Amsterdam, Netherlands	29 Aug 2014
Double sculls	6:05.36	South Africa (John Smith, James Thompson)	Amsterdam, Netherlands	30 Aug 2014
Quadruple sculls**	5:42.75	Greece (Magdanis, Giannaros, E Konsolas, G Konsolas)	Amsterdam, Netherlands	29 Aug 2014
Coxless pairs**	6:22.91	Switzerland (Simon Niepmann, Lucas Tramer)	Amsterdam, Netherlands	29 Aug 2014
Coxless fours	5:43.16	Denmark (Barsøe, Jørgensen, Larsen, Winther)	Amsterdam, Netherlands	29 Aug 2014
Eights**	5:30.24	Germany (Altena, Dahlke, Kobor, Stomporowski, Melges, März, Buchheit, Von Warburg, Kaska)	Montreal, Canada	13 Aug 1992
WOMEN	TIME	NAME & NATIONALITY	LOCATION	DATE
Single sculls	7:07.71	Rumyana Neykova (BGR)	Seville, Spain	21 Sep 2002
Double sculls	6:37.31	Sally Kehoe, Olympia Aldersey (AUS)	Amsterdam, Netherlands	29 Aug 2014
Quadruple sculls	6:06.84	Germany (Annekatrin Thiele, Carina Bär, Julia Lier, Lisa Schmidla)	Amsterdam, Netherlands	30 Aug 2014
Coxless pairs	6:50.61	Great Britain (Helen Glover, Heather Stanning)	Amsterdam, Netherlands	30 Aug 2014
Coxless fours**	6:14.36	New Zealand (Prendergast, Pratt, Gowler, Bevan)	Amsterdam, Netherlands	29 Aug 2014
Eights	5:54.16	USA (Regan, Polk, Snyder, Simmonds, Luczak, Robbins, Schmetterling, Opitz, Lind)	Lucerne, Switzerland	14 Jul 2013
LIGHTWEIGHT	TIME	NAME & NATIONALITY	LOCATION	DATE
Single sculls**	7:24.46	Zoe McBride (NZ)	Varese, Italy	20 Jun 2015
Double sculls	6:48.38	Great Britain (Charlotte Taylor, Katherine Copeland)	Varese, Italy	20 Jun 2015
Quadruple sculls**	6:15.95	Netherlands (Woerner, Paulis, Kraaijkamp, Head)	Amsterdam, Netherlands	29 Aug 2014
Coxless pairs**	7:18.32	Australia (Eliza Blair, Justine Joyce)	Aiguebelette-le-Lac, France	6 Sep 1997

** Denotes non-Olympic boat classes

SPEED SKATING – LONG TRACK

MEN	TIME/POINTS	NAME & NATIONALITY	LOCATION	DATE
500 m	33.98	Pavel Kulizhnikov (RUS)	Salt Lake City, USA	20 Nov 2015
2 x 500 m	1:08.11	Pavel Kulizhnikov (RUS)	Salt Lake City, USA	20–22 Nov 2015
			Calgary, Canada	13–15 Nov 2015
1,000 m	1:06.42	Shani Davis (USA)	Salt Lake City, USA	7 Mar 2009
1,500 m	1:41.04	Shani Davis (USA)	Salt Lake City, USA	11 Dec 2009
3,000 m	3:37.28	Eskil Ervik (NOR)	Calgary, Canada	5 Nov 2005
5,000 m	6:03.32	Sven Kramer (NLD)	Calgary, Canada	17 Nov 2007
10,000 m	12:36.30	Ted-Jan Bloemen (CAN, b. NLD)	Salt Lake City, USA	21 Nov 2015
500/1,000/500/1,000 m	136.790 points	Michel Mulder (NLD)	Salt Lake City, USA	27 Jan 2013
500/3,000/1,500/5,000 m	146.365 points	Erben Wennemars (NLD)	Calgary, Canada	12–13 Aug 2005
500/5,000/1,500/10,000 m	145.742 points	Shani Davis (USA)	Calgary, Canada	18–19 Mar 2006
Team pursuit (eight laps)	3:35.60	Netherlands (Blokhuijsen, Kramer, Verweij)	Salt Lake City, USA	16 Nov 2013
WOMEN	**TIME/POINTS**	**NAME & NATIONALITY**	**LOCATION**	**DATE**
500 m	36.36	Lee Sang-hwa (KOR)	Salt Lake City, USA	16 Nov 2013
2 x 500 m	1:12.93	Lee Sang-hwa (KOR)	Salt Lake City, USA	15–16 Nov 2013
1,000 m	1:12.18	Brittany Bowe (USA)	Salt Lake City, USA	22 Nov 2015
1,500 m	1:50.85	Heather Richardson-Bergsma (USA)	Salt Lake City, USA	21 Nov 2015
3,000 m	3:53.34	Cindy Klassen (CAN)	Calgary, Canada	18 Mar 2006
5,000 m	6:42.66	Martina Sáblíková (CZE)	Salt Lake City, USA	18 Feb 2011
500/1,000/500/1,000 m	147.735 points	Heather Richardson-Bergsma (USA)	Calgary, Canada	20 Jan 2013
500/1,500/1,000/3,000 m	155.576 points	Cindy Klassen (CAN)	Calgary, Canada	15–17 Mar 2001
500/3,000/1,500/5,000 m	154.580 points	Cindy Klassen (CAN)	Calgary, Canada	18–19 Mar 2006
Team pursuit (six laps)	2:55.79	Canada (Kristina Groves, Christine Nesbitt, Brittany Schussler)	Calgary, Canada	6 Dec 2009

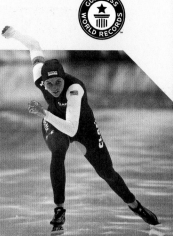

Fastest 1,500 m speed skating (female)

On 21 Nov 2015, Heather Richardson-Bergsma (USA) recorded a time of 1 min 50.85 sec in the women's 1,500 m speed skating contest at an ISU Speed Skating World Cup event in Salt Lake City, Utah, USA.

SPEED SKATING – SHORT TRACK

MEN	TIME	NAME & NATIONALITY	LOCATION	DATE
500 m	39.937	John "J R" Celski (USA)	Calgary, Canada	21 Oct 2012
1,000 m	1:22.607	Semion Elistratov (RUS)	Dresden, Germany	6 Feb 2016
1,500 m	2:09.041	Noh Jin-kyu (KOR)	Shanghai, China	10 Dec 2011
3,000 m	4:31.891	Noh Jin-kyu (KOR)	Warsaw, Poland	19 Mar 2011
5,000 m relay	6:30.958	Canada (Michael Gilday, Charles Hamelin, François Hamelin and Olivier Jean)	Calgary, Canada	19 Oct 2012
WOMEN	**TIME**	**NAME & NATIONALITY**	**LOCATION**	**DATE**
500 m	42.504	Fan Kexin (CHN)	Salt Lake City, USA	9 Nov 2014
1,000 m	1:26.661	Shim Suk-hee (KOR)	Calgary, Canada	21 Oct 2012
1,500 m	2:16.729	Zhou Yang (CHN)	Salt Lake City, USA	9 Feb 2008
3,000 m	4:46.983	Jung Eun-ju (KOR)	Harbin, China	15 Mar 2008
3,000 m relay	4:06.215	South Korea (Park Seung-hi, Kim Alang, Shim Suk-hee, Cho Ha-ri)	Kolomna, Russia	17 Nov 2013

FIGURE SKATING

MEN	POINTS	NAME & NATIONALITY	LOCATION	DATE
Combined total	330.43	Yuzuru Hanyu (JPN)	Barcelona, Spain	12 Dec 2015
Short programme	110.95	Yuzuru Hanyu (JPN)	Barcelona, Spain	10 Dec 2015
Free skating	219.48	Yuzuru Hanyu (JPN)	Barcelona, Spain	12 Dec 2015
WOMEN	**POINTS**	**NAME & NATIONALITY**	**LOCATION**	**DATE**
Combined total	228.56	Kim Yuna (KOR)	Vancouver, Canada	25 Feb 2010
Short programme	78.66	Mao Asada (JPN)	Saitama, Japan	27 Mar 2014
Free skating/ Long programme	150.10	Evgenia Medvedeva (RUS)	Boston, USA	2 Apr 2016
PAIRS	**POINTS**	**NAME & NATIONALITY**	**LOCATION**	**DATE**
Combined total	237.31	Tatiana Volosozhar & Maxim Trankov (RUS)	Detroit, USA	20 Oct 2013
Short programme	84.17	Tatiana Volosozhar & Maxim Trankov (RUS)	Sochi, Russia	11 Feb 2014
Free skating	154.66	Tatiana Volosozhar & Maxim Trankov (RUS)	Detroit, USA	20 Oct 2013
ICE DANCE	**POINTS**	**NAME & NATIONALITY**	**LOCATION**	**DATE**
Combined total	195.52	Meryl Davis & Charlie White (USA)	Sochi, Russia	17 Feb 2014
Short dance	78.89	Meryl Davis & Charlie White (USA)	Sochi, Russia	16 Feb 2014
Free dance	118.17	Gabriella Papadakis & Guillaume Cizeron (FRA)	Boston, USA	31 Mar 2016

Highest score in free skating – long programme (female)

Evgenia Medvedeva (RUS) scored 150.10 at the ISU World Championships in Boston, Massachusetts, USA, on 2 Apr 2016. Her outstanding performance secured her the gold medal at the competition, even though she had come only third in the short programme.

SWIMMING

SWIMMING – LONG COURSE (50 M POOL)

MEN	TIME	NAME & NATIONALITY	LOCATION	DATE
50 m freestyle	20.91	César Cielo Filho (BRA)	São Paulo, Brazil	18 Dec 2009
100 m freestyle	46.91	César Cielo Filho (BRA)	Rome, Italy	30 Jul 2009
200 m freestyle	1:42.00	Paul Biedermann (DEU)	Rome, Italy	28 Jul 2009
400 m freestyle	3:40.07	Paul Biedermann (DEU)	Rome, Italy	26 Jul 2009
800 m freestyle	7:32.12	Zhang Lin (CHN)	Rome, Italy	29 Jul 2009
1,500 m freestyle	14:31.02	Sun Yang (CHN)	London, UK	4 Aug 2012
4 x 100 m freestyle relay	3:08.24	USA (Michael Phelps, Garrett Weber-Gale, Cullen Jones, Jason Lezak)	Beijing, China	11 Aug 2008
4 x 200 m freestyle relay	6:58.55	USA (Michael Phelps, Ricky Berens, David Walters, Ryan Lochte)	Rome, Italy	31 Jul 2009
50 m butterfly	22.43	Rafael Muñoz (ESP)	Malaga, Spain	5 Apr 2009
100 m butterfly	49.82	Michael Phelps (USA)	Rome, Italy	1 Aug 2009
200 m butterfly	1:51.51	Michael Phelps (USA)	Rome, Italy	29 Jul 2009
50 m backstroke	24.04	Liam Tancock (GBR)	Rome, Italy	2 Aug 2009
100 m backstroke	51.94	Aaron Peirsol (USA)	Indianapolis, USA	8 Jul 2009
200 m backstroke	1:51.92	Aaron Peirsol (USA)	Rome, Italy	31 Jul 2009
50 m breaststroke	26.42	Adam Peaty (GBR)	Kazan, Russia	4 Aug 2015
100 m breaststroke	57.92	Adam Peaty (GBR)	London, UK	17 Apr 2015
200 m breaststroke	2:07.01	Akihiro Yamaguchi (JPN)	Gifu, Japan	15 Sep 2012
200 m medley	1:54.00	Ryan Lochte (USA)	Shanghai, China	28 Jul 2011
400 m medley	4:03.84	Michael Phelps (USA)	Beijing, China	10 Aug 2008
4 x 100 m medley relay	3:27.28	USA (Aaron Peirsol, Eric Shanteau, Michael Phelps, David Walters)	Rome, Italy	2 Aug 2009
WOMEN	**TIME**	**NAME & NATIONALITY**	**LOCATION**	**DATE**
50 m freestyle	23.73	Britta Steffen (DEU)	Rome, Italy	2 Aug 2009
100 m freestyle	52.07	Britta Steffen (DEU)	Rome, Italy	31 Jul 2009
200 m freestyle	1:52.98	Federica Pellegrini (ITA)	Rome, Italy	29 Jul 2009
400 m freestyle	3:58.37	Katie Ledecky (USA)	Gold Coast, Australia	23 Aug 2014
800 m freestyle	8:06.68	Katie Ledecky (USA)	Austin, USA	17 Jan 2016
1,500 m freestyle	15:25.48	Katie Ledecky (USA)	Kazan, Russia	4 Aug 2015
4 x 100 m freestyle relay	3:30.98	Australia (Bronte Campbell, Melanie Schlanger, Emma McKeon, Cate Campbell)	Glasgow, UK	24 Jul 2014
4 x 200 m freestyle relay	7:42.08	China (Yang Yu, Zhu Qian Wei, Liu Jing, Pang Jiaying)	Rome, Italy	30 Jul 2009
50 m butterfly	24.43	Sarah Sjöström (SWE)	Borås, Sweden	5 Jul 2014
100 m butterfly	55.64	Sarah Sjöström (SWE)	Kazan, Russia	3 Aug 2015
200 m butterfly	2:01.81	Liu Zige (CHN)	Jinan, China	21 Oct 2009
50 m backstroke	27.06	Zhao Jing (CHN)	Rome, Italy	30 Jul 2009
100 m backstroke	58.12	Gemma Spofforth (GBR)	Rome, Italy	28 Jul 2009
200 m backstroke	2:04.06	Missy Franklin (USA)	London, UK	3 Aug 2012
50 m breaststroke	29.48	Rūta Meilutytė (LTU)	Barcelona, Spain	3 Aug 2013
100 m breaststroke	1:04.35	Rūta Meilutytė (LTU)	Barcelona, Spain	29 Jul 2013
200 m breaststroke	2:19.11	Rikke Møller Pedersen (DNK)	Barcelona, Spain	1 Aug 2013
200 m medley	2:06.12	Katinka Hosszú (HUN)	Kazan, Russia	3 Aug 2015
400 m medley	4:28.43	Ye Shiwen (CHN)	London, UK	28 Jul 2012
4 x 100 m medley relay	3:52.05	USA (Missy Franklin, Rebecca Soni, Dana Vollmer, Allison Schmitt)	London, UK	4 Aug 2012

Fastest long course 4 x 100 m freestyle relay (female)

On 24 Jul 2014, Australia (Bronte Campbell, Cate Campbell, Emma McKeon and Melanie Schlanger) won the women's long course 4 x 100 m freestyle relay in 3 min 30.98 sec. The record-breaking swim took place at the 2014 Commonwealth Games in Glasgow, UK. Above, Bronte Campbell greets her sister Cate as their team-mates look on.

Fastest long course 100 m freestyle (female)

Germany's Britta Steffen recorded a time of 52.07 sec in the women's long course 100 m freestyle at the World Aquatics Championships held in Rome, Italy, on 31 Jul 2009. In doing so, she broke her own record of 52.22 sec, set just four days earlier.

Fastest long course 200 m medley (female)

Katinka Hosszú (HUN) completed the long course 200 m medley in just 2 min 6.12 sec at the 16th FINA World Swimming Championships in Kazan, Russia, on 3 Aug 2015. She shaved 0.03 of a second off the previous record, which was set at the World Aquatics Championships in 2009.

SWIMMING – SHORT COURSE (25 M POOL)

MEN	TIME	NAME & NATIONALITY	LOCATION	DATE
50 m freestyle	20.26	Florent Manaudou (FRA)	Doha, Qatar	5 Dec 2014
100 m freestyle	44.94	Amaury Leveaux (FRA)	Rijeka, Croatia	13 Dec 2008
200 m freestyle	1:39.37	Paul Biedermann (DEU)	Berlin, Germany	15 Nov 2009
400 m freestyle	3:32.25	Yannick Agnel (FRA)	Angers, France	15 Nov 2012
800 m freestyle	7:23.42	Grant Hackett (AUS)	Melbourne, Australia	20 Jul 2008
1,500 m freestyle	14:10.10	Grant Hackett (AUS)	Perth, Australia	7 Aug 2001
4 x 100 m freestyle relay	3:03.30	USA (Nathan Adrian, Matt Grevers, Garrett Weber-Gale, Michael Phelps)	Manchester, UK	19 Dec 2009
4 x 200 m freestyle relay	6:49.04	Russia (Nikita Lobintsev, Danila Izotov, Evgeny Lagunov, Alexander Sukhorukov)	Dubai, UAE	16 Dec 2010
50 m butterfly	21.80	Steffen Deibler (DEU)	Berlin, Germany	14 Nov 2009
100 m butterfly	48.44	Chad le Clos (ZAF)	Doha, Qatar	4 Dec 2014
200 m butterfly	1:48.56	Chad le Clos (ZAF)	Singapore, Singapore	5 Nov 2013
50 m backstroke	22.22	Florent Manaudou (FRA)	Doha, Qatar	6 Dec 2014
100 m backstroke	48.92	Matt Grevers (USA)	Indianapolis, USA	12 Dec 2015
200 m backstroke	1:45.63	Mitch Larkin (AUS)	Sydney, Australia	27 Nov 2015
50 m breaststroke	25.25	Cameron van der Burgh (ZAF)	Berlin, Germany	14 Nov 2009
100 m breaststroke	55.61	Cameron van der Burgh (ZAF)	Berlin, Germany	15 Nov 2009
200 m breaststroke	2:00.48	Dániel Gyurta (HUN)	Dubai, UAE	31 Aug 2014
100 m medley	50.66	Markus Deibler (DEU)	Doha, Qatar	7 Dec 2014
200 m medley	1:49.63	Ryan Lochte (USA)	Istanbul, Turkey	14 Dec 2012
400 m medley	3:55.50	Ryan Lochte (USA)	Dubai, UAE	16 Dec 2010
4 x 100 m medley relay	3:19.16	Russia (Stanislav Donets, Sergey Geybel, Evgeny Korotyshkin, Danila Izotov)	St Petersburg, Russia	20 Dec 2009

WOMEN	TIME	NAME & NATIONALITY	LOCATION	DATE
50 m freestyle	23.24	Ranomi Kromowidjojo (NLD)	Eindhoven, Netherlands	7 Aug 2013
			Indianapolis, USA	12 Dec 2015
100 m freestyle	50.91	Cate Campbell (AUS)	Sydney, Australia	28 Nov 2015
200 m freestyle	1:50.78	Sarah Sjöström (SWE)	Doha, Qatar	7 Dec 2014
400 m freestyle	3:54.52	Mireia Belmonte (ESP)	Berlin, Germany	11 Aug 2013
800 m freestyle	7:59.34	Mireia Belmonte (ESP)	Berlin, Germany	10 Aug 2013
1,500 m freestyle	15:19.71	Mireia Belmonte (ESP)	Sabadell, Spain	12 Dec 2014
4 x 100 m freestyle relay	3:26.53	Netherlands (Femke Heemskerk, Inge Dekker, Ranomi Kromowidjojo, Maud van der Meer)	Doha, Qatar	5 Dec 2014
4 x 200 m freestyle relay	7:32.85	Netherlands (Femke Heemskerk, Inge Dekker, Ranomi Kromowidjojo, Sharon van Rouwendaal)	Doha, Qatar	3 Dec 2014
50 m butterfly	24.38	Therese Alshammar (SWE)	Singapore, Singapore	22 Nov 2009
100 m butterfly	54.61	Sarah Sjöström (SWE)	Doha, Qatar	7 Dec 2014
200 m butterfly	1:59.61	Mireia Belmonte (ESP)	Doha, Qatar	3 Dec 2014
50 m backstroke	25.67	Etiene Medeiros (BRA)	Doha, Qatar	7 Dec 2014
100 m backstroke	55.03	Katinka Hosszú (HUN)	Doha, Qatar	4 Dec 2014
200 m backstroke	1:59.23	Katinka Hosszú (HUN)	Doha, Qatar	5 Dec 2014
50 m breaststroke	28.80	Jessica Hardy (USA)	Berlin, Germany	15 Nov 2009
100 m breaststroke	1:02.36	Rūta Meilutytė (LTU)	Moscow, Russia	12 Oct 2013
		Alia Atkinson (JAM)	Doha, Qatar	6 Dec 2014
200 m breaststroke	2:14.57	Rebecca Soni (USA)	Manchester, UK	18 Dec 2009
100 m medley	56.70	Katinka Hosszú (HUN)	Doha, Qatar	5 Dec 2014
200 m medley	2:01.86	Katinka Hosszú (HUN)	Doha, Qatar	6 Dec 2014
400 m medley	4:19.86	Mireia Belmonte (ESP)	Doha, Qatar	3 Dec 2014
4 x 100 m medley relay	3:45.20	USA (Courtney Bartholomew, Katie Meili, Kelsi Worrell, Simone Manuel)	Indianapolis, USA	11 Dec 2015

Fastest short course 100 m backstroke

Matt Grevers (USA) swam the short course 100 m backstroke in 48.92 sec in Indianapolis, Indiana, USA, on 12 Dec 2015. Grevers broke the record during the Duel in the Pool competition between the European All-Stars and the USA.

Fastest short course 200 m backstroke

Australia's Mitch Larkin completed the short course 200 m backstroke in 1 min 45.63 sec in Sydney, Australia, on 27 Nov 2015. Larkin set the record at the Australian Short Course Championships.

Fastest short course 100 m freestyle (female)

At the Australian Short Course Championships in Sydney on 28 Nov 2015, Cate Campbell (AUS) broke the 100 m freestyle record during a 200 m exhibition swim. Her split time at 100 m was clocked at 50.91 sec, 0.8 sec faster than the previous record.

WEIGHTLIFTING, SPORTS MARATHONS & WATERSKIING

WEIGHTLIFTING

MEN	CATEGORY	WEIGHT	NAME & NATIONALITY	LOCATION	DATE
56 kg	Snatch	139 kg	Wu Jingbiao (CHN)	Houston, USA	21 Nov 2015
	Clean & jerk	171 kg	Om Yun-Chol (PRK)	Houston, USA	21 Nov 2015
	Total	305 kg	Halil Mutlu (TUR)	Sydney, Australia	16 Sep 2000
62 kg	Snatch	154 kg	Kim Un-Guk (PRK)	Incheon, South Korea	21 Sep 2014
	Clean & jerk	183 kg	Lijun Chen (CHN)	Houston, USA	22 Nov 2015
	Total	333 kg	Lijun Chen (CHN)	Houston, USA	22 Nov 2015
69 kg	Snatch	166 kg	Liao Hui (CHN)	Almaty, Kazakhstan	10 Nov 2014
	Clean & jerk	198 kg	Liao Hui (CHN)	Wrocław, Poland	23 Oct 2013
	Total	359 kg	Liao Hui (CHN)	Almaty, Kazakhstan	10 Nov 2014
77 kg	Snatch	176 kg	Lü Xiaojun (CHN)	Wrocław, Poland	24 Oct 2013
	Clean & jerk	210 kg	Oleg Perepetchenov (RUS)	Trenčín, Slovakia	27 Apr 2001
	Total	380 kg	Lü Xiaojun (CHN)	Wrocław, Poland	24 Oct 2013
85 kg	Snatch	187 kg	Andrei Rybakou (BLR)	Chiang Mai, Thailand	22 Sep 2007
	Clean & jerk	218 kg	Zhang Yong (CHN)	Ramat Gan, Israel	25 Apr 1998
	Total	394 kg	Andrei Rybakou (BLR)	Beijing, China	15 Aug 2008
94 kg	Snatch	188 kg	Akakios Kakiasvilis (GRC)	Athens, Greece	27 Nov 1999
	Clean & jerk	233 kg	Ilya Ilyin (KAZ)	London, UK	4 Aug 2012
	Total	418 kg	Ilya Ilyin (KAZ)	London, UK	4 Aug 2012
105 kg	Snatch	200 kg	Andrei Aramnau (BLR)	Beijing, China	18 Aug 2008
	Clean & jerk	246 kg	Ilya Ilyin (KAZ)	Grozny, Russia	12 Dec 2015
	Total	437 kg	Ilya Ilyin (KAZ)	Grozny, Russia	12 Dec 2015
105+ kg	Snatch	214 kg	Behdad Salimi Kordasiabi (IRN)	Paris, France	13 Nov 2011
	Clean & jerk	264 kg	Aleksei Lovchev (RUS)	Houston, USA	28 Nov 2015
	Total	475 kg	Aleksei Lovchev (RUS)	Houston, USA	28 Nov 2015
WOMEN	CATEGORY	WEIGHT	NAME & NATIONALITY	LOCATION	DATE
48 kg	Snatch	98 kg	Yang Lian (CHN)	Santo Domingo, Dominican Republic	1 Oct 2006
	Clean & jerk	121 kg	Nurcan Taylan (TUR)	Antalya, Turkey	17 Sep 2010
	Total	217 kg	Yang Lian (CHN)	Santo Domingo, Dominican Republic	1 Oct 2006
53 kg	Snatch	103 kg	Li Ping (CHN)	Guangzhou, China	14 Nov 2010
	Clean & jerk	134 kg	Zulfiya Chinshanlo (KAZ)	Almaty, Kazakhstan	10 Nov 2014
	Total	233 kg	Hsu Shu-ching (TPE)	Incheon, South Korea	21 Sep 2014
58 kg	Snatch	112 kg	Boyanka Kostova (AZE)	Houston, USA	23 Nov 2015
	Clean & jerk	141 kg	Qiu Hongmei (CHN)	Tai'an, China	23 Apr 2007
	Total	252 kg	Boyanka Kostova (AZE)	Houston, USA	23 Nov 2015
63 kg	Snatch	117 kg	Svetlana Tsarukaeva (RUS)	Paris, France	8 Nov 2011
	Clean & jerk	146 kg	Wei Deng (CHN)	Houston, USA	25 Nov 2015
	Total	261 kg	Lin Tzu-chi (TPE)	Incheon, South Korea	23 Sep 2014
69 kg	Snatch	128 kg	Liu Chunhong (CHN)	Beijing, China	13 Aug 2008
	Clean & jerk	158 kg	Liu Chunhong (CHN)	Beijing, China	13 Aug 2008
	Total	286 kg	Liu Chunhong (CHN)	Beijing, China	13 Aug 2008
75 kg	Snatch	135 kg	Natalya Zabolotnaya (RUS)	Belgorod, Russia	17 Dec 2011
	Clean & jerk	164 kg	Kim Un-ju (PRK)	Incheon, South Korea	25 Sep 2014
	Total	296 kg	Natalya Zabolotnaya (RUS)	Belgorod, Russia	17 Dec 2011
75+ kg	Snatch	155 kg	Tatiana Kashirina (RUS)	Almaty, Kazakhstan	16 Nov 2014
	Clean & jerk	193 kg	Tatiana Kashirina (RUS)	Almaty, Kazakhstan	16 Nov 2014
	Total	348 kg	Tatiana Kashirina (RUS)	Almaty, Kazakhstan	16 Nov 2014

56 kg snatch

The heaviest weight lifted in the men's 56 kg snatch weightlifting competition is 139 kg, by Wu Jingbiao (CHN) at the IWF World Weightlifting Championships in Houston, Texas, USA, on 21 Nov 2015.

His feat broke a 14-year-old record. The previous holder, Halil Mutlu (TUR), had lifted 138 kg in Antalya, Turkey, on 4 Nov 2001.

58 kg total

Boyanka Kostova (AZE) lifted a weight of 252 kg in the 58 kg category at the International Weightlifting Federation (IWF) World Weightlifting Championships in Houston, Texas, USA, on 23 Nov 2015.

On the same day, she also recorded the **heaviest weight lifted in the 58 kg snatch category (female)**: 112 kg. In all, nine records were broken during that year's championships.

63 kg clean & jerk

Wei Deng of China achieved a lift of 146 kg in the women's clean & jerk (63 kg weight class) at the 2015 IWF World Championships in Houston, Texas, USA, on 25 Nov. Wei took gold in the 63 kg snatch, clean & jerk and combined events at the Championships.

LONGEST SPORTS MARATHONS

SPORT	TIME	NAME & NATIONALITY	LOCATION	DATE
Aerobics	39 hr 20 min	Esther Featherstone (UK)	Haywards Heath, UK	15–17 Sep 2012
Baseball	70 hr 9 min 24 sec	56 amateur baseball players from Tom Lange Company and Dinos Logistics (USA)	Sauget, USA	21–24 May 2015
Basketball	120 hr 1 min 7 sec	Walang Iwanan & Bounce Back (PHL)	Manila, Philippines	24–29 Mar 2014
Basketball (wheelchair)	27 hr 32 min	South West Scorpions Wheelchair Basketball Club (UK)	Bristol, UK	11–12 Aug 2012
Bowling (tenpin)	134 hr 57 min	Stephen Shanabrook (USA)	Plano, USA	14–19 Jun 2010
Bowls (indoor)	40 hr	Lyn Atkinson, Rob Atkinson, Peter Harry, Lorraine Missingham, Laurie Munro and Liz Munro (AUS)	Roxburgh Park, Australia	17–19 Apr 2013
Bowls (outdoor)	172 hr 7 min	Six members of Cambridge Bowling Club (NZ)	Cambridge, New Zealand	19 Mar 2016
Cricket	150 hr 14 min	Loughborough University Staff Cricket Club (UK)	Loughborough, UK	24–30 Jun 2012
Curling	79 hr 15 min 3 sec	Rocks Around the Clock – Coldwater & District Curling Club (CAN)	Coldwater, Canada	17–20 Oct 2014
Darts (doubles)	48 hr	Kevin Bryan, Matthew Cook, Adam Roberts and Ben Roper (UK)	Shepshed, UK	4–6 Sep 2013
Darts (singles)	50 hr 50 min 50 sec	Mark Dye and Wayne Mitchell (UK)	Bromley, UK	13–15 Mar 2014
Dodgeball	41 hr 3 min 17 sec	Right to Play @ Castleton Club (USA)	Castleton, USA	27–29 Apr 2012
Floorball	26 hr	Lappeenranta University of Technology and Urheilu Koskimies Team (FIN)	Lappeenranta, Finland	12–13 Jul 2013
Hockey (ice)	247 hr 59 min 30 sec	The Oilympics (CAN)	Chestermere, Canada	4–15 May 2014
Hockey (indoor)	60 hr	Floor Hockey for Blake (CAN)	Calgary, Canada	27–30 Jun 2014
Hockey (inline/roller)	30 hr	I H Samurai Iserlohn (DEU)	Iserlohn, Germany	13–14 Feb 2016
Hockey (street)	105 hr 17 min	Molson Canadian and Canadian Tire teams (CAN)	Lethbridge, Canada	20–24 Aug 2008
Hurling	24 hr 14 min 2 sec	Cloughbawn GAA Club (IRL)	Castleboro, Ireland	22–23 Jun 2012
Korfball	30 hr 2 min	Kingfisher Korfball Club (UK)	Larkfield, UK	14–15 Jun 2008
Netball	72 hr 5 min	Generation Netball Club (AUS)	Launceston, Australia	9–12 Jul 2015
Pétanque (boules)	52 hr	Gilles de B'Heinsch (BEL)	Arlon, Belgium	18–20 Sep 2009
Pool (singles)	100 hr	David Miles, Keith Pulley, Drew Rieck and Shawn Terrell (USA)	Colorado Springs, USA	6–10 Dec 2013
Skiing	202 hr 1 min	Nick Willey (AUS)	Thredbo, Australia	2–10 Sep 2005
Snowboarding	180 hr 34 min	Bernhard Mair (AUT)	Bad Kleinkirchheim, Austria	9–16 Jan 2004
Soccer	105 hr	Craig Gowans Memorial Fund (UK)	Edinburgh, UK	4–8 Jul 2015
Soccer (five-a-side)	70 hr 3 min	Lee Knight Foundation (UK)	Wirral, UK	30 Jul–2 Aug 2015
Table soccer	61 hr 17 min	Alexander Kuen, Manuel Larcher, Bernd Neururer and Dietmar Neururer (AUT)	Innsbruck, Austria	29 Aug–1 Sep 2012
Table tennis (doubles)	101 hr 1 min 11 sec	Lance, Mark and Phil Warren, Bill Weir (USA)	Sacramento, USA	9–13 Apr 1979
Table tennis (singles)	132 hr 31 min	Randy Nunes and Danny Price (USA)	Cherry Hill, USA	20–26 Aug 1978
Tennis (doubles)	57 hr 32 min 27 sec	Sipke de Hoop, Rob Hamersma, Wichard Heidekamp and Andre Poel (NLD)	Zuidlaren, Netherlands	16–18 Aug 2013
Tennis (singles)	63 hr 27 min 40 sec	Dennis Groissl and Niklas Jahn (DEU)	Bargteheide, Germany	7–9 Jul 2015
Volleyball (beach)	25 hr 39 min	Mateusz Baca, Wojciech Kurczyński, Sebastian Lüdke and Tomasz Olszak (DEU)	Görlitz, Germany	3–4 Jul 2010
Volleyball (indoor)	85 hr	SVU Volleybal (NLD)	Amstelveen, Netherlands	27–30 Dec 2011
Wiffle ball	25 hr 39 min 33 sec	Chris Conrad, Julian Cordle, Gary Dunn, Donny Guy and Tom Mercier versus Bobby Heiken, Josh McDermott, Jeff Multanen, Rich Rosenthal and Cameron Williams (USA)	Medford, USA	10–11 Aug 2013

WATERSKIING

MEN	RECORD	NAME & NATIONALITY	LOCATION	DATE
Slalom	2.5 buoy | 9.75 m line | 58 km/h	Nate Smith (USA)	Covington, USA	7 Sep 2013
Barefoot slalom	20.6 crossings of wake in 30 sec	Keith St Onge (USA)	Bronkhorstspruit, South Africa	6 Jan 2006
Tricks	12,570 points	Alexi Zharnasek (BLR)	Isles of Lake Hancock, USA	29 Apr 2011
Barefoot tricks	12,150 points	David Small (GBR)	Adna, USA	12 Jun 2010
Jump	76.2 m (250 ft)	Freddy Krueger (USA)	Isles of Lake Hancock, USA	1 May 2014
Barefoot jump	29.9 m (98 ft 1 in)	David Small (GBR)	Brandenburg, Germany	11 Aug 2010
Ski fly	95.1 m (312 ft)	Freddy Krueger (USA)	Michigan, USA	7 Aug 2015
Overall	2,818.01 points*	Jaret Llewellyn (CAN)	Seffner, USA	29 Sep 2002

WOMEN	RECORD	NAME & NATIONALITY	LOCATION	DATE
Slalom	3.25 buoy | 10.25 m line | 55 km/h	Regina Jaquess (USA)	Cedar Ridge Lake, USA	7 Jun 2014
Barefoot slalom	17.2 crossings of wake in 30 sec	Ashleigh Stebbings (AUS)	Perth, Australia	8 Oct 2014
Tricks	10,460 points	Erika Lang (USA)	Crystal Point, USA	10 May 2014
Barefoot tricks	10,100 points	Ashleigh Stebbings (AUS)	Mulwala, Australia	13 Mar 2014
Jump	59.1 m (193 ft 10 in)	Jacinta Carroll (AUS)	Groveland, USA	17 May 2015
Barefoot jump	21.7 m (71 ft 2 in)	Ashleigh Stebbings (AUS)	Mulwala, Australia	16 Mar 2014
Ski fly	69.4 m (227 ft 8.2 in)	Elena Milakova (RUS)	Pine Mountain, USA	26 May 2002
Overall	3,126.52 points**	Natalia Berdnikova (BLR)	Groveland, USA	19 May 2012

*5@11.25 m, 10,730 tricks, 71.7 m jump   **3@11.25 m, 9,740 tricks, 58.0 m jump

Farthest distance waterski flying

Freddy Krueger (USA) covered 312 ft (95.1 m) in Grand Rapids, Michigan, USA, on 7 Aug 2015. On 1 May 2014, he had made the **farthest waterski jump**: 250 ft (76.2 m).

ON THE ROAD!

LIVE! ON TOUR

Guinness World Records LIVE! is your opportunity to have a go at a genuine GWR record attempt and perhaps even get your name in the world's best-selling annual book. GWRLIVE! inspires ordinary people to do extraordinary things, and it's coming to an event near you…

Not all record-breaking is done in an Olympic swimming pool or a scientific laboratory. To prove that anyone can be the best at something, we've gone on the road with GWRLIVE! to bring record-breaking to the masses.

Most cobblestone collected in 3 minutes (Minecraft Pocket Edition): 127 by Ryan Hughes (UK, pictured), later beaten by Omar Siraj (UK) with 137.

Most treats balanced on a dog's nose at one time: 29, by George and handler Dima Yeremenko (UK)

Most dog treats balanced on a human's nose at one time: minimum of 10 not achieved within 30-sec time limit

LONDON PET SHOW

Humans and their pets got the chance to take part in six GWRLIVE! record challenges at the London Pet Show held at ExCeL on 9 May 2015.

MINECON

We went to MINECON 2016 – the **largest convention for a single videogame** (10,000 visitors) – where the GWRLIVE! team approved eight new records.

Fastest time to stack 20 large LEGO® bricks: target not achieved within 20-sec time limit

Most swimming trunks pulled on over clothing in 30 seconds: 12 by Oscar Whybrow (UK), narrowly beating his sister Matilda's record of 10 set earlier that day

SPORT RELIEF 2016

GWRLIVE! joined in the Sainsbury's Sport Relief Games at London's Queen Elizabeth Olympic Park in Mar 2016 for some record-breaking.

MEADOWHALL

Meadowhall shopping centre's 25th birthday celebrations saw GWRLIVE! as the star turn, with Sheffield shoppers taking part in three record attempts.

Find out where our *GWRLIVE!* team are visiting next…

Look out for our team of roving coaches and adjudicators in shopping malls, conference centres, holiday resorts and at sporting events. The GWRLIVE! team has selected records that are easy to attempt... but not necessarily easy to beat! Here we present some of the highlights from the past year. As you'll see, not every attempt results in a record – but it's about challenging yourself and enjoying the thrill of having a go!

Fastest five-cone slalom by a spherical robot toy: Richard Beckett (UK), 15.26 sec

GADGET SHOW LIVE

At the Gadget Show Live in 2016, there were 20 official attempts, more than six live adjudications and eight GWR titles achieved.

Most sandcastles built in an hour: existing record of 2,230 not broken

Fastest time to pass through 10 rubber rings: 27.60 sec by Adam Kaufman (UK)

HAVEN HOLIDAYS

Haven Holidays hosted live record-breaking at all 36 of their parks to give customers a chance to break records by the seaside.

HOW TO BREAK A RECORD AT GWRLIVE!

1. PRACTISE

In the practice phase, challengers get the chance to familiarize themselves with the record's rules. The coach is there to advise and encourage challengers, and help them to hone their skills to achieve the best possible score.

2. QUALIFY

Once the challenger is ready, they can move on to set their best qualifying time. This is recorded by the coach and the result placed on the leaderboard. Whoever is at the top of the board at the end of qualification goes through to the next stage.

3. ATTEMPT

The official Guinness World Records adjudicator is then invited to the champions' arena to adjudicate the official attempts of all the qualifying challengers from the record-breaking stations.

4. CELEBRATE

During the results service, the official adjudicator announces any new GWR titles that have been set or broken. If that's happened, it's time for the challenger and crowd to celebrate!

WATCH US ON TV!

Rebecca Peache (UK) and Donovan Jones (USA): **Most hand spins on a Spanish web in 30 seconds (52)**

OFFICIALLY AMAZING

AS SEEN ON BBC

Linsey Lindberg (aka "Mama Lou", USA): **Most card decks ripped in one minute (5)**

Cherry Yoshitake (aka "Mr Cherry", JPN): **Most baked beans eaten with chopsticks in one minute (71)**

Where better to catch up with the latest and greatest Guinness World Records titles *as they're being broken* than on our super-cool CBBC show, *Officially Amazing*!

Your host Ben Shires takes you on a journey of discovery that explores everything from martial arts and free-running to jet-skiing and jelly eating… with your feet! See if you can find your favourite.

Dan Rowan (UK): **Most barrel rolls on an aquabike in two minutes (15)**

"Mr Cherry" Yoshitake: **Most water moved with the hands in 30 seconds** (2,274 ml; 76.9 US fl oz)

"Mr Cherry" Yoshitake attempting the record for the **largest plastic cup pyramid made in 30 minutes**

CHLOE BRUCE

In the recent series of Officially Amazing, martial-arts performer and stuntwoman Chloe Bruce (UK) set the record for the **most scorpion kicks in one minute** (39, inset). Chloe's amazing talents have landed her roles in some of Hollywood's biggest hit movies, including *Star Wars: The Force Awakens* (USA, 2015). Said Chloe: "Being able to achieve Guinness World Records titles has brought some of the proudest moments of my career so far and I hope to achieve many more in the future."

BEN SHIRES

"There's something special about every record and record-breaker I've been lucky enough to encounter. And hosting Officially Amazing, I've encountered a few! I've been around the world and back to witness it all, meeting the people (and animals) willing to strive that extra mile for excellence (and the occasional doggy biscuit or two). I've discovered first-hand that records have the power to thrill, terrify and inspire, often all at the same time. Truly, if the world is a marvellous place, then the world of record-breaking makes it all the more marvellous, madcap and magical."

INDEX

Bold entries in the index indicate a main entry on a topic; **BOLD CAPITALS** indicate an entire chapter.

INDEX

ACKNOWLEDGEMENTS

Editor-in-Chief Craig Glenday	**Head of Pictures & Design** Michael Whitty	**VP Publishing** Jenny Heller	**Cover Development** Paul Deacon
Senior Managing Editor Stephen Fall	**Deputy Picture Editor** Fran Morales	**Director of Procurement** Patricia Magill	**Cover Production** Spectratek Technologies, Inc (Terry Conway and Mike Foster), API Laminates Ltd (Steven Emsley), GT Produktion (Bernd Salewski)
Layout Editors Rob Dimery, Alice Peebles	**Picture Researchers** Saffron Fradley, Wilf Matos	**Publishing Manager** Jane Boatfield	
Project Editors Ben Hollingum, Adam Millward	**Talent Researchers** Jenny Langridge, Victoria Tweedy	**Production Assistant** Thomas McCurdy	**Reprographics** Res Kahraman at Born Group
Gaming Editor Stephen Daultrey	**Design** Christian Gilliham (CGcreate), Paul Wylie-Deacon, Richard Page at 55design.co.uk	**Production Consultants** Roger Hawkins, Dennis Thon	**Original Photography** Richard Bradbury, Al Diaz, James Ellerker, Carley Garantziotis, Paul Michael Hughes, Ranald Mackechnie, Kevin Scott Ramos
Proofreading/fact-checking Ben Way, Matthew White		**Printing & Binding** MOHN Media Mohndruck GmbH, Gütersloh, Germany	
Indexer Marie Lorimer	**Artworkers** Billy Waqar, Sue Michniewicz, Jim Howard, Robin Stannard		

British Library Cataloguing-in-publication data: a catalogue record for this book is available from the British Library

UK: 978-1-910561-3-24
US 10: 1-910561-33-9
US 13: 978-1-910561-33-1
Middle East: 978-1-910561-51-5
Canada: 978-1-897553-48-0

This book is dedicated to the memory of Kenneth Crutchlow, founder of the Ocean Rowing Society

Records are made to be broken – indeed, it is one of the key criteria for a record category – so if you find a record that you think you can beat, tell us about it by making a record claim. Always contact us before making a record attempt.

Check www.guinnessworldrecords.com regularly for record-breaking news, plus video footage of record attempts. You can also join and interact with the Guinness World Records online community.

Sustainability
The paper used for this edition is manufactured by UPM Plattling, Germany. The production site has forest certification and its operations have both ISO14001 environmental management system and EMAS certification to ensure sustainable production.

UPM Papers are true Biofore products, produced from renewable and recyclable materials.

Guinness World Records Limited has a very thorough accreditation system for records verification. However, while every effort is made to ensure accuracy, Guinness World Records Limited cannot be held responsible for any errors contained in this work. Feedback from our readers on any point of accuracy is always welcomed.

Guinness World Records Limited uses both metric and imperial measurements. The sole exceptions are for some scientific data where metric measurements only are universally accepted, and for some sports data. Where a specific date is given, the exchange rate is calculated according to the currency values that were in operation at the time. Where only a year date is given, the exchange rate is calculated from 31 Dec of that year. "One billion" is taken to mean one thousand million.

Appropriate advice should always be taken when attempting to break or set records. Participants undertake records entirely at their own risk. Guinness World Records Limited has complete discretion over whether or not to include any particular record attempts in any of its publications. Being a Guinness World Records record holder does not guarantee you a place in any Guinness World Records publication.

OFFICIALLY AMAZING

CORPORATE OFFICE
Global President: Alistair Richards

Professional Services
Chief Financial Officer: Alison Ozanne
Financial Controller: Andrew Wood
Accounts Receivable Manager: Lisa Gibbs
Assistant Accountant: Jess Blake
Accounts Payable Assistant: Victoria Aweh
Finance Managers: Shabana Zaffar, Daniel Ralph
Trading Analysis Manager: Elizabeth Bishop
Head of Legal & Business Affairs: Raymond Marshall
Legal & Business Affairs Manager: Terence Tsang
Legal & Business Affairs Executive: Xiangyun Rablen
Head of HR: Farrella Ryan-Coker
HR Assistant: Mehreen Saeed
Office Manager: Jackie Angus
Director of IT: Rob Howe
IT Development Manager: James Edwards
Developer: Cenk Selim
Junior Developer: Lewis Ayers
Desktop Administrator: Ainul Ahmed / Alpha Serrant-Defoe
SVP Records: Marco Frigatti
Head of Category Management: Jacqui Sherlock / Shantha Chinniah
Information & Research Manager: Carim Valerio
Records Managers: Adam Brown, Corrinne Burns, Sam Golin, Victoria Tweedy, Tripp Yeoman
Records Consultants: Sam Mason, Tom Ibison

Global Brand Strategy
SVP Global Brand Strategy: Samantha Fay

Global Product Marketing
VP Global Product Marketing: Katie Forde
Director of Global TV Content & Sales: Rob Molloy
Senior TV Distribution Manager: Paul Glynn
Senior TV Content Executive: Jonathan Whitton
Digital Product Marketing Manager: Veronica Irons
Online Editor: Kevin Lynch
Social Media Manager: Dan Thorne
Digital Video Producer: Matt Musson
Online Writer: Rachel Swatman
Brand & Consumer Product Marketing Manager: Lucy Acfield
Designer: Rebecca Buchanan Smith
Junior Designer: Edward Dillon
Product Marketing Assistant: Victor Fenes

EMEA & APAC
SVP EMEA APAC: Nadine Causey
VP Creative: Paul O'Neill

Attractions Development Manager: Louise Toms
PR Director: Jakki Lewis
Senior PR Manager: Doug Male
Senior Publicist: Madalyn Bielfeld
B2B PR Manager: Melanie DeFries / Juliet Dawson
UK & International Press Officer: Amber-Georgina Gill
Head of Marketing: Justine Tommey
B2B Marketing Manager: Mawa Rodriguez
B2C Marketing Manager: Christelle Betrong
Content Marketing Executive: Imelda Ngouala
Head of Publishing Sales: John Pilley
Sales & Distribution Manager: Richard Stenning
Licensing Manager, Publishing: Emma Davies
Head of Commercial Accounts & Licensing: Sam Prosser
Commercial Account Managers: Lucie Pessereau, Jessica Rae, Inga Rasmussen, Sadie Smith
Commercial Account Executive: Fay Edwards
Commercial Representative, India: Nikhil Shukla
Country Manager, MENA: Talal Omar
Head of RMT, MENA: Samer Khallouf
B2B Marketing Manager, MENA: Leila Issa
Commercial Account Manager, MENA: Khalid Yassine
Head of Records Management, Europe & APAC: Ben Backhouse
Records Managers: Mark McKinley, Christopher Lynch, Matilda Hagne, Antonio Gracia, Daniel Kidane
Customer Service Managers: Louise McLaren / Janet Craffey
Senior Project Manager: Alan Pixsley
Project Managers: Paul Wiggins, Paulina Sapinska
Official Adjudicators: Ahmed Gamal Gabr, Anna Orford, Glenn Pollard, Jack Brockbank, Kimberley Dennis, Lena Kuhlmann, Lorenzo Veltri, Lucia Sinigagliesi, Pete Fairbairn, Pravin Patel, Rishi Nath, Şeyda Subaşı Gemici, Sofia Greenacre, Solvej Malouf, Swapnil Dangarikar

AMERICAS
SVP Americas: Peter Harper
VP Marketing & Commercial Sales: Keith Green
Director of Latin America: Carlos Martinez
Head of RMT – North America: Kimberly Partrick
Senior Account Managers: Nicole Pando, Ralph Hannah

Head of Client Services: Amanda Mochan
Account Managers: Alex Angert, Lindsay Doran, Lisa Tobia, Giovanni Bruna
Project Manager: Casey DeSantis
PR Manager: Kristen Ott
PR Coordinator: Sofia Rocher
B2B Marketing Executive: Tavia Levy
Publishing Sales Manager: Lisa Corrado
Records Managers: Michael Furnari, Hannah Ortman, Kaitlin Holl, Raquel Assis, Sarah Casson
HR & Office Manager: Kellie Ferrick
Official Adjudicators: Christina Flounders Conlon, Evelyn Carrera, Jimmy Coggins, Michael Empric

JAPAN
VP Japan: Erika Ogawa
Office Manager: Fumiko Kitagawa
Director of RMT: Kaoru Ishikawa
Project Manager: Aya McMillan
Records Managers: Mariko Koike, Yoko Furuya
Designer: Momoko Cunneen
Senior PR & Sales Promotion Manager: Kazami Kamioka
PR Manager: Sawako Wasada
Digital & Publishing Content Manager: Takafumi Suzuki
Commercial Sales & Marketing Director: Vihag Kulshrestha
Senior Marketing Executive: Asumi Funatsu
Account Manager: Takuro Maruyama
Senior Account Executive: Daisuke Katayama
Account Executive & Event Co-ordinator: Minami Ito
Official Adjudicators: Justin Patterson, Mai McMillan, Rei Iwashita, Gulnaz Ukassova

GREATER CHINA
President: Rowan Simons
Commercial Director: Blythe Fitzwiliam
Senior Account Manager: Catherine Gao, Lessi Li
Account Manager: Chloe Liu
Digital Business Manager: Jacky Yuan
Head of RMT: Charles Wharton
Records Manager: Alicia Zhao
Records Consultant: Lisa Hoffman
External Relations Manager: Dong Cheng
Records Manager / Project Co-ordinator: Fay Jiang
HR & Office Manager: Tina Shi
Office Assistant: Kate Wang
Head of Marketing: Wendy Wang
B2B Marketing Manager: Iris Hou
Marketing Executive: Tracy Cui
Content Director: Angela Wu
Official Adjudicators: Brittany Dunn, Joanne Brent, John Garland

Guinness World Records would like to thank the following for their help in compiling this edition:

Professor Gregory Ablavsky (Stanford Law School); Hans Åkerstedt (Vice President, Ballooning Commission (CIA), FAI Fédération Aéronautique Internationale); Dr Buzz Aldrin; Andrea Bánfi; Oliver Beatson; Bechallenged (Australia); Tom Beckerlegge; Akenabah Begay (US Census Bureau); Jacques Berlo; Bizgroup (UAE); Casey Blossom (LEGO); Bluehat Group (Fiona Craven); Brandon Boatfield; Joseph Boatfield; Luke Boatfield; Ryan Boatfield; Charlie Bolden (NASA); Brighouse High School; Rick Broadhead; Saul Browne; Alex Burrow; Dr Randall Cerveny (World Meteorological Organisation); Katie Clark; Prof John Collier (Central Laser Facility); Creative Urban Projects Inc.; Nedra Darling (Bureau of Indian Affairs); Mrs M E Dimery; Marcus Dorsey; Joshua Dowling; Roger Edwards (NOAA); Erden Eruç; European Space Agency (Jules Grandsire, Alessandra Vallo), Benjamin Fall; Rebecca Fall; Jonathan de Ferranti; FJT Logistics Ltd (Ray Harper, Gavin Hennessy); Forncett St Peter CE VA Primary School; Filomena Gallo; Marshall Gerometta; Sam Gibbes (GIS Research Associate, World Resources Institute); Damien Gildea; Jordan Greenwood; Victoria Grimsell; Chris Hadfield (Cheryl-Ann Horrocks, Julia Ostrowski) Markus Haggeney (Sports and Marketing Director, FAI Fédération Aéronautique Internationale); Sophie Alexia Hannah; Amy Cecilia Hannah; Haven Holidays (Lucy Bargent, Steve Donnelly and Danny Hickson); Bob Headland; The Himalayan Database; Tamsin Holman; Marsha K Hoover; Alan Howard; Dora Howard; Tilly Howard; Colin Hughes; Integrated Colour Editions Europe (Roger Hawkins, Susie Hawkins); Invisible Means Management (David Ross); Res Kahraman; Harry Kikstra; Christina Korp; Megan Krentz (WhiteWater); Denise Lalonde; Kristina Langenbuch; Orla Langton; Thea Langton; Frederick Horace Lazell; LEGO® (LEGO, BIONICLE and the LEGO Minifigure are trademarks of the LEGO Group, used here by permission); Wolfgang Lintl (President, Microlight and Paramotor Commission (CIMA), FAI Fédération Aéronautique Internationale); Rüdiger Lorenz; Bruno MacDonald; Alexander, Dominic and Henrietta Magill; Christian de Marliave; Chris Martin; Missy Matilda; Dave McAleer; Prof John Monterverdi (San Francisco State University); Steven Munatones (Open Water Source); Glen O'Hara; Oakleigh Park School of Swimming (especially Jamie, Matt and Polly); OK Go (Bobbie Gale); Robert Pearlman (collectSPACE.com); Teddi Penland (Bureau of Indian Affairs); Rachael Petersen (Research Analyst, World Resources Institute); Play With A Purpose (USA); Carmen Alfonzo Portillo; Winter D Prosapio (Schlitterbahn Waterparks and Resorts); James Proud; Robert Pullar; Martyn Richards; Perry Riggs (Navajo Nation Washington Office); Ripley Entertainment (Phyllis Calloway, John Corcoran, Lydia Dale, Brian Garner); Eric Sakowski; Tore Sand; Susanne Schödel (Secretary General, FAI Fédération Aéronautique Internationale); Milena Schoetzer (Team Assistant, FAI Fédération Aéronautique Internationale); Dr Nancy Segal; Natasha Sheldon; Bill Slaymaker; Glenn Speer; Bill Spindler; Spotify (Alison Bonny and Martin Vacher); St Chads CE VA Primary School; Ray Stevenson; SynCardia Systems Inc. (Don Isaac); Martyn Tovey; Julian Townsend; Steven Trim BSc CBiol MRSB (Venomtech Limited); Bon Verweij; Clemens Voigt; Rich Walker; Wensum Junior School; Sevgi and Lara White; WhiteWater West Industries Ltd (Megan Krentz); Beverley Williams; WKF (Sara Wolff); World Puzzle Federation (Hana Koudelkova); Stephen Wrigley; Madeleine Wuschech; Garrett Wybrow

ENDPAPERS

Front/row 1:
1. Largest gathering of people dressed in Tracht dress
2. Largest camel race
3. Largest ball bath
4. Most jewels on a guitar
5. Largest gathering of brides
6. Most skips of a rope wearing swim fins in five minutes
7. Fastest time to stack a set of dominoes (team of two)

Front/row 2:
1. Most tandem parachute jumps in 24 hours
2. Longest duration hopping on a treadmill
3. Largest crustacean sculpture
4. Fastest 100 km barefoot
5. Largest gathering of people dressed as princesses

6. Most flowers picked up with the mouth in a contortion backbend in one minute
7. Largest gathering of pirates

Front/row 3:
1. Largest firework display
2. Driving to highest altitude (motorcycle)
3. Largest free-floating soap bubble (indoors)
4. Largest drum ensemble
5. Largest collection of Scooby Doo memorabilia
6. Largest sock monkey
7. Tallest rugby union posts

Front/row 4:
1. Longest non-stop three-rope cable car
2. Largest collection of lip balms
3. Largest gathering of people dressed as Albert Einstein

4. Largest hand-knitted jumper (sweater)
5. Fastest 100 m on roller skates with a football balanced on the head
6. Most shaker cups juggled
7. Stair-climbing by bicycle – most steps

Front/row 5:
1. First father and daughter to summit Everest
2. Largest flaming image using torches
3. Most cereal boxes toppled
4. Most neckties worn at once
5. Longest duration spinning a basketball on a toothbrush

Back/row 1:
1. Largest cheese sculpture
2. Most motorcycles driven over the body while laying on a bed of nails (two minutes)
3. Largest aerial acrobatic display
4. Longest usable golf club
5. Longest stand-up paddleboard (SUP) ride on a river bore by a human-dog pair
6. Most bridesmaids to a bride
7. Lowest limbo skating over 25 m

Back/row 2:
1. Longest underwater walk with one breath
2. Tallest house of cards in 12 hours
3. Longest time controlling a football with the soles while on the roof of a moving car
4. Most people sitting on one chair

5. Tallest stack of pancakes
6. Largest mascot race
7. Most people bouncing tennis balls on tennis rackets

Back/row 3:
1. Largest umbrella
2. Most consecutive pinky pull-ups
3. Highest jump on a hydrofoil
4. Longest tandem ATV side-wheelie
5. Most consecutive bunny hops on a bicycle
6. Longest football scarf
7. Longest bicycle

Back/row 4:
1. Most people on unicycles
2. Largest rice cracker
3. Most simultaneous Scrabble opponents
4. Largest projected image

5. Longest journey on a golf buggy
6. Most fire torches lit and extinguished in 30 seconds
7. Tallest dice column to perform a pistol squat on

Back/row 5:
1. Largest piggy bank
2. Longest squash marathon (singles)
3. Longest wedding dress train
4. Most combine harvesters working simultaneously (single field)
5. Largest gathering of people dressed as leprechauns

For more details on these records, see
www.guinnessworldrecords/insidecover

CONTRIBUTORS

Dr Mark Aston
FRAS; CPhys; MInstP; Hon Research Fellow of University College, London
Mark has served as a Science & Technology consultant for *GWR* since 2010. He brings nearly 30 years of experience of high-technology science and engineering to the task of ensuring that cutting-edge record submissions are correct and interesting. Mark's experience of working both in academia and with professional companies has led to a lively career in optics development – a field in which he is responsible for a number of patented inventions.

Professor Iain Borden
BA; MA; MSc; PhD; Hon FRIBA
Iain is Professor of Architecture & Urban Culture, and Vice-Dean Education, at The Bartlett, University College London. An active skateboarder, photographer, film watcher and urban wanderer, he has written more than 100 books and articles both on these subjects and on architects, buildings and cities. A former resident of Oxford and Los Angeles, he now lives in London.

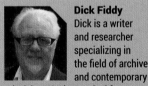

Dick Fiddy
Dick is a writer and researcher specializing in the field of archive and contemporary television. Having worked for a period of time as a television comedy scriptwriter, Dick has subsequently gone on to serve as a consultant to organizations that include the BBC and the British Film Institute (BFI).

David Fischer
Since 2006, David has acted as a senior US sports consultant for *Guinness World Records*. He has written for *The New York Times* and *Sports Illustrated for Kids*, and has worked at *Sports Illustrated*, *National Sports Daily* and NBC Sports. David is the author of *The Super Bowl: The First Fifty Years of America's Greatest Game* (2015) and *Derek Jeter #2: Thanks for the Memories* (2014). He was also the editor of *Facing Mariano Rivera* (2014).

Mike Flynn
Mike is the author of a number of best-selling books, award-winning websites and ground-breaking exhibitions. A former curator at the Science Museum in London, UK, Mike has published widely in the fields of science, technology, mathematics, history, popular culture and music. His work as a writer for galleries and museums can currently be viewed across three continents.

Justin Garvanovic
Having co-founded The Roller Coaster Club of Great Britain in 1988, Justin went on to create the magazine *First Drop* for roller-coaster fans. In 1996, he founded The European Coaster Club, a not-for-profit organization that promotes the enjoyment of riding roller-coasters. He has been involved in the designs of several roller-coasters, and takes photographs of them for a number of parks and ride manufacturers.

Ben Haggar
Ben has a rich family background in the film industry, extending back more than 100 years. His great-great-grandfather was a pioneer of silent film in Wales. Ben's own love of film began at the age of three, when he saw *The Jungle Book* in his father's cinema. Today, he continues to spend as much time as he can immersed in movies, whether learning about, writing about or – most importantly – watching them. Ben currently lives in London, UK, with his wife and two cats, and can generally be found obsessing over some obscure aspect of European, Japanese, British or Mexican cinema when he knows he really should be doing something more useful.

Stuart Hampton-Reeves
Stuart is Professor of Shakespeare Studies at the University of Central Lancashire and Head of the British Shakespeare Association. He has written several books on Shakespeare in performance and on Shakespeare's history plays. Stuart also serves as the General Editor of the book series *Shakespeare in Practice* and frequently gives lectures and writes articles about the Bard of Avon.

Ralph Hannah
Fascinated by sports and stats since childhood, Ralph combines both in his role as one of *GWR*'s sports consultants. A *Guinness World Records* veteran of nine years, when not contributing to the book he helps grow the company's presence in Latin America. Ralph lives in Luque, Paraguay, with his wife and two daughters. His favourite record is the **longest unbeaten run in the Premier League** – 49 games – held by his beloved Arsenal FC.

Dave Hawksett
For 16 years, Dave has been our principal science consultant and contributor. He has a background in astrophysics and planetary science and is passionate about communicating scientific issues to wide audiences. He has also worked in television, education, government policy and the commercial space sector. Dave is founder of the UK Planetary Forum.

John Henderson
Known variously to those he torments as Enigmatist, Nimrod, Elgar and Io, John is nearing the end of his fourth decade of compiling crosswords for the UK national press. As well as editing the weekly "Inquisitor" crossword, he writes bespoke crosswords for special occasions and has joined the question-writing team for BBC TV's *Only Connect*. He has not won the *Times* Crossword Championship on quite as many occasions as Mark Goodliffe, but does boast the Championship record of having solved a *Times* crossword in a time of 2 min 53 sec.

Eberhard Jurgalski
Eberhard has been fascinated by mountains since early childhood, and in 1981 he began formally chronicling the high mountains of Asia. He has developed the system of "Elevation Equality" – a universal method to classify mountain ranges and peaks – and his website, www.8000ers.com, has become the primary source of statistics for altitude in the Himalaya and Karakorum ranges. Eberhard is also the co-author of *Herausforderung 8000er* – regarded as the definitive guide to the world's 14 mountains over 8,000 m.

Rohan Mehra
BSc (Hons) in Cybernetics and Computer Science; MSc in Science Communication
By his own admission, Rohan is easily excited by new feats of science and technology – so covering a range of cutting-edge science stories for *Guinness World Records* is a dream come true! As he has extensive knowledge of innovations that employ 3D printing, Rohan covered the topic for this year's edition of *GWR*. He is a science journalist and enjoys writing about physics, engineering and nature. He also covers science in the developing world.

Bruce Nash/ The Numbers
Bruce runs Nash Information Services, LLC, which is regarded as the leading provider of movie-industry data and research services. The company operates the websites The Numbers (www.the-numbers.com) and OpusData, in addition to providing research services to a range of the biggest – and smallest – film studios and production companies.

Ocean Rowing Society International (ORS Int.)
The Ocean Rowing Society was established in 1983 by Kenneth F Crutchlow and Peter Bird, later joined by Tom Lynch and Tatiana Rezvaya-Crutchlow. It keeps a record of all attempts to row the oceans and major bodies of water such as the Tasman Sea and Caribbean Sea, as well as rowing expeditions around Great Britain. The society also classifies, verifies and adjudicates ocean-rowing achievements.

Dr Paul Parsons
DPhil in Theoretical Cosmology
Paul now has almost 20 years' experience as a science writer and journalist. He is a former editor of the popular BBC science magazine *Focus* and is author of *The Science of Doctor Who* (2006). When not writing, he enjoys applying the laws of mathematics and statistics to solve the greatest puzzle of all: horse racing.

Dr Clara Piccirillo
PhD in Materials Science
Clara has been working in research for more than 20 years. Her main fields of expertise are materials, biotechnology and environment/sustainable development. She is also greatly interested in the communication of science to the general public and, to that end, writes for a website dedicated to science dissemination (www.decodedscience.org/author/clara-piccirillo). She has collaborated with *GWR* for around four years.

James Pratt
A life-long chess player, James was Britain's youngest chess journalist in 1980. He has been the editor of magazines including *The Chess Parrot* and the *British Chess Magazine*. He lives with 700 chess books in Basingstoke, UK.

Will Shortz
Will is the crossword editor of *The New York Times*, puzzlemaster for National Public Radio (NPR) and founder/director of the American Crossword Puzzle Tournament. He founded the World Puzzle Championship in 1992 and is chairman of the World Puzzle Federation, which oversees the championship. He holds the world's only college degree in Enigmatology – the study of puzzles – which he earned in a self-designed programme at Indiana University in 1974. Will is the author or editor of more than 500 puzzle books, including *Brain Games*, *The Puzzlemaster Presents* and numerous best-selling volumes of sudoku.

Dr Karl P N Shuker
BSc (Hons) in Zoology from the University of Leeds; PhD in Zoology and Comparative Physiology from the University of Birmingham; Scientific Fellow of the Zoological Society of London; Fellow of the Royal Entomological Society; Member of the Society of Authors
Karl works as a freelance zoologist and media consultant. He is also the author of 25 books and many hundreds of articles covering all aspects of natural history. Karl's work has a particular emphasis on anomalous animals – including new, rediscovered and unrecognized species, superlative (record-breaking) animals and the beasts of mythology, folklore and legend.

Matthew White
Guinness World Records' music, cricket and tennis consultant has pored over an estimated 36,000 published records as proof-reader during the course of nine editions (2009–17) of the world's **best-selling annual publication**. A whistle-stop tour of Matthew's own favourite records would include the mind-boggling **largest island in a lake on an island in a lake on an island** (Taal Lake in the Philippines), St Simeon the Stylite's **longest pole-sitting vigil** (an extraordinary 39 years) and any record featuring the bludgeoning blade of West Indian cricketer Chris Gayle. Now to find a pub quiz where such random knowledge can be utilized...

Robert D Young
MA in Gerontology; MA in History
Robert serves as *Guinness World Records'* senior consultant for gerontology, the study of various aspects of ageing. He has maintained lists of the world's oldest people for the Gerontology Research Group (GRG) since 1999, and has worked with the Max Planck Institute for Demographic Research and the International Database on Longevity. Robert became Director of the Supercentenarian Research and Database Division for the Gerontology Research Group in 2015. He is also the author of *African-American Longevity Advantage: Myth or Reality?* (2009).

COUNTRY CODES

ABW	Aruba
AFG	Afghanistan
AGO	Angola
AIA	Anguilla
ALB	Albania
AND	Andorra
ANT	Netherlands Antilles
ARG	Argentina
ARM	Armenia
ASM	American Samoa
ATA	Antarctica
ATF	French Southern Territories
ATG	Antigua and Barbuda
AUS	Australia
AUT	Austria
AZE	Azerbaijan
BDI	Burundi
BEL	Belgium
BEN	Benin
BFA	Burkina Faso
BGD	Bangladesh
BGR	Bulgaria
BHR	Bahrain
BHS	The Bahamas
BIH	Bosnia and Herzegovina
BLR	Belarus
BLZ	Belize
BMU	Bermuda
BOL	Bolivia
BRA	Brazil
BRB	Barbados
BRN	Brunei Darussalam
BTN	Bhutan
BVT	Bouvet Island
BWA	Botswana
CAF	Central African Republic
CAN	Canada
CCK	Cocos (Keeling) Islands
CHE	Switzerland
CHL	Chile
CHN	China
CIV	Côte d'Ivoire
CMR	Cameroon
COD	Congo, DR of the
COG	Congo
COK	Cook Islands
COL	Colombia
COM	Comoros
CPV	Cape Verde
CRI	Costa Rica
CUB	Cuba
CXR	Christmas Island
CYM	Cayman Islands
CYP	Cyprus
CZE	Czech Republic
DEU	Germany
DJI	Djibouti
DMA	Dominica
DNK	Denmark
DOM	Dominican Republic
DZA	Algeria
ECU	Ecuador
EGY	Egypt
ERI	Eritrea
ESH	Western Sahara
ESP	Spain
EST	Estonia
ETH	Ethiopia
FIN	Finland
FJI	Fiji
FLK	Falkland Islands (Malvinas)
FRA	France
FRG	West Germany
FRO	Faroe Islands
FSM	Micronesia, Federated States of
FXX	France, Metropolitan
GAB	Gabon
GEO	Georgia
GHA	Ghana
GIB	Gibraltar
GIN	Guinea
GLP	Guadeloupe
GMB	Gambia
GNB	Guinea-Bissau
GNQ	Equatorial Guinea
GRC	Greece
GRD	Grenada
GRL	Greenland
GTM	Guatemala
GUF	French Guiana
GUM	Guam
GUY	Guyana
HKG	Hong Kong
HMD	Heard and McDonald Islands
HND	Honduras
HRV	Croatia (Hrvatska)
HTI	Haiti
HUN	Hungary
IDN	Indonesia
IND	India
IOT	British Indian Ocean Territory
IRL	Ireland
IRN	Iran
IRQ	Iraq
ISL	Iceland
ISR	Israel
ITA	Italy
JAM	Jamaica
JOR	Jordan
JPN	Japan
KAZ	Kazakhstan
KEN	Kenya
KGZ	Kyrgyzstan
KHM	Cambodia
KIR	Kiribati
KNA	Saint Kitts and Nevis
KOR	Korea, Republic of
KWT	Kuwait
LAO	Laos
LBN	Lebanon
LBR	Liberia
LBY	Libyan Arab Jamahiriya
LCA	Saint Lucia
LIE	Liechtenstein
LKA	Sri Lanka
LSO	Lesotho
LTU	Lithuania
LUX	Luxembourg
LVA	Latvia
MAC	Macau
MAR	Morocco
MCO	Monaco
MDA	Moldova
MDG	Madagascar
MDV	Maldives
MEX	Mexico
MHL	Marshall Islands
MKD	Macedonia
MLI	Mali
MLT	Malta
MMR	Myanmar (Burma)
MNE	Montenegro
MNG	Mongolia
MNP	Northern Mariana Islands
MOZ	Mozambique
MRT	Mauritania
MSR	Montserrat
MTQ	Martinique
MUS	Mauritius
MWI	Malawi
MYS	Malaysia
MYT	Mayotte
NAM	Namibia
NCL	New Caledonia
NER	Niger
NFK	Norfolk Island
NGA	Nigeria
NIC	Nicaragua
NIU	Niue
NLD	Netherlands
NOR	Norway
NPL	Nepal
NRU	Nauru
NZ	New Zealand
OMN	Oman
PAK	Pakistan
PAN	Panama
PCN	Pitcairn Islands
PER	Peru
PHL	Philippines
PLW	Palau
PNG	Papua New Guinea
POL	Poland
PRI	Puerto Rico
PRK	Korea, DPRO
PRT	Portugal
PRY	Paraguay
PYF	French Polynesia
QAT	Qatar
REU	Réunion
ROM	Romania
RUS	Russian Federation
RWA	Rwanda
SAU	Saudi Arabia
SDN	Sudan
SEN	Senegal
SGP	Singapore
SGS	South Georgia and South SS
SHN	Saint Helena
SJM	Svalbard and Jan Mayen Islands
SLB	Solomon Islands
SLE	Sierra Leone
SLV	El Salvador
SMR	San Marino
SOM	Somalia
SPM	Saint Pierre and Miquelon
SRB	Serbia
SSD	South Sudan
STP	São Tomé and Príncipe
SUR	Suriname
SVK	Slovakia
SVN	Slovenia
SWE	Sweden
SWZ	Swaziland
SYC	Seychelles
SYR	Syrian Arab Republic
TCA	Turks and Caicos Islands
TCD	Chad
TGO	Togo
THA	Thailand
TJK	Tajikistan
TKL	Tokelau
TKM	Turkmenistan
TMP	East Timor
TON	Tonga
TPE	Chinese Taipei
TTO	Trinidad and Tobago
TUN	Tunisia
TUR	Turkey
TUV	Tuvalu
TZA	Tanzania
UAE	United Arab Emirates
UGA	Uganda
UK	United Kingdom
UKR	Ukraine
UMI	US Minor Islands
URY	Uruguay
USA	United States of America
UZB	Uzbekistan
VAT	Holy See (Vatican City)
VCT	Saint Vincent and the Grenadines
VEN	Venezuela
VGB	Virgin Islands (British)
VIR	Virgin Islands (US)
VNM	Vietnam
VUT	Vanuatu
WLF	Wallis and Futuna Islands
WSM	Samoa
YEM	Yemen
ZAF	South Africa
ZMB	Zambia
ZWE	Zimbabwe

STOP PRESS

The following new entries were approved and added to our records database after the official closing date for this year's submissions.

Most people showering at once (single venue)
A group of 331 individuals showered simultaneously in an event held by Delta Faucet (USA) in Crawfordsville, Indiana, USA, on 27 Jun 2015.

Most shark attacks in one year
According to the International Shark Attack File (ISAF), the year 2015 saw 98 unprovoked shark attacks against humans, from a total of 164 reported incidents. The ISAF is compiled annually by the Florida Museum of Natural History at the University of Florida, USA, under the auspices of the American Elasmobranch Society.

Most drink cans placed on the head using air suction
Jamie Keeton (USA) "suctioned" eight drink cans to his head on the set of *CCTV – Guinness World Records Special* in Beijing, China, on 11 Jan 2016. Jamie appears to have a rare skin condition that makes his skin pores function like suction cups.

Largest solar oven cooking class
A group of 4,780 people, each equipped with their own solar oven, assembled for a cooking class in an event organized by Simplified Technologies for Life and Chamber of Marathwada Industries & Agriculture (both IND) in Aurangabad, India, on 12 Jan 2016.

Largest collection of *Little Mermaid* memorabilia
Jacqueline Granda (ECU) owns 874 items relating to *The Little Mermaid* (USA, 1989), as verified in Quito, Ecuador, on 16 Jan 2016.

Fastest 100 m rope skipping
Rohollah Doshmanziari (IRN) skipped 100 m in a time of 14.43 sec in Iran's Shahid Beheshti Stadium in Bushehr on 21 Jan 2016.

Most slender tower
The British Airways i360 is 160.47 m tall by 3.9 m wide (526 ft 5 in x 12 ft 9 in) – a slenderness ratio of 41.15 to 1 – as verified on 26 Jan 2016 in Brighton, UK.

Oldest cockatiel
At 32 years old, Sunshine was the world's oldest cockatiel as of 27 Jan 2016. He lives in Albuquerque, New Mexico, USA, with his owner, Vickie Aranda (USA), who acquired him in Colorado in 1983. Sunshine has been moving around with Vickie ever since.

Largest snow dome igloo
Sponsored by Volvo (SWE), the 18-person-strong Iglu-Dorf building crew (CHE) constructed a snow dome igloo with an internal diameter of 12.9 m (42 ft 4 in) in Zermatt, Switzerland, on 30 Jan 2016.

Longest marathon hosting a radio talk show (team)
From 2 to 4 Feb 2016, Jessy Abu Faysal (LBN) and Amjad Hijazin (JOR) hosted a radio talk show for 60 hr 52 min 8 sec at Sawt El Ghad studios in Amman, Jordan.

Most chin-ups in 24 hours
On 6–7 Feb 2016, Joonas Mäkipelto (FIN) performed 5,050 chin-ups at Ideapark shopping centre in Lempäälä, Finland.

Tallest stack of pancakes
On 8 Feb 2016, Center Parcs Sherwood Forest (UK) raised a 1.01-m-tall (3-ft 4-in) stack of pancakes in Rufford, Newark, UK. James Haywood and Dave Nicholls (both UK) made and stacked the 213 pancakes.

Longest continuous vocal note
Alpaslan Durmuş (TUR) held a note for 1 min 52 sec at the Kipdaş Mühendislik engineering office, Istanbul, Turkey, on 8 Feb 2016.

Most players in an ice hockey exhibition match
Loblaw Companies Ltd (CAN) staged an exhibition match with 433 players at Richcraft Sensplex (Ottawa East) in Ottawa, Ontario, Canada, on 9 Feb 2016.

Most players in a netball exhibition match
England Netball (UK) assembled 1,322 netball players for an exhibition match in London, UK, on 15 Feb 2016.

Largest handball lesson
Ravindra Gaikwad (IND) organized a handball lesson with 678 players in Solapur, Maharashtra, India, on 28 Feb 2016.

Longest motorcycle burn-out
Joe Dryden (USA) achieved a 2.22-mi (3.58-km) burn-out on a 2017 Victory Octane at Orlando Speed World Dragway in Florida, USA, on 29 Feb 2016.

Longest zip wire
The Monster is a zip wire at Toro Verde Adventure Park in Orocovis, Puerto Rico, with a single unbroken span of 2.205 km (1.37 mi) – longer than 20 American football fields. It was opened on 2 Mar 2016.

Most rugby passes in a minute (pair)
Drew Mitchell and Matt Giteau (both AUS) made a total of 98 rugby passes in 60 sec for *Sky Sports Rugby* in Toulon, France, on 3 Mar 2016.
On the same day, and at the same location, Mitchell ran the **fastest 100 m in clogs** in a time of just 14.43 sec.

Largest camel race
On 7 Mar 2016, a total of 1,108 people completed a camel race organized by the Administrative Office of the Governor of Ömnögovi Aimag (MNG) in Dalanzadgad, Mongolia.

Most pull-ups in one hour (female)
Eva Clarke (AUS) performed 725 pull-ups in one hour at Al Wahda Mall in Abu Dhabi, UAE, on 10 Mar 2016.

Longest picnic table
On 11 Mar 2016, Flags for Managing and Organizing Exhibitions and Conferences (KWT) unveiled a 194.7-m (638-ft 9-in) picnic table at Kuwait Shooting Club in Kuwait City.

Most jewels on a guitar
Aaron Shum Jewelry Ltd (HKG) set 16,033 jewels on a Fender Jazz Bass, as verified in Basel, Switzerland, on 11 Mar 2016.

Largest women's marathon
In all, 19,607 runners took part in the Nagoya Women's Marathon in Nagoya, Aichi, Japan, on 13 Mar 2016.

Largest beer tasting
On 15 Mar 2016, The Publican Awards (UK) saw 1,236 individuals gather to taste beer in London, UK.

Most people filling out a sports tournament bracket simultaneously
On 15 Mar 2016, a total of 298 people filled out a sports tournament bracket – a tree diagram showing the progression of games in a knockout tournament – concurrently. The event was arranged by Bing (USA) in Bellevue, Washington, USA.

Fastest time to complete the Iditarod Trail
Dallas Seavey (USA) finished the Iditarod Trail sled-dog race in 8 days 11 hr 20 min 16 sec in Nome, Alaska, USA, on 15 Mar 2016.

Tallest house of cards built in 12 hours
LG Electronics (KOR) and Bryan Berg (USA) collaborated to raise a 48-level house of cards in 12 hr in Seoul, South Korea, on 15–16 Mar 2016.

Youngest billionaire (current)
As of 16 Mar 2016, Norway's Alexandra Andresen had an estimated wealth of $1.18 bn (£829,800,000), according to Forbes. She was 19 years old at the time.

Largest dance fitness class
Balanga City (PHL) set up a dance fitness class for 16,218 people in Bataan, Philippines, on 18 Mar 2016.

Most people dressed as *Doctor Who* characters
On 19 Mar 2016, TV channel Syfy Latinoamérica (MEX) assembled 491 people dressed as *Doctor Who* characters at La Mole Comic-Con in Mexico City.

Fastest time to pump up a bicycle tyre
On 20 Mar 2016, in London, UK, Steven Smith (UK) took just 20.50 sec to inflate the inner tube of a bicycle tyre with a hand pump.

Fastest 4 x 50 m unicycle hurdle relay
On 20 Mar 2016, "Voodoo Unicycles", aka Jason Auld, Simon Berry, Mike Taylor and Rob Terry (all UK), finished a 4 x 50 m unicycle hurdle relay in 1 min 33.49 sec in London, UK.

Largest confetti mosaic
Kurobe International Cultural Center (JPN) created a confetti mosaic measuring 32.16 m² (346.16 sq ft) at the Kurobe International Cultural Center (JPN) in Toyama, Japan on 21 Mar 2016.

Longest paper chain made in one hour by a team
A team from the Hong Kong Jockey Club (HKG) produced a 3.74-km-long (2.32-mi) paper chain during the Riding High Together Festival at Sha Tin Racecourse in Hong Kong, China, on 26 Mar 2016.

Longest rail grind ski
On 27 Mar 2016, Tom Wallisch (USA) performed a 422-ft 1-in-long (128.65-m) rail grind on skis at the Seven Springs Mountain Resort in Seven Springs, Pennsylvania, USA.

Highest bicycle speed on a Wall of Death
Shanaze Reade (UK) cycled at 42.94 km/h (26.68 mph) around a Wall of Death on the set of Channel 4's *Guy Martin's Wall of Death: Live* (North One TV, UK) in Louth, UK, on 28 Mar 2016.
On the same date, and at the same location, Guy Martin (UK) achieved the **highest speed on a Wall of Death** – 125.77 km/h (78.15 mph) on a self-built "bitsa" motorcycle with a BSA engine. He experienced forces of 5.2 *g* on his ride.

Longest line of postcards
The Shanghai Town & Country Club (CHN) lined up 11,863 postcards in Shanghai on 19 Apr 2016.

Answer to puzzle on p.151

Most game shows produced
Harry Friedman (USA) had produced 11,128 game shows in Los Angeles, California, USA, as of 31 Mar 2016.

Largest floral chandelier
National Parks Board (SGP) created a floral chandelier 16.84 m (55 ft 2.8 in) long by 10.29 m (33 ft 9 in) wide and 8.16 m (26 ft 9.3 in) tall. Consisting of 60,000 flowers, it was crafted in Marina Square Atrium, Singapore, on 1 Apr 2016.

Largest human fingerprint
Storebrand Livsforsikring (NOR) arranged 313 people into the whorled shape of a fingerprint in Fornebu, Norway, on 2 Apr 2016.

Oldest cat living
Scooter (b. 26 Mar 1986) was 30 years 13 days old as of 8 Apr 2016. He lives with his owner, Gail Floyd (USA), in Mansfield, Texas, USA.

Largest bobblehead
A 4.69-m-tall (15-ft 4.75-in) bobblehead of a St Bernard dog was unveiled on 8 Apr 2016 in Orlando, Florida, USA. It was created by scenic prop shop Dino Rentos Studios for the Applied Underwriters insurance firm (both USA).

Most people sewing simultaneously
On 9 Apr 2016, a group of 606 people gathered to sew in an event organized by Mostwell Sdn Bhd (MYS) at the Auditorium Cempaka Sari in Putrajaya, Malaysia.

Largest vegan cake
Essentis Biohotel Berlin (DEU) made a 388.9-kg (857-lb 6-oz) vegan cake in Berlin, Germany, on 9 Apr 2016. It took 31 people 26 hr to complete it.

Longest usable golf club
On 9 Apr 2016, a 7.65-m-long (25-ft 1-in) golf club made by Ashrita Furman (USA) was measured and demonstrated in Jamaica, New York City, USA.

Longest marathon watching television
Alejandro "AJ" Fragoso (USA) watched TV for 94 hr in New York City, USA, on 12 Apr 2016.

Fastest hole of golf (team of four)
Raphaël Jacquelin, Alex Lévy, Grégory Havret and Romain Wattel (all FRA) took just 34.87 sec to play the 4th hole of the Valderrama Golf Course in Sotogrande, Spain, on 12 Apr 2016.

Heaviest vehicle pulled with an arm-wrestling move
Kevin Fast (CAN) pulled a 31,900-lb (14,470-kg) fire truck more than 12 in (30.4 cm) with his arm – while resting his elbow on an arm-wrestling table – in Cobourg, Ontario, Canada, on 13 Apr 2016.

Most lit candles on a cake
On 13 Apr 2016, Mike's Hard Lemonade (USA) lit 50,151 candles on a cake in Los Angeles, California, USA.

Largest chocolate bar
Čokoladnica Cukrček (SVN) prepared a 142.32-m² (1,531.9-sq-ft) bar of chocolate, which was measured in Radovljica, Slovenia, on 15 Apr 2016.

Largest merengue lesson
The merengue is a Dominican dance. Osteo Bi-Flex (USA) organized an event in which 252 people took part in a merengue lesson at the Fremont Street Experience in Las Vegas, Nevada, USA, on 15 Apr 2016.

Largest spring mattress
Lijun Hou and his team (all CHN) have built a spring mattress 20 m x 18.18 m (65 ft 7.4 in x 59 ft 7.75 in) in size. It was measured in Harbin, Heilongjiang, China, on 15 Apr 2016.

Largest simultaneous flying disc throw
On 16 Apr 2016, a group of 958 participants let loose their flying discs in Miura, Kanagawa, Japan. The event was arranged by Miura Beach 900 Challenge Executive Committee (JPN).

Most hits of a golf ball on a golf club in 30 seconds
Ashrita Furman (USA) achieved 94 hits of a golf ball on a golf club in 30 sec in Jamaica, New York City, USA, on 16 Apr 2016.

Largest profiterole
Associazione Cons.erva, in collaboration with Etica Del Gusto, Despar, Uova Pascolo Fantoni and Crespi (all ITA), unveiled a 150-kg (330-lb 11-oz) profiterole at Gemona del Friuli in Udine, Italy, on 17 Apr 2016.

Most people playing boomwhackers
A boomwhacker is a hollow plastic tube tuned to a musical pitch; tubes of various length are struck in order to produce melodies. P&G European Planning Service Center (POL) staged an event in which 661 individuals played the song "Eye of the Tiger" on boomwhackers in Serock, Poland, on 18 Apr 2016.

Largest naan bread
Loblaw Companies Ltd (CAN) produced a naan bread weighing 32 kg (70 lb 8.76 oz) in Toronto, Ontario, Canada, on 19 Apr 2016. The naan measured 4.96 m (16 ft 3.27 in) long and 1.26 m (4 ft 1.6 in) wide.

Oldest message in a bottle
It was announced on 20 Apr 2016 that a message in a bottle found at Amrum Island, Germany, on 17 Apr 2015 was the oldest ever discovered. It had been at sea for 108 years 138 days, having been set adrift in the North Sea by the UK's Marine Biological Association (MBA) on 20 Nov 1906. Inside was a postcard asking the finder to list where and when the bottle was found and post the card back to the MBA.

First person to climb the Seven Summits and cross the Seven Seas
Martin Frey (USA) climbed the highest mountain on each continent from 21 Aug 2005 to 5 Dec 2012 and crossed the Seven Seas by sailboat between 25 Feb 2013 and 17 Apr 2016.

Most people making s'mores simultaneously
On 21 Apr 2016, a group of 423 people on Huntington Beach in California, USA, made s'mores – a roasted marshmallow and layer of chocolate between two crackers. The event was sponsored by Hollister and SeriousFun Children's Network (both USA).

Largest wave surfed (paddle-in)
The tallest wave surfed without a tow was 19.2 m (63 ft) from trough to crest and was ridden by Aaron Gold (USA) off Maui in Hawaii, USA, on 15 Jan 2016. The feat was confirmed at the 2016 World Surf League Big Wave Awards gala at the Grove Theater in Anaheim, California, USA, on 24 Apr 2016.

First twins born in different countries
Katherine Joanne Baines (née Roberts) and Heidi Hilane Gannon (both UK) were born on 23 Sep 1976. Heidi arrived at 9:05 a.m. at Welshpool Hospital in Wales; Jo followed at 10:45 a.m. after their mother had been moved to the Royal Shrewsbury Hospital in England, owing to complications. In Apr 2016, Dr Nancy Segal, Professor of Psychology and Director at the Twin Studies Center in California State University, confirmed that the twins were identical.

Largest robot competition
VEX Worlds (USA) attracted 1,075 teams to its annual robot contest in Louisville, Kentucky, USA, held from 20 to 23 Apr 2016. Hailing from 30 countries, the teams comprised students from primary school to university level.

Fastest time to run the London Marathon (male)
Eliud Kipchoge (KEN) finished the 2016 Virgin Money London Marathon in 2 hr 3 min 5 sec in London, UK, on 24 Apr 2016.

Oldest continuously operating cinema
The State Theatre in Washington, Iowa, USA, opened on 14 May 1897. It had been in operation for 118 years 348 days, as of 26 Apr 2016.

Fastest 50 m walking on hands with a soccer ball between the legs
Zhang Shuang (CHN) covered 50 m (164 ft) while inverted and clenching a soccer ball between his legs in 26.09 sec. He attempted the record at the China West Normal University in Nanchong, Sichuan, China, on 30 Apr 2016.

Most concurrent albums in the US Top 10
On the *Billboard* 200 albums chart of 14 May 2016, Prince (b. Prince Rogers Nelson, USA) had five posthumous entries in the Top 10: *The Very Best of Prince* (No.2), *Purple Rain* (No.3), *The Hits/ The B-Sides* (No.4), *Ultimate* (No.6) and *1999* (No.7). During the week of 21–28 Apr 2016, Prince's back catalogue (including albums and individual tracks) sold a total of 4.41 million units in the USA following the news that the star had died at his Paisley Park home in Minnesota, USA, on 21 Apr 2016. He was aged 57.

Largest rise in position for a Premier League soccer team in consecutive seasons
Leicester City FC (UK) finished 14th in the 2014/15 Premier League season. On 2 May 2016, however, "The Foxes" were confirmed as champions, finishing 13 places higher up the table.

Most Tony Award nominations for a musical
Lin-Manuel Miranda's (USA) biographical musical *Hamilton*, about the life and death of US Founding Father Alexander Hamilton, received 16 Tony nominations on 3 May 2016, including Best Musical.

Oldest living person
On the day we went to press (12 May 2016), Susannah Mushatt Jones (b. 6 Jul 1899) – the last 19th-century American – passed away at the age of 116 years 311 days. The title is currently being researched by consultant Robert Young but is most likely to be Italy's Emma Morano Martinuzzi (b. 29 Nov 1899), aged 116 years 165 days as of 12 May.

THE FULL FORCE OF RECORD-BREAKING IN YOUR HANDS!

10th EDITION · OVER 4 MILLION COPIES SOLD

GUINNESS WORLD RECORDS 2017

GAMER'S EDITION

STAR WARS SPECIAL

Most difficult level created in *Super Mario Maker*
Alex Tan

Most popular female on Twitch
Sonja Reid

Most views for a *Minecraft* video channel
Dan the Diamond Minecart

WWW.GUINNESSWORLDRECORDS.COM/2017